D1799338

SIMEON & CHURCH ORDER

A View from St MARY's Church
CAMBRIDGE

THE REVEREND CHARLES SIMEON PREACHING BEFORE
THE UNIVERSITY

From a coloured print by R. Dighton at Eton College

SIMEON & CHURCH ORDER

*A Study of the Origins of the Evangelical Revival
in Cambridge in the Eighteenth century*

THE BIRKBECK LECTURES FOR 1937-8

BY

CHARLES SMYTH

*Fellow and Dean of Chapel, Corpus Christi College, Cambridge
Honorary Canon of Derby*

His ideas were far more catholic than is usually
taken for granted; and the influence which he
had, and which his opinions are probably still
exercising, on the Christian world was more extensive and salutary than is generally supposed.

*Recollections of the Conversation Parties
of the Rev. Charles Simeon, M.A.*
Abner William Brown (1863), p. ix.

CAMBRIDGE

AT THE UNIVERSITY PRESS

1940

UXORI DILECTISSIMÆ
CUIUS SINE AUXILIO
OPUS VIX PERFECTUM ESSET

CAMBRIDGE
UNIVERSITY PRESS

University Printing House, Cambridge CB2 8BS, United Kingdom

Cambridge University Press is part of the University of Cambridge.

It furthers the University's mission by disseminating knowledge in the pursuit of education, learning and research at the highest international levels of excellence.

www.cambridge.org
Information on this title: www.cambridge.org/9781107458826

© Cambridge University Press 1940

This publication is in copyright. Subject to statutory exception and to the provisions of relevant collective licensing agreements, no reproduction of any part may take place without the written permission of Cambridge University Press.

First published 1940
First paperback edition 2014

A catalogue record for this publication is available from the British Library

ISBN 978-1-107-45882-6 Paperback

Cambridge University Press has no responsibility for the persistence or accuracy of URLs for external or third-party internet websites referred to in this publication, and does not guarantee that any content on such websites is, or will remain, accurate or appropriate.

Contents

Chapter I. RELIGION IN THE HOME, pp. 1–43

Three funerals—Pusey, Lowder, Simeon. S.'s ecclesiastical statesmanship. Use of printed sources. The theme of all Church History. S.'s home not 'a religious home': daily services—the High Church tradition: S. introduces family worship: family prayers—the Puritan tradition: Evangelical clergy admit their parishioners: prayer-meetings or conventicles: importance of the revival of family worship in the history of the Evangelical Movement: the High Church and the Evangelical tradition compared—liturgical and non-liturgical. S. 'finds trials in his own family': death of his eldest brother: S. prepares to leave Cambridge: his father obdurately prejudiced against 'Methodism': S. presented to Holy Trinity, Cambridge: conversion of his elder brothers, Edward and John: triumphs of the Evangelical Revival among 'the public school class'.

Appendix. Parlour Religion Exemplified (1794).

Chapter II. RELIGION IN THE SCHOOL, pp. 45–96

Condition of the public schools: S. as a boy at Eton (1767–79): the Montem of 1778: S. on the state of religion and morals at Eton during his school days. The archetypal controversy regarding Public School Religion (1799–1802), concerned with the disproportion of Classical to religious instruction: Jones of Nayland, *Considerations on the Religious Worship of the Heathens* (1799): Dr Vincent, Head Master of Westminster, replies privately: Dr Rennell's Charity Sermon (1799): Dr Vincent remonstrates: the Bishop of Meath's Charity Sermon (1801): Dr Vincent publishes his *Defence of Public Education* (1802): Dr Vincent is rewarded with the Deanery of Westminster, to which he adds a country rectory. But how far was Eton covered by his *Defence*? Religious observance and religious instruction at Eton in 1766: gradual reforms (1809–37): Confirmation and Holy Communion in public schools: Sermons. Rowland Hill at Eton (1753–64): his conversion (1762): forms 'a religious society'. S. seriously impressed by the Fast Day of 1776. The foundation of the Newcastle Scholarship (1829) establishes divinity as a subject in its own right in the curriculum. Second controversy regarding Public School Religion (1830–34), concerned with compulsory chapel at Eton.

Appendix A. Dr Randolph.

     B. Rev. Thomas Gisborne.

     C. Dr Vincent (Syllabus of Religious Instruction at Westminster and at Winchester in 1802).

Chapter III. RELIGION IN THE UNIVERSITY, pp. 97–147

Inadequacy of the curriculum in the two Universities, regarded as theological seminaries: Pusey's criticisms (1833): demand for reform: Professor Marsh (1792): Bishop Porteus (1767). Heterodoxy at Cambridge: Professor Watson: the Subscription Controversy: Socinianism and Latitudinarianism: Professor Hey: 'Clergymen's Doubts': Porson: Tyrwhitt, Jebb, Palmer, Frend: Robert Robinson. Compulsory Chapel: 'necessary to have some kind of muster-roll': undergraduate irreverence: the Fellows conspicuous by their absence. The Holy Communion: some measure of compulsion: this the instrument of S.'s conversion (1779): 'the Terminal Sacrament': details of collegiate use. Revival of the Subscription Controversy (admission of Dissenters to degrees) in 1833: Professor Turton's opposition: Thirlwall's *Letter to Turton* (1834) denounces compulsory chapel: Whewell replies: Thirlwall resigns his Assistant Tutorship under protest. Undergraduate behaviour in Chapel much improved: but the Fellows still negligent in their attendance: Trinity College, Society for the Prevention of Cruelty to Undergraduates (1838). S. and services in King's College Chapel. Few sermons in College Chapels. Attendance at the University Sermon generally very sparse: some popular preachers—Scott, Marsh, S.: improved attendance in the early nineteenth century: favourite preachers: 'Scraping'. Attendance of undergraduates at parish churches: the Evangelical strongholds: contrast with earlier period: Dr Ogden. S., converted, seeks a spiritual home and a spiritual father: this the explanation of much of his own subsequent activity. S. attends St Edward's: Christopher Atkinson introduces him to John Venn: S. meets Henry Venn, Rector of Yelling (1782): so terminates his quest.

Appendix A. Romilly's Diary.

     B. Canon Wordsworth's recollections.

Chapter IV. BERRIDGE OF EVERTON, pp. 149–200

Academic Clergy: Pastor Moritz at Oxford (1782): Sunday-evening Clubs: pastoral ministrations: Bishop Keene's Charge of 1771: Farmer, Unwin, Bennet, Venn, Thomas Robinson, Henry Martyn. John Berridge, Fellow of Clare: Curate of Stapleford (1749): Vicar of Everton (1755): his conversion (1757). The Everton Revival (1758–59): visits from Whitefield and John Wesley: 'violent outward symptoms': Berridge joined by Hicks of Wrestlingworth: open-air preaching: eye-witness narratives: scenes at Everton: Berridge and Hicks itinerate: visit from Lady Huntingdon's chaplains: scene at Stapleford: Dr John Green is scornful: further visits from Wesley:

CONTENTS

Berridge preaches before the University: forms acquaintance with Rowland Hill and other undergraduates (1764-71): Lady Huntingdon introduces Berridge to 'the religious circles of the metropolis'. Berridge's mode of living and of preaching. The Calvinistic Controversy: Berridge's controversy with Fletcher (1773-74): relations with Wesley strained since 1760: Berridge becomes a Calvinist: Fletcher's tribute to him: reconciliation (1776): Berridge's final views on religious controversy. Church-work at Everton: Venn comes to Yelling (1771): John Venn introduces S. tô Berridge (1782). Berridge in old age: eccentricities: failing powers: death (1793): S. preaches his funeral sermon: epitaph.

Appendix. Sermon by Berridge.

Chapter V. CADOGAN OF READING, pp. 201–247

S. a purchaser of livings (1836): his object: the problem of Continuity. The Rev. the Hon. W. B. Cadogan appointed Vicar of St Giles', Reading (1774), prior to his ordination: and then also Rector of St Luke's, Chelsea (1775). His predecessor at St Giles', the Rev. William Talbot. Cadogan's appointment resented: he dismisses his predecessor's curate, the Rev. John Hallward. Hallward's previous history: his association with the Six Students of St Edmund Hall, Oxford: visit from Rowland Hill: Whitefield's interest: expulsion of the Six Students (1768): a war of pamphlets. Hallward's subsequent career and death (1826). Dispersal of Mr Talbot's congregation: Lady Huntingdon opens a Chapel: others join the Baptists: Cadogan criticised by members of his congregation: Hallward's tribute to Mr Talbot's memory: Mrs Talbot opens her house for religious exercises. Cadogan retires to Chelsea: shows energy and zeal: his popularity wanes: he returns to Reading. Cadogan's early history: Westminster and Christ Church: religious impressions: internal conflict: friendship with Mrs Talbot: altered religious sentiments: psychological reaction: illness: marriage. Cadogan an exemplary parish priest at Chelsea and Reading. The Evangelicals attached too much importance to the ministry of preaching: Cadogan's letter to the Bishop of London. Signs of trouble in store at Reading: death of Cadogan (1797): S. preaches his funeral sermon: Cadogan succeeded at Reading by the Rev. Joseph Eyre: his congregation dissipated by successive schisms (1797-1839). Erasmus Middleton, Cadogan's curate at Chelsea: one of the Six Students: obliged to leave by Cadogan's successor, the Rev. Charles Sturges. Difficulty of maintaining continuity: Wallingford (Pentycross): Berridge's letter to Lady Huntingdon: William Hey: Huddersfield (Venn). Other problems, such as recruitment and training, ordinations, presentations, secondary to this problem of securing continuity of teaching. Purchase of livings the solution: John and Henry Thornton: the Simeon Trust: dangers of this policy.

Chapter VI. SIMEON AND CHURCH ORDER, pp. 249–312

The problem of Church Order. Undenominationalism: Watson, Berridge. Distinction drawn between 'gospel labourers' and the main body of the clergy. Danger of secession. Itinerancy the crux: divergence between

CONTENTS

Illustrations

Preface

IN November 1936, I was invited by the Editor of the *Church Times* to contribute a full-page article on Charles Simeon to mark the centenary of his death. In some degree, this book has grown out of that article.[1] But the invitation, as coming from the Editor of a distinctively Anglo-Catholic religious periodical, was also suggestive and significant in itself. I suppose that never within my life-time have the traditional party divisions in the Church of England been less harmful or more beneficial than in the years immediately preceding the present War. It is true that to Simeon himself the existence of ecclesiastical parties appeared regrettable; 'nor', he declared, in the Preface to his *magnum opus*, the *Horae Homileticae* (standard ed., 21 vols. 1832–3), 'would any thing under heaven be more grateful to him than to see names and parties buried in eternal oblivion, and primitive simplicity restored to the Church.'[2] Yet such a statement reveals a startling misconception of the history of the Primitive Church. For, as Disraeli once pointed out, 'Parties in the Church have always existed. They existed in the Church at Jerusalem. They existed in the Church at Ephesus. They existed always in the Church at Rome. And it would be most wonderful indeed if in a country like England, where party has always been recognized as the most efficient and satisfactory means of conducting public affairs, party should not be found in the Church alone. My Lord, what is Party? Party is organized opinion. And so long as the nature of man is of that various and varying character which we all know it is, so long will there be various and varying modes by which it will express itself, or by which it may be counselled, upon religious matters.'[3] Harmony—harmony, even at the risk

---

[1] 'Charles Simeon: 1759–1836.' *Church Times*, Nov. 13, 1936 (vol. cxvi, pp. 567–8).   [2] *Horae Homileticae*, vol. i (1832), Preface, p. xxi*n*.

[3] Speech on 'Church Policy' at a meeting in aid of the Oxford Diocesan Society for the Augmentation of Small Benefices, held at Oxford, Nov. 25, 1864, the Bishop [Samuel Wilberforce] of Oxford presiding. *Vide* '*Church and Queen': Five Speeches delivered by the Rt. Hon. B. Disraeli, M.P.*, 1860–4, edited, with a preface, by a Member of the University of Oxford (1865), pp. 68–9.

of intermittent and momentary discords, since that risk is inevitable where any measure of speculative independence is to be
conceded in the pursuit of truth—but harmony, and not unison,
is the distinctive character of the piety of the English Church.
'Englishmen have always preferred the recognition of all the
facts of any case, however irreconcilable they may seem, to the
sacrifices which a perfect logical system invariably demands,
before it can square to its required limits the complex variety of
human nature and human life.'[1] Of this attitude in theology,
Charles Simeon was himself a notable exemplar.

> The Author is no friend to systematizers in Theology.... He has no
> doubt but that there is a system in the Holy Scriptures (for
> truth cannot be inconsistent with itself); but he is persuaded that
> neither Calvinists nor Arminians are in *exclusive* possession of that
> system. He is disposed to think that the Scripture system, be it what
> it may, is of a broader and more comprehensive character than some
> very exact and dogmatical Theologians are inclined to allow: and that,
> as wheels in a complicated machine may move in opposite directions
> and yet subserve one common end, so may truths *apparently opposite*
> be perfectly reconcilable with each other, and equally subserve the
> purposes of God in the accomplishment of man's salvation.... He
> bitterly regrets that men will range themselves under human banners
> and leaders, and employ themselves in converting the Inspired
> Writers into friends and partisans of their peculiar principles. Into
> this fault he trusts that he has never fallen. One thing he knows,
> namely, that pious men, both of the Calvinistic and Arminian
> persuasion, approximate very nearly when they are upon their
> knees before God in prayer.... And what both these individuals
> are upon their knees, it is the wish of the Author to become in his
> writings....[2]

Or, as he expressed himself more jocularly on the same subject
in a private letter to a clerical acquaintance (9 July 1825): 'The
truth is *not in the middle*, and *not in one extreme; but in both
extremes*.... So that if extremes please you, I am your man; only
remember that it is not *one* extreme that we are to go to, but *both*

---

[1] *Masters in English Theology* (1877), Historical Preface by the editor,
Canon Alfred Barry, D.D., p. xvi.
[2] *Horae Homileticae*, vol. i (1832), Preface, pp. xxiii–xxiv.

ontromoo.'[1] Plainly, it would be hazardous to erect this particular observation into an universal rule. Yet they are as grievously in error who mistake for compromise what is really comprehension, as are those who use the principle of toleration as a license for broadmindedness.

It is indeed one of the historic glories of the Church of England that she is able to comprehend within her body divergent—yet not essentially conflicting—schools of thought, and that her formularies are tolerant, within certain necessary limits, of more than one variety of theological approach to sacred truth. Of course it is true that when schools of thought develop into Church Parties, and when any single Party claims that *it is* the Church of England and that its standards of belief and practice must be accepted as the norm from which no deviations are permissible, party divisions inevitably become embittered, and the life of the Church is disturbed, distorted and distressed by noisy internecine feuds. But that, for the time being, is past history. The real issue is no longer between the High Church, Low Church, Broad Church parties, between Anglo-Catholics, Evangelicals and Modernists. Fanaticism, indeed, in all its varying modes and phases—Communist,[2] Fundamentalist, Pacifist, Millennarian, and British Israelite, as well as Papalist or Protestant—is a perennial problem, but it is peripheral, and in any case it is a matter rather for the psychopathologist than for the ecclesiastical historian: admittedly there is an issue here, but it is not the real issue, and its significance is easily exaggerated. The real issue at the present time lies not between orthodoxy and fanaticism, nor does it lie between the three traditional

---

[1] W. Carus, *Memoirs of the Rev. Charles Simeon* (2nd ed. 1847), p. 600.

[2] 'The Church of England has suffered much...from those "political" incumbents who seek a psychological compensation for their failure in pastoral love and duty towards the individual members of their flocks, in an embittered passion for Humanity at large'—and for the U.S.S.R. in particular (*The Priest as Student*, ed. H. S. Box, 1939, p. 274.)—It is indeed remarkable that those Anglican clergymen who talk most passionately about the ideals of universal brotherhood and 'the Christian Revolution' are generally those who show themselves conspicuously unable to get on with their colleagues or, what is much less pardonable, with their own parishioners. Their love for suffering humanity seems to stop short of the actual human beings they draw a salary to look after.

parties, but between those in all three parties who are essentially Anglican in their loyalties, and those who are not.[1]

It is for this reason that a historical study of the origins of the Evangelical Party and of its initial problems may be of service. For, as the Editor of *Theology* (the Rev. A. R. Vidler) has rightly pointed out, 'what the Church is to-day can be understood only in the light of its history. It is notorious that foreigners find the Church of England an enigmatic institution. It is scarcely less enigmatic to Englishmen who try to make sense of it without regard to its history. Those outside the Church, if they know its history and feel its spell, often show a keener appreciation of its character and even a warmer attachment to it as an institution than some of its members who judge and despise it for its failure to conform to some upstart ecclesiastical fashion imported from another tradition, or improvised without any traditional reference at all'.[2] If certain of the Anglo-Catholic clergy err in the former sense, it is no less true that certain of the Evangelical clergy err quite as cheerfully in the latter. In either case, the pretext is usually that of 'a higher loyalty', whether, in the one case, to an entirely irrelevant authority (euphemistically described as 'Catholic Tradition'), or, in the other, to their own peculiar insight into, or psychological sensitiveness regarding, the Mind of Christ. It is not of course intended to deny that such men frequently 'do very good work'. But that is not the point. The real issue in our own day, as in Charles Simeon's, is not con-

---

[1] It should be unnecessary to add that, for a loyal member of the Church of England, this presentation of the issue presupposes the position stated by the Archbishops and Bishops of the Anglican Communion at the Lambeth Conference of 1930:

'. . . The time has come for us to make some explicit statement of the ideal before us and of the future to which we look forward.

'Our ideal is nothing less than the Catholic Church in its entirety. Viewed in its widest relations, the Anglican Communion is seen as in some sense an incident in the history of the Church Universal. It has arisen out of the situation caused by the divisions of Christendom. It has indeed been clearly blessed of God, as we thankfully acknowledge; but in its present character we believe that it is transitional, and we forecast the day when the racial and historical connections which at present characterise it will be transcended, and the life of our Communion will be merged in a larger fellowship in the Catholic Church.' *Lambeth Conference Report*, 1930, p. 153 (*The Anglican Communion: its Ideal and Future*).

[2] *Theology*, Jan. 1940 (vol. xl), Editorial, p. 2.

cerned merely with 'good work', but with Church Order as the precondition of 'good work'. In the words of a great Evangelical bishop, Handley Moule, 'It was Simeon, more than even the greatest of his predecessors, who taught and exemplified the fact that the warmest Evangelical, without any real sacrifice of inter-denominational fraternity in Christ, can and should be watchfully loyal to the order and the organization of the English Church in the normal exercise of his energies'.[1] And, if Simeon's experience is any precedent, it may be premised that it is in the theological seminaries that the issue between Church Order and Enthusiasm must be decided.

In the period covered by these lectures, the two trends in contemporary Evangelicalism in the Church of England—the Anglican and the un-Anglican—have their representatives in Charles Simeon on the one hand, and John Berridge on the other: and this brief account of the respective ministries of those two good men may in some degree illuminate our present problems. Emphatically, it was not written for that purpose. But it may serve it.

The first four lectures represent an attempt to sketch the historic background of Simeon's ministry in the Church of England. Of these, the third (*Religion in the University*) may partially supply the place of what was intended to be the third volume of the late Canon Christopher Wordsworth's trilogy on University Life and Studies in England during the Eighteenth Century:[2] and here I have gratefully to acknowledge the kindness of the Rev. W. A. Wordsworth and Miss Wordsworth in allowing me to make use of their father's MS. notebooks (2) and also of the MS. Diary (October 1793–March 1801) of their great-grandfather, Dr Christopher Wordsworth, Master of Trinity from 1820 to 1841, very full extracts from which are printed in Canon Wordsworth's *Social Life at the English*

---

[1] H. C. G. Moule, *The Evangelical School in the Church of England: its men and its work in the nineteenth century* (1901), p. 12.
[2] *Social Life at the English Universities in the Eighteenth Century* (Le Bas Prize Essay), 1874: *Scholae Academicae: some account of the Studies of the English Universities in the Eighteenth Century*, 1877: the concluding volume was to have dealt with 'The RELIGIOUS LIFE in its personal and social aspects' (*Social Life*, p. 4).

Universities, App. G, pp. 584–98. (The Diary has since been presented to the Library of Trinity College, Cambridge.) I am also greatly indebted to my cousin, the Rev. Dr F. W. B. Bullock, late Vice-Principal of Ridley Hall, for allowing me to consult the MS. of his *History of Ridley Hall*, which is now in the press.

The two concluding lectures deal more directly with the two major problems by which Simeon found himself confronted: the problem of Continuity, and the problem of Church Order.

My thanks are due to the Master and Council of Trinity College, Cambridge, for the privilege of delivering the Birkbeck Lectures for 1937–8: and to all who have been kind enough to supply me with many useful details of information, among whom I may mention particularly Mr D. A. Winstanley, Vice-Master of Trinity College; Dr J. A. Venn, President of Queens' College; the Rev. Canon C. Tremayne, Secretary of the Elland Society; Mr R. A. Austen Leigh, the Editor of *Etoniana*; the Rev. F. M. Yglesias; the Rev. F. N. Davey; and the Rev. Dr. Newton Flew, Principal of Wesley House. Nor can I omit to record my gratitude to the Staff of the University Library, and in particular to Mr Pink of the Anderson Room.

This book does not pretend to be a new Life of Simeon, nor is it designed to supersede the standard lives by Carus (1847) and Moule (1892). It will, however, be found to contain a good deal of supplementary material.[1] I have been at pains to supply very full references, chiefly in the hope of saving time and trouble to any future church historians who may be attracted to a field in which there is still plenty of work to be done. There is room, for instance, for a far more extensive treatment of the history of the reform of theological studies in this University. There is room for a new edition of Berridge's letters, many of which are scattered through the files of defunct religious periodicals. There is room for a series of biographical sketches of the Cambridge Evangelicals of the period, Simeon's con-

[1] I may also be allowed to mention that a discussion of Simeon's influence on the development of Anglican homiletics will be found in my *Art of Preaching: A Practical Survey of Preaching in the Church of England, 747–1939* (S.P.C.K., 1940).

PREFACE

tomporaries and disciples When these, and similar under-
takings, have been accomplished, the time will be ripe for a new
biography of Simeon himself. For the meanwhile, it is hoped
that these pages may be a not unworthy tribute to his memory.

'*My covenant was with him of life and peace; and I gave them
to him for the fear wherewith he feared me, and was afraid before
my name. The law of truth was in his mouth, and iniquity was not
found in his lips: he walked with me in peace and equity, and did
turn many away from iniquity.*' (Malachi, ii, 5, 6.)

CHARLES SMYTH

Corpus Christi College, Cambridge
   January 30, 1940

Select Bibliography

*Recollections of the Conversation Parties of the Rev. Charles Simeon, M.A.,
Senior Fellow of King's College, and Perpetual Curate of Trinity
Church, Cambridge. With Introductory Notices,* by Abner William
Brown, M.A., formerly of Queens' College, Cambridge, Vicar of
Gretton, Northamptonshire, and Honorary Canon of Peter-
borough. 1863. [= Brown.]

*Memoirs of the Life of the Rev. Charles Simeon, M.A., late Senior Fellow
of King's College, and Minister of Trinity Church, Cambridge. With
a selection from his writings and correspondence.* Edited by the
Rev. William Carus, M.A., Fellow and Senior Dean of Trinity
College, and Minister of Trinity Church, Cambridge. (1847.)
2nd ed. 1847. [= Carus.]

Charles Simeon. By H. C. G. Moule, M.A. (English Leaders of
Religion.) 1892. [= Moule.]

*Memoranda of the Rev. Charles Simeon, M.A., late Minister of Trinity
Church, and Fellow of King's College, Cambridge.* (Reprinted,
'with very little variation', from *The Christian Observer*, Jan.,
April, May, 1837, pp. 56 ff., 235 ff., 353 ff.) By Matthew Morris
Preston, M.A., Vicar of Cheshunt, late Fellow of Trinity College,
Cambridge. 1840. [= Preston.]

*A brief Memoir of the Rev. Charles Simeon, M.A., late Senior Fellow of
King's College, Cambridge.* By the Rev. J. Williamson, M.A.,
Incumbent of Theale, Somerset. 1848. [= Williamson.]

Sermons on the Death of the Rev. Charles Simeon (1836), by the
Rev. William Dealtry, D.D., Chancellor of Winchester, and
formerly Fellow of Trinity College; by the Rev. James Scholefield,
M.A., Regius Professor of Greek; by the Rev. George Hodson,
M.A., Archdeacon of Stafford, late Fellow and Tutor of Magdalen
College, Cambridge (these three, together with obituary notices,
etc., are reprinted in *The Pulpit*, vol. xxix, 1837, pp. 17–29): by the
Rev. Francis Close, Incumbent of Cheltenham (reprinted in his
Occasional Sermons preached in the Parish Church of Cheltenham,
1844, pp. 179–218); by the Rev. William Mandell, B.D., Fellow of
Queens' College; by the Rev. J. B. Cartwright, Minister of the
Episcopal Jews' Chapel, Bethnal Green, London; and by Samuel
Thodey, Minister, at the Downing Street Meeting-House,
Cambridge.

Charles Simeon: An Interpretation. Addresses delivered at the Centenary Celebrations, Cambridge, November 1936 (by the Archbishop of Canterbury, the Bishops of Ely, Worcester, Truro, and Croydon, the Provost of Bradford, Prebendary W. Wilson Cash, Prebendary F. E. Murphy, the Rev. C. M. Chavasse, the Rev. H. Earnshaw Smith, and the Rev. C. J. Morton). 1936.

The Works of the Rev. John Berridge, M.A., late Fellow of Clare Hall, Cambridge, Vicar of Everton, Bedfordshire, and Chaplain to the Right Honourable the Earl of Buchan. With an enlarged Memoir of his Life: numerous Letters, Anecdotes, Outlines of Sermons, and Observations on Passages of Scripture; and his Original Sion's Songs. By the Rev. Richard Whittingham, Vicar of Potton, Bedfordshire. 1838. [*Works*, etc. = Berridge's *Works*: Whittingham's biogr. *Memoir* = Whittingham.]

Memoirs of the Honourable and Reverend William Bromley Cadogan, M.A., late Rector of St Luke's, Chelsea; Vicar of St Giles's, Reading; and Chaplain to the Right Honourable Lord Cadogan. By Richard Cecil, A.M., Minister of St John's Chapel, Bedford Row. In Cadogan's *Discourses* (1798), pp. iii–cxxxii [= Cecil, *Mem.*]: reprinted with slight alterations in *The Works of the Rev. Richard Cecil*, 2nd ed. 1816, vol. i, pp. 167–276.

Memoirs of Mr Coxe Feary, first Pastor of the Baptist Church at Bluntisham, in Huntingdonshire. With an Account of the Rise and Formation of that Church. By John Audley. 1823. [= Feary.]

The Life of the Rev. Rowland Hill, A.M. By the Rev. Edwin Sidney, A.M. 1834. [= Sidney, *Rowland Hill.*]

The Life and Times of Selina, Countess of Huntingdon. By a Member of the Houses of Shirley and Hastings [Aaron Crossley Hobart Seymour]. (2 vols., 1839–40.) 4th thousand, 1840. [= *Countess of Huntingdon.*]—Index, compiled by Francis M. Jackson, in *Proc. Wesley Hist. Soc.*, vol. v, 1906, Supplement.

The Life and a selection from the Letters of the late Rev. Henry Venn, M.A., successively Vicar of Huddersfield, Yorkshire, and Rector of Yelling, Huntingdonshire, Author of "The Complete Duty of Man", etc. The Memoir of his Life drawn up by the late Rev. John Venn, M.A., Rector of Clapham, Surrey. Edited by the Rev. Henry Venn, B.D., Incumbent of Drypool, Yorkshire; late Fellow of Queens' College, Cambridge. 1834. [= Venn.]

Annals of a Clerical Family: being some account of the family and descendants of William Venn, Vicar of Otterton, Devon, 1600–1621. By John Venn, F.R.S., F.S.A., Fellow and President of Gonville and Caius College, Cambridge. 1904. [= *Venn Family Annals.*]

I

RELIGION IN THE HOME

✠

Family religion is of unspeakable importance.

On Family Worship
(*Works* of the Rev. Richard Cecil, M.A.
2nd ed. 1816, vol. iii, p. 430.)

Chapter One

RELIGION IN THE HOME

THE HISTORY OF THE CHURCH OF ENGLAND in the nineteenth century is punctuated by three funerals, upon the significance of any one of which it would be possible to expatiate at length. All three were, in their different ways, spectacular and memorable and significant: and in each case the man thus honoured in his death was one who throughout the greater part of his life had been the object of a storm of obloquy, derision, and mistrust, and who, in his years of most laborious and most fruitful service, had been widely regarded as an open traitor to the doctrine and discipline of the Church he served.

There can be little difficulty in identifying the three funerals to which I have alluded. Probably the most obvious is the funeral of Dr Pusey in Christ Church, Oxford, on St Matthew's Day, Sept. 21, 1882; the most obvious, because the memory of the scene has been preserved for ever in one of the most deathless pages of Scott Holland's incomparable prose. '...At last, the end, so long delayed as to have become almost incredible, had come. The old man was dead. And up from every corner of the country came creeping the old men still left to whom his name had been a watchword and an inspiration. It seemed the last act of the historic Movement....We younger men watched the long procession of men whose names had been familiar, but whom we had never before seen in the flesh. Here they were— bowed, grey, tottering, making their final effort, delivering their witness to the end....As they turned away from the grave, they knew that they would never meet again in such a company, on this earth....So we buried him: and, with him, we buried a whole generation, which could never quite recur. As we turned from the grave, we passed into another atmosphere with another perspective. We had left an epoch behind us.'[1]

[1] H. Scott Holland, *A Bundle of Memories* (1915), pp. 99–101.—It is instructive to compare with this Dean Church's account of Mr Keble's

Two years earlier, in what was then one of the most squalid and vicious districts in the East End of London, there had taken place another funeral, which differed from the former not only in being utterly unacademic, but also in the circumstance that it marked the birth, and not the death, of a magnificent tradition. The funeral of Charles Lowder, formerly Vicar of St Peter's, London Docks, took place on Sept. 17, 1880. 'We have called it a funeral in compliance with established phraseology', said *The Church Review* (Sept. 24, 1880), 'but in truth it was a triumphal progress through the crowded streets of East London, such as England has never before seen in this 19th century.'[1] Of the history that lay behind it—the riots at St George's-in-the-East, the cholera epidemic of 1866, the years of devotion and self-sacrifice—there can be little need to speak. The significance of Father Lowder's funeral was that it stereotyped the tradition of the Anglo-Catholic slum priest: and there are those who will remember the echo of it in the funeral of Father Stanton of St Alban's, Holborn, in the days before the War.[2]

The span of almost half a century separated the funeral of Dr Pusey from that of the Rev. Charles Simeon, who was buried in King's College Chapel on Saturday, Nov. 19, 1836. If

funeral at Hursley, April 6, 1866. 'It was more like a festival than anything else, though there was black and white about. But the sun and the fresh keen air, and the flowers just coming out, and the beauty of the place and the church, and the completeness of that which had come to its last stage here, put all the ordinary thoughts of sorrow, not aside, but in a distinctly subordinate place. There were some seventy or eighty people, I should think, at the eight o'clock celebration, with *him* in the midst of us, once more in his chancel, and before the altar. At the service and funeral itself the church was crowded, and Rogers, Dean Hook, and I were glad to get a school children's bench in the corner. Yet it was a strange gathering. There was a meeting of old currents and new. Besides the people *I* used to think of with Keble, there was a crowd of younger men, who no doubt have as much right in him as we have, in their way—Mackonochie, Lowder, and that sort. Excellent good fellows, but who, one could not help being conscious, looked upon us as rather *dark* people, who don't grow beards, and do other proper things.' (*Life and Letters of Dean Church*, ed. Mary C. Church, 1894, p. 172.)

[1] Quoted in *St Peter's, London Docks, Parish Magazine*, Oct. 1930, p. 128. Cf. *Charles Lowder: A Biography* [by M. Trench], pp. 358 ff.

[2] Cf. photographs reproduced in *Arthur Stanton: A Memoir*, by the Right Hon. G. W. E. Russell (1917), p. 312.—'No living was ever offered to him except one in Chicago, but *omnia vincit amor*, and when he died, thousands of men uncovered, and women knelt down, to watch the progress of crucifix and coffin from Holborn to Waterloo Bridge' (*Further Letters from A Man of No Importance*, 1932, p. 73).

Dr Pusey's funeral marked the end, and Father Lowder's the beginning, of a movement, the funeral of Charles Simeon may be said to mark a movement in mid-career. And if Dr Pusey's funeral was academic, and Father Lowder's was parochial, the funeral of Charles Simeon combined both characters. The antechapel was packed with townspeople, parishioners and members of his congregation at Holy Trinity, 'the greater part ladies and respectable females',[1] while more than 1500 gownsmen, according to Dean Close's estimate,[2] thronged into the building, the undergraduates, all in mourning, standing throughout the service in the space between the coffin and the Communion rails. Many were turned away, unable to obtain admittance. The day was cold and wet, intensifying the sepulchral gloom of the proceedings. 'The funeral was not designedly public; Simeon had desired that it should be very simple.'[3] Yet Bishop Moule is surely right in saying that 'probably Cambridge never saw quite such a funeral as Simeon's'.[4] 'The procession round the quadrangle, used on the burial within the precincts of a College resident, was very striking. The persons who made up the procession, walking three or four abreast, nearly extended round the four sides of the quadrangle.'[5]

It was headed by the choristers, with their surplices, followed by the Scholars and Fellows in hat-bands of long silk, and large silk scarfs covering their gowns; last of these came the Provost of the College, Dr Thackeray, in deep mourning. The principal mourner, Sir Richard Simeon, a nephew[6] of the deceased, followed the bier,

---

[1] Account in the *Standard* of Nov. 21, reproduced in *The Pulpit*, vol. xxix (1837), p. 218: also in Williamson, p. 134.

[2] Cited by Moule, p. 275. Cf. however *A Brief Sketch of the Character and Last Days of the Rev. C. Simeon, A.M.*, in Close's *Occasional Sermons preached in the Parish Church of Cheltenham* (1844), p. 193, where he says: 'One thousand members of the University followed him to the grave.' The paper cited by Moule is dated 1882.—The most detailed accounts of the funeral will be found in *The Pulpit*, vol. xxix, pp. 215, 217–18. For other contemporary descriptions by eye-witnesses, vide Carus, pp. 827–8 (by Dr Dealtry: Moule, p. 274); *Life and Letters of Rowland Williams*, vol. i, pp. 32–3; also A. R. Pennington, *Recollections of Persons and Events*, pp. 192–4.

[3] Moule, p. 272; Carus, p. 827.

[4] Moule, p. 274.   [5] Dealtry, in Carus, pp. 827–8.

[6] Son of Charles Simeon's elder brother, Sir John Simeon, Bart. In 1814 Charles Simeon had received from another brother, Edward, a legacy of £15,000: of this, he spontaneously transferred £10,000 to his nephew's account when the latter was returned to Parliament in 1832 as Member for

which was borne upon the shoulders of six men; among the other mourners were the trustees of his livings, and many of the incumbents that filled them; and the rear was brought up by an immense body of the Members of the University, among whom were the Professors, and many of the Heads of Houses, and a very large number of Fellows of Colleges and resident Masters of Arts. Last of all came a long array of Under Graduates, who indeed, though last, constituted, from their number, the largest part of the procession....[1]

According to one estimate,[2] eight Heads of Houses, six Professors, about 100 Masters of Arts, 100 Bachelors of Arts and 500 undergraduates were present. Less than forty years earlier, it had been a University crime to speak to Simeon, and was reported to parents;[3] and Dr Dealtry could remember one occasion when he had been hissed in the Senate House on going up to vote.[4] But on Nov. 19, 1836, all the shops in the principal parts of the town were closed during the funeral, although it was market-day, and twelve out of every fourteen respectable people that were seen in the streets were in mourning; 'and, what was an unusual mark of respect in the University, in almost every College the Lectures were suspended'.[5] 'Thus', wrote the Dean of Jesus (who had not himself been present, owing to the inclemency of the weather), 'is buried a true servant of God; one who (like us all) had his failings, but who has been enabled to do more good for the Church of Christ in England than any person now living.'[6] It was therefore with a good deal of justification that Mrs Butler rebuked her feckless offspring—the future Butler of Wantage, then a scholar of Trinity—for his omission to be present: 'I should have been better pleased had you on the day of Mr Simeon's funeral made the attendance upon it instead of your water excursion.'[7]

the Isle of Wight (Moule, p. 176). Sir Richard does not seem to have been extravagantly grateful (cf. Brown, p. 40).

[1] *The Pulpit*, vol. xxix, p. 217; Williamson, pp. 133–4.
[2] *The Pulpit*, vol. xxix, p. 215.
[3] Brown, p. 117.—As late as 1817, Moule's father, a freshman at St John's, 'was warned not to enter Trinity Church because of the bad character of its fanatical minister' (H. C. G. Moule, *The Evangelical School in the Church of England*, p. 8). [4] Pennington, p. 179. [5] Carus, p. 827.
[6] *Memorials of G. E. Corrie, D.D.*, ed. M. Holroyd (1890), p. 62.
[7] *Life and Letters of W. J. Butler, late Dean of Lincoln, and sometime Vicar of Wantage* (1897), p. 14. [Letter misdated Nov. 30, 1838 (for 1836).]

I apologise for what may appear to be a somewhat morbid avenue of approach to the subject of these lectures, albeit one perhaps not wholly inappropriate to All Souls' Day.[1] But if my course required or deserved a sub-title, I should be inclined to borrow it from the title of the Funeral Sermon preached by the Rev. Thomas Scott (the Biblical Commentator) in commemoration of Mr Pentycross of Wallingford: namely, *The Duty and Advantage of remembering Deceased Ministers*.[2] For the history of the Evangelical Revival is essentially a history of personalities, rather than of opinions. And the outstanding personality in that Revival, after the heroic age of Whitefield and the Wesleys and the formidable Lady Huntingdon, is the Rev. Charles Simeon. I doubt whether the genius of that man as an ecclesiastical statesman has ever received sufficient recognition. He seems to me to rank with Samuel Wilberforce, Bishop of Oxford—the Remodeller of the Episcopate, as Burgon calls him[3]—as one of the Founding Fathers, or Remodellers of the Church of England in the nineteenth century. Now, there are two types of statesmanship, whether ecclesiastical or secular. There is the statesmanship which, confronted by a succession of problems, discovers the solution for each one of them (ignoring those that do not matter), and, what is more—and this is where the quality of statesmanship comes in—succeeds in keeping these solutions consistent with each other, by framing each in turn in strict consistency with some body of fixed principles which provides, under all circumstances, the criterion of thought and action. The other type of statesmanship is that which does not wait for problems to confront it, but, having excogitated the solution, then manufactures the particular problem to which the solution is to be applied. Again, there is the same reference to fixed principles: the difference lies in the fact that the solution anticipates and deliberately evokes the problem, instead of being

---

[1] This lecture was delivered on Nov. 2, 1937.
[2] *The Duty and Advantage of remembering Deceased Ministers: being the substance of a Funeral Sermon, preached in the church of St Mary, Wallingford, on Hebrews xii. 7, 8; for the Rev. Thomas Pentycross, A.M., during more than thirty years vicar of that parish.* By Thomas Scott, Rector of Aston Sandford, Bucks. (1808).
[3] In *Lives of Twelve Good Men*.

anticipated and evoked by it. The latter type of statesmanship reveals, perhaps, a higher order of genius: but it is far more dangerous to apply, because it leads so often to what Bishop Creighton, with unerring judgment, stigmatised as the principal ingredient in the failure of Archbishop Laud, namely, the fatal tactic of fighting 'for great principles on small issues, a method which still survives, and which makes the history of religious thought in England so obscure and difficult to follow'.[1] Simeon's statesmanship was of the former—the more pedestrian, yet probably the more effective—type; and his career may be regarded as one of the supreme examples of its application. 'As to Simeon,' wrote Lord Macaulay in 1844, 'if you knew what his authority and influence were, and how they extended from Cambridge to the most remote corners of England, you would allow that his real sway in the Church was far greater than that of any primate.'[2]

It is necessary, therefore, that these lectures on the Origins of the Evangelical Revival in Cambridge in the eighteenth century should concern themselves primarily with the incidents and with the issues of that remarkable career, and that they should find in Simeon both their *terminus ad quem* and also their *terminus a quo*. Or, if I may be permitted, not so much to vary as, rather, to confuse that metaphor, Simeon was the bottle-neck upon which those Origins converged. There were by-passes, of course: but the main stream of traffic passed through that bottle-neck before it deployed upon the swelling plain of Victorian religion. This may explain, if it does not excuse, the somewhat unorthodox and discursive treatment which my material seems to have forced upon me. I propose in each instance to take, as my point of departure, Simeon's contact with a problem: and, if not in the actual delivery, at least in the preparation of these lectures, I have worked backwards and forwards from that point.

It may also be a heartening thought to those of us who are, or

---

[1] Mandell Creighton, *The Mind of St Peter, and other sermons* (1904), p. 98 (*The Failure of Laud*).

[2] Letter to his sister on Sir James Stephen's *Edinburgh Review* article on the Clapham Sect: quoted in Sir G. O. Trevelyan's *Life and Letters of Lord Macaulay* (ed. 1908), p. 50 *n*.

who are to be, professional historians, that these lectures have been compiled almost without any recourse at all to manuscript sources. I mention this, because I have for some time felt very passionately that, at this stage of things, anyone who produces a competent piece of research without reference to any unprinted documents is striking a real blow for academic freedom. I have not the audacity to suggest that these lectures are going to constitute such a blow: for one thing, I am not altogether persuaded that they are a competent piece of research: and, for another, there are in fact one or two manuscript references in them for which I am indebted to the generosity of my friends. It would of course be silly (and no doubt, for a mediaevalist, impossible) to make a fetish of not using manuscript sources. But the temptation which doth so easily beset us as historians is not this, but rather the temptation to make a fetish of invariably and even ostentatiously using manuscript sources, however trivial, and of virtually denying the name 'research' to any piece of work in which they have not been employed. We are, I think, in real danger of capitulating without a struggle to the tyranny of archives.[1] Clearly I do not mean that the historian is entitled to neglect primary sources—memoirs, autobiographies, correspondence, reports, and so forth. But what is intolerable is the glossing of the word 'primary' with the word 'unprinted'. For in a subject such as this—and it is a field in which a vast amount of research is still waiting to be done—the printed authorities are sufficiently overwhelming both in quantity and in bulk, and, although some are more valuable than others, it is clear that between them they do contain most, if not all, of the really important stuff. And when this condition of affairs obtains, the historian whose time is limited will be ill-advised to go out of his way to hunt for manuscripts merely to give his work a *cachet* which academically-minded critics might be disposed otherwise to deny to it.

[1] Cf. Hilary Jenkinson, *Manual of Archive Administration* (2nd ed. revised, 1937), p. 1: 'It is hardly necessary to say that History, as it is understood now, has become very largely dependent on Archives.... It is more than doubtful if any authoritative historical work will ever again be published without copious notes referring to verifiable manuscript sources....'

My second point concerns not so much the writing of history in general as, rather, the writing of ecclesiastical history in particular. I need not say that I felt deeply sensible of the honour when, as an assistant curate in the town, I found myself invited by the Council of this College to deliver the Birkbeck Lectures for this year. At the same time, I could not help but feel that there was something peculiarly appropriate in the invitation, not of course as regards my personal qualifications, but as regards my calling. For the parochial clergy are, after all, in every age the primary material of Church History: and our knowledge of the eighteenth century, in particular, has been distorted in the past by a preoccupation with bishops and doctrinal controversies, to the neglect of any adequate examination of the life and labours of what Professor Seeley used to call 'the average clergyman'.[1] Professor Norman Sykes' memorable Birkbeck Lectures of 1931–3, on *Church and State in England in the Eighteenth Century*, did much to redress the balance, and thereby to correct, if not to revolutionise, our notions of the Hanoverian epoch in the Church of England. But if the parochial clergy are the primary material of Church History, it follows that they have a right to be heard in the interpretation of that material. Any intelligent atheist could write a perfectly competent, although probably a somewhat biassed history of Popes and Councils and all that sort of thing. But Church History is something other than the record of ecclesiastical statecraft and diplomacy or even of those great doctrinal controversies by which it is so much conditioned and controlled. And I would go so far as to say that nobody can write Church History who is not either a parish priest or at least a person who has some real understanding of the problems of the parish priest. Indeed I would go even farther by suggesting, in all humility, that the right place in which to begin to learn to understand Church History is not the library, but the confessional, or its equivalent.

For the central theme of Church History—and, as I myself should naturally claim, of all human history—is Sin and Redemption. This theme is not always visible, not always on the

[1] J. R. Seeley, *Lectures and Essays* (1870), pp. 255, 256, 285.

surface: but it is never absent. And every now and then, whether in the life of the individual, or of the parish, or of the diocese, or of the Church, there is a moment of crisis—that is, of judgment—at which the theme becomes apparent and articulate. In order to illustrate my meaning, I beg leave to quote from J. B. Mozley's essay on Carlyle's Cromwell, in the first volume of his *Essays Historical and Theological*, the celebrated passage in which he analyses the character of the Protector's speeches. 'Has any one of our readers ever had the curiosity, at a wild-beast show, to give a pebble to a rhinoceros? His large heavy jaws take it in, and work it from side to side with a heavy seesaw motion; the stone just makes its appearance near the lip, and then an immediate sweep of the large tongue engulfs it in the recesses of a cavernous mouth. The subject of one of Cromwell's speeches fares much in the same way. He rolls it, buried underneath his tongue, from side to side, sometimes just showing a corner of it, and then covering it again. An interminable rolling motion goes on; and the wide jaws move before the solemn assembly for their appointed time. With large quotation of Scripture, and reference to chapter and verse; with endless allusion to "Providences", "Mercies", "Deliverances", "Dispensations", "Witnessings"; with proofs from the Psalms, the Prophets, the Epistles; with sentimental allusions to his own grief at being compelled to bear the burden of power; with long parentheses about no ascertainable subject-matter; with the heavy, swaying movements and the inarticulate rumbling noises of a bituminous volcanic lake; he comes at last to a conclusion, quite clear, and level to the plainest capacities—"Mr Speaker, I do dissolve this Parliament."'[1]

So is it also with Church History. There are long and almost unintelligible passages, choked with statecraft, priestcraft, piety, controversy, accommodation, churches being built and churches being burned, the hubbub of apocalyptic language, apologetic language, dogmatic language, pietistic language, clergymen being broad-minded and clergymen being narrow-minded, conflict and battle, with confused noise and garments rolled in blood, or

---

[1] J. B. Mozley, *Essays Historical and Theological* (1878), vol. i, p. 295.

equally enigmatic periods of tranquillity, prosperity, and even apathy: and then suddenly, like a lightning flash, the theme of all Church History—Sin and Redemption—breaks through, and illuminates what had hitherto appeared chaos, disorder, and futility: and that is κρίσις, Judgment: and he who sees it is not ignorant that he himself also stands beneath it. Often it is the poet who sees it first: and I am thinking now of T. S. Eliot's *Murder in the Cathedral*, and of Charles Williams' *Cranmer of Canterbury*, and even of the strangled orthodoxy of the younger men.[1] But the parish priest acquires, by virtue of his training and his ministry, something of the same prophetic insight: and therefore he also, however stupid or inarticulate he may seem to be, has something to say about Church History to the professional historian. It is no mere coincidence that the two English historians whose writings are conspicuous beyond those of any other for the quality of moral judgment, had both been country parsons.[2] And although I can no longer claim to stand before you in the character of a parish priest, I may at least express the humble confidence that, as the Captain of Hampshire Grenadiers was not useless to the historian of the Roman Empire, so also the Curate of St Giles', Cambridge—of St Saviour's, Upper Chelsea —and of St Clement's, Barnsbury, in the Rural Deanery of Islington—may be of service to the Birkbeck Lecturer for 1937–8.

I propose, then, to proceed with the subject of the Origins of the Evangelical Revival in Cambridge in the eighteenth century by investigating, in the first instance, the problems by which Charles Simeon found himself confronted. And of these problems the first, in order of emergence, were those pertaining to the environment of his earlier years: namely, the problems of the Home—the School—the University.

The peculiar thing about the conversion of Charles Simeon is that it appears to have been entirely independent of the normal

[1] Cf. art. 'Life, Life, Eternal Life', by Brother George Every, S.S.M., in *The Student World*, April 1938.
[2] Stubbs was Vicar of Navestock, Essex, from 1850 to 1866. Creighton was Vicar of Embleton, Northumberland, from 1875 to 1884.

influences of environment. It cannot be explained as the natural outcome of such influences as were brought to bear upon him either at home or at school: nor, on the other hand, is it to be explained in terms of a violent reaction from, a conscious and deliberate defiance of those influences. It did indeed involve such a reaction: but this reaction was the consequence of the conversion, and not the occasion of it. The implications of this statement will become apparent if we examine the nature of these influences to which we have alluded, and they are relevant, not only to the development of Simeon himself, but also to the development of the Evangelical Revival, particularly in this University: for of those who, as undergraduates of Cambridge, found themselves confronted by the moral and intellectual challenge of the Evangelical theology, a considerable proportion, whether they heard or whether they forbore, were themselves the products of a home like that of Simeon, and of a school which, if not actually the same, was at least of the same type as that at which he had received his education.

Of Simeon's home and of his relations with his family it is significant that we know extremely little. An almost unbroken silence shrouds that department of his life. In Canon Abner Brown's invaluable *Recollections of Simeon's Conversation Parties* (1827–30) there is one reference to his brother Edward,[1] but none to any other member of his family: while the only two allusions to his father, printed in the Correspondence in Carus' biography,[2] permit us categorically to confirm the inferences that we must already have been obliged to draw from a reserve so obstinate and so forbidding.

The objective facts are simple. Charles Simeon was born at Reading on Sept. 24, 1759, and was the fourth, and youngest, son of Richard Simeon, Esq., of that town. He had ecclesiastical blood in his veins, for his paternal grandfather and great-grand-father had both been country parsons, and his mother's family (Hutton) had produced two Archbishops of York since the Reformation.[3] It is likely that his mother died when he was very young, although I have not succeeded in discovering any

---

[1] *Op. cit.* (1863), p. 338.   [2] Carus, pp. 507, 596–7.   [3] *Ibid.* p. 1.

positive evidence to that effect.[1] His father was a prosperous attorney in the town[2] and a gentleman of some independent means: he was an upright man, adhering, in matters of religion, to the Established Church: his sons were all baptised in the parish church of St Lawrence, where the Simeon family rented a pew.[3] The Simeons were deservedly respected in the neighbourhood: but the old house in the Forbury[4] was not what succeeding generations would have recognised as 'a religious home'.

Archdeacon Cunningham, in his Birkbeck Lectures (1909) on *Religion in the Eighteenth Century*, characterised Puritanism as the religion of the State; Wesleyanism as the religion of the heart; the Evangelical Movement as the religion of the home; and the Oxford Movement as the religion of the Church.[5] Such generalisations can never, perhaps, be wholly adequate or unexceptionable: but the justice of that emphasis on Evangelicalism as the religion of the home will be admitted by anyone who has had, as I have had, the privilege of an upbringing that was still essentially Evangelical, however mellowed by the humaner standards of a later age.

The home of Charles Simeon was emphatically not a home of this description. About his boyhood, apart from a few stray references to his school-days at Eton, we know very little. But we do know that when he returned from Cambridge in the long vacation (1779) a converted man, he introduced a new, an unfamiliar, and on the whole a disturbing and obnoxious element into his domestic circle.

It was not, however, until a slightly later stage that the tension became acute. 'As yet, and indeed for three years after, I knew not any religious person, and consequently continued to have

---

[1] Mr J. J. Cooper, in *Some Worthies of Reading* (1923), p. 101, supports this view.

[2] 'A wealthy and respectable lawyer, at Reading, in Berkshire.'—Rev. T. Pentycross to John Thornton, July 28, 1783 (*Congregational Magazine*, Dec. 1842, vol. vi, n.s., p. 826).

[3] *A History of the Municipal Church of St Lawrence, Reading*, by the Rev. Charles Kerry (1883), p. 83.

[4] J. J. Cooper, *Some Worthies of Reading*, p. 100.

[5] From a MS. note-book of the late Sir Geoffrey Butler, now in my possession.

my society among the world. When the races came, I went to them, as I had been used to do, and attended at the race-balls as usual, though without the pleasure which I had formerly experienced. I felt them to be empty vanities; but I did not see them to be sinful; I did not then understand those words, "*be not conformed to this world*".[1] On the other hand, he now began, and continued all the following vacations until his entry into Holy Orders, 'to attend the parish-church at Reading every afternoon, and frequently in a morning; and I used to find many sweet seasons of refreshment and comfort in the use of the stated prayers'.[2]

In this, however, there was nothing to distinguish him from a devout High Churchman. The daily offices of matins and even-song were far better attended, and the former, at least, more generally supplied, in the eighteenth century, than they are to-day: and this was true even after the middle of the century, when, despite the personal example of King George III, the custom was beginning to die out,[3] although pious individuals of

[1] Carus, pp. 11–12.
[2] *Ibid.* p. 14.
[3] Casual mention of the performance of the daily offices in parish churches will be found in *The Torrington Diaries: containing the Tours through England and Wales of the Hon. John Byng (later fifth Viscount Torrington) between the years 1781 and 1794*, ed. C. Bruyn Andrews (1934–38), as under: vol. i, Dolgelle (Wednesday, July 7, 1784), p. 147; Caversham, nr. Reading (Friday, July 30, 1784: 'Prayers at church in the morning; I was not there on Wednesday, so went to-day'), p. 197: vol. iv, Faversham, Kent (Friday, Sept. 24, 1790), p. 167. It would seem that by this time the daily offices were seldom performed during the week except on Wednesdays and Fridays (cf. vol. ii, p. 238), and not always then (vol. iii, p. 230). Byng has also a good deal to say about the daily services in cathedrals, of which Southwell was the most exemplary (vol. iv, p. 141), and Llandaff the most disgraceful (vol. i, p. 282): the attendance was generally very poor (cf. vol. ii, pp. 347, 400).—But 'the due order of daily prayer in some of the London churches was not yet discontinued' when William Stevens (1732–1807), Treasurer of Queen Anne's Bounty, attended constantly (except on Nov. 5) at St Vedast's, Foster-lane: there was, however, 'a considerable falling-off in these observances'. 'Meeting there one day with Mr Sikes [a banker in the City] to their mutual surprise, the Church being otherwise nearly empty, he said with much good humour to him as they went out: "Never mind; if you will not tell of me, I will not tell of you."' (E. Churton, *Memoirs of Joshua Watson* (1861), vol. i, p. 30; [Sir J. A. Park], *Memoirs of William Stevens, Esq.* (1812), pp. 55–6.)—Cf. *Reflections upon the Education of Children in Charity Schools*, by Mrs Trimmer (1792): 'The children, in most Charity Schools...go to church twice every Sunday, and, where there is weekly duty performed, they attend also on Wednesdays, Fridays, and Holidays' (p. 30).—The Rev. Henry Gauntlett, Vicar of Olney (1815–34), 'made several attempts to introduce the occasional

the laity, both men and women, used, whether privately or in their families, to read the psalms and lessons appointed for each day.[1]

A considerable amount of evidence relating to the observance of the duty of daily service in the eighteenth century will be found in that magnificent repository of High Anglican traditions, Dr Wickham Legg's *English Church Life from the Restoration to the Tractarian Movement*.[2] The custom, in its fullness, dated from the great revival of the Anglican piety after the Restoration: and the readiness with which the people welcomed the recovery of the Book of Common Prayer is evidence, not only of their negative weariness of Presbyterian and Independent preachings, but also of their positive recognition of the value and importance of the public Liturgy in what we may describe, in the cant phrase of our own day and age, as 'everyday religion'. Of more than local interest in this connection is the letter addressed by Dr Turner, Bishop of Ely, to Mr Say of Caxton (Sept. 11, 1686),[3] exhorting him particularly, because his parish lay on the Great North Road, to provide daily prayers, preferably at six or seven in the morning, 'for our churches Honor and for the consolation of well dispos'd Travellers'. Dr Wickham Legg mentions a Derbyshire squire, William Coke of Trusley (1679–1718), who was as zealous a churchman as he was a keen fox-hunter, and who used invariably to attend matins, read by the rector of Trusley, before he went out with his pack of harriers, and to return home again in time for evensong.[4] A Cheshire squire of the 1840's harked back to the same tradition: Mr Row-

services on days when they had been long entirely omitted; particularly in the Passion week. But these efforts were not very successful; as few persons were able or willing to redeem time from their ordinary occupations, in order to attend divine worship on the morning of a week-day.' (*Memoir*, prefixed to *Sermons by the late Rev. Henry Gauntlett, Vicar of Olney, Bucks.* vol. i, p. cci).—Cf. further, Overton, *The English Church in the Nineteenth Century* (*1800–1833*), pp. 142–4.

[1] Cf. *Tracts for the Times*, No. 18 (*Thoughts on the benefits of the System of Fasting enjoined by our Church*), by E. B. P[usey], 1833, p. 8: 'Since our Daily Service has been nearly lost, many pious individuals, it is well known, have habitually read just that portion which the Church has allotted.'— Other refs. in Wickham Legg, *English Church Life* (1914), p. 107.

[2] Ch. iv (*Observance of the Duty of Daily Service*), pp. 77–118.

[3] Printed in *Christianity and Politics*, by W. Cunningham (1916), p. 129 *n.*

[4] *Op. cit.* p. 98: J. Charles Cox, *Derbyshire* (1903), p. 250.

land Egerton Warburton, of Arley Hall, the author of a well-known volume of *Hunting Songs* which earned him the kindly title of 'the Poet Laureate of the Tarporley Hunt'.[1] When Mr Warburton rebuilt Arley Hall, he added a private chapel. 'And in the days when daily prayer was scarcely heard of', writes 'Mother Kate' of Haggerston in her anonymous *Memoirs of a Sister of S. Saviour's Priory*, 'all the household assembled within its walls and a surpliced choir chanted choral Matins. Never was the squire missing from his place, and on hunting mornings he always appeared in scarlet and buckskins.'[2] That is, no doubt, an isolated instance: Surtees, we know, was a churchwarden, but it seems improbable that the creator of *Jorrocks* carried his piety to the same extreme. Nevertheless, the case of Squire Warburton shows that the memory of the old High Anglican tradition had persisted even into the nineteenth century.

Thus far, then, Charles Simeon stood in the great High Church tradition; in that tradition out of which, in its declining period, the Evangelical Revival may properly be said to have arisen. But what construction are we to place upon his introduction of Family Prayers into his father's household, since this was already in some measure, and was soon conspicuously to become, the badge of an Evangelical allegiance?

He had already experimented with it, apparently quite independently. 'From the time that I found peace with God myself', he wrote, 'I wished to impart to others the benefits I had received': and therefore, very innocently and indeed ingenuously (as he afterwards admitted), he told his bed-maker at King's 'that as she and the other servants were prevented almost entirely from going to church, I would do my best to instruct them on a Sunday evening, if they chose to come to me for that purpose. Several of them thankfully availed themselves of the offer, and came to me; and I read some good book to them, and used some of the prayers of the Liturgy for prayer; and though I do not know that any of them ever received substantial benefit to their souls, I think that the opportunities were not lost upon

---

[1] *The Sport of our Ancestors...*, ed. Lord Willoughby de Broke (1921), p. 37.
[2] *Op. cit.* [by Katharine Anne Egerton Warburton], 1903, p. 9.

myself; for I thereby cultivated a spirit of benevolence, and fulfilled in some measure that divine precept, "Freely ye have received, freely give".

'In the long vacation I went home; and carried with me the same blessed desires. I had then a brother [Richard], eight years older than myself, living with my father, and managing, as it were, his house. I wished to instruct the servants, and to unite with them in family prayer; but I had no hope that a proposal to that effect would be acceded to either by my father or my brother: I therefore proposed it to the servants, and established it myself, leaving to my brother to join with us or not, as he saw good. To my great joy, after it was established, my brother cordially united with me, and we statedly worshipped God, morning and evening, in the family. I take for granted that my father knew of it; but I do not remember that one word ever passed between him and me upon the subject.'[1]

What is peculiarly interesting here is that Simeon evidently did not get the idea out of a book, nor was he copying anybody. His practice in this regard arose out of a concrete situation, and represents a serious and courageous attempt to tackle a concrete problem. It is my own conviction that the whole of Simeon's life, the whole of his ecclesiastical statesmanship, requires to be interpreted by the same formula. Charles Simeon was not an academic theorist: he was essentially a practical man confronting practical difficulties, and dealing with them boldly and resolutely, in the light of common sense. That is one of the reasons why he made such an admirable parish priest. He had an undoubted gift for recognising the practical issues in pastoral work, and for discovering how best to resolve them. Here, for example, the terms of reference were, on the one hand, the necessity that was laid upon him to preach the Gospel, and, on the other, the lack of adequate religious instruction and assistance for the domestic servant class.

This flair for recognising and resolving practical issues was one of the reasons why Simeon became one of the great religious leaders of his time. But it was not, of course, the only reason.

---

[1] Carus, pp. 10–11.

RELIGION IN THE HOME

Had that been his only talent, Simeon might well have been a mere opportunist. He was indeed accused, or at least suspected, of opportunism, particularly in connection with his purchase of livings. It is admittedly difficult for any statesman, whether secular or ecclesiastical, entirely to escape that charge. But what redeemed the whole of Simeon's ecclesiastical statesmanship from the taint of opportunism was that it was invariably conceived and developed with reference, whether deliberate or unconscious, to a clearly defined body of fundamental principles which themselves lay always under the judgment of the Word of God. Thus, in this instance, his conduct found its ultimate reference in the Dominical precept, 'Freely ye have received, freely give'. And yet, writing in 1813, he could speak of his Sunday evening prayer-meeting for the bed-makers as 'a measure...which perhaps a more matured judgment might have disapproved':[1] the explanation being that, the older he grew, the more marked became his attachment to the principle of order, and his unwillingness to flout it: and the Divine injunction, 'Freely ye have received, freely give', was seen to leave the amateur evangelist poised upon the brink of antinomianism unless it was qualified by that other principle, 'The powers that be'—that is, in this case, the authorities of his College, and of the University, and in the context of the long and complicated history that lay behind the attitude of Authority towards conventicles and towards anything that even looked like a conventicle—'are ordained of God'. When we say, therefore, that Simeon's pastoral strategy, or, on a wider plane, his ecclesiastical statesmanship, was essentially realist, we mean, not only that he was not a mere theorist, but also that he was not a mere opportunist. Practice without principle is only more deadly than principle without practice: and it was in the unusually strong and effective combination of coherent principle with consistent practice that Simeon's genius is most clearly seen.

This is the key to the life-history of the one man who, more than any other, inspired and promoted the Evangelical Revival in the second and third generations of its course. If Simeon ever

[1] *Ibid.* p. 11.

18

took up a thing, we may be certain that it was something that met the needs of the age. That such needs were often confused and inarticulate goes without saying: the needs of every age are generally confused and inarticulate until someone diagnoses them, and writes a book, or launches a movement, or evolves a policy, or creates an organisation; and then the corresponding needs of his age become clarified, conscious, and effective, under the stimulus of the means provided for their satisfaction. The individuals who are capable of discharging this function in society are always rare, but Simeon was one of them: that was the secret of his influence. And 'family worship' was obviously one of the things that met the spiritual needs of his generation.

To-day that pious custom is virtually extinct:[1] not only because the Victorian piety is virtually extinct, but also because the Victorian family is virtually extinct.

...A few minutes more and we could hear screams coming from the dining-room, across the hall which separated the drawing-room from the dining-room, and knew that poor Ernest was being beaten.

'I have sent him up to bed', said Theobald, as he returned to the drawing-room, 'and now, Christina, I think we will have the servants in to prayers', and he rang the bell for them, red-handed as he was.

CHAPTER TWENTY-THREE

The manservant William came and set the chairs for the maids, and presently they filed in. First Christina's maid, then the cook, then the housemaid, then William, and then the coachman. I sat opposite them, and watched their faces as Theobald read a chapter from the Bible. They were nice people, but more absolute vacancy I never saw upon the countenances of human beings.

Theobald began by reading a few verses from the Old Testament, according to some system of his own. On this occasion the passage came from the fifteenth chapter of Numbers....

When Theobald had finished reading we all knelt down and the Carlo Dolci and the Sassoferrato looked down upon a sea of upturned backs, as we buried our faces in our chairs....

[1] The Archbishop of Canterbury has lately pleaded for its revival at a public united meeting in the Caxton Hall. 'There was no way comparable to the great and honourable custom of family prayer to bring the remembrance of God right into the heart of the home life from beginning to end.' Vide *The Times*, Wednesday, Feb. 2, 1938.

...My thoughts wandered...I heard Theobald beginning 'The grace of our Lord Jesus Christ' and in a few seconds the ceremony was over, and the servants filed out again as they had filed in.[1]

It is a serious matter that there must be a very high proportion of people at the present time whose only knowledge of family worship in an English household is derived from the elaborately odious presentation of it in the twenty-third chapter of *The Way of All Flesh*.[2] For Evangelicalism was the religion of the Home: and in the revival of family worship it won the most signal and the most gracious of its triumphs. It may well be that this revival was virtually restricted to the upper and middle classes of society, especially the latter: but within these limits it was so widely spread that in 1889 the Provost of King's, in a circular letter addressed to the undergraduates of that College on the subject of voluntary attendance at morning Chapel, could write: 'You, most of you, come from homes where family prayers are the custom.... Our 8 A.M. service is simply the family prayers of the College....'[3] When Whewell had employed a similar analogy in 1834, it is noticeable that he was thinking principally of the family pew.[4]

Yet he also speaks more generally of 'the practice of social worship' in a well-ordered family, as distinct from 'the regular attendance at stated services':[5] and by the time at which he was writing, this pious custom was already strongly entrenched in the households of the Evangelicals, not only of the clergy, but also of the laity. Cowper, with a pathetic diffidence, had adopted

[1] *The Way of All Flesh: A Novel*. By Samuel Butler. (Published post-humously, 1903). An oil-painting, 'Family Prayers', painted by Butler in 1864, and reminiscent of his early days at Langar Rectory, Notts., is in the possession of St John's College, Cambridge: it is reproduced in Henry Festing Jones' *Samuel Butler: A Memoir* (1919: frontispiece to vol. ii).
[2] For a more kindly description, cf. Edith Olivier, *Without Knowing Mr Walkley: personal memories* (1938), ch. iv (*Family Prayers*): or Henry W. Nevinson, *Between the Acts* (1904), ch. i (*A London Merchant*).
[3] *Augustus Austen Leigh*, ed. William Austen Leigh (1906), pp. 248–9.
[4] *Remarks on some parts of Mr Thirlwall's Letter on the Admission of Dissenters to Academical Degrees* and *Additional Remarks*.—It is not without significance that this fine distinction has frequently been missed: cf. Mrs Stair Douglas, *The Life and selections from the Correspondence of William Whewell* (1881), p. 165; J. Willis Clark, *Old Friends at Cambridge and Elsewhere* (1900), p. 118.
[5] *Additional Remarks*, p. 5.

it in February, 1768.[1] Under the year 1785, the private Journal of William Wilberforce contains two curt and characteristic entries:[2]

Nov. 28th... Began this night constant family prayer, and resolved to have it every morning and evening, and to read a chapter when time.

Nov. 30th...(Forgot to set down that when my servants came in the first time to family prayer, I felt ashamed.)

Again, when Mr William Hey, the surgeon, of Leeds, 'married and became the head of a family', he 'conceived it to be not less his duty to provide for the spiritual advantages of those over whom he presided, than to supply their bodily wants. He accordingly established the regular worship of God in his family, morning and evening; at which his apprentices, pupils, and servants, were always expected to be present; and he communicated to them, at other times, such religious instruction as he judged to be best suited to their respective capacities and situations.'[3] A crowning mercy was vouchsafed when the exemplary Mr Sumner, Chaplain-in-Ordinary to the King, the 'little Methodist parson' of Princess Lieven's letters, succeeded

---

[1] '...We are at last settled in our own Mansion [Orchard Side, Olney: now the Cowper Museum]....We had no sooner taken Possession...than I found myself called to lead the Pray'rs of the Family, a formidable undertak'g you may imagine to a Temper & Spirit like mine. I trembled at the Apprehension of it, and was so dreadfully harrass'd in the Conflict I sustain'd upon this Occasion in the first Week, that my Health was not a little affected by it. But there was no Remedy, and I hope the Lord brought me to that point, to chuse Death rather than a Retreat from Duty. In my first Attempt he was sensibly present with me, and has since favour'd me with every perceptible Assistance. My Fears begin to wear off, I get rather more Liberty of Speech at least, if not of Spirit, and have some Hope that having open'd my Mouth he will never suffer it to be closed again, but rather give Increase of Utterance and Zeal to serve him. How much of that Monster Self has he taken Occasion to shew me by this Incident. Pride Ostentation, and Vain glory have always been my Hindrance in these Attempts. These be at the Root of that Evil Tree which the world good natur'dly calls Bashfullness. Evil indeed in the Character of a Disciple of Christ. May our gracious Teacher mortify them all to Death and never leave me 'till he has made the Dumb to speak, and the Stammering Tongue like the Pen of a ready Writer!...'—Cowper to his aunt, Mrs Madan, Olney, March 1, 1768. (*The Unpublished and Uncollected Letters of William Cowper*, ed. Thomas Wright, 1925, pp. 20–2.)

[2] *The Life of William Wilberforce*, by his sons, Robert Isaac Wilberforce and Samuel Wilberforce, vol. i (1838), pp. 91, 93.

[3] *The Life of William Hey, Esq., F.R.S.*, by John Pearson (1822), pt. ii, p. 20.

in inducing George IV to have family prayers for his household at Cumberland Lodge.[1]

There is an ingenuous description of family prayers in Wilberforce's household in the third volume of the Farington Diary
(July 19, 1806).

> Abt. a quarter before 10 oClock, the family assembled to prayers,
> which were read by Wilberforce in the dining room. As we passed
> from the drawing room I saw all the servants standing in regular
> order, the woemen ranged in a line against the wall & the men the
> same. There were 7 woemen & 6 men.—When the whole were
> collected in the dining room, all knelt down each against a chair or
> Sopha, and Wilberforce knelt at a table in the middle of the room, and
> after a little pause began to read a prayer, which He did very slowly
> in a low, solemnly awful voice. This was followed by 2 other prayers
> & *the grace*. It occupied abt. 10 minutes, and had the best effect as
> to the manner of it.
>
> After prayers were over, a long table covered with cold meat, tarts,
> &c. was drawn to a Sopha on which sat Mrs Wilberforce & Miss
> Hewit.—Wilberforce had boiled milk and bread, and tasted a little
> brandy & water which at night He sd. agrees better with Him than
> wine. Bowdler & myself made up the party.[2]

The procedure varied a good deal in different households. It is
recorded, for example, that Samuel Wilks, Esq., Examiner of
Indian Correspondence for the East India Company, a friend of
Berridge and a noted philanthropist, used for many years to
compose a hymn regularly every morning, and another every
evening, for the purpose of family prayer. He left behind him
twenty-seven manuscript volumes, beautifully written out, containing four thousand, two hundred, and thirty-seven compositions, ranging from six to twelve stanzas each, besides a volume
containing more than four hundred hymns, which he had printed
for private distribution.[3] Most heads of families felt a certain
diffidence about undertaking to pray extempore: for them,

[1] Cf. *The Private Letters of Princess Lieven to Prince Metternich (1820–
1826)*, ed. Peter Quennell (1937), p. 147; *Life of Charles Richard Sumner,
D.D., Bishop of Winchester*, by G. H. Sumner (1876), p. 79; *George the
Fourth*, by Roger Fulford (1935), pp. 258–9, 264–5.
[2] *Farington Diary*, ed. J. Greig, vol. iii, p. 285.
[3] *Vide* Berridge's *Works*, p. 399 n.

EVENING PRAYERS

From Eugène Lami, *Voyage en Angleterre*, 1829

manuals of family devotion were quickly multiplied, of which Henry Thornton's *Family Prayers* reaped the most general popularity: first published in 1834, nineteen years after its author's death, it ran through thirty-one editions in two years, and G. W. E. Russell mentions the use of it as 'a distinctive sign of true Evangelicalism'.[1] There were also older compilations, of which the most notable was Benjamin Jenks' *Prayers and Offices of Devotion for Families, and for particular Persons upon most occasions*, 1st ed. 1697: altered and improved by Charles Simeon in 1808, it entered on a new lease of life. Toplady's little *Course of Prayer for each Day in the Week, suitable to every Christian Family*, was also based on Jenks. David Simpson's father, a reputable Yorkshire farmer, although he 'made no religious profession beyond attention to the duties of morality', kept up the form of family prayer, 'aided by a short formula, adapted to the use of families, in a little work called the Christian's Monitor'.[2] Mr Hey's method was to read

a section of Doddridge's Family Expositor (omitting the paraphrases and critical notes,) with the improvement, every morning, about eight o'clock; the family then united in singing a psalm or hymn; and Mr Hey prayed, sometimes extempore, and at other times he used an approved form of prayer. His family assembled again between nine and ten o'clock in the evening, when he read a psalm, or a portion selected out of the Old Testament, concluding with singing and prayer as in the morning.

The manner in which he conducted the family devotions was serious and most impressive; he read the portion of Scripture slowly and reverently, now and then offering a very short and pious remark on any particular text that occurred. His prayer was offered up with a devout solemnity and reverence, which indicated his due recollection of the greatness and majesty of Him whom he was addressing. The whole service rarely exceeded twenty, or twenty-five minutes; for he was careful not to make the duties of religion wearisome by protracting them too long.[3]

[1] G. W. E. Russell, *The Household of Faith* (1st ed. 1902), p. 241 (*Recollections of the Evangelicals*).
[2] *Memoirs of the late Rev. David Simpson, M.A.*, by Edward Parsons, prefixed to Simpson's *A Plea for the Deity of Jesus, and the Doctrine of the Trinity* (1812), p. iv.
[3] Pearson's *Life of Hey*, pt. ii, pp. 20–1.

In that solicitude Hey was representative of the pious heads of families of his generation. Quite frequently in the literature of the Evangelical Movement the reader finds himself reminded that such worship must be kept short if it is to do good. 'In families professing godliness, it is very desirable that family prayer be considered rather a delightful privilege, than a wearisome duty—the infirmities of the weakest or youngest member, should ever be borne in mind; the use of tedious lectures or commentaries, often becomes a burden, and engenders a distaste for that, which may and ought to be, the happiest part of the day's occupation; every thing tending to weariness should by all means be avoided, as the evil consequences are often severely felt. After a short prayer or hymn, I believe a regular portion of the Sacred Scriptures, elucidated and enforced, perhaps, by an occasional remark, will be found the best introduction to the morning and evening devotions. The language of Scripture is for the most part intelligible, interesting, and impressive, and peculiarly attractive to the minds of children. This, experience will convince us, is not the case with that of almost any of our commentators, and I doubt much, whether benefit will be found to result from reading long portions of these, at family prayer. I would not be understood in the least degree to undervalue the many excellent aids for biblical study, with which the Church of God is now blessed, but I consider other times more suited to their perusal, and I venture to offer the suggestion, with an earnest desire to promote the enjoyment of family worship, as the great means of preserving true religion in the world.'[1]

So far was this the prevailing temper that the saintly Thomas Scott of Aston Sandford, whose family worship was unusually lengthy—morning prayers often occupied three-quarters of an hour or even more, although his evening prayers were a good deal shorter—felt bound, in his autobiographical memoir, to defend his practice in the matter. 'Though the time which I have allotted to this service has been, for many years, far

---

[1] Editor's Preface to a new edition of Toplady's *Family Prayers* (Dublin, 1852: ed. J. J. C.), pp. v–vi.—Cf. Richard Cecil's *Works* (2nd ed. 1816), vol. iii, pp. 430–4, *On Family Worship* ('The old Dissenters wearied their families'); Henry Gauntlett's *Sermons* (1835), vol. i, p. cxii.

longer than is generally deemed sufficient or expedient, yet, by a punctual observance of an appointed hour, and the adjustment of domestic affairs to the plan, as known and invariable, no inconvenience worthy of notice has resulted from it. Nor have I, as many complain in excuse for great brevity, found my domestics in general show symptoms of weariness and inattention.'[1] On the other hand, his grandson has confessed, with a commendable restraint, that 'family prayers at Aston Rectory were formidable, particularly to a child. They lasted a full hour, several persons from the village usually attending'.[2]

It should here be noted that many of the Evangelical clergy used to throw open their domestic worship at least one evening in the week, if not more often, to those of their parishioners who cared to attend it. Conyers of Helmsley erected a room adjoining to the parsonage, which was every morning and evening opened for all who thought proper to be present at his domestic religious exercises: on Monday, Tuesday, Wednesday, and Friday evenings he was accustomed to read and expound a chapter in the Old Testament, and on Saturday and Sunday evenings he commented on a chapter in the New.[3] Berridge of Everton admitted 'the serious people of the parish' to his vicarage on Saturday evenings for a like purpose.[4] Cadogan of Reading invited his parishioners to join in his family prayers on Tuesday evenings, only to find that they availed themselves of his invitation in such numbers that it became necessary to adjourn to the chancel of St Giles'.[5] Isaac Milner, whether at the President's Lodge in Queens' College, Cambridge, or at the Deanery, Carlisle, was used occasionally to admit one or more of his intimate friends to his domestic worship. 'In these little friendly meetings, Dr Milner was always ready and willing to expound any passage concerning which he might be requested to give his thoughts, but there were portions of Scripture upon which his

---

[1] *The Life of the Rev. Thomas Scott, Rector of Aston Sandford, Bucks.*, by John Scott (5th ed. 1823), pp. 73, 609.
[2] *Personal and Professional Recollections*, by the late Sir George Gilbert Scott, R.A. (1879), p. 28.
[3] *Evangelical Magazine*, vol. ii (1794), pp. 402–3.
[4] *Works*, ed. Whittingham, p. 491.
[5] *Evangelical Magazine*, vol. vi (1798), p. 11.

own choice frequently fell. Among these were the first psalm, the sermon on the mount, and parts of the fifth, sixth, seventh and eighth chapters of the Epistle to the Romans. It should be added, that he occasionally chose for the subject of his exposition ' the general Confession in the order for Morning and Evening Prayer, 'a composition which he regarded as among the most excellent of uninspired writings'.[1]

Examples might indeed be multiplied of the way in which the Evangelical clergy turned their family prayers into parochial prayer meetings. No doubt these pious exercises had an exemplary character: the laity learned, by the example of their ministers, how to conduct such worship in the bosoms of their own families. But it has also to be remembered that there was only a very narrow margin between prayer meetings and pro- phesyings: and of prophesyings the authorities of the Church of England had always been advisedly suspicious. Archbishop Whitgift, in his eleven Articles touching Preachers and other orders for the Church (1583), laid down 'That all preaching, reading, catechising, and other such-like exercises in private places and families, *whereunto others do resort, being not of the same family*, be utterly inhibited, seeing the same was never permitted as lawful, under any Christian magistrate, but is a manifest sign of schism, and a cause of contention in the Church'.[2] The accuracy of the concluding statement had indeed been verified in the experience of the Church of England, and the lesson had not been forgotten. The problem of Church Order was thus directly involved: and the Rev. Thomas Scott himself wrote to his son, a freshman at Magdalene, in Nov. 1795, warning him to be cautious before engaging himself to join some undergraduate society which met in college or Sunday evenings for religious exercises. '. . . I do not quite understand whether your friends actually keep out of the reach of the Conventicle Act, or not. If no more than *five* meet in one place, I can see no manner of objection on the score of ecclesiastical irregularity. If they do

[1] *Life of Milner*, pp. 598, 709–12.
[2] Gee and Hardy, *Documents illustrative of English Church History* (1896), p. 481.

26

meet in greater numbers, the matter demands more careful consideration. I look on that Act as a direct opposition of human authority to the word of God; and I cannot deem myself bound, *in foro conscientiæ*, to obey it: but at the same time expediency may often suggest obedience....'[1] Moreover, prayer-meetings, as Simeon himself was subsequently to discover, were liable to get out of hand.

But that is a separate problem, and one which may for the moment be ignored: whereas, when it is recognised how important a part the revival of Family Worship played in the history of the Evangelical Movement in the Church of England, it may well be argued that much of the spiritual power of Evangelicalism came from this source. There is a very significant letter from Butler of Wantage to Archdeacon Manning, dated Aug. 29, 1848—written, that is, at a period when the Evangelical Movement is generally regarded as having passed its zenith—in which he says: 'The evangelical party seem more saturated with spirituality'[2] than the 'High Church' school.

The question here arises: How far was family prayer, like the saying of the daily offices in church, a survival from the old High Church tradition?

This question is easier to propound than it is to answer. Of these two forms of religious exercise, the former might be accepted, more or less reluctantly, as a substitute for the latter. Thus, for example, in 1866, a young High Churchman, Mandell Creighton, expanding or defending a statement in a previous letter, in which he had declared himself 'adverse to family prayers, on the ground that you ought to send all your servants to daily service', writes as follows:

[1] *Life of the Rev. Thomas Scott*, by John Scott (5th ed. 1823), p. 332.—Cf. also a letter from the Rev. R. W. Sibthorp, Fellow of Magdalen College, Oxford, to Simeon ('I write for information and advice....I am designing to open my rooms once a week for what I may call, in one sense, an evening party....But the tea is only introductory to an exposition of Scripture which I propose to give myself....Allow me to ask whether you open or close with prayer? With prayer, should the number exceed twenty, are we not in danger of being considered *conventiclers*?...'), quoted by Moule, p. 205; and Simeon's answer (Dec. 9, 1829), Carus, pp. 641–2. For Sibthorp's subsequent career in and out of the Church of England, *vide* R. D. Middleton, *Magdalen Studies* (1936), pp. 193–228.

[2] *Life and Letters of Dean Butler* (1897), p. 66.

You understand that in all the violent sentiments I give vent to, I do not at all mean that I would act up to them; e.g. in the case of family prayers, I always read them at home, because, though theoretically they are untenable and do a great deal of harm by reconciling people's consciences to not attending daily service, still in practice the advantages in individual cases are so great as to counterbalance the general wrongfulness of the proceeding; and moreover, though I do read them myself at home because I don't attend daily service, still if I was head of a household I would not allow my family or those of my servants who did go to daily service to attend them, and so would keep clearly before the eyes of the rest the purely provisional nature of the proceeding, and so to some extent remind them of the existence of a church.[1]

So also, a century earlier, Bishop Butler, in his *Charge delivered to the Clergy at the Primary Visitation of the Diocese of Durham, in the year 1751*, had insisted that 'the conscientious attendance upon [the Divine service] ought often to be inculcated upon the people, as a plain precept of the gospel, as the means of grace, and what has peculiar promises annexed to it. But external acts of piety and devotion, and the frequent returns of them, are moreover necessary to keep up a sense of religion, which the affairs of the world will otherwise wear out of men's hearts. And the frequent returns, whether of public devotions, or of anything else, to introduce religion into men's serious thoughts, will have an influence upon them, in proportion as they are susceptible of religion, and not "given over to a reprobate mind" [Rom. i. 28]. For this reason, besides others, the service of the Church ought to be celebrated as often as you can have a congregation to attend it.'

But since the body of the people, especially in country places, cannot be brought to attend it oftener than one day in a week; and since this is in no sort enough to keep up in them a due sense of religion; it were greatly to be wished they could be persuaded to anything which might, in some measure, supply the want of more frequent public devotions, or serve the like purposes. Family prayers, regularly kept up in every house, would have a great and good effect.[2]

[1] Letter dated Sept. 18, 1866, in *Life and Letters of Mandell Creighton, D.D., sometime Bishop of London*, by his wife, vol. i, p. 26.
[2] *The Works of Bishop Butler*, ed. J. H. Bernard (1900), vol. i (*Sermons, Charges, etc.*), p. 295.

More light is thrown upon the problem by a long paragraph in the Life of Dr Humphrey Prideaux, Dean of Norwich from 1689 to 1724,[1] where it is stated that 'till the breaking out of the Civil War, in the year 1641, which proved destructive to all order in Religion, as well as every thing else, family devotion was kept up all over the Nation, and the Deity worshipped by prayer every morning and evening; the Master of the family (where there was no Minister) always officiating herein. Such as were able often composed forms of their own; others for the most part used those, which are in the *Practice of Piety*,[2] a book then in much repute. Thus it continued till those unhappy wars, when the Puritanical party prevailing, carried this duty to an extravagant excess, and by their long extempore prayers, which were stuffed with absurd cant, and downright nonsense, brought family devotion itself into disrepute with many, who justly disliked such a nauseous and unsuitable a manner of addressing the Deity, but instead of avoiding and reforming the abuse, went into the contrary extream, and omitted all prayer whatsoever with their families. And this happened especially after the Restoration of King *Charles* the second; for Episcopacy and the Church being then again restored, many, to pay their court to what was uppermost, and shew their aversion to the sectaries, who had hitherto reigned, carried the matter too far, and branded many things with the imputation of phanaticism, only because those people had used them in a phanatical manner. Of this kind was family prayer, which many, in compliance with the prevailing vogue, from this time omitted.[3] And there was another cause, which derived its original from the same times, and helped to produce the same ill effect; that during the reign of these Sectaries, and the prevalence of Puritanism throughout the

---

[1] *The Life of the Reverend Humphrey Prideaux, D.D., Dean of Norwich*... (1748).—This work is extensively quoted in *A Chinese Fragment: containing an Enquiry into the Present State of Religion in England* (1786), by an Evangelical layman, Ely Bates, Esq.: *vide* footnotes to Section IV (*Family Worship*). On Ely Bates, *vide* Pearson's *Life of Hey*, pt. ii, pp. 27–9 *n*.

[2] *The Practice of Piety, directing a Christian how to walk that he may please God*, by Lewis Bayly, Bishop of Bangor (1st ed. 1619).—Vide *D.N.B.* (Bayly).

[3] Cf. also Sermon L (*Concerning Family-Religion*: 1684) in Archbishop Tillotson's *Fifty-Four Sermons and Discourses* (8th edn. 1720: pp. 513–20).

Nation, the Book of Common-Prayer being extravagantly run down, on the change of times, and the Restoration of the Church, it was as extravagantly cryed up by those of the High-Church Party, as if no other form of prayer was to be used in families, any more than in the Churches: and this notion growing more and more fashionable, the consequence of it was, that whereas these prayers are many of them proper only to be read by men in orders, many families of the Gentry and Nobility, where there were no Chaplains, began to disuse them; and nothing being substituted in their room, this was in a great many families the occasion of totally neglecting this duty.'[1] 'A family-book' had therefore been compiled, with a view to its authorisation by the Convocation which had been summoned to meet in 1689: 'it contained directions for family-devotions, with several forms of prayer for worship every morning and evening, suited to the different circumstances of the families, in which they were to be used'.[2] But the opportunity was missed: and some years later Dean Prideaux pressed Archbishop Tenison very strongly to publish this Family-Book on his own authority; 'but the Archbishop, though he was sensible of the great occasion there was for it, and the service it might do Religion, thought it had best be done with the concurrence of the Convocation, which would make it be received with greater authority, and said, that there were then some thoughts of speedily calling one'. This Dean Prideaux thought very ill-advised, in view of the uncertain and factious temper of the Lower House. However, the Archbishop was not to be persuaded. The manuscript was then lent to the Bishop of Chichester (Williams), who somehow mislaid it among his papers: and when he died, it most unfortunately could not be found.[3]

This extract from the Life of Dean Prideaux is extraordinarily illuminating. One inference to be drawn from it is that the nobility and gentry were beginning to economise in the matter of keeping domestic chaplains: and this is confirmed by Jonas Hanway, who in his *Reflections* (1761) recalls the time when 'every *great family* had a *chaplain*, and almost every little one,

---

[1] *Op. cit.* pp. 61–3.   [2] *Ibid.* p. 61.   [3] *Ibid.* pp. 64–5.

a stated time for prayer. This custom is still observed in some large families, in a few counties in this kingdom; but the number, upon the whole, I fear, is small: I am not happy enough to hear of more than *five* about *London*, and one of them is an *Archbishop's*.'[1] Nevertheless, in some great houses, when the family was in residence, the local vicar, or (if the vicar were nonresident) his curate, would come in periodically to read prayers in the private chapel: Thomas Hutchinson, the exiled Governor of Massachusetts Bay, mentions that at Lord Hardwick's place at Ampthill a clergyman to whom his lordship had given a living in the adjoining parish used thus to officiate three times a week:[2] while at Lord Gage's seat at Firle in Sussex, it was the custom every Sunday evening to summon the entire household 'into the Hall, where Lady Gage read the Evening Service of the Church with great propriety, the whole family joining in the Responses. She then read, as well, a sermon from Dr Tillotson, and dismissed the Assembly with the usual Collect and Blessing', apparently indifferent as to whether there was a clergyman in the company or not.[3] By contrast, the Countess of Huntingdon's domestic worship, although she had her Chaplains, was manifestly non-liturgical. 'On the week-days her kitchen was filled with the poor of the flock, for whom she provided suitable instruction; and on the Sabbath the rich and the noble were invited to spend the evening in her drawing-rooms, where Mr Whitefield and other eminent ministers of Christ proclaimed all the words of this life, and with eloquence which was exceeded only by their faithfulness and affection.'[4]

The contrast is significant. Indeed, the essential point about this extract from the Life of Dean Prideaux is that it supplies us with the clue to our riddle. The good High Churchmen were, at least in many cases, no less solicitous than the Evangelicals for the keeping up of family worship: but the High Churchmen

---

[1] *Reflections, Essays and Meditations on Life and Religion*, vol. ii, p. 554. Cf. J. H. Hutchins, *Jonas Hanway* (1940), pp. 11, 123.
[2] *The Diary and Letters of His Excellency Thomas Hutchinson, Esq., Captain-General and Governor-in-Chief of His Late Majesty's Province of Massachusetts Bay*, ed. P. O. Hutchinson (1883), vol. i, p. 516 (1775).
[3] *Ibid.* pp. 224–5, 523 (1774–5). Cf. Disraeli's *Venetia*, bk. 1, ch. iv.
[4] *Countess of Huntingdon*, vol. i, p. 103; cf. pp. 111, 228.

stipulated that it should be liturgical, and taken from the Prayer Book,[1] whereas the Evangelicals were better satisfied with extempore prayer and exposition or with the use of any edifying book. It is true that Dr Prideaux himself, in one of his Visitation Charges as Archdeacon of Suffolk, admonished the clergy of his Archdeaconry to obey the rubric at the beginning of the Prayer Book *Concerning the Service of the Church*, and to read morning and evening prayers daily, if not in their own churches ('this being impracticable in Country parishes, by reason of the difficulty of getting the people together, from their several distant habitations'), then at least in their own families, and even in any house where they might happen to be lodging, if the family 'should not be otherwise provided for that duty . . . : and should they refuse to hearken to him therein, let him look on that house, as unfit for a Clergyman to make his abode in, and avoid it accordingly'.[2] But this applied only to members of the clerical profession.

The essential difference between the High Church and the Evangelical modes of family prayer is clearly seen when one compares *The Whole Duty of Man* (1st ed. 1657)—'the most popular book of devotion that England has known'[3]—with the revised edition of it, *The New Whole Duty of Man*, published almost a century later. At the end of *The Whole Duty of Man* you will find a section headed, *Private Devotions for several*

---

[1] To judge from the curious description by the King of Saxony's Physician, family prayers in Trinity Lodge when Whewell was Master conformed to the High Church pattern. 'It is the custom for the whole household to assemble; the servants come in and seat themselves upon a row of seats near the windows. The master of the household takes his seat at a small table, with the Bible and prayer-book before him, reads a prayer, and then some chapters from the Bible; next, whilst all kneel, he reads a long, long litany, which in almost the whole of its parts corresponds with that of the Catholic Church. The service finished, all rise, the servants depart, and then comes the breakfast, which in England, as is well known, is a very rich and multifarious affair. As for myself, the custom was interesting for *once*; as a question of daily use, it must become tedious and ineffective, and presumes much time to spare.' *The King of Saxony's Journey through England and Scotland in the year 1844*, by Dr Carl Gustav Carus (tr. S. C. Davison), 1846, p. 153.—Cf. also *A Morning Prayer for a Family, An Evening Prayer for a Family* (compiled from prayers and collects in the Book of Common Prayer) in *The Practice of True Devotion*, by Robert Nelson, Esq. (3rd ed. 1716), pp. 281–92.
[2] *Life of Prideaux*, pp. 69–71.
[3] Wickham Legg, *English Church Life*, p. 338.

occasions, ordinary and extraordinary. But these are, literally, private devotions: they are written in the first person singular: and they are prefaced by this note:

Christian Reader,

I have, for the help of thy Devotions, set down some FORMS *of* PRIVATE PRAYER, *upon* several occasions; *if it be thought an omission, that there are none for* Families, *I must answer for myself, That it was not from any opinion, that God is not as well to be worshipped in the Family as the Closet; but because the Providence of God and the Church hath already furnished thee for that purpose, infinitely beyond what my utmost care could do; I mean the* PUBLICK LITURGY *or* COMMON PRAYER, *which for all public addresses to God (and such are Family Prayers) are so excellent and useful, that we may say of it as* David *did of* Goliah's *sword,* I Sam. xxi, 9. There is none like it.

Whereas, if you turn to the corresponding section in *The New Whole Duty of Man*, you will discover that the title has been altered to *Devotions for the Use of Families and Particular Persons*: the prefatory note has been omitted, and in place of it we find:

☞ *Note*, When the Prayers for *Morning* or *Evening* are to be used with a *Family*,

Instead of
$\begin{Bmatrix} I \\ me \\ my \\ I\ was \\ I\ am \\ myself \end{Bmatrix}$
say
$\begin{Bmatrix} we \\ us \\ our \\ we\ were \\ we\ are \\ ourselves \end{Bmatrix}$

And, in the body of the work, the section headed 'Sunday VII' now includes a paragraph inculcating the duty of Family Prayer, without any reference to the Prayer Book.

It is, I think, to be inferred that the family worship which Charles Simeon instituted and conducted in his father's house at Reading during the vacations conformed rather to the High Church than to the Puritan tradition. As he had anticipated, the head of the family studiedly ignored it: but that his eldest brother, Richard, should have condescended to unite with him was an uncovenanted mercy. This was in the summer of 1779. There was more definite unpleasantness three years later, after his ordination to the diaconate (Trinity Sunday, May 26, 1782). During that Long Vacation, he was taking duty for Mr Atkinson at St Edward's, Cambridge: and, full of pastoral zeal, he appears to have addressed a letter to his family, with a view to effecting their conversion. This letter has not been preserved: but we are fortunate in having John Simeon's answer to it, which is probably more interesting. It is the sort of letter that a young man of the world might write to-day to a younger brother who had suddenly gone Groupy.

Dear Charles,

To argue with you upon the effects of over zeal in desiring to serve a good cause, I am fully sensible will but confirm you in your plan of reformation, and by that very means prevent a reform in our family, if it is so necessary amongst us as you seem to apprehend. I will therefore tell you exactly what effect your well-meant letter had upon me and Ned (who are the two heretics in the family you will say), and leave you to judge, whether you would not do well to adopt a different mode of advising; and even to confine yourself to the duties of your office within the bounds, which the best men have prescribed to themselves. We laughed and looked serious alternately, under the apprehension that you should lose that valuable gift called common sense, in endeavouring to furnish your mind with ideas of one sort only....I should add, that Dick, though left to his own observations on the subject, and not in the enjoyment of that pride of health which makes us all so thoughtless—(though I have the pleasure of telling you that he is much mended since his return to Reading)—only smiled....

It is natural for young people to be zealous in anything new; and therefore I trust that in the common course of things your zeal will slacken a little, being well assured that you will have full enough to serve your Master with efficacy, after a considerable abatement. In hopes therefore of seeing this period, which I consider much more favourable to the cause you mean to serve, than the enthusiasm by which you at present seem to be influenced,

I remain yours very affectionately,

J. SIMEON.[1]

Charles Simeon's impassioned answer to this letter may be read in Carus.[2] But our attention may be concentrated rather

---

[1] Carus, pp. 30–1.   [2] *Ibid.* pp. 31–7.

upon John Simeon's brotherly remonstrance, because it exhibits so clearly the mentality that was one of the most formidable obstacles to the progress of the Evangelical Revival. It is symbolic of the attitude of the men of the upper middle classes generally towards that Movement. Other examples could be given: for instance, the domestic trials of Rowland Hill, or of the Rev. the Hon. W. B. Cadogan, or of Mrs Mary Fletcher; or the Duke of Wellington's commendation of an Army Chaplain —'Mr Briscoll, by his admirable conduct and good sense, got the better of Methodism, which had appeared among the soldiers and once among the officers'; or, perhaps most difficult of all, the detached and not unkindly banter of *The Spiritual Quixote*.[1] It is so much a known fact of history that Evangelicalism made enormous inroads upon the guarded and formal piety of that class of man, that we tend to take that fact too much for granted. The strength of Evangelicalism among the upper middle classes at the time of Simeon's death, or after, is one of the most remarkable phenomena of religious history, for it was built up in the teeth of social and religious prejudice which it had laboriously to undermine. Evangelicalism did undermine that prejudice, because it went deep enough to do so. It got down to fundamentals: and, in particular, to those fundamental spiritual needs of men in which there is no distinction between the upper and the lower classes of society. But, in so doing, it had to encounter from the gentry a sharp antagonism compounded of ingredients of social pride, historical tradition, and ordinary worldliness: and of this antagonism, the attitude of the Simeon family is eloquent. 'From the time that I set myself to seek the Lord, and more especially from the time that I began to minister in holy things, I found trials in my own family.'[2]

The tension shortly became painful, for Richard Simeon, the eldest son, was dying: and when Charles Simeon intended

---

[1] *The Spiritual Quixote: or, the Summer's Ramble of Mr Geoffry Wildgoose. A Comic Romance* [by the Rev. Richard Graves, Rector of Claverton, near Bath, and sometime Fellow of All Souls], 3 vols. 1773. (New ed. in 2 vols. with introd. by Charles Whibley, 1926.)—Cf. Overton and Relton, *History of the English Church from the Accession of George I to the End of the Eighteenth Century (1714–1800)*, pp. 271–2.

[2] Carus, p. 596.

going to him, his two other brothers strove to prevent him, 'lest I should disturb his mind'.[1] Richard Simeon died at the beginning of October 1782. With great magnanimity, Charles offèred to leave Cambridge for ever in order to take his brother's place at home. So he wrote to his friend John Venn (Oct. 13, 1782): 'I have offered to live with my dear and aged father, who has hitherto declined it: whether he may alter his wishes I cannot tell; most certainly if he does, I shall think it both my duty and my happiness to render his few remaining years as comfortable as I can.'[2] It appears that the suggestion emanated from his other brothers, John and Edward. For Charles it involved a very considerable sacrifice, not merely of worldly prospects, but of private happiness: for he and his father did not hit it off, and their relations were continually strained and difficult and embarrassed. Many years later, Charles Simeon reproached himself for not having sufficiently endeavoured 'to bear with him, and feel for him, and try to win him. I was always so unhappy in his company, that I could not put on sufficient ease and cheerfulness: and I seem to think, that if he were now alive, I would try more the effect of such condescension on my part; yet I doubt much, whether as quite a young man I could safely venture to do all that I might at a more advanced age. I think we ought to feel towards such persons as we should towards our beloved Monarch, if we now saw him beating his head against a wall.'[3] Of all the family, old Mr Simeon was the most unreasonably 'prejudiced against Methodism as it is called'.[4] In particular, he had ordered Charles to renounce the friendship of the Rev. the Hon. W. B. Cadogan, the Evangelical vicar of St Giles', Reading, to whom Venn's father had given him an introduction: this Charles refused to do, although from filial piety he obeyed him 'so far as not to preach for Mr Cadogan, because I had no particular call to *that*'.[5] Nevertheless, 'feeling the indispensable necessity of serving

---

[1] Carus, p. 37.   [2] *Ibid.* p. 38.
[3] *Ibid.* pp. 507–8 (letter dated March 9, 1819).
[4] *Ibid.* p. 596.
[5] *Ibid.* p. 596.—Cf. Pentycross to John Thornton, July 28, 1783 (*Congreg. Mag.* Dec. 1842, vol. vi, n.s., p. 826).

God according to my conscience, and of seeing my acquaintance without restraint', he stipulated that if he was to come and live at home 'I should have a part of the house to myself, where I might see my friends without interfering with my father. Everything was settled: my books, &c. were just going to be packed up; and in a fortnight I was to leave College for good.' The omens for the future were decidedly not propitious. 'But behold! in that juncture an event took place that decided the plans of my whole life.'[1] Simeon's fidelity had been tested, and had not been found wanting: and God accepted the intention of the sacrifice, and spared the victim.

'I had often, when passing Trinity Church, which stands in the heart of Cambridge, and is one of the largest churches in the town, said within myself, "How should I rejoice if God were to give me that church, that I might preach his Gospel there, and be a herald for him in the midst of the University!" But as to the actual possession of it, I had no more prospect of attaining it, than of being exalted to the See of Canterbury. It so happened, however, that the incumbent of it (Mr Therond) died just at this time, and that the only bishop, with whom my father had the smallest acquaintance, had recently been translated to the see of Ely. I therefore sent off instantly to my father, to desire him to make application to the bishop for the living on my behalf. This my father immediately did':[2] and the application proved successful.[3] No doubt the old gentleman hoped that if his son was given

---

[1] *Ibid.* p. 40. [2] *Ibid.* pp. 40–1.

[3] The parishioners petitioned the Bishop to bestow the living on the Rev. John Hammond, Fellow of Queens', who had been Therond's curate, and in any case appointed him to the lectureship (established in 1610) which normally went with it, 'concluding that the living without the lectureship would not be worth any one's acceptance; it being, even with the surplice-fees, not worth more than forty guineas per annum'. Seeing that the parish was 'so extremely violent for Mr H.', Simeon offered to stand down: but the Bishop 'did not like that mode of application', and intimated his determination not to license Mr Hammond under any circumstances, whereupon Simeon accepted the proffered charge. Hammond occupied the lectureship for about five years, and was succeeded by another clergyman, equally independent (the Rev. Mr Berry, elected lecturer, Feb. 5, 1787): not until 1794 was Simeon elected to it.

Cole preserves another tradition, which may also contain an element of truth. 'In Nov. 1782, the Bishop of Ely presented Mr Simeon A.B. and Fellow of King's to this vicarage. He was then Vicar (*sic*) of St Edward's, a much followed preacher and inclined to Methodism. Mr Hammond, Fellow

37

a benefice it might cure him of his nonsense. In this he was rudely disappointed. The troubles at the outset of Charles Simeon's ministry greatly upset him. 'Mr Simeon's father', wrote Henry Venn (Jan. 23, 1783), '...is all gall and bitterness. I should not wonder if he were to disinherit him.'[1] However, they were completely reconciled a few months later (May 1783),[2] although old Mr Simeon could never be induced to look more tolerantly on his son's religious views and habits.[3] He seems to have died not long after.[4]

Charles Simeon was more successful with his brothers. Edward, who became a London merchant and a Director of the Bank of England, was completely won over: his name began to figure largely in subscription lists: and when he died on Dec. 14, 1812, he left Charles a legacy of £15,000.[5]

of Queens' College, who had served the cure for Mr Therond was elected lecturer by the parish in Nov. 1782, and would probably have been vicar had not Dr Plumtre, the Mr. of his college, with whom he was on ill terms, and Dr Cooke, Dean of Ely, Sollicited the BP. for Mr Simeon.' (*William Cole of Milton*, by W. M. Palmer, M.D., F.S.A. (1935), p. 147.)—Gunning insinuates (vol. i, p. 239) that Hammond was one of the unbiddable men of whom Isaac Milner succeeded in purging Queens' during his forty years' supremacy.

It may be noted that Simeon was still only in deacon's orders (having been ordained on the title of his fellowship on May 26, 1782, although he was four months short of the canonical age of twenty-three). His institution, however, was not irregular, since it was technically only to a curacy-in-charge held for the Bishop. Cf. *The Pulpit*, vol. xxix (1837), p. 212.

[1] Carus, p. 47.   [2] *Ibid.* p. 47.

[3] 'Unhappily my poor father retained his prejudices to the last' (*ibid.* p. 597).

[4] Moule, p. 4.

[5] Technically, as Mr D. A. Winstanley points out (*Unreformed Cambridge*, 1935, p. 233), Simeon ought to have resigned his fellowship on accepting this legacy, for 'by the statutes of the college, which he had sworn to observe, an annual income of £5, however expended, disqualified for a fellowship; and though the value of money had greatly changed since those statutes were framed, it had not changed sufficiently to justify Simeon's conduct. That such a pious and high-minded man should have so acted is a significant indication of the academic attitude towards statutory obligations.' His defence was, that he regarded himself only as a trustee on behalf of the numerous charitable organisations and causes to which his brother had contributed liberally in his life-time: he goes into the matter at some length in an exculpatory memorandum, dated Oct. 19, 1836, and quoted in part by Mr Winstanley, in which he is also careful to place on record that the whole thing was perfectly open and above-board, and that the circumstances were known to his colleagues (Carus, pp. 433–5).—'He once told me himself', says Dean Close, 'that he retained his college fellowship for no other reason than that it enabled him to live more economically, and to devote more to the Lord' (*Occasional Sermons*, p. 202).

How, then, was Edward Simeon won over? The answer is to be found in Canon Abner Brown's invaluable *Recollections of Simeon's Conversation Parties*. 'My brother disregarded deep religion, and said to me, "You ask too much". I prayed much for him, and one day said, "Is it too much to love God with all your heart, and your neighbour as yourself?" He said, "No!" "Then", said I, "I will never ask more of you than this." I had thus his assent to a simple truth, which I could explain by Scripture, and this simple remark was made by God the means of my brother's conversion.'[1] In this incident we can, I think, discern the strength of Evangelicalism, and the principal causes of its triumph. The Evangelicals were men of that indomitable moral earnestness which has its roots in prayer and in that real pastoral love for men and women in which prayer finds a proper outlet. Their appeal was addressed directly to the conscience: it was simple, profound, and radical: and it based itself on Scripture proofs.

The only evidence for John Simeon's conversion is contained in a memorandum relating to his brother Richard's death, in which Charles Simeon records how John and Edward 'strove to keep me away, lest I should disturb his mind. Blessed be God, both these brothers lived to embrace and honour that Saviour whom I had commended to them.'[2] Intellectually, John Simeon was the ablest of the four brothers. From Eton, where he was a King's Scholar, he went up to Merton College, Oxford, in 1775; in 1779 he was elected to a Fellowship at All Souls.[3] In the same year he was called to the Bar: he rose to be Senior Master in Chancery, and was one of the Commissioners appointed to manage the real and personal property of George III: in recognition of his services, he was created a Baronet in 1815. He sat as Tory M.P. for Reading (of which he was also Recorder, 1779–1807) from 1797 to 1802, and again from 1806 to 1818, and is said to have been unusually solicitous for the interests of his constituents. He was also the author of a treatise on the Law of Elections (1789: 2nd ed. 1795). He died in 1824, at the age of

[1] *Op. cit.* p. 338. [2] Carus, p. 37.
[3] *Ibid.* p. 720. (Not mentioned in Foster's *Alumni Oxonienses (1715–1886)* or in *D.N.B.*)

sixty-eight. By a curious irony his grandson, the third Baronet, a gentle, ineffective creature, who had been an undergraduate at Christ Church at the time of his great-uncle Charles' funeral, went over to the Church of Rome in 1851.[1]

These domestic details, trivial in themselves, are yet significant as illustrating one of the greatest difficulties and one of the most signal triumphs of the Evangelical Revival: namely, the way in which, in spite of the most formidable psychological antagonism, it did succeed in winning over, at least to a remarkable extent, what we should call 'the public school class'. The limits of that class were then, admittedly, both narrower and wider than they are to-day. Nevertheless, all the Simeon brothers except the eldest, Richard, who seems to have been delicate, were Old Etonians: and therefore it is appropriate to proceed directly from the problem of Evangelicalism and the Family to the problem of Evangelicalism and the Public Schools.

---

[1] *Notice of Sir John Simeon* in *Miscellanies of the Philobiblon Society*, vol. xii, 1868–69.—Cf. Manning's observation: 'Every Evangelical name is now inscribed in the Catholic Church—Wilberforce, Owen, Ryder, Cunningham, Simeon, Woodward, Sargent, and many more....' (Shane Leslie, *Henry Edward Manning*, p. 478).

APPENDIX TO CHAPTER I

[From *The Evangelical Magazine* for February 1794 (vol. ii, pp. 69–72)]

PARLOUR RELIGION EXEMPLIFIED IN THE PRACTICE
OF HONORIO AND HIS FAMILY AND FRIENDS

THOSE to whom the Lord has given a plenty of the good things of this world, have it in their power to anticipate something of the employments and enjoyments of heaven, so far as the imperfection of the present state will permit; for they have all things richly to enjoy, they may chuse their company, their time, and entertainments, and in all things follow the pious disposition of their hearts. It is an happiness for a religious man to visit, or to be in a house, that has a good man at its head. Such a house is that of Honorio.

In the morning the parlour is decently prepared, and warmed for the reception of the pious heads of the family, who come from their chamber smiling with gratitude to God, and good-humoured with their diligent servants. The little family during their infancy are in the nursery, and every thing that might interrupt, is prohibited from entering the parlour, which is at this hour a chapel for devotion. The clock having struck the well-known hour, Honorio and his beloved wife are seated, with the Book of God before them; the servants enter with looks expressive of the happiness they feel in having the privilege of being God's free men, and joining their master and mistress in his service. Under the direction of Honorio, a song of praise to God for his mercies is offered up by this primitive church; and a portion of Scripture is read, that their minds may become more familiarly acquainted with the sacred oracles. This being done, they all bow their knees to Him by whom the whole family in heaven and earth is named, and the good Honorio calls upon his Lord and Master in heaven, with expressions of profound homage and humility; blessing him for the favours of the past night, and the pleasure of seeing the light of the returning day. Like the great High-priest he bears on his heart all his family before God, and intreats for particular mercies according to the known state of his household, and puts himself and all his affairs, both temporal and spiritual, into the hands of his heavenly Father. He then gives them his benediction, and they all rise. The happy servants, cheered and warmed with the aids of devotion, return to their duty, each according to his place, and the heads of the family, with their guests (if such are present), sit down to breakfast on the overflowing bounty of God's providence. Business, or works of piety, perhaps, call the master away, and the mistress, having given directions in her family, takes her usual seat and employment in her parlour. The Bible is laid near her, to be referred to as her best friend and director, her richest cordial in trouble, and most faithful monitor in doubtful cases. Nor is she fearful that any visitor should find her with this companion, for she desires no company but those who love the Scriptures. She is rather of the sentiments of a well-known female, who brought her family Bible into her parlour, and laying it on the table, said, 'Lie there, thou best of books, and keep thy place whoever comes in'. A pious visitor or two, or a minister of Christ perhaps, drops in, in the forenoon. If so, the time is not wasted in unprofitable talk, but the parlour is honoured by being changed into the similitude of the holy mount. This heavenly woman and her guests enter into discourse, as Moses and Elias did, on what once passed at Jerusalem, when Jesus gave his life a ransom for many; and their experience so confirms their interest in that work of love, that their hearts burn within them, and, like St Peter, they find it good to be there.

The hour to dine being come, Honorio returns, and probably brings a religious friend or two to his hospitable mansion. The table being spread with plenty, without ostentation, the provision is sanctified by the prayers of Honorio, penetrated with a sense of having forfeited every thing by sin, but having recovered all by the merit of his great Saviour, a remembrance of whose love makes every thing more sweet and refreshing. Having used, but not abused, the bounties of Providence, grateful acknowledgments are returned to the great Giver of every good gift; and the pious few mingle profitable discourse with their wine, or concert some plan for supplying the wants of those who are in distressing circumstances. Towards evening, a select company grace the tea-table; and the interests of the Gospel, with the best means of spreading its influence around them, become the subjects of this conversation. Should national affairs happen to be introduced, they express their loyalty towards their lawful sovereign, and their thankfulness to God for the many invaluable privileges enjoyed by Englishmen. The hour of parting being come, the praises of God introduce the devotion of the evening, in which, as in the morning, the Scriptures are read, and all the family called to unite. Care is taken not to protract this service to an immoderate length, lest the children, on account of their tender years, and the servants, wearied with the labour of the day, might be inclined to sleep when their minds ought to be attentive. Nor is it hurried over as though it were of no importance; but sufficient time is taken reverently and decently to thank God for his goodness, earnestly to intreat him to pardon their sins, and to commit themselves into his care and protection.

O ye worldlings! what can ye produce in the scenes of your lives that is worthy to be compared with this? 'The curse of God', says the Scripture, 'is in the dwellings of the wicked.' Your parlours have no blessings in them. Your children and servants never hear the name of God mentioned in them, unless it be to blaspheme it. Your tables are unblessed. At your banquets, intemperance reigns, and modesty is put to the blush. The parlours I have been describing are types of heaven, where due returns are made to God for his bounty. Ye are deluded by what you call rational amusements. Like children you divert yourselves in foolish play, night after night, wasting your time and substance. 'And the God in whose hands your breath is, and whose are all your ways, you have not glorified.' Any thing that is serious and useful to your souls, you will not once hear, much less will you hear it repeated. 'And what will ye do in the end thereof?' O that ye were wise, that ye would consider your ways, and at last make some returns of gratitude to a gracious God for all his benefits bestowed upon you!

PROBUS.

43

II

RELIGION IN THE SCHOOL

❂

'Boarding schools in general', writes the Dean, 'unless under very particular and favourable circumstances, I exceedingly disapprove.'

Life of Isaac Milner, p. 462.

After I left St James's-place, I spent the afternoon with Mrs Peckwell, a precious woman, and a living instance of what grace can do. Some little gloom hung upon her countenance, but a cheerfulness appeared in her speech and manner.... The daughter is the very image of the father, and the son pleased me much. At five he came from school, and I asked him whether he had learned to swear. He answered, No. I asked him further, has no one tried to make you swear? Yes, he said, many had tried, and once he was offered a guinea to make him swear, but would not. What nurseries of vice are public schools! and the next nursery is an university.

Rev. JOHN BERRIDGE TO JOHN THORNTON, Esq.
Tabernacle, March 2, 1782.
(*Congregational Magazine*, vol ix, n.s. 1845, p. 741.)

45

Chapter Two

RELIGION IN THE SCHOOL

CHARLES SIMEON entered Eton at the age of seven, in 1767. Following in the footsteps of his brother John (King's Scholar, 1771), he was elected onto the Foundation in 1773; and, fortunate in not being disappointed of a vacancy at the appropriate time, migrated to Cambridge in January 1779 as a scholar of King's.[1]

Notoriously, the condition of the public schools in the latter part of the eighteenth century and at the commencement of the nineteenth left much to be desired. Thus, for example, the Rev. George Gretton, D.D., Fellow of Trinity College, Cambridge, in conversation with Mr Joseph Farington, R.A. (Sept. 26, 1806), 'described the Characters of three great Schools by saying that the youth at *Eaton are dissipated gentlemen*;—those at *Westminster* dissipated with a little of the Black guard;—and those at *St Pauls School* the most depraved of all.—He said *Eaton* at present is upon a sad footing; the Master, Dr Goodall, having lost much of His Authority from want of resolution.... —He said *Rugby School* is also upon a bad footing. In it are many of the Sons of Gentlemen, but more of those who are the Sons of Manufacturers at Birmingham, Wolverhampton &c. who having little sentiment of the disgrace of anything dishonorable act as their inclinations lead them.—...At Harrow ..., He said, the Boys are gentlemen.—'[2] Dr Gretton kept a private school at Taplow, and therefore can hardly be regarded as an impartial witness: but there were other critics of the system whose censures were equally severe. 'I am no friend of public schools', wrote Southey (Aug. 3, 1798). 'Where they are bene-

---

[1] *Eton College Register: 1753–1790*, ed. R. A. Austen Leigh (1921), p. 475.
[2] *Farington Diary*, ed. J. Greig, vol. iv, p. 6.—Dr Gretton was himself an Old Reptonian. (*Admissions to Trinity College, Cambridge*, ed. W. W. Rouse Ball and J. A. Venn, vol. iii, p. 232.)

ficial to one they are ruinous to twenty.'[1] And Wilberforce, reporting a conversation with Bowdler (Oct. 26, 1807), noted: 'Much talk about education. He agreed that public school inadmissible, from its probable effects on eternal state.'[2]

From various sources it is possible to construct a tolerably vivid and convincing picture of Simeon as an Eton schoolboy. His profile was distinguished, but not handsome: his nickname was 'Chin Simeon':[3] and on one occasion Porson, who was a school contemporary, and who disliked him intensely, wrote some satirical verses addressed 'to the ugliest boy in Dr Davies's dominions', and threw them over a wall. They were picked up, and brought to Simeon, who was furious, and took infinite pains to detect the writer, even going to the length of comparing the handwriting of all the boys in his form, and soliciting the assistance of the monitors; but he could discover nothing, ' "nor was it likely that he should", said Porson, (who never *directly* acknowledged such compositions), "for it was written with the left hand." '[4] Simeon was, in fact, in early life, grotesquely, whimsically ugly: and, like other ugly boys, he instinctively sought compensation in an extravagance in dress. There is a reference to this in a letter written by Henry Venn, on the occasion of his ordination in 1782, and clearly based on information from Simeon himself: 'This is the young man so vain of dress, that he constantly allowed more than £50 a year for his own person. Now he scruples keeping a horse, that the money may help the saints of Christ.'[5] The scruple was, in fact, sur-

---

[1] *Selections from the Letters of Robert Southey*, ed. J. W. Warter (1856), vol. i, p. 60.

[2] *The Life of William Wilberforce*, by his sons, Robert Isaac Wilberforce and Samuel Wilberforce, vol. iii, p. 348.—Cf. also Edward C. Mack, *Public Schools and British Opinion: 1780 to 1860* (1938), pp. 151 ff.

[3] So Mr Farington was told by his friend Mr J. Wells of Bickley who had been at Eton with Charles Simeon (*Farington Diary*, vol. vii, p. 280).

[4] E. H. Barker, *Parriana* (1829), vol. ii, p. 701 *n.*: J. S. Watson, *Life of Porson* (1861), p. 21. The antipathy persisted into later years. Porson called Simeon 'a coxcomb in religion' (Watson, p. 21). Simeon said: 'I never could make up my mind to agree with Porson in any matter of Divine truth. I could agree with him in a Greek criticism, but I feared to lend my mind to anything on Divine truth which Porson said, for I knew his moral character.' Yet he inclined to believe that Porson was right in his controversy with Travis on I John v. 7, 8. (A. W. Brown, *Recollections of Simeon's Conversation Parties*, p. 356.)   [5] Carus, p. 27.

mounted: and it is also true that throughout his life Charles Simeon was remarked for a punctilious neatness of dress and personal appearance.[1]

In other respects, he seems to have been a perfectly normal boy of rather athletic type: many years later, his school friend, Provost Goodall, could write to him (Sept. 29, 1833): 'I much doubt if you could *now* snuff a candle with your feet, or jump over half-a-dozen chairs in succession. *Sed quid ego haec revoco?* —at 73, *moniti meliora sequamur*.'[2] In point of fact, Simeon kept up his reputation for strenuous physical activity until well past middle age. 'Horsemanship was his favourite exercise; and few persons, it is well known, were better judges of the merits of a horse, or more dexterous and bold in the management of one.'[3] The luxuries in which he indulged himself in later life were few, but it is characteristic that, instead of availing himself of the College stables, he kept a private stable of his own:[4] and the author of *Alma Mater* (1827) recounts an anecdote of 'the gay old cushion-thumper' riding on the Gogmagogs, leaping the ditches, and making his servant follow him: 'one, however, which he took, the servant dared not attempt, at which the fine old fellow roared out, "You cowardly dog, why don't you follow?" This scene took place in the "Senior Wranglers' Walk", even at the time when it was crowded by Simeonites.'[5]

Of intellectual ability there was less promise. 'There was nothing remarkable abt. Him to signify superiority of talents': he was, however, ambitious 'to acquire distinction in some way or other'.[6] At a later date he used to maintain that emulation was good for schoolboys, better, at any rate, than listlessness: it brought the best boys to the top, although admittedly it was

---

[1] 'He was fastidious in his attention to his person, dress, and furniture, and over-punctilious in his observance of whatever he conceived to belong to the address and manners of a gentleman.'—*Memoirs of the Rev. Charles Jerram* (1855), p. 124.

[2] Carus, p. 3.　　　　　　　　　　[3] *Ibid.* p. 3.

[4] A. C. Benson, *Fasti Etonenses* (1899), p. 241. 'He came with a servant and two very fine horses, on which he places a high value': *Autobiography of Arthur Young* (July 13, 1804), ed. M. Betham-Edwards (1898), p. 399.

[5] *Alma Mater; or, Seven Years at the University of Cambridge*, by a Trinity-Man [J. M. F. Wright] (1827), vol. i, pp. 56–7.

[6] *Farington Diary*, vol. vii (Oct. 7, 1814), p. 280.

liable to make them petulant and impudent,[1] Ambition coupled with application certainly carried Simeon into the Sixth Form: and in the Speech List of 1778—the earliest Eton Speech List still extant—appears this entry:

SIMEON, K.S.... to M. Marcellus *Cicero*[2]

The occasion was remarkable for the presence of the King and Queen and of the Royal Family, as well as of the Archbishop of Canterbury and of the Prime Minister, Lord North. It was remarkable also for a brilliant performance by Lord Wellesley, who declaimed Strafford's speech before his execution with such pathos as to draw tears from the whole audience.[3]

The Royal visit was a great success: the King, on taking leave, assured the Provost that this should not be his last visit to the College, and from this time continued to bestow upon it that royal interest and partiality which, more than any other single factor, enabled Eton to wrest the hegemony from Westminster. The success of the previous Royal visit on Whit Tuesday of the same year had been more qualified. The occasion of it was the Montem.[4]

This was, in essence, a quasi-military procession to a mound called Salt Hill, near Slough, in the course of which tribute (known as 'salt') was more or less forcibly levied from all spectators on behalf of the Captain of Montem (who was always the senior King's Scholar) to help him in his University career: the money taken ran into several hundred pounds, but the Captain had also to bear the expenses of the day, which were very considerable. Besides the Captain, there were other officers —the Marshal, the Ensign, the Lieutenant, two Salt-bearers, and so forth—chosen from among the Scholars by mutual

[1] Brown, p. 322.
[2] *Etoniana* [ed. R. A. Austen Leigh], No. 37 (Oct. 1, 1924), p. 581.
[3] *A History of Eton College (1440–1910)*, by Sir H. C. Maxwell Lyte (4th ed. revised, 1911), pp. 343–4.
[4] The best account of Eton Montem is to be found in Maxwell Lyte, *op. cit.* ch. xxi. Cf. also Brand's *Observations on Popular Antiquities*, ed. Henry Ellis (1813), vol. i, pp. 337–49; Disraeli's *Coningsby* (1844), bk. i, ch. xi; [W. H. Tucker's] *Eton of Old* (1892), pp. 1–10; and G. C. Green's *Eton Montem: A Memory of the Past*, in *Eton in the Forties*, by an Old Colleger [A. D. Coleridge] (1896), pp. 229–66.

arrangement: the Captain of the Oppidans was also an ex-officio Salt-bearer. Montem was always something of an interruption and a nuisance, the more so as it became increasingly elaborate: originally annual, it was made triennial in 1775, and was finally abolished by Provost Hawtrey in 1847, six years after the opening of the Great Western Railway had had the undesirable effect of bringing down promiscuous hordes of vulgar sightseers.[1] Nevertheless, in Simeon's time it must have been a brave sight, with the officers and upper boys in their red coats and military uniforms, and even the lower boys in gala dress. Disraeli, through the character of Madame Colonna, described it as 'a Protestant Carnival', and regretted that it did not last forty days. The description was ingenious rather than exact, for Montem was an unmistakable survival from the Middle Ages, whether or not connected with the mummeries of the Boy Bishop: and as late as 1778, the official ceremony terminated, after the waving of the standard by the Ensign on the summit of Salt Hill at the conclusion of the march amid cries of 'Floreat Etona', with a distinctly blasphemous performance in which two of the Collegers, dressed as a Parson and a Clerk, gabbled some mock prayers in Latin, at the end of which the Parson, to the uproarious amusement of the bystanders, proceeded to kick the Clerk down to the bottom of the hill. At the Montem of 1778, the Clerk occasioned much additional merriment by dressing himself according to the *ton* of 1745, and by acting his part with as minute a consistency as he had dressed the character.[2] Unhappily, the Queen was not amused: and, at her particular request, this part of the ceremony was discontinued. The remaining twenty-two Montems concluded decorously with the waving of the flag.

A contemporary drawing of their Majesties at the Eton Montem of 1778 is reproduced in Sir H. C. Maxwell Lyte's

[1] Appropriately enough, the Old Etonian opposition to its abolition was headed by Lord John Manners (the 'Lord Henry Sidney' of *Coningsby*), 'always an anxious guardian of ancient institutions'.—Cf. Charles Whibley, *Lord John Manners and His Friends* (1925), vol. i, pp. 263–70.

[2] Brand, *Popular Antiquities*, ed. Henry Ellis (1813), vol. i, p. 338 *n.* (quoting a contemporary account, signed 'Etonensis', from the *Public Advertiser*).

History of Eton College.[1] The popular interest attaching to this occasion, from our point of view, lies in the fact that Simeon was Marshal for that year, while his friend Goodall was the Ensign.[2] It is indeed a strange coincidence that the future hero of the Evangelical Revival should have assisted at the last performance of this mediaeval burlesque of mediaeval piety. For the religion of the Middle Ages had its scurrilous side: and it is perhaps significant that at Eton in the eighteenth century it was the indecorous aspect of mediaeval familiarity with the things of God that had persisted when the decorous and devotional aspect had virtually become effaced.

What, then, was the state of religion at Eton during Charles Simeon's school-days?

His own recollections of it are, to say the least, decidedly unfavourable. Admittedly, his censures are levelled primarily at himself: admittedly also, the saints in their reminiscences tend to take a disproportionately gloomy view of the misdemeanours of their childhood. 'And is this the innocence of boyhood?' cries St Augustine, after a brief recital of his boyish peccadilloes. 'Not so, Lord, not so; I cry Thy mercy, O my God.'[3] So also Simeon's biographer is at pains to emphasise that the opening paragraph of his autobiographical Memoir, written in 1813, represents the standpoint 'of an advanced Christian, recording with matured views his judgment of the unprofitableness of his youth'. The Memoir opens thus:

> I begin then with *my early life.*—But what an awful scene does that present to my view! Never have I reviewed it for thirty-four years past, nor ever can I to my dying hour, without the deepest shame and sorrow. My vanity, my folly, my wickedness, God alone knoweth, or can bear to know. To enter into a detail of particulars would answer no good end. If I be found at last a prodigal restored to his Father's house, God will in no ordinary measure be glorified in

---

[1] *Op. cit.* p. 507. From a drawing by S. H. Grimm in the British Museum.

[2] Brand, *Popular Antiquities*, vol. i, p. 339 *n.* Simeon was a visitor at the Montem on May 17, 1796, when he had the pleasure of introducing his Scotch Presbyterian friend, Dr Buchanan of Edinburgh, to the spectacle (Carus, p. 114).

[3] *The Confessions of S. Augustine*, tr. E. B. Pusey, bk. i, c. xxviii, 30. (Library of the Fathers, vol. i, 1840, p. 18.)

me: the abundance of my sinfulness will display in most affecting colours the superabundance of his grace.[1]

It is therefore, surely, in the light of this self-accusation that we have to read his statement to old Mr Venn in 1782, at the time of his ordination to the diaconate, that Eton was 'so profligate a place, that he told me he should be tempted to murder his own son (that was his word) sooner than let him see what he had seen'.[2] Again he seems to have avoided entering into detail. Forty-five years later, however, he wrote to his old friend and contemporary, Joseph Goodall, now Provost of Eton, upon a concrete issue. He also enclosed a copy of Wilberforce's *Practical View*[3] as a small pledge of his regard. Unfortunately Mrs Goodall temporarily mislaid the packet, and when the Provost, after a courteous reminder, at last acknowledged it, his answer was evasive. The point complained of was the disproportionate amount of time allotted to the study of the Classics in the curriculum of the school, compared with the instruction given in the Christian religion. 'It is often with me a matter of regret', wrote Simeon (Sept. 4, 1827), 'that the atmosphere of Eton is so unfavourable for the health of the soul; and that amidst all the attention that is paid to the Poets and Philosophers of Greece and Rome, scarcely ever by any chance is the name of our blessed Saviour heard, especially in a way of admiration and love; and that whilst earthly honours are held up as proper objects of our ambition, so little is spoken of heaven as worthy of our pursuit....'[4] The regret thus felt by Simeon was by no means peculiar to him: had not the poet Cowper complained long since in his *Tirocinium: or, a Review of Schools* (1784) that

[1] Carus, p. 4.
[2] *Ibid.* p. 27.—A brief and inconclusive correspondence regarding the morals of the school will be found in the *Gentleman's Magazine*, Feb., April, May 1798 (vol. lxviii, pt. 1, pp. 95, 282–6, 383–4): it is patent that we cannot build anything material on MONTEM's hints respecting '*the systematic arrangement of a* FIFTH-FORM SERAGLIO'(p.95), or even upon the admission of PHILO ETONENSIS that 'the immorality predominant at Eton, &c. at the present time, exceeds that of any former period' (p. 286).
[3] *A Practical View of the Prevailing Religious System of Professed Christians in the higher and middle classes of this country, contrasted with Real Christianity*, by William Wilberforce, Esq., Member of Parliament for the County of York (1797).
[4] Carus, p. 609.

a public school education supplied no intellectual defence against the teachings of infidel philosophers who cant of 'Reason', 'Priestcraft', and the like, since public school boys are

> ...taught at school much mythologic stuff,[1]
> But sound religion sparingly enough[2]?

But this particular indictment had been popularised, or had at least been brought before the general notice of the public, by what is surely the original and archetypal controversy regarding Public School Religion, a controversy which raged from 1799 to 1802, and was not even then extinguished.

The controversy was inaugurated by the Rev. William Jones of Nayland, a man to-day remembered chiefly as one of the few eighteenth-century links in the chain which couples the old Anglo-Catholicism with the new, who in the last year of his life (March 1799) addressed to the Rev. William Vincent, D.D., Head Master of Westminster School, and *doyen* of the educational profession, an open letter entitled *Considerations on the Religious Worship of the Heathens as bearing unanswerable testimony to the Principles of Christianity.*[3]

It transpired that Mr Jones had had his observation drawn to the case of 'an amiable youth, of the first fashion', who, most regrettably, 'was found to have kept loose company very early in life; from which every bad consequence was to be apprehended'. There was nothing very unusual in this, as the Old Boy himself admitted. But what had impressed him, had indeed 'struck him to the heart', in this particular example, was the observation made on it by the young man's father, who

accounted for the evil in the following manner: that his son, having been accustomed at school to the loose ideas, communicated by

---

[1] ['The author begs leave to explain.—Sensible that, without such knowledge, neither the ancient poets nor historians can be tasted, or indeed understood, he does not mean to censure the pains that are taken to instruct a school-boy in the religion of the heathen, but merely that neglect of Christian culture which leaves him shamefully ignorant of his own.']

[2] *Op. cit.* ll. 197–8. Cowper's *Poetical Works*, ed. H. S. Milford (3rd ed. 1926), p. 246.

[3] *The Theological and Miscellaneous Works of the Rev. William Jones, M.A., F.R.S.*, ed. William Stevens (new ed. 1810), vol. vi, pp. 189–208. Cf. also Jones' *Life of Bishop Horne*, ibid. pp. 38–40.

Horace and other Heathen poets, had carried their principles into his own practice; and was therefore only in a train with other young men of his age and education. Good GOD! said I to myself, is this the case? and are we asleep about it? Do we sit still, and see Christians, under the light of the Gospel, sinking into worse than heathen corruption? This led me to consider, whether it be not possible to turn this evil into some good, by showing young men of learning, that, as the false religion of Heathens was borrowed from the true religion of Revelation, and is a witness to its authority, it ought rather to confirm us in the truth than draw us into evil. I thought, if this could be shown, something might be done toward the preservation of our youth, without breaking in upon the established forms of education: that the attempt would be laudable, and merit the thanks of parents, who see this matter in a proper light; that no learned teachers, if Christian, could be offended; and that, at all events, he that should give notice of the evil, might deliver his own soul by it.[1]

There is no need to enter into the ensuing demonstration that the religion of the Heathens, with all its limitations, was at least clean contrary to Deism and Infidelity and Low Church principles.[2] From it, the author had two inferences to make. 'I. That, if Heathen books give this testimony to Divine Revelation, we should use them for the best end they are capable of answering, the confirmation of our own faith': and if our teachers of youth would but give their pupils such hints occasionally, as would acquaint them with this use of Heathenism as a never-failing testimony to an original Revelation (from which it had apostatised), and therefore as a never-failing argument against Infidelity, 'we shall not then be long under the dominion of profligate scholars, who use their heathen learning for no end, but as an instrument of evil, to corrupt and destroy the Christian world; increasing all that misery daily, which abounds too much already'. Secondly, he would also recommend 'that the deplorable consequences of a departure from the true God should be pointed out to all school-boys, as the Apostle has displayed them in the first chapter to the Romans: which was extended as

---

[1] *Ibid.* pp. 191–2.
[2] 'No Heathens were what we now call Low Churchmen: they carried things to such a height on the contrary part, that I wonder Infidels do not burn their books for teaching Tory principles, and bearing such testimony against themselves.'—*Ibid.* p. 193.

a warning against the corruptions of Heathenism, and should never be forgotten to the end of the world. It is full as necessary now, as when the Apostle wrote it': perhaps more necessary than ever, in the light of the parallel apostasy in the French nation; an apostasy worse, both in its guilt and in its fruits, than the original departure to Heathenism. 'All that the apostle has said of the antient Heathens and their abominable morals may now be applied to the French, in whom it is fully verified, so that they are become the very pests of the earth, and their metropolis, in the literal sense of the words, a second Sodom.' What was requisite, therefore, was that the rising generation should be continually reminded of the dreadful effects of Heathenism, both in the time of the Apostle, and in their own.[1]

The sting of the pamphlet lay in the phrase: 'From the common forms of school-education, our youth are in danger of returning back from the purity of Christians to the impure manners of Heathens.'[2]

Dr Vincent replied to these admonitions in a private letter, in which he courteously denied the allegation that the study of the Heathen poets was turning his pupils into budding libertines or full-fledged Jacobins, and explained to Mr Jones the course of religious instruction employed at Westminster. The Old Boy was on the brink of death, and very feeble: but he dictated a reply, in which he gladly exculpated Dr Vincent from these strictures, approved the propriety and consistency of his method, and cheered his labours with his blessing.[3]

From this exchange of courtesies one point emerges which will probably become even clearer in the course of these lectures, but which may be noted here. Humanly speaking, the revival of Christianity in England in the nineteenth century was precipitated by events across the Channel. 'I have heard persons of great weight and authority,' wrote Mr Gladstone, 'such as Mr Grenville, and also, I think, Archbishop Howley, ascribe the beginnings of a reviving seriousness in the upper classes of lay society to a reaction against the horrors and impieties of the

---

[1] *Ibid.* p. 207.   [2] *Ibid.* p. 191.
[3] *A Defence of Public Education, addressed to the Most Reverend the Lord Bishop of Meath*, by William Vincent, D.D....(2nd ed. 1802), pp. 23-4.

first French Revolution in its later stages.'[1] To Jones of Nayland belongs the credit of having been one of the first to face that challenge. As Dr Vincent subsequently explained: 'The circumstances of the times operated more powerfully on his mind, than on others who were possessed of less fervency and zeal. He had lived to see the Christian religion overwhelmed in France, and altars erected to Liberty, and Reason, and Nonsense. He saw the grossness of Heathenism, as he thought, reviving in the caprice of imagination, and he wished to warn his own countrymen against a similar catastrophe.'[2]

The attack on Public School Religion was renewed a few months later by the Master of the Temple, Dr Thomas Rennell, in a Sermon preached in St Paul's Cathedral on Thursday, June 6, 1799, on the occasion of the Yearly Meeting of the Children educated in the Charity Schools in and about the Cities of London and Westminster.[3] Dr Rennell was himself connected with the Hackney phalanx: and, like Jones of Nayland, he had been impressed, in the light of the French revolutionary outbreak, with the precariousness of any civil polity that did not rest upon the deep and firm foundation of 'the genuine religion of Jesus Christ'. 'There is no occasion to dwell upon events before us all. It is sufficient to say, that what *superstition* was incapable of doing in France and Italy, the Christianity of this PROTESTANT nation has here effected. To the principles therefore diffused by the labours of this Society [the Society for

---

[1] G. W. E. Russell, *Collections and Recollections* (1st ed. 1898), p. 77.—Cf. *The Annual Register* (1798), p. 229: 'The French Revolution illustrated the connection between good morals and the order and peace of society more than all the eloquence of the pulpit and the disquisitions of moral philosophers had done for many centuries. The upper ranks in society, the generality of men of rank and fortune, not always the most inquisitive and penetrating on other subjects, were among the very first to take alarm at those irreligious and profligate doctrines by which the French democracy sought to shelter the profligacy of its conduct. In this country, royal proclamations were issued for paying a decent and due regard to Sundays.... The churches were well attended, and sometimes even crowded. It was a wonder to the lower orders, throughout all parts of England, to see the avenues to the churches filled with carriages. This novel appearance prompted the simple country-people to inquire what was the matter?'

[2] *Op. cit.* p. 26.

[3] Cf. M. G. Jones, *The Charity School Movement: a study of eighteenth-century Puritanism in action* (1938).

Promoting Christian Knowledge], we are, under God, principally to look for the preservation of the country.... All we have seen, all we have feared, all we have felt for these last ten years, leads us to promote the furtherance of that religion' which teaches 'the obedience due, from *christian subjects*, to *christian magistrates*'.[1]
Then followed the peccant paragraph.

Another circumstance of the times which renders the labours of this Society of peculiar exigency, is the most lamentable and notorious defectiveness of christian education in many of our public schools, and other great seminaries of this nation. In those happy times, when men in the higher and middle ranks *necessarily* imbibed in the course of their education the essential principles of the Gospel, while these were made an *integral* part of the systems of general instruction, every master of a family in his turn became a teacher to his domestics, to his children, and to his neighbours. What he *freely* received he *freely* imparted. But all who are acquainted with the elementary ignorance of christianity, in which young men are permitted to remain, in the greater part of our public institutions, (and it is impossible to be much conversant in them without knowing this) will see how necessary the exertions of *this* Society are for preserving the light of the Gospel, among the lower ranks of men. Ignorance and irreligion are extremely apt to descend from the high to the low; and therefore when the reservoirs which used to diffuse these salutary streams among those of elevated rank are choaked and dried up, the charitable hand which supplies the deficiency among the poor, is peculiarly grateful to God and beneficial to mankind.[2]

The offence thus given was aggravated by a lengthy Note[3] in the appendix to the sermon.

The *general* state of public education in this country, with regard to religion, appears to require much attention. We cannot but lament, that in *very few* of our best endowed seminaries, the study of Christianity has that portion of time and regard allotted to it, which

[1] *A Sermon preached in the Cathedral Church of St Paul, London, on Thursday, June 6, 1799: being the time of the Yearly Meeting of the Children Educated in the Charity Schools, in and about the Cities of London and Westminster.* By Thomas Rennell, D.D., F.A.S., Master of the Temple. *Published at the Request of the Society for promoting Christian Knowledge, and of the Trustees of the several Schools* (1799), p. 6.
[2] *Ibid.* pp. 7–8.   [3] *Ibid.* pp. 18–19.

57

the welfare of society, the progress of delusive and ruinous errors, and the true interest of sound learning itself, seems at the present time, *peculiarly* to call for. In some of them, and those not of *small* celebrity or importance, *all* consideration of the revealed will of God is passed over with a resolute, systematic, and contemptuous neglect, which is not exceeded in that which the French call their *national institute*.

The consequences for learning itself might easily be apprehended, were indeed beginning to be evident, in the increase of 'indolence and dissipation, even in *these* retreats', the disappearance of 'even the very *form* and *external* appearance of discipline and instruction', the decay of '*industry* and *dignity* in those who *teach*, and *subordination* and *modesty* in those who *learn*'.

But in the present moral and political state of human affairs, the consequences are *immediately* alarming. Young men of rank and talents are dismissed into the world, without *one single* safeguard against those plausible and tremendous theories, which have turned more than one quarter of the world into an Aceldama, or field of blood! Of religion, its evidences, doctrines, and motives, they are utterly and grossly ignorant: No check therefore, restraint or corrective is afforded from hence; they are therefore, not unfrequently, hurried on by heated imaginations and enflamed pride, *aggravated* rather than *controuled* by the learning they have acquired, to turn the arms of eloquence and genius to the subversion of order, and the destruction of their native country.

Dr Rennell then paused to quote a passage from Cicero, and continued:

This evil, however, for which PAGANISM supplied no remedy, CHRISTIANITY, by abating the presumption, and softening the affections of men, would, if inculcated at an *early* period of life, effectually counteract. CHRISTIANITY alone can peculiarly, in the present disposition of the minds of men, turn learning and talents into a blessing to this country. There is scarcely an *internal* danger which we fear, but what is to be ascribed to a *pagan* education, under *Christian establishments*, in a *Christian* country.

He concluded by expressing the hope that those who presided over our public seminaries might be 'awakened to their deep responsibility in this important duty to GOD, their KING, and their COUNTRY'; and by quoting 'the awful words of the reverend and venerable Mr *Jones*' in his *Considerations on the Religious Worship of the Heathens*, in which he alluded to 'the dominion of profligate scholars, who use their heathen learning for no end, but as an instrument of evil, to corrupt and destroy the Christian world; increasing all that misery daily, which abounds too much already'.[1]

This was a much more serious matter, because, whereas the normal demand for a published sermon, even by a preacher of such eminence as the Master of the Temple, was seldom capable of exhausting an edition of 500 copies, the annual Sermon on behalf of the Charity Schools was always bound up with the Annual Report of the S.P.C.K., which had a circulation of 3000.[2] Moreover, the reference to Mr Jones' pamphlet, which was addressed personally to Dr Vincent in the advertisement and on the title page, incited that combative and conscientious pedagogue to construe Dr Rennell's discourse as a personal attack.[3] Accordingly, he prepared to publish his defence. But certain mutual friends and members of the Board of the S.P.C.K. intervened to effect a reconciliation: and the Master of the Temple was induced to write to the Head Master of Westminster, explaining that he had not in the least intended to cast aspersions upon the religious instruction enjoyed by Dr Vincent's pupils, and explicitly excepting Westminster from his blanket indictment of the English public schools. 'I no sooner received his letter, with the exception in my favour, than I returned an answer by the same post, expressed in cordial terms, that I was contented to be silent. I was not a little surprized to find afterwards, that another letter was written by Dr Rennell to the Board, much less favourable to me, and much more resolute in censuring Public Schools and Universities, than even his publication. I repented of my acquiescence, but my word was passed, and I made no further complaint. Dr Rennell will feel the value of this sort of moderation, when I acquaint him that

---

[1] Rennell, pp. 18–19. [2] Vincent, p.
[3] *Ibid.* pp. 21–2.

my Defence was ready for publication, and could have gone to the press the next morning.'[1]

But if Dr Vincent had thus put back his sword into its scabbard, it was not destined to remain there very long: for two years later the Bishop of Meath, preaching from the same pulpit upon a similar occasion, adopted and reiterated the indictment. Taking as his text Matt. xi. 5—*And the Poor have the Gospel preached to them*—Dr O'Beirne suggested, by a glancing innuendo, that he was dubious whether 'the system of education for the higher and wealthier classes' was built upon the same foundation. 'I had proposed to myself', he wrote, in a footnote[2] to the printed edition of his Sermon, 'to say a few words on the sad degeneracy of our public schools in this most important part of education, and their systematic neglect, for such it is now become, of that religious instruction, which, in the earlier periods of the reformation, and even to a much later date, was so carefully provided for the higher and wealthier classes of the British youth; but I found the subject anticipated by Dr Rennell, in his Sermon on this Anniversary, and I could add nothing to what that zealous and eloquent preacher has there urged to call the public attention to this portentous evil.'

Indignant that this libel on the Public Schools of England should once more 'be propagated from the Liffey to the Ganges, as the opinion of the Society, adopted on the authority of Dr Rennell and [the Bishop of Meath]',[3] Dr Vincent applied for permission to circulate with this Annual Report, containing his Lordship's discourse, a Note requesting the members to suspend

---

[1] Vincent, pp. 9–10.

[2] *A Sermon preached in the Cathedral Church of St Paul, London, on Thursday, May 21, 1801: being the time of the Yearly Meeting of the Children Educated in the Charity Schools, in and about the Cities of London and Westminster.* By the Most Reverend Thomas Lewis [O'Beirne], Lord Bishop of Meath.... (1801), p. 39 *n.*—The sermon is in itself an interesting specimen of that flowery eloquence by which the sober, rational preaching of the Hanoverian Establishment was occasionally relieved, particularly in the later decades of the eighteenth century, and of which the Bishop of Meath was a conspicuous exponent. Cf. [Edward Mangin's] *Piozziana* (1833), p. 137 ('His style, without being in the slightest degree gorgeous, was never less than elegant...').—There is a brief account of Dr O'Beirne in Beloe's *Sexagenarian*, vol. ii, pp. 170–4. Cf. *History of the Church of Ireland*, ed. W. Alison Phillips (1933), vol. iii, pp. 273, 289.

[3] Vincent, p. 8.

RELIGION IN THE SCHOOL

their judgment on the point in question until he could be heard in his own defence. The secretary (the Rev. George Gaskin, D.D., Rector of St Bene't Grace-church) admitted that he had merely passed on the Bishop's manuscript to the printer, and had not actually read it until it was in print: he added, however, 'very coldly', that he was but little acquainted with Public Schools, but had heard similar reports. He might well have done so, for, as Dr Vincent noted,[1] the same outcry was to be found in several of the religious and moral writers of the day, including the poet Cowper, and Dr Randolph of Bath,[2] and the Rev. Thomas Gisborne (who blamed the parents),[3] and the indefatigable Mrs Trimmer. On the other hand, considering that Dr Gaskin had seen Dr Vincent's letter to Mr Jones and had himself actually written the reply at the Old Boy's dictation, it was natural for the Head Master of Westminster to feel that he had a grievance. One remedy alone remained to him: publication.

Dr Vincent's *Defence of Public Education* is one of the most spirited pamphlets of its age. It begins by pointing out that the Bishop's sweeping allegations as to the systematic neglect of religious instruction in the public schools rested upon no more substantial basis than the rhetoric of Dr Rennell, which, without any knowledge of his own, without enquiry or examination, his Lordship had accepted as incontrovertible. Yet the charge was of a very serious character, and might well be as abundant in mischief as it was deficient in proof: 'the fact is, if the world credits your assertions, in a very few years no man will be enabled to live by the emoluments of a Public School.'[4] Moreover the terms of the indictment had not been modified by repetition: where Dr Rennell had spoken of the 'notorious defectiveness of Christian education in many of our Public

[1] *Ibid.* p. 32.
[2] *Sermons, preached at Laura-Chapel, Bath, during the season of Advent 1799.* By the Rev. Francis Randolph, D.D., Prebendary of Bristol, and Chaplain to H.R.H. the Duke of York (1800), pp. 12, 193–4. *Vide* Appendix A.
[3] 'The principal fault, when faults exist, is not in the preceptor, but in the parent. The former is to water the plant; the latter must sow the seed.' *A Familiar Survey of the Christian Religion....* By Thomas Gisborne, A.M. (2nd ed. 1799), p. iv. *Vide* Appendix B.
[4] Vincent, p. 5.

Schools', the Bishop of Meath, omitting the word '*many*', spoke of the 'sad degeneracy of our Public Schools', and of their 'systematic neglect' of religious instruction.[1] But what did they intend to comprise under the expression of Public Schools?

Are we to understand only Winchester, Eton, and Westminster? or, are we to extend our notion, as we ought to do, to the three other great schools in the Metropolis; to Harrow, Rugby, Manchester, Wakefield, and many more of equal magnitude in the North?[2] If all these are to plead guilty to the charge, the rising generation is ripe for the machinations of a Voltaire, a Diderot, a d'Alembert, a Condorcet, or a Lepaux; and we may expect a revolution in Church and State, as soon as ever a prime agitator shall start up in this country to set the conspiracy in motion. I do not think, my Lord, that either you or Dr Rennell, carry your impeachment to this extent. If you do, I must maintain that your enquiries and your information will not bear you out in the event; for even in the three schools, which I suppose your accusations in reality to comprehend, your investigation is miserably deficient.[3]

On the subject of religious instruction at Westminster, Dr Vincent, having taught there for the past forty years, from the day that he 'sat as Usher at the first form',[4] could speak with an authority in no way shared by his antagonists. He was also in a position to supply a reassuring, though imperfect, outline of what was done at Winchester.[5] As to conditions at Eton, he confined himself to pointing out that Dr Rennell was himself an Old Etonian, and that his only son was at that very moment a pupil on the same foundation: 'And why is the family of the Rennells alone to escape the contagion of these Pagan principles, while thousands bred in the same celebrated Seminary are all tainted with the infection?'[6]

[1] Vincent, p. 12.
[2] Cf. Edward C. Mack, *Public Schools and British Opinion: 1780 to 1860* (1938), p. xiii *n*. ('Englishmen have never been very consistent at any period in their use of the word Public School...').
[3] Vincent, pp. 12–13.
[4] *Ibid.* p. 36. Dr Vincent, himself an Old Westminster scholar (1748–57), returned as an Usher in 1762, became Under-Master in 1771, and Head Master in 1788. (He was elected to a minor fellowship at Trinity College, Cambridge, in 1763, and to a major fellowship in the following year.)
[5] 'Winchester I know enough of, generally, to believe that the accusation is groundless.' *Ibid.* pp. 14, 48. *Vide* also Appendix C.
[6] *Ibid.* pp. 14, 29–30.

Having completed these preliminary observations, Dr Vincent then proceeded to analyse the charge against the public schools, recurring for this purpose to Dr Rennell's discourse, 'because your Lordship has not descended to particulars'. The charge amounted, in effect, to three specific allegations:

I. That a preference is due to the religious education in Charity Schools, compared with instruction in Public Seminaries.

II. That the Paganism taught in Public Schools, is noxious to the cause of Christianity; and,

III. That Public Schools are guilty of a systematic neglect of all religious instruction.[1]

Upon the first head, he retorted that Dr Rennell had entirely failed to prove his case. As for the Universities, since these were apparently included, their Presses had published greater treasures of Theology in the past thirty years than in any period of equal length since the Reformation, while the lectures given in Divinity were so far compulsory that no Bishop would ordain a candidate without a certificate of attendance from the Professor. But he might leave the Universities to supply their own defenders.[2] What, then, of the Public Schools? Wherein consisted this lamentable and notorious *defectiveness* of religious education, which could be counterbalanced only by preserving the light of the Gospel among the lower orders of society? The teaching in the public schools was almost exclusively in the hands of men who belonged to the same profession as their accuser ('And does Dr Rennell deny faith and ability to every Churchman but himself?'), and who, unlike the instructors of the poor, had received, and in their turn transmitted to their pupils, what foreigners themselves allowed to be the most liberal education known in Europe.[3] The masters in the Charity Schools, bred to the instruction of youth by an apprenticeship, were indeed estimable men: Dr Vincent's own parish clerk, for instance, who presided in the parish school with which both he and Dr Rennell were connected, as Rectors of adjoining parishes,[4] was

---

[1] *Ibid.* pp. 14–15.   [2] *Ibid.* p. 16.
[3] *Ibid.* p. 17.
[4] Dr Vincent was Rector of All Hallows the Great and Less, Thames Street: Dr Rennell was Rector of St Magnus the Martyr, London Bridge.

a sober, discreet, and laborious teacher: but, useful as they were in their own rank, why should they be supposed to be more willing to execute their trust than those whom the public voice, and the discernment of their nominators or electors, had appointed to the management of the first seminaries in the kingdom? And why should the public school masters be degraded by a comparison with teachers who had never had similar means of acquiring knowledge, or equal advantages in life, manners, and education?

But this is not sufficient; the inferior is to be raised above the superior; the children of the poor are to be told, that they have better instruction than those above them; and the teachers of the poor are taught to believe, that their's is the pre-eminence; that they are to atone for the neglect, and compensate for the deficiency of all that are engaged in the education of the higher orders. If the children who heard this discourse understood it, I should imagine, that their respect for the rank above them must be greatly diminished, and their resistance to subordination greatly increased; and if they were capable of drawing a conclusion, the natural consequence ought to be, that, as they are wiser and better than their superiors, they ought to govern, and their superiors obey.[1]

Incidentally, Dr Rennell's rhetorical enthusiasm for Charity Schools might give a somewhat misleading impression of his active interest in their work. He and Dr Vincent happened to be Rectors of contiguous parishes, connected with the same Charity School. In the course of the past twenty years, Dr Vincent had preached in favour of the institution almost annually, while Dr Rennell had afforded his assistance only once. Dr Vincent had taken an active part in the management: Dr Rennell had never attended a single meeting. Dr Vincent had given the master his constant encouragement and support: Dr Rennell hardly knew his name or his person. Dr Vincent habitually catechised the children: Dr Rennell never asked them a question. Dr Vincent had expounded the catechism, either privately or publicly, almost every year: Dr Rennell had never condescended to so humble an office. 'We will leave it to the judgment of the

---

[1] Vincent, p. 18.

Public, which of the two was the greater advocate for the general system? and which of the two was the more zealous supporter of the school under their common protection?'[1]

It is not meant to detract from the services of Dr Rennell at St Paul's: they were important and meritorious; but he ought not to arrogate all merit to himself: he ought not to assume a right of censuring every other species of education, but the one he was to recommend: he ought not to have flattered the poor at the expence of the rich: he ought not to have elated the poor above their condition, by enhancing the value of their acquirements, and depreciating those of every other order in society: he ought not to have told the instructors of these children, that they were more able, or at least more willing, to do their duty than his brethren of the Clergy, who were engaged in the higher departments, and the more arduous office of educating the children of the wealthy and the noble. Our service is sufficiently painful in itself: why is our estimation to be lessened in the eyes of the people, by the intemperance of a man who thinks he has no equal among his equals? If we do not fulfil our duty, we are amenable: but not before the tribunal of Dr Rennell. He is not yet my Diocesan or my Principal, and I am thankful that he is neither.[2]

The second allegation was that the Public Schools inculcated Paganism instead of Christianity. In bringing it forward, Dr Rennell had exhibited a certain disingenuousness: for he must know perfectly well that the reading of Pagan Authors is not the same thing as a Pagan Education. 'For who is a disciple of Fo, because he learns Chinese? or a Bhuddist, because he reads Sanskreet? If the wild mythology of Hindostan is thought an object worthy of the labours of a Sir W. Jones, a Wilkins, or a Maurice, to explore; if some men of the most consummate learning have dedicated their lives to investigate the extravagancies of the Egyptian, Persian, Peruvian, or Druidical system; does it follow that they are tainted with the respective superstitions?—but it will be said these are men, and we teach children; be it so. Yet I assert, that I never yet found a child of ten years old, who believed in the transformation of Jupiter into a bull, or a swan, or a shower of gold; nor a child, in the nursery, convinced that crows sung, or trees talked, or asses played on the

---

[1] *Ibid.* pp. 19–20.   [2] *Ibid.* p. 20.

fiddle.... I do aver once more, that I never found a child in the lower forms ideot enough to want guarding against the seduction of his mind by the Gods or Metamorphoses of Ovid.... Are all who read the Koran disposed to become Mahometans? All who read Iamblichus, Mysticks? or all who read Manetho, Astrologers? These, indeed, are depths of corruption which we do not fathom; but we assert, that our pupils are no more liable to delusion from the miracles of Livy, or the oracles of Herodotus, than men are from these seductions of deeper research....'[1] Nor should the fact be overlooked that 'the luminaries of the Church in all ages, from Bede to Roger Bacon, from Bacon to the Reformation, and from the Reformation to the present hour, were all formed upon classical instruction'. 'Chrysostom, Gregory Nazianzen, and Jerom' were all versed in the elegancies of classical literature: Tillotson, Pearson, Butler, Sherlock, not to mention Dr Rennell himself, 'were all trained under this execrable Pagan institution, which is continued in our schools, both public and private, to the present hour'.[2] Moreover, the authors read at Westminster were not selected by the Head Master, but prescribed by the statutes. 'I am not authorised, if I were willing, to substitute Prudentius for Virgil, or Gregory Nazianzen for Homer:—but I have not the will more than the power; for our authors are not intended to teach Paganism, but to set before our youth the best models of writing that the world affords.'[3] At the same time, no master worth his place would fail to compare the teaching of the Classical philosophers with the fullness of the Christian Revelation, or to impress upon his pupils how far their doctrines approach the truth, and how infinitely they fall short of the Word of God. 'Upon such opportunities as authors or sentiments like these afford, I remember to this hour, the tone, the manner, the elevated warmth of my own preceptor, the venerable Metropolitan of York;[4] and I feel at this moment, that I owe the firmest principles of my mind, and my first reverence of the Scriptures, to his instruction.'[5]

[1] Vincent, pp. 22–3, 26, 28.   [2] *Ibid.* pp. 27–8.
[3] *Ibid.* p. 24.
[4] William Markham, Head Master of Westminster, 1753–64; Archbishop of York, 1777–1807.   [5] Vincent, p. 25.

Thus far, Dr Vincent had acquitted himself valiantly, and had drawn a good deal of blood from his antagonists, even if it might be retorted that he had either failed to see, or failed to face, the real points at issue. But it is the concluding section of his vindication that is the most impressive and the most effective. The third article of the indictment was that the Public Schools were guilty of a systematic neglect of all religious instruction, and Dr Vincent met it simply by describing what was done at Westminster. The statutes required prayers (including the graces) to be said ten times a day: this had indeed been slightly modified, inasmuch as the Latin prayers at six o'clock in the morning had been discontinued:[1] but the English prayers at noon and at five, with the Latin prayers at eight in the evening, were performed regularly[2] (apart from holidays and half-holidays), and 'with as much external decency as can be exacted, allowing for the natural impatience of boys under restraint, and the levity of youth'.

If it shall be asked, what effect this service has upon the morals of our youth? for the present I shall answer, that the habit of prayer is a good habit. I am now only contending against the resolute and contemptuous neglect of our duty with which we are charged; and I maintain, that whatever the effect may be, here is a *resolute* and *persevering* attendance on the offices prescribed.[3]

A Confirmation was held every alternate year, the boys being prepared for it by 'a catechetical lecture, continued for four, five, or six days'.[4] The Supper of the Lord was celebrated, as prescribed by statute, four times a year, and was preceded by a whole week of painful and energetic preparation, including the daily use of specially selected prayers, 'and upon one day in

---

[1] 'The omission of early prayers in this, and other foundations, has arisen from the manners of the age; those who are not in bed early, cannot rise early. Our ancestors retired with the curfew; and yet Matthew Paris complains, that, in performing the *Ante-lucan* service, the Monks of his Abbey (St Alban's) were asleep, and the reader was unintelligible from dispatch.'—*Ibid.* p. 33 *n.*

[2] '...from five to nine times every day, when we attend school twice, with a remission on one day only in the week; for this neglect, which is confessed, I must expect your Lordship's reprehension; but the world, in general, will perhaps think that the office is still too frequent.'—*Ibid.* p. 34.

[3] *Ibid.* pp. 34–5.　　　　　　　　[4] *Ibid.* p. 38.

that week, a lecture, or rather affectionate address' from the Head Master: an office which had been proved to be acceptable, salutary, and efficacious, and for which he had received the thanks of several, after they had been many years removed from his tuition.[1]

The next object of our statutes is to put the Scriptures into the hands of our scholars, from the day on which they enter the School, to the day they leave it: they commence with translating the Psalms [into Latin] almost daily; they proceed to the Gospels; then to a collection of Sacred Exercises, appropriate to the School;[2] and finally, to produce a composition in verse, from the Psalms, every Monday. This is the business of the lower School [i.e. of boys from 8 to 12 years of age]. In the higher classes, the Sacred Exercise is still used for compositions in verse, the Greek Testament, Grotius [*De Veritate Christianæ Religionis*], and the Hebrew Psalms; and throughout the year, on Saturday, a History, or other portion out of the Scriptures, is appointed for a Bible exercise in verse: added to this, the Catechism, or Bishop Williams's exposition,[3] is as regularly repeated on Monday morning, in the lower forms, as in a Parish School; attended with such an oral explanation as might instruct the Parish Teacher, as well as those he teaches.[4]

Thus the first part of Christian education—'to make young people acquainted with the Scriptures'—was provided for by the statutes, and the second part—'to explain the doctrines, and apply the precepts'—by the practice and attention of the instructors.[5] The Catechism was not only taught by rote, but

[1] Vincent, pp. 39–40.
[2] These Sacred Exercises 'were collected and drawn up by the late Mr Wilcox, son of the Bishop of Rochester, a most pious and devout Christian, and one of the most elegant scholars of his time. They consist of Lessons with appropriate Collects, and comprehend many of the moral and poetical passages from the Prophets, Ecclesiastes, and the Book of Wisdom.'—*Ibid. Postscript*, p. 44.
[3] *A brief Exposition of the Church-Catechism, with Proofs from Scriptures* (1689). By John Williams (afterwards Bishop of Chichester). Dedication ' *To his honoured Friend, the Reverend Dr Busby.*—After so pious a Design as you have laid, in Founding and Endowing a Catechetical Lecture in *Westminster-Abbey*, for the Instruction of the Youth under your Care, and my Three Years Employment therein; It may seem to be a mean account of it, to publish such an Exposition of our *Church-Catechism* as this is...'.— Busby was Head Master of Westminster, 1638–95.
[4] Vincent, p. 35. *Vide* also Appendix C.
[5] *Ibid.* p. 40.

carefully expounded; the application of every passage in Holy Scripture, 'the moral and religious tendency of the subject, as well as its arrangement for poetical composition', laboriously explained: while in the highest class the Grotius lesson (Christian apologetics) on Monday mornings employed more time, and was enforced with more earnestness, than any other lesson in the week.[1] Furthermore, 'in Passion Week, it is the custom of the School to take our lesson, for the highest class, from some peculiar subject of the New Testament: sometimes, it is the History of Paul, from the Acts; sometimes, the Abrogation of the Ceremonial Law, from the Epistle to the Galatians; at other times, the Sacrifice and Atonement, with the doctrine of Faith and Works, from the Epistle to the Romans; and our last subject was, the Sermon on the Mount'.[2]

But here, my Lord, I expect to be told that all this may be done without effect; that the mere performance of this task is nothing, without the will, the mind, the example, the fervency, the zeal of the instructor. On this head I have nothing to offer for myself; but on this head I must observe, that neither Dr Rennell or your Lordship are authorised to be my judges. To my own master I am to stand or fall, and whether my foundation is gold, wood, or stubble, must be determined before that tribunal, where I must plead no merit of my own, but appear with conscious trembling, for my imperfections, negligences, and omissions, and feel that there is but one hope of pardon for me and for you.

Or it will be said, that all this is without effect, because vice still exists. Doubtless it does, in schools as well as nations. Education can no more extinguish vice than law; but every good government, and every good institution of learning aim at the correction of the governed. And if you ask whether we perceive the immediate effect of our endeavours, I must answer with hesitation. For we cast our bread upon the waters, but we do not expect to find it till after many days. We experience no instantaneous conviction or conversion, nor do we hope it; and if we asserted it, it might justly be replied, that it is easy to make boys as well as men hypocrites, but very difficult to make them religious. As far as my own observation serves, it is the seed sown which is to ripen for the harvest, when the age of reflection shall arrive. Men, even young men, feel the want and consolation of religion; and it is when those thoughts present themselves, that

[1] *Ibid.* p. 37.   [2] *Ibid.* p. 38.

memory will suggest the precepts and principles proposed to them in their youth. It is to that period we look forward for success; for though the majority among us is always on the side of virtue, I dare not say that the principles of religion are as evident now as we hope them to be hereafter.[1]

Dr Vincent modestly concluded by asking the Bishop for a public withdrawal of the charge of systematic neglect of religious instruction in the English public schools.[2]

It does not appear that Dr O'Beirne gave him the satisfaction that he demanded. But the effect of the *Defence* was irresistible: it ran through three editions in a surprisingly short time, and, unlike its author's more learned publications, actually returned a profit, which he good-humouredly presented to Mrs Vincent as the first fruits of his authorship. Furthermore, he had the gratification afterwards of knowing that the King himself had been particularly pleased to have his public schools defended, and still more pleased with the spirit and effect of the defence. Another of his admirers was Mr Addington, the Prime Minister, himself a Wykehamist, who had the happiness of recommending Dr Vincent to his Majesty, to succeed Bishop Horsley (lately translated to St Asaph) in the Deanery of Westminster, as 'a public reward for public services'. The King did not fail to declare his satisfaction in giving the appointment, which was indeed as unsolicited as it was unexpected; and, at a subsequent opportunity, was pleased even to express regret that the See of Rochester had not, as in many former instances, gone with the Deanery.[3] Some such thought seems also to have crossed the mind of the Rev. Prebendary Beloe, whose *Recollections* exude that quiet worldliness which is traditionally, if not altogether justly, regarded as the characteristic spirit of the Hanoverian Establishment. To him it seemed extremely odd that a man of Dr Vincent's scholarship should never have been made a bishop.

Various are the branches of science which his pen illustrated and adorned; indeed all his publications may be considered as truly

[1] Vincent, pp. 40–2.   [2] *Ibid.* p. 42.
[3] *Life of Dr Vincent*, by the Rev. Robert Nares, Archdeacon of Stafford, prefixed to Vincent's *Sermons on Faith, Doctrines, and Public Duties* (1817), vol. i, pp. xlvii–xlviii.

valuable, and highly important. The intricacies of the Greek verb, peculiarities relating to the military tactics of the ancients, many arduous and obscure points, both in ancient and modern geography, a most powerful and effective vindication of the system of national education, with various other contingent appendages to learning, have been elucidated by his learning, and embellished by his taste.

The question may naturally be asked why, with such an accumulation of claims, did he not ascend to the highest gradation of his profession? The interrogatory is more easily proposed than answered. Perhaps it is true, that with all his great attainments, and love of literature, the Prime Minister of that day was so occupied with political perplexities and difficulties, that he considered the pursuits of the Muses, as trifling and subordinate, and conferred distinction and reward on those only and their connections, and adherents, who were most useful and necessary to him in the prosecution of his views.

However, the honours which were bestowed, were communicated in the handsomest manner possible, and if inadequate to the merits of the receiver, there is great reason to suppose that they satisfied his utmost ambition.[1]

That, indeed, is true. Delighted and surprised at his translation from 'the tedium of treading the same dull round daily through a life of perpetual labour, confinement, and anxiety';[2] delighted also to be rewarded in the very place where he had so long laboured to deserve reward; the new Dean of Westminster often frankly declared, and even, in the warmth of his gratitude, told Mr Addington himself, that, if all the preferments in the gift of the Crown could have been laid before him, the Deanery of Westminster was that which he would have chosen.[3] Characteristically also, the first use he made of his advancement was

to obtain the presentation of a living, for a curate who had been his assistant at All-Hallows twenty-four years. His own eldest son was then in orders, and totally unbeneficed; but he paid, what he considered as a debt of gratitude, before he would consent to think of his own more immediate concerns. For this forbearance he was soon rewarded; and in the second year after his promotion, the Rectory of St John's, Westminster, came to his choice; and when he accepted it

[1] *The Sexagenarian; or, the Recollections of a Literary Life.* [By William Beloe] (1817), vol. ii, pp. 93-4.
[2] Vincent, p. 11.
[3] Nares, *Life of Dr Vincent, loc. cit.* p. xlviii.

for himself, he had the satisfaction of obtaining the living of All-Hallows for his son. He might have continued to hold it, but he preferred resigning it in that manner. He held St John's only about two years, when he exchanged it for the Rectory of Islip, Oxfordshire, which is also in the patronage of the Church at Westminster. He was presented to it by the Chapter in 1805.

The acquisition of this living formed another fortunate epoch in his life. He had always been accustomed to pass his summer holidays in the country; a change quite necessary for his health, while confined to the school; and desirable, when he had no longer that tie. But his only resource on these occasions had hitherto been in temporary lodgings. He had now a country residence of his own, to which, when he had once made it suitable to his convenience, he could at any time retire. This advantage he felt, at least to the utmost of its value. Islip is not a place which an admirer of rural beauty would make his choice, nor has the neighbouring scenery any peculiar charms. The Dean, however, was not only contented, but delighted, with it. He attached himself to the parish, attended to its business, and still more to its wants; entered into its antiquities, and collected documents respecting its former rectors, particularly the famous Dr South, who built the house; and since whose time it had never been regularly inhabited. The vicinity of Islip to Oxford was a circumstance peculiarly grateful to him, by giving him access both to the dead and living learning of that university. Oxford, on her part, was happy to enrol so illustrious a neighbour among her adopted sons; in consequence of which he was appointed to preach the annual sermon for the benefit of the Radcliffe Infirmary, in July 1808.

The Rectory House at Islip, though a well-built stone mansion, was not, when he came to it, exactly suited to modern notions of convenience; and his first task was to make it so. It was not his habit to do any thing in a narrow or illiberal way: and being aided by a handsome sum which was due for dilapidations, he expended more than twice as much, to make the house commodious for himself and future Rectors. When so altered, he enjoyed it with the utmost satisfaction; and never thought of passing the period, in which the country is desirable for its own sake, any where but among his parishioners at Islip.[1]

With that last touch, the picture is complete. 'He had an income equal to all his wants; and sufficient, with such continuance of life as might very reasonably be hoped, to secure a

---

[1] Nares, *loc. cit.* pp. l–lii.

decent provision for his family; and more he did not anxiously desire.[1] Taken by and large, it was not a bad reward for a pamphlet of slightly less than fifty pages in defence of the English public schools.

It was, however, still possible to argue that the defence was incomplete, and therefore inconclusive: for even if Westminster were thus exemplary in the religious education which was afforded there, this in itself proved nothing with regard to the other public schools.[2] True, the strictures of the Bishop of Meath might be discounted, since, as Dr Vincent had gently indicated, he spoke without any knowledge of his own:[3] the son of a Roman Catholic farmer in County Longford, Dr O'Beirne had received most of his education in the diocesan school of Ardagh, and the rest of it in the seminary at St Omer before his abandonment of the religion of his fathers. Nor could the name of Mrs Trimmer carry much weight in this particular field of controversy. Cowper was an Old Westminster, but of an earlier generation (1742–9). Gisborne was an Old Harrovian (1773–6): he had, however, 'excepted the place of his own education from the deficiency which he temperately remarked in others'.[4] But Dr Randolph was an Old Etonian (1764–72), as was also Dr Rennell (1767–72), who had a son there at this very time (1799–1806): and the accusing finger, so far as it pointed anywhere in particular, appeared to point more definitely in that direction than in any other.

So we are brought back to our original enquiry: What was the state of religion at Eton during Charles Simeon's school days?

Unfortunately the material for an answer to this question is more scanty than it would be if we were dealing with a slightly later period. We know a good deal about the religious condition of Eton under Dr Keate (Head Master, 1802–34), but comparatively little about its religious condition under Simeon's Head Masters, the unlucky Dr Foster (1765–73), son of a

[1] *Ibid.* p. lii.
[2] 'His defence... is confined to one School only, if allowed to be complete, even as to that.'—*Remarks on the Rev. Dr Vincent's Defence of Public Education...*, by a Layman (1802), p. 25.
[3] Vincent, p. 3.
[4] *Monthly Review*, Jan. 1818, vol. lxxxv, p. 38.

Windsor tradesman, under whom numbers fell rapidly, after the great Rebellion of 1768, from 522 to 230, and Dr Jonathan Davies, 'a learned, pleasant, generous, open-hearted man, but in conversation too much of a Stentor', who succeeded him on his resignation in 1773, and ruled the School for eighteen years with moderate success.[1] We are, however, fortunate in possessing a MS. Account of the Eton Discipline and Education[2] drawn up in 1766—the year before Simeon entered Eton—by Thomas James, and annotated by him in the course of the next five years. James must have been still a boy at Eton when he wrote it, since he was not admitted to King's College, Cambridge, until Feb. 21, 1767. He was subsequently to acquire a great reputation as Head Master of Rugby. Mr Austen Leigh conjectures that the Account was written for the guidance of a preparatory school. Here we are concerned only with that part of it which relates to religious observance and instruction.

The Eton time-table was immensely complicated by the ecclesiastical calendar, inasmuch as each red-letter festival had to be observed as a holiday, and its vigil as a half-holiday. On ordinary whole school-days, the Latin prayers (Preces *horâ sextâ* Matutinâ, et *undecimâ*, et *horâ quintâ* Vespertinâ) from the school prayer book—*Preces quotidianæ in usum Scholæ Collegii Regalis apud Etonam*—were read in school by the Fifth Form Praepostor a little before 7 a.m., at noon, and at 6 p.m. respectively. On a 'play-at-four' other than a Saturday, the evening prayers were read at the end of 3.0 o'clock school. The Collegers had prayers in the Lower School at 8 p.m. (Preces in Longo Cubiculo—formerly read in the Long Chamber—*horâ octavâ* Vespertinâ), also read by the Fifth Form Praepostor: after a collect, the Lord's Prayer, versicles and responses, and the Apostles' Creed, the boys sang the Compline hymn,

> *Salvator mundi, Domine,*
> *Qui nos servasti hodie,*

[1] Maxwell Lyte, pp. 342–3, 351.
[2] Printed in extenso in *Etoniana*, Nos. 7, 8 (July 3, Nov. 30, 1906), pp. 97–108, 113–19, ed. R. A. Austen Leigh: summary in Maxwell Lyte, ch. xvi. Cf. Malim's *Consuetudinarium* (*c.* 1560), *Etoniana*, No. 5 (Dec. 6, 1905), pp. 65–71; Maxwell Lyte, ch. viii; A. K. Cook, *About Winchester College* (1917), App. VII.

followed by versicles and responses, collects, and the Prayer of St Chrysostom. All the prayers were in Latin. On whole holidays, the boys attended Church at 11.0 and at 3.0, and on half-holidays at 3.0. Court days (or anniversaries of the births, marriages, etc., of the principal members of the Royal Family) and Founder's days were observed as whole holidays.

On Sundays, the boys boarding in the town were not allowed out of their houses until the time of the morning service in Church, which was at 10 a.m.: but the Collegers had to go into the Upper School, when they sang the 100th Psalm, after which the Fifth Form Praepostor repeated the Morning Prayers, and the Sixth Form Praepostor took a roll call. The Master did not come in until all this was over. Then the entire school went to Church. After Church, the Oppidans went back to their houses and the Collegers to their Chamber or study. The Collegers dined in Hall at noon, dinner being preceded and concluded by the reading of the Latin grace from the school prayer book by one of the boys. From Hall the Collegers retired to their Chamber where they were 'supposed to be reading something sacred or instructive'. The entire school reassembled in the Upper School at 2 o'clock, their names being marked by the Praepostors, and one of the Fifth Form boys was told off to read four or five pages from *The Whole Duty of Man*. The boys then went back to their houses or Chambers, from which they emerged only for Church at 3.0, and in summer (but not in winter) for Absence at 6.0. The Collegers had supper at 5.0, and sat in Hall from 7.0 to 8.0 under the eye of the Captain of the School, who noted any absentees and reported them to the Master. During this time they were supposed to read. At 8.0 they went into the Lower School, where the Sixth Form Praepostor took another roll call, and the Fifth Form Praepostor read the Evening Prayers. These being ended, they were locked up in their Chambers for the night.

From this outline, the sacred character of the day would appear to have been marked chiefly by the recurrence of roll calls and the denial of any opportunity for reasonable recreation, although it does not seem to have struck the writer in that light.

The religious instruction, as distinct from the religious observance, appears to have been conceived upon a far less generous scale. On Mondays at 8 a.m. boys in the Fifth and Sixth Forms, which together constituted the Head Master's division, went into school, and were expected 'to Repeat about 20 verses in the Greek Testament; one boy saying 6 or 7 verses & then another repeating as many, but this is as the Master pleases', these verses having been set the previous Saturday at 2 o'clock school. The Fourth Form were required to parse and construe twelve verses of the Greek Testament at 8.0, and to repeat them at 11.0. In the Lower School, the Latin Testament was substituted for the Greek, the boys being required to learn a page by heart—the Second Form were let off with eight verses—and to be able to construe and parse it. But the First Form, who learned nothing but the Latin Grammar, appear to have been disqualified by their linguistic ignorance from any contact whatsoever with Holy Writ. These Scripture periods were in any case confined to Monday mornings, the remainder of the week being devoted to the study of the Classics: except that the Lower School boys had to say the Catechism on Saturdays at 2.0. No further religious instruction of any kind appears to have been given: although it may be noted that in the Easter holidays, which lasted a fortnight, and began on the Monday in Holy Week, the holiday task consisted of 'some short chapter of Jeremiah,...to be turned into Long Verses or Long & Short verses or Asclæpiads, or Alcaics, or Iambics, or whatever Metre the boys chuse. Many of which Tasks beg Half Holydays, if the boys take pains with them.' In the other holidays—a month at Christmas, and a month in August—the tasks allotted were purely secular in character and utilitarian in purpose.

It is sufficiently apparent that, apart from the retention of the early morning prayers (if this were an advantage), the system of religious observance and instruction at Eton under Dr Foster compared unfavourably with that at Westminster under Dr Vincent.

The author of *Remarks on the Rev. Dr Vincent's Defence of*

RELIGION IN THE SCHOOL

Public Education (1802) quotes a communication from an Old Etonian which, in its main particulars, bears out this general impression.

At Eton the oppidans lived mostly in dames' houses, or with their tutors; a few lodged in the town. At my dame's there never were any prayers, or any graces: I believe other dames' houses were exactly the same in this respect.

We went into chapel on an average six times a week, viz. twice on Sunday, twice on the whole holiday, and once on each of the half holidays; and the conduct of the boys there, was certainly disorderly. I understand Dr Goodall has introduced decency into Chapel. There were no prayers at any time in the upper School, except that on Sundays the fifth or sixth forms went to hear the theme set, when something was read, but not heard.

Religious instruction, in the upper School, we never had any. On a Monday morning the fifth and sixth forms had to say by heart fifteen verses of the Greek Testament. The fourth form used once a week to say twelve verses, which they had previously construed and parsed. I do not recollect ever to have heard the spirit of any passage explained, or inculcated. There was another form called the Remove, but in this I think there was no appearance of Religious instruction.[1]

Reform was slow in coming. Perhaps it may be considered an improvement that in the days of Dr Keate (1809–34) the Sunday afternoon period was devoted to an exercise known to the School as 'Prose' but which Keate himself insisted on calling 'prayers', and that, instead of one of the Fifth Form boys reading aloud to the whole School four or five pages of *The Whole Duty of Man*, the Head Master himself read 'a short discourse on abstract morality taken from Blair's *Sermons*, from the *Spectator*, or from the works of some pagan writer like Epictetus, and then gave out to the Fifth and Sixth Forms the subject for their Latin theme for the ensuing week':[2] but the proceedings were even less edifying than this account suggests, for although Tucker (who was at Eton from 1811 to 1822) pays tribute to 'five minutes of very splendid reading by Keate in "Prose" from Blair's sermons',[3] there is evidence at a later date to show that

---

[1] *Op. cit.* (by 'A Layman'), pp. 38–9.   [2] Maxwell Lyte, p. 389.
[3] *Eton of Old, or Eighty Years Since (1811–1822)*, by an Old Colleger [William Hill Tucker].

77

Prose was one of the two occasions—the other being evening school on the day of the Windsor Fair—on which not even Keate himself was able to control the situation. The most vivid description is to be found in the reminiscences of 'Hang Theology' Rogers—the Rev. William Rogers, Rector of St Botolph's, Bishopsgate—who entered the school in 1830.

At two o'clock, immediately after dinner, Keate came into the Upper School with a book, generally 'Blair's Sermons', under his arm. By the time he had read aloud two or three sentences his voice was always lost in the uproar. He would then violently stamp his foot, dash his cocked hat on the desk, and call out, 'I will declare it immediately'. What exactly he was to declare nobody could ever make out, but the confusion was quelled by the announcement of themes, or that the members for Windsor had asked for a holiday, or some other school arrangement.[1]

Even some of the boys themselves were not unconscious of the inadequacy of the religious instruction. An Old Etonian, writing in 1821, could not 'refrain from mentioning the great satisfaction with which all the old Etonians at Oxford have viewed the slight alteration that took place last Christmas in the Eton system in favour of Sacred Knowledge. It had always been a subject of regret, that, although a good foundation had been laid in the lower parts of the school by the reading of "Watts's Scripture History", and the "Harmony of the Gospels", no superstructure was afterwards raised. On the contrary, this branch of study was utterly neglected; for the "Burnet" in Lent[2] was a mere drop of fresh water in the ocean.'[3] This seems to indicate some measure of improvement since 1766, apart from and anterior to 'the slight alteration', whatever this latter may have been; possibly the introduction into the Fifth and Sixth Form syllabus of some standard work on Christian Evidences, for when an Edinburgh Reviewer in 1830, in an attack on Eton,

---

[1] *Reminiscences of William Rogers* (1888), p. 12. Cf. Maxwell Lyte, p. 389.
[2] 'During Lent an additional public schooltime is set apart for reading Burnet De Fide et Officiis' (*The Eton System of Education vindicated: and its capabilities of improvement considered, in reply to some recent publications,* 1834, p. 22).—But cf. Tucker, *Eton of Old*, p. 129.
[3] *Letters from Oxford*, No. 111 [by Henry Neech], in *The Etonian* (4th ed. 1824), vol. iii, p. 135.

ashly declared that the religious instruction there was 'confined
to reading once in the week a portion of the Greek Testament,
and a chapter of Bishop Tomline's book on the Thirty-nine
Articles...nor is there read any work on the Evidences of
Christianity',[1] 'Etonensis' was able to correct him: Tomline on
the Thirty-nine Articles was *not* read at Eton, being quite unsuitable, 'as something above the ordinary capacity of boys': but

the fifth or sixth form read the Greek Testament, and some English
work, explanatory of the doctrines and evidences of Christianity: at
present, they are reading Secker's Sermons on the Catechism; and
the book which they read before that, was Porteus's Evidences. The
remove boys read the Greek Testament. The fourth form, Watts's
Scripture History. The remaining forms, which contain but few, and,
for the most part, very young boys, the Westminster Catechism.
Besides this, every Tutor gives his *private* pupils, at *all* events, if not
all his pupils, instruction in divinity.[2]

Whatever this last was worth, it certainly marked an improvement on the system under which J. B. Sumner (afterwards
Archbishop of Canterbury), as an Assistant Master (1802–17),
found himself practically debarred from saying a single word
about God or Christianity to his pupils.[3] In other directions
also there was a notable advance: Edward Coleridge, despite the
conservative disapproval of his father-in-law, Dr Keate, introduced family prayers into his boarding house,[4] and his example
was gradually followed: while, in College, prayers in English
were substituted for prayers in Latin.[5] In his *Self-Formation; or,
the History of an Individual Mind* (1837)[6] Capel Lofft averred
that when he was a boy at Eton (1814–25) 'we were thought
sufficiently trained, if we were trained to scholarship; or I should
say, not to it, but in the way of it; as to religion we were left to
get it as we could...': and this is corroborated by Mr Gladstone

[1] Art. *Public Schools of England—Eton*, in the *Edinburgh Review*, April
1830, vol. li, p. 78.
[2] *Observations on an article in the last number of the Edinburgh Review...*,
by Etonensis (1830), p. 16.—'There is also a private lesson in the houses of
the Masters on every Sunday morning, in which the Gospel is read and
explained' (*The Eton System of Education vindicated*, 1834, p. 22).
[3] Maxwell Lyte, p. 388.   [4] *Ibid.* p. 388 *n.*
[5] *The Eton System of Education vindicated* (1834), p. 8.
[6] *Op. cit.* ('by a Fellow of a College', i.e. Capel Lofft), vol. ii, pp. 54–5.

(1821–27): 'the actual teaching of Christianity was all but dead, though happily none of its forms had been surrendered.'[1] But, Capel Lofft continued, 'in this respect a great change has taken place at Eton within a few years. Recently it has become regenerate. A new life, a very soul, has been breathed into the system. Religion has been vindicated to its rights. It is at length a Christian school, and a school of Christianity.'

In all these records and reminiscences of Eton in the bad old days, mention of Confirmation and of Holy Communion is conspicuous by its absence. But in 1897 Mr Gladstone communicated to A. C. Benson his recollections of his confirmation in the eighteen-twenties. 'I told my father that I did not wish to be confirmed at Eton, but the fiat went out that I was to be included among the candidates. The order was given us all for a book of sermons—but we never got it, though our parents paid for it, and Pote [the school bookseller] had the money. We were never asked if we read it.—I went three times to Knapp, my tutor. He came out of his study—took up a volume of Sinclair's sermons—there was not an ounce of Christianity in them—read a couple of pages, shut up the book with a snap—said "you can go", and walked out. Three times this happened, and never another word of advice.

'The administration of the Sacrament was a scandal. The etiquette in the School was that no one should receive except the Sixth Form, and they were obliged to. I don't suppose there was ever an official pronouncement on this—but the authorities must have noticed it, and they never contradicted the idea.'[2]

It would, however, be a mistake to suppose that Eton was exceptionally bad in these respects. Harrow, for example, was a peculiar of the archdiocese of Canterbury, and Charles Wordsworth, son of the Master of Trinity, was confirmed there by Archbishop Manners Sutton in 1824. 'I cannot remember whether the Archbishop gave us an address; if he did I am

[1] *A Chapter of Autobiography, 1861*, in W. E. Gladstone, *Gleanings*, vol. vii, p. 138.
[2] A. C. Benson, *Fasti Etonenses* (1899), pp. 499–500.—Bishop Moberly recorded that his preparation for Confirmation at Winchester in 1821 (?) 'was nil' (C. A. E. Moberly, *Dulce Domum*, 1911, p. 22).

afraid it made no impression, and previously there had been little or no preparation of the candidates. All that my tutor did for me was to ask whether I could say the Catechism; to which I answered in the affirmative! In no case, so far as I can remember, was Confirmation followed up by the reception of Holy Communion; in short, as regards the school, it was, I fear, a thing unknown. This is melancholy. The present generation have great reason to be thankful that in this, as in other respects, things are very different now.'[1] At Winchester, on the other hand, the Prefects were apparently required to receive the Sacrament, whether they had been confirmed or not. Though contrary to modern usage, the practice of admitting to Communion those who were 'ready and desirous to be confirmed' was widely developed in the eighteenth century (when confirmations were still of necessity infrequent[2]), and it is covered by the rubric.[3] But the Master of Trinity did not like it, and wrote accordingly to his son Christopher, who had just been made a Prefect. '...On the subject of your last letter, it is very gratifying to me that you feel it so seriously. You are of age and of understanding to be confirmed, and when an opportunity offers, I should wish your mind to be turned seriously to that subject, and that you should appear before the Bishop with a good purpose, through God's help and power, to take upon yourself the vows and engagements, that you may not forfeit your claim and title to the blessings of a Christian. But, till you have been confirmed, it is more correct that you should not receive the sacrament, and I have written therefore to Dr Gabell [the Head Master], to beg him, if it be not wholly inconsistent with the rules of the school, that he will dispense with your attendance....'[4]

[1] *Annals of my Early Life: 1806–1846*, by Charles Wordsworth, Bishop of St Andrews (1891), p. 21.
[2] Cf. N. Sykes, *Church and State in England in the Eighteenth Century* (1934), pp. 115–146.
[3] At the end of the Order of Confirmation.—Thus, e.g., Daniel Wilson, afterwards Bishop of Calcutta, made his first communion on Oct. 1, 1797, but was not confirmed until June 7, 1799 (Josiah Bateman, *Life of Daniel Wilson*, 1860, vol. i, pp. 27, 55, 56). Cf. also G. W. E. Russell, *A Short History of the Evangelical Movement* (1915), p. 141.
[4] Letter dated Trinity College, Cambridge, Sept. 25, 1823: *Christopher Wordsworth, Bishop of Lincoln (1807–1885)*, by J. H. Overton and Elizabeth Wordsworth (1888), p. 23.

At Winchester, although it was part of the duty of the *Hostiarius*, or Second Master, to catechise every Sunday and to read a Monthly Sacramental Lecture, these duties had long since fallen into abeyance, although they continued to be paid for—£1. 6*s*. 8*d*. for catechising, and £10. 7*s*. 0*d*. (from Mr Taylor's benefaction) for the Sacramental Lecture—until 1873.[1] 'There never was a sermon till Mr Barter came [as Warden, in 1832]; he undertook to do it every Sunday.'[2] At Eton, on the other hand, sermons were preached on Sunday mornings by the Fellows: but these

were weary work. They were intolerably long, as was the custom of the age. They were mumbled and jumbled by aged men with weak, smothered voices; not one word of which could be heard except by those immediately under them, and that imperfectly, so that it is impossible to say whether or not they were suited to our capacity or welfare. The ladies, if any, absorbed the whole profit derivable from them, as all the wives and daughters of Fellows and Masters were lodged in a large pew which abutted on the Pulpit.[3]

'It may be said without disparagement to the system', writes Mr Tucker in conclusion of the whole matter of religious instruction and observance at Eton in the earlier decades of the nineteenth century, 'that unless there had been an innate religious feeling in the greater part of the boys, which there certainly was in those years, a rather plentiful crop of indifference would have gone forth into the world, if nothing worse.'[4]

But most children, if not all, have a religious instinct, more or less developed: and when it is strong, it is extremely difficult to destroy. Thus even in this desert of scholastic Anglicanism at its most arid there blossomed the youthful piety of Rowland Hill. We may add, in passing, that, of the two, the normal public schoolboy is less likely to be choked off Christianity by the arid than by the lush variety of public school religion; and

---

[1] *About Winchester College*, by A. K. Cook (1917), p. 254 *n*.
[2] Evidence of the Rev. G. Moberly, D.C.L., Head Master of Winchester, before the Royal Commission on Public Schools, May 30, 1862 (*Report*, 1864, vol. iii, p. 355). Cf. A. K. Cook, *op. cit.* p. 255.
[3] [W. H. Tucker], *Eton of Old*, pp. 121, 125.
[4] *Ibid.* p. 130.

his religious instincts are better calculated to persist against the background of such stiff and formal exercises of devotion as Simeon and his contemporaries endured at Eton—'Prayers read, scandalously quick and mechanical; choral on Saints' days'[1]— than if half-choked by the luxuriant undergrowth of those bastard extra-liturgical devotions in vogue during what may be called the Norwood-Dearmer phase of public school religion,[2] with their profound misunderstanding both of the piety of the Church of England and of the psychology of the normal boy. It is a matter of historic record that Charles Simeon was led to think seriously about religion by the school observance of a National Fast Day in 1776, when the tide of battle in the American Colonies was beginning to turn against the armies of the Mother Country. It is more than doubtful whether the same result could have been produced by any number of sermons about 'Service' or collects about 'gallant and high-hearted happiness' or litanies of thanksgiving for 'the ecstasy of swift motion' and similar delights.

Rowland Hill was a good deal senior to Charles Simeon, for he left Eton in 1764. But during his time there he became converted. The influence of his school had nothing to do with it: it happened in the holidays, in 1762, when his elder brother, Richard, who had in effect become a Methodist in 1757, read him a sermon of Bishop Beveridge, probably that on John i. 29: 'Behold the Lamb of God, which taketh away the sins of the world.'[3] On his return to school, he marked the change in his religious sentiments by writing to ask his brother to procure him a copy of the works of Archbishop Leighton: and, in the teeth of a good deal of ridicule and a little persecution, he began to make proselytes among his schoolfellows. He appears even to have formed what Sidney calls 'a religious society': it languished somewhat after he had gone up to Cambridge, but was revived again, and certain rules and directions were drawn up by the

---

[1] *Ibid.* p. 121.
[2] Cf. art. *Christianity and the Public Schools*, in *Theology*, June 1939, vol. xxxviii, p. 440 and *n.*
[3] Cf. *Sensibility at the Fall of Eminence: A Sermon preached in Surrey Chapel, at the Funeral of the Rev. Rowland Hill, A.M.*: William Jay, *Works* (1843), vol. vii, p. 425.

members of it for their guidance: Sidney quotes one of these at length, as being 'not only interesting as the production of these pious boys, but intrinsically excellent'.

Fifthly, let us take notice of the manner in which our time is spent, and of the strain which runs through our discourse. How often the former is lost in trifles—how often the latter evaporates in vanity! Let us attend to the principles from which our actions flow; whether from the steady habitual love of God, or from some rambling impulse, and a customary propensity to please ourselves? How frequently we neglect to glorify our Creator, to edify our fellow-creatures, and to improve ourselves in knowledge and holiness! Let us observe the frame of our spirits in religious duties—with what reluctance they are undertaken, and with what indevotion they are performed, with how many wanderings of thoughts, and how much dullness of desire. How often in the common affairs of life we feel the inordinate sallies of passion, the workings of an evil concupiscence, or the intrusion of foolish imaginations. Let us be careful to register those secret faults, which none but the all-seeing eye discerns. Often review these interesting memoirs. Let us frequently contemplate ourselves in this faithful mirror.[1]

Sidney's *Life of Rowland Hill* (1834) was published in the heyday of the Evangelical Revival: and to a generation that took a peculiar delight in instances of precocious piety, the intrinsic excellence of such a document was no doubt more striking than the discrepancy between the maturity of its tone and the immaturity of its compilers. To us it seems distinctly priggish. Yet it is difficult to see how it could have been otherwise in that environment: and, before we pass judgment on this ebullition of youthful earnestness, we should do well to recall the private journals of Henry Martyn and of Hurrell Froude. What is true, however, is that earnest youth tends to be unduly critical of the shortcomings of its elders and contemporaries: and so we find Richard Hill admonishing his younger brother, 'in a very long letter, dated Sept. 30, 1763', that 'even they, who are really the children of God by faith in Christ Jesus, have their spots,

---

[1] *The Life of the Rev. Rowland Hill, A.M.*, by the Rev. Edwin Sidney (1834), p. 17.—Cf. *Memoirs of the Life, Ministry, and Writings of the Rev. Rowland Hill, M.A., late Minister of Surrey Chapel*, by William Jones (1834), pp. 10–16.

and do too often act greatly below the high dignity unto which they are called'.[1] Partly on this account, partly on others, such private religious societies have seldom been regarded with much enthusiasm by sensible schoolmasters. Nor are they generally of long continuance. The little cell of pietists founded by Rowland Hill at Eton began to break up the moment that it was deprived of his own forceful leadership: and although it was revived by his immediate disciples, we may doubt whether it persisted beyond the close of that scholastic year. Certainly there is no evidence of anything of the sort at Eton when Charles Simeon came there as a new boy three years after Rowland Hill had left.

Yet, in looking back upon his schooldays, Simeon could recall, amid much vanity and sinful folly, 'one remarkable circumstance' which left a deep impression on his mind and on his conduct. On the Fast Day in 1776, the School attended chapel twice, and heard a sermon from the Provost, Dr Barnard. Few of them had any clear notion of the meaning of a fast, except that they were to abstain from meat and from amusement until the afternoon after the second service.[2] But Simeon

was particularly struck with the idea of the whole nation uniting in fasting and prayer on account of the sins which had brought down the divine judgments upon us: and I thought that, if there was one who had more displeased God than others, it was I. To humble myself therefore before God appeared to me a duty of immediate and indispensable necessity. Accordingly I spent the day in fasting and prayer. But I had not learned the happy art of 'washing my face and anointing my head, that I might not appear unto men to fast'. My companions therefore noticed the change in my deportment, and immediately cried out Οὐαί, οὐαὶ ὑμῖν, ὑποκριταί (Woe, woe unto you, hypocrites), by which means they soon dissipated my good desires, and reduced me to my former state of thoughtlessness and sin. I do not remember that these good desires ever returned during my stay at school; but I think that they were from God, and that God would at that time have communicated richer blessings to me, if I had not resisted the operations of his grace, and done despite to his blessed Spirit.[3]

---

[1] Sidney, *op. cit.* p. 18.
[2] Carus, p. 5 (Rev. J. H. Mitchell).—Moule is clearly mistaken in identifying this 'second service' as the Holy Communion (*Simeon*, p. 5 *n*.).
[3] Carus, p. 5: cf. p. 700.

Here Simeon's recollection was at fault. The impression thus solemnly received was not so easily effaced. One of his school contemporaries writes: 'His dress and manners from this time became more plain and unfashionable....We learnt also that he kept a small box with several divisions, into which, on having been tempted to say or do what he afterwards considered as immoral or unlawful, it was his custom to put money for the poor.[1]—His habits from that period became peculiarly strict.—We used to have a song about him, ridiculing his strictness and devotion: and the chorus of that song, referring to his box, I am ashamed to say I once joined in: and it haunts me to this day.'[2]

Another thing that Simeon remembered from his schooldays was the neglect of religious, and the comparative excess of classical instruction. Here the reform for which he pleaded in his letter to Provost Goodall (Sept. 4, 1827)[3] was secured by the munificence of the Duke of Newcastle. For when the Newcastle Scholarship was founded in 1829, it was especially provided by the founder that a certain standard of knowledge in divinity[4] should be a preliminary and indispensable condition of success: with such remarkable results that, as 'Etonensis', in his vindication of the system of religious instruction against the criticisms of the *Edinburgh Review*, was happy to point out, 'the examiners...expressed themselves highly satisfied with the manner in which the boys acquitted themselves; and one of them, (Mr Archdeacon Baillie,) a gentleman, I believe, in the habit of examining candidates for orders, declared, that the boys knew enough divinity to pass a Deacon's examination. After this, I do not know that much more need be said on the matter.'[5]

Mr Archdeacon Baillie may have been too kind. But the establishment of divinity as a subject *in its own right* in the

[1] After his ordination, Simeon used the same method to enforce upon himself the duty of early rising: Moule, p. 83.
[2] Rev. J. H. Mitchell, quoted, Carus, p. 6.   [3] *Vide* p. 52 *supra*.
[4] 'The first day of the examination is exclusively devoted to this subject. The candidate is examined in one of the Gospels, the Acts of the Apostles, the History of the Old Testament, Paley's Evidences, &c.'—*The Eton System of Education vindicated: and its Capabilities of Improvement considered, in reply to some recent publications* (1834), p. 21.
[5] *Observations on an article in the last number of the Edinburgh Review....* by Etonensis (1830), p. 17.

curriculum, and with its own rewards, did indeed constitute a revolution, and one of which the consequences were finally decisive. Hitherto it might well have been suspected, and with ample reason, that when the Fourth Form were required to parse and construe twelve verses of the Greek Testament each Monday morning, it was not 'for the sake, or with the possibility of promoting religion, but for the inoculating them with the virus of Greek Grammar rules';[1] while even to the author of *The Eton System of Education vindicated*, it was apparent that the application of the Sunday evenings to Latin prose could but habituate the mind to a practical profanation of the day. 'It should be stated that a moral subject is invariably proposed, and often, portions of a sermon are given to be translated; but it is evident that, in the composition of a Latin exercise, whatever the subject may be, the attention of the author will be more directed to the proprieties of grammatical construction than to the tendencies of the subject. The display of profane learning will be the aim and object of his study.'[2] But the foundation of the Newcastle Scholarship, even if it directly affected 'only the more industrious and talented scholars',[3] did at least establish the position of divinity as a subject to be studied for its own sake, and not simply as subordinate or ancillary to the acquisition of a working knowledge of Greek and Latin; and thereby inculcated a measure of intellectual respect for sacred learning such as the pre-1829 curriculum had done little to encourage. It was, moreover, peculiarly fortunate that Eton at this date had on its staff a number of very able private tutors, good Christian men, who made the most of their advantage.[4]

Consequently, when next the searchlight of public criticism was turned upon the religious life of Eton, it was observable that the critics were transferring, or had transferred, their criticisms to a different target. No longer was it a question simply, or even primarily, of 'a *pagan* education, under *Christian*

[1] *Some Remarks on the present Studies and Management of Eton School.* By a Parent (1834), p. 17.
[2] *The Eton System of Education vindicated* (1834), p. 26.
[3] *Ibid.* p. 35.
[4] Maxwell Lyte, p. 388.

establishments, in a *Christian* country', or of the 'systematic neglect of religious instruction' in the public schools. The real point at issue now was whether compulsory chapel served any useful purpose, or whether in fact it did not do more harm than good. It was the *Edinburgh Review* (April 1830) that first raised the question, in a characteristically offensive tone: 'The very objectionable habit of converting chapel into a roll-call is...kept up, in spite of arguments, to the number and strength of which we could add nothing; and a portion of time, which might be devoted to valuable instruction, is wasted, we will not say in the pretence of devotion, for pretence of the kind there is none.'[1] Here 'Etonensis' found himself, for once, in full agreement:

> The Reviewer is quite right in his strictures on the impropriety of sending the boys to Chapel as a mere roll-call, on Holidays; it is a custom that cannot be too severely reprehended. It is greatly to be feared, that this habit engenders a disinclination to going to Church in after life, even in pious minds; and I think every man, who has been bred up at a public School, will (if he be honest) confess that he has some difficulty in persuading himself to look upon going to Church otherwise than as a restraint; in fact, it is impossible that it should be otherwise. The Eton Masters cannot but be sensible of this, and must regret it; but the removal of so great an evil is in the discretion of the Provost: and it is certainly matter of wonder, that, with the public opinion running so strong as it does upon the subject, no inclination should have been manifested to amend the system.[2]

In effect, the controversy regarding Public School Religion was entering into its second phase: and there was an extraordinary unanimity among the controversialists, who, whether they wrote in praise of Eton or in blame, agreed in condemning the system of compulsory chapel as it stood. 'A Parent', in his *Remarks on the present Studies and Management of Eton School* (1834), reiterated the indictment with unusual feeling:

> ...Nor do I complain solely of the omission of what is good, but of the practice of that which is positively evil. The boys are not only

---

[1] Art. *Public Schools of England—Eton*, in the *Edinburgh Review*, vol. li, p. 78.
[2] *Observations on an article in the last number of the Edinburgh Review...*, by Etonensis (1830), p. 22.

defectively instructed in the nature and doctrines of Christianity, but are most perniciously taught to regard some of its highest duties as a matter of annoyance and coercion. They are COMPELLED to attend chapel, exclusive of Sundays, at the least four, very often five, sometimes even six, times in the week. The evil might, in some degree, be mitigated, if worship on the week days were devoutly performed; but the boys are neither expected to bring Prayer Books into Church, nor to join in the service. The prayers are read in a slovenly manner, being usually accomplished in 25 minutes. Very frequent COMPULSORY attendance on Divine Worship, even if *properly* done, can have none but a bad effect on MEN—and men, too, of religious minds; but upon the YOUNG the consequences are incalculably disastrous.

Upon the young, who generally mistake associations of ideas for opinions, and with whom inveteracy of custom is equivalent to energy of conviction, the effects of this system are doubly deplorable. Attendance on church becomes, in after life, an irksome and uncomfortable duty, and that which was intended by a merciful Creator to be an everlasting memorial of his care and benevolence to man— to be the medicine of sorrow, and the purification of thought, is converted, by a stupid and obstinate adherence to forms, whose single claim to respect consists in the longevity of their mischief, into an uneasy and unprofitable ceremony; thus God is robbed of his mercy, and man of his consolation....[1]

All that the author of *A Few Words in Reply* could find to say to this was that it was not fair to pick on Eton, 'as if it alone were acting upon statutes by which every collegiate foundation is bound. There are other public schools following the same plan', not to mention the Universities, where 'attendance in our college chapels is far less reverently paid, and consequently far more injurious to the morals, and destructive of the religious sense, than it ever is at Eton. The reasons are obvious. I wish to be understood, not as defending the system, (it will not admit of defence,) but merely as stating the fact, that other collegiate establishments are exposed to the same charge, and must equally bear its weight.' For himself, he was 'anxiously desirous that another plan should be acted upon', 'admitting fully, as I do, the possibility of weakening the religious sense in young minds by a compulsory attendance upon Divine worship, of wearing

[1] *Op. cit.* pp. 15–16.

away the reverence, which the holy place should inspire, by frequent and unprofitable meetings within its walls'.[1]

'An Etonian', in *The Eton Question reconsidered*, echoed the language of the *Edinburgh Review* in his denunciation of the abuse of 'making the house of God answer the purpose of a muster-roll. Of religion there is not in this matter a pretence; not even among the masters, whose office it is to enforce the attendance of the boys at six weekly chapels at the lowest—or at an average of seven: all that can possibly be offered in its favour by the authorities is, that it is in accordance with the statutes: but the great majority of the boys are not on the foundation, and therefore only the Eton Montem motto of *Mos pro Lege* can, in their case, be quoted: and for the Collegers, inasmuch as has already been hinted at, the statutes are occasionally violated, this particular point might be added to other conceded ones.'[2]

The author of *The Eton Abuses considered*—a pamphlet which, as was duly pointed out, was 'evidently the work of a young person whose feelings are still embittered with the fancied indignities of some school-discipline, which, to judge from his tone of writing, may have been well deserved, though it certainly failed of its desired effect'[3]—went even further.

There is one point which I have much at heart, and to which I implore the Masters of Eton to turn their most serious attention; I mean the compulsory attendance upon Divine Worship, but most particularly on holydays, when the idea, which is uppermost in a boy's mind, is, how soon he shall be out of church, and how he shall enjoy himself when he is out. This is not the frame of mind in which a human being should wait upon his Maker. Indeed, it is a well-known fact, that those boys who are not under the immediate eye of the Masters, are not unfrequently employed in cutting out their names on the benches, reading light works, or composing the exercises of the week:[4] if a whole day is too long a period for a boy to be

---

[1] *A Few Words in Reply to 'Some Remarks upon the present System and Management of Eton School'.* By Etonensis (1834), pp. 15–16.
[2] *The Eton Question reconsidered.* By an Etonian. *Dedicated by permission to His Grace the Duke of Newcastle, K.G. &c. &c. &c.* (1834), p. 44.
[3] *The Eton System of Education vindicated* (1834), p. 4.
[4] Cf. also Tucker on 'Church sock', *Eton of Old*, pp. 123–5.

left to his own resources, I can see no reason why church service on holydays should not be abolished, and the time given up to science.[1]

The argument put forward in *A Few Words in Reply*, namely, 'that the same system is still acted upon at other Collegiate foundations', seemed to him a very lame defence: for 'if the system is bad, (and bad he confesses it to be), I can discover no reason why Eton should not take the lead in setting a better example. She stands high among our Collegiate Institutions— her authority is likely to be influential—and the system is allowed to be pernicious,—why then should she not take the lead? I am sure that it would have its effect.'[2]

Finally, the author of *The Eton System of Education vindicated: and its Capabilities of Improvement considered, in reply to some recent publications*, while defending the system of compulsory chapel at the Universities, recognised that compulsory chapel at Eton stood upon an entirely different footing.

...It is not there, as at the Universities, a service that commences and closes each successive day, composed of a short and appropriate form of prayer, and incorporated with the daily routine of college business—circumstances to which I would attribute the beneficial workings of the system—but an occasional and variable service, during the course of the day, without any appropriate meaning, considered only as the marks of a holiday or day of indulgence, and apparently enforced only as an useful occupation in the place of school-times. The service, moreover, is not suited to the occasion, being a repetition of the entire service of the Church, which is evidently too long and too comprehensive for a daily office, and which, from its very nature, is not adapted to the capacities of the far greater number of the scholars. It has been remarked by Archbishop Whateley, that our Liturgy is not adapted or designed for children. It may at least be affirmed that our public orders of prayer, from their length and composition, are not suited, as daily offices, for persons of the early age within which the majority of the scholars may be classed....

---

[1] *The Eton Abuses considered: in a letter addressed to the author of Some Remarks on the Present Studies and Management of Eton School* (1834), p. 22.
[2] *Ibid.* (2nd ed.), p. 23.

But the last thing that the writer wished to advocate was the abandonment of the principle

of daily congregational prayer. I consider that this custom, if appropriately observed, may become of essential benefit in the training up of a child, nay more, that it is the most effectual means to implant and mature a sense both of his true dependence on his Maker, and of his brotherly connexion with his fellow Christians. These impressions, to be permanently fixed in our moral being, or rather, to be produced at all, must be made a compulsory part of our daily existence; and this can be effected only by an appropriate observance, of this custom. While, therefore, I willingly admit the necessity of an alteration in the system now pursued at Eton, I deny the propriety of its total abolition. The change required is, to adjust the forms and time of prayer to the capacities of the scholars and the daily routine of business, in such a manner as to make the observance preparatory to the more advanced principles of the University system. It will not, I hope, be considered irrational or presumptuous, if I suggest, in case of any alteration, the adoption of regular morning and evening prayers, at which the office to be used should be arranged expressly for the occasion. The evening prayers now in use among the scholars on the Foundation, might become the model on which such a system could be framed....[1]

Much of this language has a very modern ring. Yet it is significant that, in this second phase, the controversy regarding public school religion marched *pari passu* with a corresponding controversy, with which it can scarcely have been unconnected, regarding religion in the University.

[1] *Op. cit.* pp. 14–16.

Appendix A

[From *Sermons, preached at Laura-Chapel, Bath, during the season of Advent 1799*. By the Rev. FRANCIS RANDOLPH, D.D., Prebendary of Bristol, and Chaplain to His Royal Highness the Duke of York (1800), pp. 12, 193–4.]

...And from studies which might adorn, but should not be made the basis, of a christian education, what evils have originated in a christian land, for which the most extensive learning never can compensate!...

[*Note.*] It is with painful remark I here confess to allude to the system of public education; and reflecting, as I do, that after many years employed in classical attainments, in seeking knowledge in the Lyceum, the Portico, and the Academy, I had not advanced a step in the only knowledge that was to make me wiser, or happier, or better; I most cordially join my voice to that of my friend and school-fellow, Dr Rennell, as well as to that of another champion in the Christian cause, who followed us in the same mistaken paths of science, and with whose sentiments I am proud to concur, in depre-cating that inattention to serious concerns which is so visible in our greatest and best-endowed seminaries. I scruple not to affirm, that our senate and bar are now exhibiting, in many instances, the fatal consequences of this neglect; and that amidst the exertion of the noblest faculties, the display of the brightest talents, religion has too often to weep over a total indifference to her duties, an habitual disregard for the providence of GOD, the gospel of his Son, and the sacred institutions of his service.[1]

[1] Vide note to Dr Rennell's admirable sermon before the Society for promoting Christian Knowledge; and the preface to Mr Gisborne's last publication, though not least in fame, "A Familiar Survey of the Christian Religion".

Appendix B

[From *A Familiar Survey of the Christian Religion, and of History as connected with the introduction of Christianity and with its progress to the present time. Intended primarily for the use of young persons of either sex, during the course of Public or of Private Education*. By THOMAS GISBORNE, A.M. (2nd ed. 1799), pp. iii–v, vii.]

To the REVEREND
BENJAMIN HEATH, D.D.
Fellow of Eton College, etc.

DEAR SIR,

If I venture to assert that more than customary attention might advantageously be allotted to the inculcation of Christian principles and knowledge on the youth of this country; let me not be thought desirous of loading their instructors with harsh and indiscriminate censure.

My own personal experience might lead me to a more equitable conclusion. Nearly six of the earlier years of my education were consigned to the care of a clergyman (*a*); whose life exemplified the religious lessons, which he endeavoured to impress on his pupils. The years intervening between private tuition and the university were passed at the very eminent public school (*b*), over which you, then presided. I recollect with pleasure that the head class, which was under your immediate superintendence, was regularly occupied one morning in the common days of the week in the study of some book of a religious nature. Nor was this the only effort pointed to the same end in the conduct of the school. But I fear that many young persons, if summoned from seminaries of repute to a public examination, would give a better account of the fabled wanderings of Ulysses and Æneas than of the heaven-directed journeyings of Moses and Saint Paul; and would display a more intimate acquaintance with the fortunes of Athens and Rome, than with the historical progress of a religion designed to be their supreme comfort and guide through life, and the means of acquiring eternal happiness.

The principal fault, when faults exist, is not in the preceptor, but in the parent. The former is to water the plant; the latter must sow the seed. But how often does the parent limit his concern for the best interests of his children to the decorum of mere morals: without impressing on their minds, perhaps without feeling on his own, a firm and habitual conviction, that there is no stable foundation on which morality can rest except a Christian fear and love of God! How often does the parent expend his solicitude in unremitting efforts to fit his children for worldly eminence; to prepare them to make their way as politicians, as merchants, as followers of lucrative professions; to be skilful seamen, intrepid soldiers, men of learning, of taste, of accomplishments, and what the world is pleased to call 'men of honour': regardless of the duty of training them up as servants of a God of holiness, and disciples of a crucified Saviour!

A work intended to facilitate the attainment of the most important knowledge will experience, I am confident, your favourable acceptance. I offer it to you with additional satisfaction, as it affords to me an opportunity of conveying to you an assurance that I retain a grateful remembrance of your instructions....

(*a*) The Rev. John Pickering, of Mackworth near Derby.
(*b*) At Harrow on the Hill.

RELIGION IN THE SCHOOL

PREFACE

Among persons who are convinced that youth, the spring-time of life, is the season when the seeds which are to occupy and fill the heart are to be sown; and who regard the acquisition of eternal happiness through Jesus Christ as the great object of human existence; it is a common, and I fear, a just complaint, that in any mode [of] education sufficient attention is too seldom devoted to religion....

Appendix C

[From *A Defence of Public Education, addressed to the Most Reverend the Lord Bishop of Meath*, by WILLIAM VINCENT, D.D. *In answer to a Charge annexed to his Lordship's Discourse, preached at St Paul's, on the Anniversary Meeting of the Charity Children, and published by the Society for promoting Christian Knowledge* (2nd ed. 1802), pp. 46–8.]

RELIGIOUS INSTRUCTION
IN WESTMINSTER SCHOOL

In the three first forms, where children are estimated from 8 to 10 years of age—The Psalms and Gospels turned into Latin, are an exercise four days in the week.

On Monday Catechism repeated.

In the two other forms of the Lower School—Sacred Exercises two days in a week.

On Mondays, alternately—Bishop Williams's Exposition, and the Catechism repeated and explained, *viva voce*.

Boys 10, 11, or 12 years of age.

UPPER SCHOOL
Fourth Form

Bible Exercise. Greek Testament. Sacred Exercises—and, at first, Greek Testament every day construed and explained.

Fifth Form, and Shell

Nearly the same; with Sacred Exercises occasionally in all three.

Sixth Form

Bible Exercise on Saturday.

Grotius Lesson on Monday, explained at large.

RELIGION IN THE SCHOOL

Grotius, Hebrew Psalter, Bible Exercise weekly.

Upper Boys receive the Sacrament four times. a year; always lectured and prepared.

Throughout the Upper School.

Greek Testament during Passion Week—the history or doctrine explained.

Confirmation once in two years—a week's lecture to explain and prepare.

Prayers in College, and at the Boarding-houses.

On Saturdays in Term, Lectures are read to the King's Scholars by a Prebendary.

This Institution[1] has produced two learned and useful Publications by Dr Heylin and Dr Blair; and the duty is now very meritoriously performed by the Rev. Mr Hughes, Prebendary.

RELIGIOUS INSTRUCTION
AT WINCHESTER

Prayers regularly morning and evening in Chapel.

Catechetical Lectures regularly read.

Upper Boys receive the Sacrament once a-month.

Grotius read and explained every Sunday evening.

This account is very imperfect.

[1] The office of Theological Lecturer was created by the Elizabethan Statutes of the Abbey: 'Lectoris munus et officium erit Sacram Scripturam ad plebis et auditorum ædificationem,...linguâ vernaculâ, in Choro Ecclesiæ nostræ, interpretari; cujus Lectionibus intersint administri et pauperes, presbyteri, clerici cæterique Ecclesiæ sub pœnâ pecuniariâ judicio Decani aut Prodecani infligendâ.' 'At present [1809], there is no audience except the school.' 'The Institution has produced few printed works.—In 1749, Dr Heylin published his Interpretation of the Four Gospels, with Lectures on select parts of St Matthew. The book is well known, and maintains its place in Ecclesiastical collections. In 1785, appeared the Lectures of Dr John Blair on the Canon of the Scriptures; a work creditable to the ability of the writer, though certainly not calculated to attract much attention from a youthful audience.' As a direct result of the controversy regarding public school religion, Dean Vincent prevailed upon Prebendary Ireland to 'support the honour of the foundation, and to offer to the school a course of Lectures which should unite the attractions of Literature with the principles and feelings of Christianity'; a task which he performed with great acceptance from 1806 to 1812.—*Vide* Prefaces to *Paganism and Christianity compared: in a course of Lectures to the King's Scholars, at Westminster, in the years 1806-7-8*. By John Ireland, D.D., Dean of Westminster. (New ed. 1825.)

III

RELIGION IN THE UNIVERSITY

✣

Be Folly and False-seeming free to affect
Whatever formal gait of discipline
Shall raise them highest in their own esteem—
Let them parade among the Schools at will,
But spare the House of God. Was ever known
The witless shepherd who persists to drive
A flock that thirsts not to a pool disliked?
A weight must surely hang on days begun
And ended with such mockery. Be wise,
Ye Presidents and Deans, and, till the spirit
Of ancient times revive, and youth be trained
At home in pious service, to your bells
Give seasonable rest, for 'tis a sound
Hollow as ever vexed the tranquil air;
And your officious doings bring disgrace
On the plain steeples of our English Church,
Whose worship, 'mid remotest village trees,
Suffers for this.

WORDSWORTH, *The Prelude*, III, 404–421.

Chapter Three

RELIGION IN THE UNIVERSITY

THE first thing to be borne in mind regarding Oxford and Cambridge in the days when Simeon was an undergraduate is that they virtually monopolised,[1] while they failed conspicuously to discharge, the functions of theological seminaries in which the future clergy of the Church of England received their training for the sacred ministry. The Theological Colleges, as we know them, were not invented until more than half a century later: Chichester (1838–39) has pride of place, with Wells (1840) a close second: both owed their inspiration, in large measure, to the astute ecclesiastical statesmanship of Archdeacon Manning. But in the eighteenth century the main idea of the training of an ordinand was that he should be as well educated as the educated laity: for which there was, indeed, a good deal to be said. With the advance of specialisation and with the ominous contraction of the employment market, the Universities within very recent years have tended increasingly to acquire, or to resume, the character of high-grade technical schools. But throughout Simeon's life-time they offered only a general education, liberally conceived, although predominantly classical at Oxford and predominantly mathematical at Cam-

[1] But they were already losing their monopoly. Cf. (e.g.) art. *Hints concerning the Universities*, in *Janus; or, the Edinburgh Literary Almanack* (1826), p. 9: '... The English universities do not educate the English clergy. Once or twice some three or four bishops have met together, and agreed that they would thenceforth ordain nobody who had not an university degree. The experiment has been tried at least twice in our own recollection, and both times it failed almost immediately. The truth is, that a vast proportion of the livings all over England are very poor; and that, besides men to hold the livings, there is a constant demand for a very large supply of curates. The man whose prospects are limited to the hope, or even the certainty, of a small living or curacy, cannot afford the expense of an education at Oxford or Cambridge; and the consequence is, that all over England, clergymen who have never been at any university are abundant; and that there are many districts, particularly in Wales, Westmoreland, and such poor provinces, where öne meets with, comparatively speaking, but few parish priests who have ever been at one.' Cf. Henry Gauntlett's *Sermons* (1835), vol. i, p. vi: '...a University degree was not at that period (1783) considered so essential a qualification for holy orders as at present it is.'

bridge. 'They have formed neither lawyers, nor physicians, nor statesmen; but they have trained the mind, and disciplined the intellect, and schooled the heart, so that those whom they sent forth should grapple with any subject which might subsequently be presented to them, with a disciplined judgment and a discerning understanding....These more general advantages the Clergy also share, nor is it a slight advantage that their habits and powers of thinking are formed in the same way with those of other educated men; that they are, until a certain point, trained up in contact with those whom they are afterwards to influence; and that the peculiarities of habits and of manners, which, on a more contracted plan of education, might impede or dull that influence, are, as far as may be, prevented. I rejoice', concluded Dr Pusey, 'that an education has been formed, calculated alike for the Christian layman, and for those who are afterwards to be ministers of Christ.'[1] What was less desirable was that this was held almost to preclude the necessity for a more specialised vocational training than that provided by the normal course for a degree in arts.

In truth, arduous as the practical duties of the Clergy always are, even to the experienced, and difficult as it must be, under any system, to reduce into practice the principles or the instruction given in the abstract, the difficulties are increased a hundred fold, when the qualifications for the ministerial office are to be learned during the discharge of its duties. It is impossible for any person, who has not either himself entered thus unprepared into the office, or been frequently consulted by young Clergy, to conceive the extent of perplexity and difficulty in which they are constantly plunged. New to every portion of their office, even the composition of a sermon or the duties of catechising, and new to their studies also, they are perpetually distracted between their active duties, and the studies which may fit them to discharge those duties, what studies to pursue, or how to pursue them.[2]

The case was the more serious when the young graduate went straight from the University to a cure of souls without, like the

---

[1] *Remarks on the Prospective and Past Benefits of Cathedral Institutions, in the promotion of sound religious knowledge, occasioned by Lord Henley's plan for their abolition.* By E. B. Pusey, Regius Professor of Hebrew, Canon of Christ Church, late Fellow of Oriel College, Oxford (1833), pp. 12–14.
[2] *Ibid.* pp. 19–20. Cf. Simeon, *Horæ Homileticæ*, Dedic., vol. i (1832), p. ii.

physician or lawyer, first serving an apprenticeship in 'some subordinate or secondary office in which his own inexperience might be corrected by another's knowledge'.[1]

The problem of how to provide, within the limits of the University curriculum, something of a more specialised vocational training for candidates for holy orders, was simply a particular aspect of the general problem of the Reform of Academic Studies. But into that historic battle-ground Simeon does not appear to have intruded. The explanation is, that he had his own method for training ordinands of his persuasion: and his fortnightly Friday Evening Conversation Parties for undergraduates, and his tuition in sermon composition and delivery, supplied those wants of which he was himself most conscious. But the neglect, or failure, of the University to cope at all adequately with the problem of training ordinands in its official system of instruction requires to be borne in mind, because this was the background of much of Simeon's work: nor was Cornelius Neale the only undergraduate to whom it appeared 'strange, that on science we should have so many lectures, syllabuses, manuscript-helps, tutors, acts, examinations, and prizes; while a person wishing to read Theology would scarcely know how to supply himself with books or a tutor'.[2]

The demand for the reform of the curriculum became insistent in the 1820's: and an anonymous pamphlet of 1822 mentions, as a notorious fact, that Bishops and their Examining Chaplains were wont to complain 'that at their examinations the majority of Cambridge candidates appear worse prepared than those from Oxford'.[3] But the demand had been articulate long before. In 1792 the Rev. Herbert Marsh, B.D., Fellow of St John's, and

[1] Pusey, *op. cit.*, p. 14.
[2] *Memoir of Cornelius Neale*, by William Jowett (2nd ed. 1835), p. 29. Cf. Francis Russel Hall, *A Letter, respectfully addressed to the Heads of Houses, and the Senior Fellows, in the University of Cambridge, on the defective state of Theological Instruction in the University, in reference to candidates for Holy Orders* (1833): James Hildyard, *The obligation of the University to provide for the professional education of its members designed for Holy Orders* (1841).
[3] *A Letter to the Right Reverend John [Kaye], Lord Bishop of Bristol, respecting an additional Examination of students in the University of Cambridge.* By Philograntus. 3rd ed., in *The Pamphleteer*, vol. xx, p. 317. (Dr Kaye was also Regius Professor of Divinity and Master of Christ's.)

RELIGION IN THE UNIVERSITY

subsequently (1807-39) Lady Margaret Professor of Divinity, published *An Essay on the Usefulness and Necessity of Theological Learning, to those who are designed for Holy Orders*.[1] 'Though the greatest number of students in the two Universities is designed for orders, the study of Divinity is regarded as a secondary consideration; it has till lately been thought sufficient to apply for a few months after the bachelor's degree without direction and without assistance, nor has it been deemed an impropriety in our mode of education, that those should be appointed to instruct others, who have never been instructed themselves.'[2] And Beilby Porteus, Bishop of Chester (1777-87: of London, 1787-1808), 'lamented exceedingly', as he told Gilbert Wakefield when he came to Stockport on his primary visitation, 'that no proper provision was made for regular lectures in *Theology*; an idea which he had formerly enforced in an excellent sermon preached by him for his *doctor's degree* at the *commencement* in 1767'.[3] Wakefield's reply was symptomatic

[1] 'The following publication, which is the substance of a Discourse lately held before the University of Cambridge, was principally occasioned by the following circumstance. The author had been frequently asked, during his residence in Germany, "What is the plan of study adopted in your Universities for those, who are designed to take Orders, to what branches of Divinity do they particularly attend, and how many years must a student have heard the different courses of theological lectures before he is admitted to an office in the church?" He was unable at that time to give a satisfactory answer, because theological learning forms no necessary part of our academical education; but he hopes that due attention will in future be given to a study that is at present more neglected than it deserves.' *Op. cit.* p. ii.—On Marsh, vide Baker's *History of St John's College*, ed. J. E. B. Mayor (1869), vol. ii, pp. 735-898. He was a man of outstanding ability and of formidable erudition, and 'conferred a signal benefit on English biblical scholarship by introducing German methods of research' (*D.N.B.*). He retained his Professorship until his death, although after his elevation to the Bench (Bishop of Llandaff, 1816; translated to Peterborough, 1819) he omitted the performance of its duties. Beverley (*Letter to H.R.H. the Duke of Gloucester*, 1833, p. 26) taxes him with having delivered only thirty-four lectures in twenty-six years. On the other hand, his inaugural course (on 'The History of Sacred Criticism', 1809), which was delivered in the University Church, instead of in the divinity schools, in order to accommodate the crowded audience, which included Town as well as Gown, constitutes an important landmark in the history of theological studies in this University.

[2] *Op. cit.* pp. 1-2. Cf. also Richard Watson, *A Collection of Theological Tracts* (1785), vol. i, Preface, pp. vii-viii.

[3] Cf. R. Hodgson, *Life of Bishop Porteus* (2nd ed. 1811), pp. 18-21, 287-90. The sermon in question ('On the advantages of an academical education') will be found in Porteus' *Sermons on several subjects*, vol. i (7th ed. 1794), pp. 171-99: note esp. pp. 190 ff.

of the new temper of the University. '...I thought *an unbiassed disposition for enquiry* into religious truth was of much higher consequence: and it was to be feared, that no lectures could be given divested of all peculiarities of opinion, which would hardly fail to introduce themselves, in spite even of the watchfulness of integrity itself, for the purpose of defending *systems* and *establishments*: and this inconvenience, I humbly thought, no advantages of instruction could compensate. The *bishop* in reply, did not think such a partiality a necessary concomitant of these lectures in proper hands.'[1]

'The prevalent Heterodoxy in the Establishment', wrote Erasmus Middleton in the Conclusion of his *Biographia Evangelica*, 'took its Rise at *Cambridge*.'[2] He was contrasting this University with his own, in which had originated, with all its happy consequences, that 'lively Promulgation of the old Truths and antient Principles of the *Church* of *England*' which some men called Methodism.[3] Certainly Latitudinarianism had particular associations with Cambridge. In this, the University probably took its tone from Richard Watson more than from any other single individual. Watson was elected Regius Professor of Divinity in October 1771, at the age of thirty-four, and continued to discharge the duties of his office in person until 1787, when, acting on medical advice, he arranged to have them discharged by a deputy: a course for which Bentley had set an unlucky precedent.[4] 'To the chair of Divinity', says Professor Sykes, 'he brought the same qualifications as hitherto to that of Chemistry: a total ignorance of the subject of his profession, an

---

[1] *Memoirs of the Life of Gilbert Wakefield, B.A., late Fellow of Jesus College, Cambridge, written by himself* (1792), p. 157.

[2] *Op. cit.* (1786), vol. iv, p. 510.

[3] "'Tis an Honor, which (notwithstanding some poor Proceedings which I wish to bury in Silence) she ought never to be ashamed of' (*ibid.* p. 511). The 'poor Proceedings' meant the expulsion of the six students of St Edmund Hall in 1768: the writer had been one of them. In spite of Middleton's pious adulation, his University took no pride in her spiritual offspring. 'I remember one highly eccentric rector hard by, a master of a college at Oxford....Of this rector I used to hear that when once led, the worse for his cups, through the quadrangle of his college, he exclaimed, "All this I do to purge my college from the stain of methodism!" (Wesley had been of his college.) This, however, was of course an extreme case....' (*Personal and Professional Recollections*, by the late Sir George Gilbert Scott, R.A., 1879, p. 11.)

[4] D. A. Winstanley, *Unreformed Cambridge* (1935), pp. 106–8.

unwearied zeal for the acquisition of knowledge, and a financial genius which raised the emoluments of the office from £300 to £1000 per annum.'[1] A Regius Professor of Divinity who is distinguished chiefly, in his academic character, by the liberality of his opinions, is never an unmixed blessing to the University: and in Watson's exercise of his official duties there was what so often goes with such broad-mindedness, namely, an almost fanatical intolerance of dogmatic orthodoxy. The nature of his influence upon the theological temper of the University may be inferred from the following passage of his posthumous *Anecdotes*:

I reduced the study of divinity into as narrow a compass as I could, for I determined to study nothing but my Bible, being much unconcerned about the opinions of councils, fathers, churches, bishops, and other men, as little inspired as myself. This mode of proceeding being opposite to the general one, and especially to that of the Master of Peterhouse, who was a great reader, he used to call me αυτοδιδακτος, the self-taught divine.—The Professor of Divinity had been nick-named *Malleus Hæreticorum*; it was thought to be his duty to demolish every opinion which militated against what is called the orthodoxy of the Church of England. Now my mind was wholly unbiassed; I had no prejudice against, no predilection for the Church of England; but a sincere regard for the *Church of Christ*, and an insuperable objection to every degree of dogmatical intolerance. I never troubled myself with answering any arguments which the opponents in the divinity schools brought against the articles of the church, nor ever admitted their authority as decisive of a difficulty; but I used on such occasions to say to them, holding the New Testament in my hand, *En sacrum codicem!* Here is the fountain of truth, why do you follow the streams derived from it by the sophistry, or polluted by the passions of man? If you can bring proofs against any thing delivered in this book, I shall think it my duty to reply to you; articles of churches are not of divine authority; have done with them; for they may be true, they may be false; and appeal to the book itself. This mode of disputing gained me no credit with the hierarchy, but I thought it an honest one, and it produced a liberal spirit in the University.[2]

Of the latter of these propositions there can be no question.

---

[1] Norman Sykes, *Church and State in England in the Eighteenth Century* (1934), p. 336.
[2] *Anecdotes of the life of Richard Watson, Bishop of Llandaff; written by himself...* (1817), p. 39.

Cambridge, when Charles Simeon came up to King's as a freshman in 1779, was still feeling the effects of the Subscription Controversy. In this University (by contrast with Oxford[1]) no religious test was, or ever had been, imposed upon undergraduates *at matriculation*: but, under royal letters received from James I in 1616, and accepted by the continuous practice of the University (except during the Civil War and Commonwealth), all persons *proceeding to a degree* were required to subscribe three articles which declared the Sovereign to be Supreme Governor of the Church, and the Book of Common Prayer and the Thirty-nine Articles to be agreeable to the Word of God. This regulation effectually excluded the Dissenters, who were thus obliged to study for degrees at Scottish universities or at academies of their own. But it also bore hardly on those members of the Church of England whose religious beliefs were of a heterodox or Unitarian cast: and it was from this quarter that the agitation came. The Feathers' Tavern Petition (1771) had been largely signed by Cambridge dons: and in June of the same year the Rev. Robert Tyrwhitt, Fellow of Jesus College, prepared to submit to the Senate a grace for the abolition of subscription at the time of taking degrees. This was unanimously rejected by the Caput, as proposing a reform which it was not within the competence of the University to make. In December, Tyrwhitt brought forward another grace for the exemption only of bachelors of arts, which met with the same fate. But the agitation continued, and there was some threat of Parliamentary interference. In order to stave off this latter danger, a grace was passed in the Senate House on June 23, 1772, providing that for the future persons

---

[1] 'When I matriculated at the University at the early age of fourteen, I was told by the Vice-Chancellor, "You are too young to take the common oath of obedience to the Statutes of the University, but you are quite old enough to subscribe the Articles of Religion"' (T. A. Nash, *Life of Lord Westbury*, 1888, vol. i, p. 14 *n*.).—Cf. William Everett, *On the Cam: Lectures on the University of Cambridge in England* (1866), p. 248: 'Indeed, I was told that Lord Loughborough, who, as Chancellor of England and Keeper of the King's Conscience, ought to understand the matter, put a purely negative interpretation on the whole matter. A young relative of his entering Oxford, wrote to protest against his being obliged to sign the thirty-nine articles. "O," wrote back the Chancellor, "it isn't supposed that you believe them, it is only a pledge that you don't hold to any other of the world's superstitions."' (Loughborough was Lord Chancellor 1793–1801.)

admitted to the degree of Bachelor of Arts should, instead of subscribing the Three Articles, sign a declaration: 'I, *A.B.*, do declare that I am *bona fide* a member of the Church of England as by law established.' This grace was not opposed: but, since it scarcely conceded anything at all, it was far from satisfying the reformers;[1] and on Dec. 27 of the same year, the Rev. John Jebb, a beneficed clergyman and a former Fellow of Peterhouse, whose lectures on the Greek Testament had been notorious for their Unitarian bias, preached an inflammatory sermon before the University from Acts xv. 10 ('Now therefore why tempt ye God, to put a yoke upon the neck of the disciples, which neither our fathers, nor we, were able to bear?').[2] This was the dying kick of the agitation: the attack was renewed in 1833, but not until 1871 was the University finally made safe for nonconformity, latitudinarianism, and infidelity.[3]

Nevertheless, the agitation left its mark. It was once customary to defend the Hanoverian Church on the ground that, however inadequate it may have been on its pastoral side, it did at least justify itself at the bar of history by its resounding intellectual triumph over Deism. That is true up to a point. The victory over the Deists was important, because an adequate theology is one of the conditions of the Church's life. Butler's *Analogy* (1736) remains one of the greatest monuments of Anglican piety

---

[1] D. A. Winstanley, *Unreformed Cambridge*, pp. 301 ff.

[2] Disney's *Memoirs of the Life of the Author* in Jebb's *Works* (1787), vol. i, p. 42; the sermon is printed in vol. ii, pp. 107–33.

[3] Universities Test Act, June 1871. But degrees at Cambridge in Arts, Law, Medicine, or Music were opened to Dissenters in 1856, although they were still precluded from becoming Members of the Senate or exercising any share in the government of the University. (Cf. A. I. Tillyard, *A History of University Reform from 1800 to the present time* (1913), passim.)—Cf. *The Letters and Memoirs of Sir William Hardman* (second series: 1863–65), ed. S. M. Ellis (1925), pp. 163–4: 'March, 1864.... The University Boat Race came off on Saturday and resulted in a tremendous licking for Cambridge: they were beaten by twelve boat lengths!!... My friend Dodson (M.P.) is vigorously endeavouring to pass a Bill for Abolition of Tests at Oxford through the House. If he succeeds, it will only place Oxford on the same footing as Cambridge, which is but fair. I attribute our recent defeats on the Thames to the admixture of Little Bethel—to the admission of Dissenters. The Physique of the University is thereby lowered, for who could reasonably expect that Salem, Ebenezer, or Bethesda, could possibly produce anything worthy of being put in a University Eight?... Unbeliever as I am, I hate Dissenters!'

and learning: and Deism collapsed abruptly about the middle of the century. But a purely intellectual triumph is always something of a Pyrrhic victory: and no sooner was Deism driven from the field, than Unitarianism—then more generally called Socinianism—began to make formidable inroads upon the citadels of orthodoxy. The Church is indeed bound to defend her faith: but she can never afford to be content with defending it only on the intellectual plane. The Evangelical Revival was conspicuously unintellectual. That was, indeed, its limitation. It was, no doubt, incapable of fighting the Socinians with their own weapons. But it turned the Socinian flank by its appeal to the hearts and consciences of men. If it tended not to appeal sufficiently to their intellects, it paid the price of that in the latter half of the nineteenth century.

The sum of the matter would appear to be that the task of Christian apologetic is both intellectual and moral: it requires to be directed both to the brains and to the consciences of men. The weakness of the Evangelical Revival was intellectual: the weakness of the Hanoverian Church was moral. To-day we are more disposed to think that the Hanoverian Church requires to be judged primarily on its pastoral side: and we are beginning to discover that in that department it can put forward a better justification than has been traditionally held. The Hanoverian Church was justified, not by its triumph over Deism, but by the lives and labours of its parochial clergy at their best. The intellectual victory was a signal victory indeed: but it was curiously sterile. As soon as Deism had been disposed of, Socinianism sprang up in its place.

It is true that Socinianism spread more rapidly among the Protestant Dissenters than among the Anglicans, who had the safeguard of the Prayer Book. The Presbyterians were particularly riddled with it: and the reason why George III opposed the relaxation of subscription for Dissenters was that there seemed to be no other way of keeping them upon a Trinitarian basis. 'I am sorry to say', he wrote to Lord North (Feb. 23, 1772), 'the present Presbyterians seem so much more resembling Socinians than Christians that, I think, the test was never so

necessary ao at present for obliging them to prove themselves
Christians.'[1] But even in Cambridge, one of the twin strongholds of Anglican orthodoxy, the prevailing religious unsettlement had its repercussions. Professor Watson's attitude was
certainly equivocal: and it was with some reason that Southey
remarked that his conversation was such as to suggest that
'certainly the articles of his faith are not all to be found among
the nine-and-thirty, nor all the nine-and-thirty to be found
among his'.[2] Some very startling observations regarding the
Athanasian Creed, collected from his published writings, will be
found in Professor Sykes' *Church and State in England in the
Eighteenth Century*:[3] and neither the exclusively Biblical nature
of his studies, nor that sincere regard for the Church of Christ
of which he speaks so movingly in his *Anecdotes*, precluded him
from allowing the name of Christian to those who denied the
Divinity of our Lord, as, for example, his friend and patron, the
Duke of Grafton, Chancellor of the University: 'If any one
thinks that an Unitarian is not a Christian, I plainly say, without
being myself an Unitarian, that I think otherwise.'[4] Nor did he
stand alone. Leslie Stephen, in his *English Thought in the
Eighteenth Century*, devotes a section to 'the accurate, the
amiable, the candid Dr Hey',[5] Norrisian Professor of Divinity
from 1780 to 1795, whose lectures, although technically
orthodox, carried the spirit of conciliation to excess. For he
contended that dogmatic statements about the Trinity should
be retained on the ground that they are meaningless and unintelligible, and therefore inoffensive to the most queasy conscience: in assenting to them for the sake of peace and order, we
neither lie to God nor injure man.[6] All this was very painful and

---

[1] *Correspondence of George III with Lord North, 1768–1783*, ed. W. Bodham Donne, vol. i, p. 89.
[2] *Selections from the Letters of Robert Southey*, ed. J. W. Warter (1856), vol. i, p. 391.
[3] *Op. cit.* p. 353.
[4] Watson's *Anecdotes*, p. 47.
[5] Memoir of the Rev. Thomas Twining by his brother (1817) in *Recreations and Studies of a Country Clergyman of the Eighteenth Century*, ed. Richard Twining (1882), p. 5: cf. pp. 186–7 for a description of Hey as a lecturer (Dec. 1793).
[6] Leslie Stephen, *op. cit.* (2nd ed. 1881), pp. 424–6.

embarrassing to Isaac Milner and his friend Professor Jowett, who had inadvertently sanctioned the publication of Hey's *Lectures in Divinity* at the University Press without realising the nature of their contents.[1]

The three Colleges in which the effects of this liberal spirit were most conspicuously marked were Jesus, Peterhouse, and Queens'. Here Gilbert Wakefield's *Memoirs* are peculiarly valuable: for Wakefield came up to Jesus in 1772, was elected to a Fellowship in 1776, and voluntarily migrated to a curacy in 1778. He mentions how one of his contemporaries, Mr Tylden, 'a most amiable person and an excellent scholar, suffered a family-living to devolve upon his brother' because he could not stomach the Thirty-nine Articles, and how one of the senior Fellows, Mr Braithwaite, was understood to refuse 'all *college-livings* upon the same conscientious scruples'.[2] It is indeed striking to observe, in the biographical records of this period and later, how one is continually coming across individuals who refused to be ordained, or to accept livings, or to move from one living to another, in consequence of difficulties about the Prayer Book and the Articles. Porson is a conspicuous example: his fellowship at Trinity, to which he was elected in 1782, was held under the obligation of resigning it at the end of ten years, unless he should take holy orders: he devoted himself conscientiously to a large course of theological reading, in order to ascertain whether he could, with satisfaction to himself, subscribe the Articles, and finally decided that he could not do so. He therefore 'so early as 1788', writes his biographer in the *Gentleman's Magazine*,[3] 'made up his mind to surrender his

---

[1] '— —'s brother, (Dr —,) who is now talked of for the next bishop, is printing his Lectures on Divinity, at the university press, and with our sanction. In these lectures he advances a most extraordinary and ****** opinion, that articles of religion, are to be considered as articles of union not of faith; and in short, that a person may subscribe anything: I really think, that I do not misrepresent. Dr Jowett, myself, and others, have inadvertently countenanced the publication, not knowing how much he has laboured this point. There are likely to be some very serious meetings of syndics on the subject.'—Milner to William Wilberforce, Jan. 1797. (*Life of Milner*, p.123.)

[2] *Op. cit.* p. 116.

[3] *Biographical Memoirs of Professor Porson*, in *The Gentleman's Magazine*, Oct. 1808, vol. lxxviii, pt. ii, p. 948.

fellowship, though, with an enfeebled constitution, he had nothing to depend upon but acquirements that are very unprofitable to their owner'. He also mortally offended the pious lady who had been one of the principal subscribers to the fund for sending him to college, and from whom he had considerable expectations. Indeed, it would be difficult to exaggerate the moral heroism required by his decision. Yet Porson was not an Unitarian: 'A friend once, in the course of conversation with him, asked him what he thought of the evidence afforded by the New Testament in favour of the Socinian doctrines. His answer was short and decisive—"If the New Testament is to determine the question, and words have any meaning, the Socinians are wrong".'[1] And, apart from his controversy with Archdeacon Travis, he always, even in his most drunken moments, spoke respectfully of the Establishment and of its clergy: and whenever he visited his sister in Norfolk, he went regularly with the family to church.[2]

Porson's scruples are in fact symbolic and significant: symbolic and significant of the Age of Doubts, which lasted roughly from the meeting at the Feathers' Tavern in 1771 to the Great War of 1914–18, and of which *Robert Elsmere* (1888) is in some respects the typical literary monument: the Age of Doubts, which has been succeeded by the Age of Doubt, the former marked by the intense assertion, the latter rather by the abdication, of the intellectual principle. For the Age of Doubts was also an age of what at its best was a pure, if slightly academic, passion for intellectual truth, and at its worst a somewhat excessive scrupulosity: and, however much we may deplore the religious unsettlement of the concluding decades of the eighteenth century, we are at the same time bound to recognise that it marks the emergence of a degree of conscientiousness which had not, perhaps, been so prominent or so oppressive in the Anglican clergy of the previous generation.

Tyrwhitt was also a victim of this new disease of Clergymen's Doubts: at least, he resigned his fellowship 'from a dissatis-

---

[1] *Quarterly Review*, Dec. 1825, vol. xxxiii, p. 99.
[2] [W. Beloe], *The Sexagenarian* (1817), vol. i, p. 220; *Life of Richard Porson*, by John Selby Watson (1861), p. 363.

faction with the doctrines contained in the *Articles* and the *Common-Prayer* of the *Church* of *England*'.[1] But, being possessed of amiable manners and some private fortune, he was permitted to retain his rooms in Jesus: and in 1788 he illustrated his wide tolerance and native courtesy by making a gift of £200 to the College 'for defraying the expense of repairing and fitting up the Inside of the College Chapel', although it was eleven years since he himself had ceased to worship there.[2] The liberal spirit of the University towards men of heterodox opinion did in fact assume a corresponding liberality on their side. Cambridge could find room for Tyrwhitt and Porson: but Jebb, who was generally obnoxious, was readily encouraged to depart in 1776 (having resigned his livings in the previous year and openly avowed himself an Unitarian):[3] Thomas Fyshe Palmer fell foul of Milner's positive determination 'to have nothing to do with Jacobins or infidels'[4] in Queens', challenged his dictatorial methods, and, having the worst of the encounter, threw up his fellowship and withdrew to an Unitarian pulpit at Montrose:[5] and in 1793 the notorious William Frend, Fellow of Jesus, and author of a bitter and subversive pamphlet entitled *Peace and Union*, was treated almost as a public enemy.[6] Yet the University

[1] Wakefield, p. 115.
[2] Arthur Gray, *Jesus College* (1902), pp. 200, 168.
[3] Disney's *Memoirs of the Life of the Author* in Jebb's *Works* (1787), vol. i, p. 110.
[4] *Life of Milner*, p. 243.
[5] He was transported for sedition in 1794 after one of the most notorious trials in Scottish history. Cf. Henry W. Meikle, *Scotland and the French Revolution* (1912), ch. vi and passim: *A Narrative of the Sufferings of T. F. Palmer and W. Skirving, during a Voyage to New South Wales, 1794, on board the Surprise Transport,* by Thomas Fyshe Palmer, late Senior Fellow of Queens' College, Cambridge (2nd ed. 1797); George Dyer's sketch of the character of T. F. Palmer, in George Thompson's *Slavery and Famine, punishments for sedition; or, an account of New South Wales, and of the miserable state of the convicts* (2nd ed. 1794).
[6] Cf. Gunning, vol. i, pp. 255–84; Henry Crabb Robinson's *Diary* (ed. T. Sadler, 1869), vol. iii, pp. 143, 401.—Frend became a convert to Unitarianism in 1787, resigned his living (Madingley), and in the following year was removed from his tutorship at Jesus: against this decision he appealed to the Visitor, but without success. After April 1793 he was forbidden to reside in College: he was, however, permitted to retain his fellowship and its emoluments until his marriage in 1808. Cf. Arthur Gray, *Jesus College*, pp. 169–80; W. Frend, *An Account of the Proceedings in the University of Cambridge against William Frend, M.A., Fellow of Jesus College, Cambridge* (1793), and *A Sequel to the Account* (1795).

where Watson was Regius Professor of Divinity was prepared to connive at heterodox opinions so long as they were accompanied by inoffensive manners. The effect of all this upon the undergraduates may be imagined. Wakefield indeed denies that Jebb and Tyrwhitt sought to make proselytes among those *in statu pupillari*: but he adds, 'It is not improbable, (but of this I have no particular recollection) that the *example* of such respectable characters, occupied in the search and the profession of religious truth, might apply *spurs* to the *willing courser*; as it certainly excited, with the publications then current, a variety of conversation and debate upon the controverted points in *Theology*, among the *Undergraduates*'.[1] To this influence may be added, at a slightly later period, that of the celebrated Robert Robinson, the Baptist minister, a man exceptionally unstable in his religious convictions, who was gravitating into Unitarianism: he died in 1790, while on a visit to Dr Priestley at Birmingham. Robinson had a considerable following among the junior members of the University, and, after the death of Dr Ogden of St Sepulchre's, was the most popular preacher in the town.[2]

Granted this background of religious unsettlement, it has to be admitted that the orthodox piety of the Church of England was not exhibited in its most attractive guise in the worship of the College Chapels. Attendance was, of course, compulsory. Wakefield seems to imply that when he was a scholar of Jesus (1772–76) this rule was rigidly enforced for undergraduates: and if he himself occasionally cut an evening chapel, he could afford to do so only on the strength of his 'uniformly punctual' attendance at other times.[3] On the other hand, the author of a pamphlet entitled *Remarks on the Enormous Expence in the Education of Young Men in the University of Cambridge; together with a Plan for the better regulation of the discipline of that University* (1788), objects that 'the young Men are actually

---

[1] Wakefield, p. 110.
[2] Cf. *The Sexagenarian; or, the Recollections of a Literary Life* [by William Beloe], 1817, vol. i, p. 51; George Dyer, *Memoirs of the Life and Writings of Robert Robinson* (1796), p. 68.
[3] Wakefield, p. 109.

allowed, without Mulct or Censure, to be absent a certain Number of Times in each Week. Of their Absence I do not so much complain, as that they cannot be absent to any good Purpose, but are running either into Vice or Expense; most probably into both.'[1] He also alleges that 'it is a Matter well understood by the young Men of Fashion, that for a certain Amercement, which varies according to the Avarice of the Society to which they belong, that they may be at Liberty not to attend their College Prayers Morning or Evening. This is a Mode of administering Discipline which I fear we are unlikely ever to see dispensed with: Inasmuch as several of the Colleges, at least several Members of the Colleges, derive from it a very considerable Part of their annual Income. I could mention a Gentleman, formerly Dean of one of the large Colleges above mentioned,[2] who had amassed a considerable Sum of Money by Fines on young Men for Non-attendance on Prayers. A Circumstance I should not have been able to have communicated to the Public had not the Gentleman been so incautious as to have boasted of it as Matter of Merit in himself.'[3] Writing twenty years later, the author of a series of articles under the general title of *The Cantab* in a scurrilous periodical, *The Satirist, or Monthly Meteor*, says: 'If a man attends *nine* times a week he escapes without notice; but should he be prevented by idleness or drunkenness from attending that number, he is punished by an order to attend *twelve* times in the succeeding week. Should he still prove refractory, he is given an imposition, *e.g.* a number of the Spectator to be turned into Latin, or a scene of Eschylus to be "done into English". Either of these, on paying the sum 1*l.* 10*s.* he can procure at Nicholson's, *alias* Map's, the bookseller's; where declamations, themes, and all the other exercises of the college can be purchased "for *ready money only*".'[4] The practice varied a little in different Colleges, and also according to seniority: 'the freshman is expected to go oftener than the junior soph, the junior soph than the senior, and the senior than

---

[1] *Op. cit.* p. 12.
[2] Trinity, Emmanuel, and St John's.
[3] *Remarks*, p. 10.
[4] *The Satirist*, May 1808, vol. ii, p. 247.

the questionist':[1] and there is more than a suspicion that Noblemen and Gentlemen-Commoners were more leniently handled than mere scholars, pensioners, and sizars.[2] 'We are very pious indeed here,' writes the author of *Letters from Cambridge, illustrative of the studies, habits, and peculiarities of the University* (1828): 'poor deluded sinners think if they go twice a week to church, and offer up their prayers in the simplicity of their hearts, they have done enough, as far as public devotion is concerned. What a fatal error!—eight times a week is considered not at all too little here, and in some Colleges more is insisted on.—"It must produce a marked effect on your conduct and demeanour."—It does produce a marked effect, and you may mark it through life, if you please. It produces listlessness and indifference, and it stifles true piety. To be plain with you, attendance at chapel is made much more a point of discipline than a point of duty; I mean religious duty. In some of the Colleges ten times, in others eight, and in none, I believe, fewer than five a week are required from all undergraduates: this is a very severe, and a very impolitic rule also. Is a true perception of the efficacy of prayer likely to be given in a compulsory abuse of its purposes?...What is the excuse? What is the plea urged?—"O, it is necessary to have some kind of muster-roll."...If a muster-roll be so necessary, why not make it at Hall?'[3]

All our authorities agree in two main points. 'The *morning* and *evening* prayers', says Wakefield, 'are much too long and attended by the generality of *undergraduates* with no seriousness of devotion, and seldom by the *fellows* at all.'[4] 'It might be supposed', observes *The Cantab*, 'that in a seminary devoted, in a very considerable degree, to the education of the clergy, the most scrupulous attention would be paid to the service of

---

[1] *Letters from Cambridge* [by E. S. Appleyard] (1828), p. 103 *n.*
[2] At C.C.C., Oxford, in the 1760's, 'the gentlemen-commoners were not obliged to attend early chapel on any days but Sunday and Thursday'. *Memoirs of Richard Lovell Edgeworth* (1820), vol. i, p. 94.
[3] *Op. cit.* [by E. S. Appleyard], pp. 102–4. Cf. *Alma Mater; or, Seven Years at the University of Cambridge,* by a Trinity-Man [J. M. F. Wright] (1827), vol. i, p. 32.
[4] Wakefield, p. 147.

religion, and that its outward ceremonies would be performed with the most impressive solemnity. It is foolish to expect that the young, the foolish, and the idle, will submit with willingness to those duties which are neglected or despised by the grave and authorized professors of religion.... A *fresh-man* learns, in the first week of his seasoning, to consider the chapel as a kind of guard-house or muster-room, where a certain number of formulary lines are to be hurried over, *secundum artem*, for the amusement of the tutor, as a kind of rotatory plaything, which serves to fill up the time *as well as any other nonsense*. His imposition he generally evades by taking out an *ægrotat*, or certificate that he is indisposed (*i.e.* to go to chapel), and thus avoids all the inconveniences of the *statutable* discipline, and may drink and frolic with the most perfect impunity.

'Many of these abuses, however, might be obviated by the regular attendance of the fellows. Were the clerical dignitaries of the college to appear more frequently at chapel, and enforce these regulations by their own example, it is possible that the first impression they excited might be, in a great degree, corrected; and that the undergraduates might really believe attendance at chapel to be a religious duty. But it is not one time in ten that these personages condescend to grace such places with their presence. Their time is, in their own opinion, more profitably employed in playing at bowls,[1] or talking scandal in the combination room. The Dean, alone, "of all this goodly train", is obliged to relinquish his pastime, or his bottle, and to administer spiritual comfort to his (sometimes *drunken*) congregation.'[2]

It was undoubtedly a serious liability that the Fellows, of whom almost all were clergymen of the Church of England, should have made themselves conspicuous by their absence from the statutory religious exercises of morning and evening

---

[1] 'The following memorandum is found in a blank page of Bentley's Ephemeris for 1701: "July 26, 1701, Saturday. Mr Hutchinson, Mr Porter, Mr Green, and Mr Leighton played at bowls in the College bowling-green all Chapel time, in the evening service: seen out of my window by me (who was then lame and could not be at Chapel) and Will. Saist."' *The Life of Richard Bentley, D.D.*, by J. H. Monk (1830), p. 160 *n*.

[2] *The Satirist*, May 1808, vol. ii, pp. 246–8.

player.[1] 'When are the Fellows, or even the Tutors, now seen at the morning service in chapel?' demanded the author of *Strictures upon the Discipline of the University of Cambridge, addressed to the Senate* (1792: 2nd ed. 1794).[2] '...Yet, can it be expected that young men should of their own accord, turn their minds to the sacred duties of religion, which they see so constantly and openly violated by their seniors, who, by their superior age and station, should be the first to join in them, and encourage others to the practice of them? Can it be expected that they should look upon their attendance in chapel in any other light than as an expedient mode of mustering them together; and that they meet there, not to offer up their prayers and thanksgivings to heaven, and to inculcate early in their minds the practices of piety; but merely to be reviewed, and to be pronounced regular or irregular, and accordingly punished or approved of by those, who by their own non-attendance declare this criterion of regularity, to be merely an imaginary and arbitrary one?'[3] So also the youthful Wordsworth, as an undergraduate at St John's, 'saw sacred services provided day after day, morning and evening, by his college, and he found that he and his fellow students were statutably bound to attend them. But he looked in vain for the presence of many of those who ate the bread of the founders, and were supposed to administer the statutes, and had bound themselves by solemn engagements to observe the laws of the college, and to be examples to the younger

[1] Cf. R. M. Beverley's *Letter to H.R.H. the Duke of Gloucester* (1833), p. 22: 'The statutes command that the Fellows should attend chapel as punctually as the Under-graduates, but the law slumbers for them, and some of the resident Fellows never go to chapel once in the whole year. The Tutors and Deans are obliged for decency's sake to attend with tolerable regularity: their absence would be too barefaced, but
   "Weary woe it is, and labour dire."'

[2] He added: 'none of those who remember what the discipline was half a century ago, will scruple to pronounce it degenerated' (pp. 10, 13).—Yet in Sept. 1704 Bentley had decreed that the penalty of three half-pence for absence from Chapel, which the statutes of Trinity imposed upon the Fellows as well as other members of the College, should be exacted as far as concerned the lower half of the sixty Fellows. 'The measure itself was nugatory; since a more regular attendance could never be enforced by the infliction of so paltry a fine. The only good which this mass of small penalties could produce, was a more liberal remuneration to the two College deans for the execution of their invidious but important office.' (Monk's *Life of Bentley*, pp. 133–4.)

[3] *Op. cit.* pp. 11–12.

8-2

members of the society, and especially to maintain that collegiate unity which cannot subsist without religious communion. He felt that there was something like hollow mockery and profane hypocrisy in this,' and, in the bitterness of his heart, 'would have suspended the daily service in the college chapels', although he came to revise his opinion in maturer years.[1]

The Cantab's mention of drunkenness at evening chapel requires a word of explanation. When Watson came up to Trinity as a sizar in 1754, and for many years after, every College dined at 12.0 noon.[2] Even this was an hour later than it had been at Oxford at the end of the previous century.[3] The hour continued to be gradually moved forward to 1.0, 1.30, 2.15, or 3.15: the reason usually given was that 'It makes a *long morning*', although Wakefield doubted whether the studies of the undergraduates were much profited thereby.[4] At Trinity in 1800 the time of Hall was moved from 2.15 to 3.15:[5] Chapel was at 5.30. By the middle of the nineteenth century, Hall was at 4.0 (with a Second Hall, for freshmen and sizars, at 5.0):[6] Chapel was at 6.0, and the intervening period was occasionally occupied by a wine-party. It was not the thing for reading men to go to evening chapel, and this was permitted by the Deans, provided that they kept five or even four weekday morning chapels and attended with unfailing regularity on Sundays, both morning and evening. On this basis, Whewell used to divide attendants at Chapel into 'orthrodox' and 'hesperodox'.[7] Morning chapel was then at 7.0.

'The indecorum attendant on this branch of discipline,' wrote Wakefield,[8] 'especially in *winter-mornings*, is even ludicrous. I

---

[1] *Memoirs of William Wordsworth*, by Christopher Wordsworth (1851), vol. i, p. 47: cf. vol. ii, pp. 265–6.
[2] Watson's *Anecdotes*, p. 22.
[3] Wakefield's *Memoirs* (2nd ed. 1804), vol. i, p. 153 *n*.
[4] Wakefield, p. 149.
[5] *Extracts from the Diary of Chris. Wordsworth, [afterward Master of] Trin. coll. Camb. Oct. 9, 1793–Mar. 8, 1801*, printed in *Social Life at the English Universities in the 18th Century*, compiled by Christopher Wordsworth (1874), p. 598.
[6] W. Everett, *On the Cam* (1866), pp. 99 ff.
[7] '*J*', by A. E. Shipley, p. 27.
[8] Wakefield's *Memoirs* (1792), pp. 147–8. The sentence about the 'sleepy devotee' was omitted in the 2nd ed. (1804).

have known a sleepy devotee delayed so long by the *drowsy god*, as to make it requisite to come at last without his clothes; and he has stood shivering with the flimsy *fig-leaf* of a *surplice* only to veil his *outward-fellow*. Nothing can be more humorous and more truly descriptive of a reality, than a stanza in the parody of *Gray's* Elegy:[1]

> Haply some friend may shake his hoary head,
> And say: "Each morn, unchill'd by frosts, he ran,
> "With hose ungarter'd, o'er yon turfy bed,
> "To reach the chapel e'er the psalms began".'

The administration of the Holy Communion retained the character of a sacramental test rather than that of a religious ordinance, and was regarded more as a political restraint than as a sacred obligation. 'Put it to the serious-minded man, and ask him what he would think, were he to be told, that not merely the regular services are so abused, but that the most awful ceremony of the Christian church, no less than the Sacrament itself, is treated in many of these establishments (some I except) with equal levity and contempt? Whenever celebration of it is enjoined, you must attend: no scruples of conscience are admissible; no sense of unworthiness can be pleaded. If you have just risen from a debauch, your senses steeped in wine, your better feelings unawakened to a sense of duty—well:—if, the bread touched, and the tremendous cup tasted, you return to the carousal you have quitted—no matter:—an imperious necessity commands, and you hope (and I trust not in vain) the shame, and the guiltiness of the deed, will rest on their heads who dragged you to it. I have said I except some: these are Trinity, Catherine Hall, and St Johns: there may be more: I shall be happy to be corrected. I do not recollect any at present.'[2]

The writer was in error: there were more, at least by the date at which he was writing: what measure of compulsion had been

---

[1] *An Evening Contemplation in a College* (1753), by J. Duncombe, M.A., Corpus Christi, or Bene't College, Cambridge: printed in *The Cambridge Tart* (1823), pp. 30 ff.; also (but quite unwarrantably) in *The Oxford Sausage* (1821), pp. 27 ff.

[2] [E. S. Appleyard], *Letters from Cambridge* (1828), pp. 104–5.

practised in the eighteenth century is less easily discoverable. But when the odious Mr Beverley, in his *Letter to His Royal Highness the Duke of Gloucester, Chancellor, on the present corrupt state of the University of Cambridge* (1833), talked wildly of 'the system of forcing the Undergraduates to attend chapel and take the sacrament', of the Established Church 'dragging the youth of England to her hated altars', and of 'troops of young profligates compelled to join in the Lord's Supper, and "eat and drink their own damnation"',[1] it was a simple matter for the vindicators of the University to retort that nowhere was Communion compulsory except 'in one or two of the lesser colleges', where 'the undergraduates are required to communicate or *leave the society*, a regulation of which they may inform themselves before they join it, and *avoid*, by choosing some other college'.[2] Yet it seems probable that the reception of the Sacrament was still in theory compulsory: even at Trinity, which had long since thrown open its gates to Nonconformists, a trifling fine continued until 1844 to be exacted from all who absented themselves from the Communion,[3] although this nominal punishment was not intended to have the force of a compulsive law;[4] and the communicants were obliged to leave their names with the Deans. But no great hardship was involved in any case,

[1] *Op. cit.* pp. 22, 23. Beverley had been admitted to Trinity as a pensioner in 1814; matriculated 1816; fellow-commoner, 1820: LL.B. 1821. His strictures were, in consequence, a trifle out of date.

[2] *A Letter to the Rt. Hon. Henry Goulburn, M.P., on the Morals and Religion of the University of Cambridge, with reference to a recent letter from R. M. Beverley, Esq.* ... By John Fuller Russell, of St Peter's College (1833), p. 14.—Cf. *Remarks upon Mr Beverley's Letter*..., by a Member of Trinity College (1833), p. 31; *Letter to R. M. Beverley*..., by an Undergraduate (1834), p.15.

[3] 'Much practical difficulty has been experienced in compelling the dissenting students to attend the sacramental services in Trinity college chapel, and the compulsory attendance of all the lay students on the sacrament, in that college, is now practically commuted into the payment of a small pecuniary fine, not exceeding sixpence or one shilling for each absence of a student from the sacramental service' (*Collection of Statutes for the University and the Colleges of Cambridge*, ed. James Heywood (1840), preface, p. xv).—Mr Winstanley informs me that the fine was abolished by the new statutes of 1844 on the initiative, not of the College, but of the Home Secretary.

[4] *Four Letters to the Editors of the* Leeds Mercury *in reply to R. M. Beverley, Esq.*, by the Rev. Adam Sedgwick, Woodwardian Professor, and Fellow of Trinity College, Cambridge (1836: not published), p. 31.

since, as was duly pointed out, 'The Lord's Supper is administered *only* once in the term, in every college'.[1]

It is true, however, that a certain measure of compulsion was applied to ordinands, in so far as 'no college will grant a man his testimonials unless he have been a partaker at this holy rite a certain number of times'.[2] The number seems later to have been fixed at three. However defensible in theory, this regulation was not wholly edifying in practice. Sir Walter Besant, as an undergraduate at Christ's (1855–59), was so little moved by the responsibilities before him that he 'forgot this requirement, and, on discovering the omission, attended all three [celebrations of the Holy Communion] in the last two terms. This was thought somewhat scandalous, and I nearly lost my college certificate in consequence.'[3] And William Everett, a young American from Harvard, was sickened by the spectacle of young men coming up to Cambridge for the week-end, long after they had taken their degrees, in order simply 'to keep their sacraments'. 'I saw many things in England that pained me as to their estimation of sacred things, but never anything like this gross levity as to the communion.'[4]

In 1834 the Rev. Adam Sedgwick, Woodwardian Professor of Geology, and Fellow of Trinity College, could solemnly aver 'that on no occasion, either public or private, have I seen this holy rite of our church performed with more solemnity or devotion than it is at the altar of a College Chapel'.[5] Yet when *The Cantab* wrote, in 1808, his picture, however violently over-coloured, may have contained more than an element of truth:

> ...Every member of the college is obliged to attend it; and neither the casual intemperance, nor the premeditated debauchery of the

[1] *A Letter to R. M. Beverley, Esq....*, by Francis Russel Hall, B.D., Rector of Fulbourn, and late Fellow of St John's College (1834), p. 27.
[2] J. F. Russell, *Letter to the Rt. Hon. Henry Goulburn*, p. 14.—Cf. *A Letter to H.R.H. Frederick, Duke of Gloucester, D.C.L., Chancellor, in vindication of the University of Cambridge from the calumnious attacks of R. M. Beverley, Esq.*, by an Undergraduate, φιλαλήθης [Alex. Watson?] (1833), p. 16; F. R. Hall, *Letter to R. M. Beverley*, pp. 26–7.
[3] *Autobiography of Sir Walter Besant* (1902), p. 91.
[4] W. Everett, *On the Cam* (1866), pp. 252–3.
[5] Sedgwick, *Four Letters to the Editors of the* Leeds Mercury, p. 31.

preceding night are considered as a sufficient apology for absence. The bread and wine are administered by the Master or the tutor with all the solemnity of deliberate b—y. The most perfect insensibility is displayed to shame and decency; and while the most solemn denunciations of divine vengeance are fulminated against those who approach the altar unworthily, it is frequently surrounded by violaters of morality, and the most deplorable victims of excess.[1]

Nevertheless, in the mysterious Providence of God, it was this obligation that was made the instrument of Simeon's conversion. He came up to King's on Jan. 29, 1779. On Feb. 2 he was notified that he would be required to attend the Lord's Supper at the division of Term, in about three weeks' time. 'What! said I, *must* I attend?' He was informed that he had no option in the matter: '*The Provost absolutely required it.* Conscience told me, that Satan was as fit to go there, as I; and that if I MUST go, I MUST repent, and turn to God, unless I chose to eat and drink my own damnation.' 'Without a moment's loss of time, I bought the old *Whole Duty of Man*, (the only religious book that I had ever heard of) and began to read it with great diligence; at the same time calling my ways to remembrance, and crying to God for mercy; and so earnest was I in these exercises, that within the three weeks I made myself quite ill with reading, fasting, and prayer. From that day to this, blessed, for ever blessed, be my God, I have never ceased to regard the salvation of my soul as the one thing needful.'[2]

But he continued: 'I am far from considering it a good thing that young men in the university should be compelled to go to the table of the Lord; for it has an evident tendency to lower in their estimation that sacred ordinance, and to harden them in their iniquities; but God was pleased to make use of that compulsion for the good of my soul, and to bring me to repentance by means, which for the most part, I fear, drive men into a total disregard of all religion.'[3]

As will have been noted, the Sacrament was administered at the division of Term: not necessarily, however, on a Sunday.

---

[1] *The Satirist*, May 1808, vol. ii, p. 249.
[2] Carus, pp. 6–7, 711. Cf. Preston, pp. 2–4.
[3] Carus, p. 7.

At Queens', it was normally administered on the Friday after the division:[1] at Trinity, on the Thursday.[2] At St John's also it was administered on a weekday, notice having been given on the Sunday immediately preceding.[3] Later, Sunday came to be generally employed for the purpose. At St Catharine's in 1828 this was the case: it was the only Sunday on which attendance at Chapel was left optional.[4] Trinity appears to have been the last College to come into line, if we may judge from an entry in Romilly's diary:[5]

Sunday, 5 March, 1843.

Last Sunday we began at Trinity to have the Terminal Sacrament on Sunday;—it used to be on the Thursday after Division.—We have now imitated the rest of the University in having it on Sunday.— We have a compulsory chapel service at the usual hour of 8, without the Communion:—then at 11 the service begins with the Communion, is followed by a Sermon, and concludes with the Sacrament.

The words, 'the Terminal Sacrament', clearly imply that even at this date there was still only one celebration in each term, apart from the three great Festivals of Christmas, Easter, and Pentecost, which did not necessarily fall in Term.

It happens that in the following year Charles Wordsworth, at that time Second Master at Winchester, anxious to discover what improvements had been introduced at Oxford under the influence of the Tractarian Movement,

employed a trusty young friend, who had recently gone up from Winchester to Oxford, to inquire at the several colleges what improvement had taken place, in regard, for instance, to a test so simple and elementary as the frequency of the administration of Holy

---

[1] *Preparation for Death enforced from the Uncertainty of Life: A Sermon, preached in the Chapel of Queen's College, Cambridge, on occasion of the Death of Basil Anthony Keck, Esq., Scholar of that Society.* By the Rev. William Mandell, B.D., Fellow and Tutor of Queen's College (1815), p. v.
[2] '*Thursday*, Feb. 26, 1801. Sacrament Day for Term. Ramsden preached [John 14, 16].' (*Extracts from the Diary of Chris. Wordsworth [afterward Master of] Trin. coll. Camb. Oct. 9, 1793–Mar. 8, 1801,* in C. Wordsworth, *Social Life at the English Universities in the 18th century* (1874), p. 599.)
[3] *History of the College of St John the Evangelist, Cambridge,* by Thomas Baker, B.D., ed. J. E. B. Mayor (1869), vol. ii, p. 1087.
[4] [E. S. Appleyard], *Letters from Cambridge,* p. 106.
[5] *Vide* Appendix A.

RELIGION IN THE UNIVERSITY

Communion. His report, comprised in two interesting letters, which are now before me (bearing date October 1844), is,·I am sorry to have to say, a very disappointing one. It appears from it that in almost all the colleges Holy Communion was still administered not more than once in a term; there were only three or four bright exceptions; and this although the Rubric plainly directs that 'In colleges, where there are many Priests and Deacons, they shall all receive the Communion with the Priest *every Sunday at the least*, except they have a reasonable cause to the contrary'. In one college it was the practice of the Master to speak to the freshmen on the subject the evening before, and at the same time to give to each of them a copy of the S.P.C.K. tract, 'Exhortation to Frequent (!) Communion. By a Layman.' At another college all the undergraduates were required to attend under pain of a guinea fine! From this it would seem that the spiritual interests of the youths whom we at Winchester and others elsewhere, had done our best to train up in the right way, were being neglected and uncared for just *when* and *where* we had a right to expect that they would be tended and fostered with greater and more skilful pains.[1]

It may also be noted that, despite Sedgwick's tribute to the edifying solemnity of a Collegiate Eucharist, so late as 1871, if not later, communicants in Trinity College Chapel were still communicated in their stalls. This was also the practice at Christ Church, Oxford, up to 1856: the communicants remained in their seats—it is to be presumed that they knelt—while the celebrant walked round to communicate each in turn: Dr Pusey, of all men, used to administer in this way.[2] On the other hand, the ancient practice of bowing to the altar still survived in certain College Chapels, at least at Oxford, well into the nineteenth century.[3] But these details of collegiate use, although

[1] *Annals of my early life, 1806–1846*, by Charles Wordsworth, D.D., Bishop of St Andrews (1891), pp. 346–7.
[2] Francis Bond, *The Chancel in English Churches* (1916), pp. 122–3. Cf. Appendix B.
[3] Cf. Brand's *Observations on Popular Antiquities*, ed. Henry Ellis (1813), vol. ii, p. 219 n.: *Of Bowing towards the Altar or Communion Table on entering the Church*. '...A regard for impartiality obliges me to own that I have observed this practice in College Chapels at Oxford. I hope it is altogether worn out in every other place in the kingdom: and, for the credit of that truly respectable Seminary of Learning and religious Truth, that it will not be retained there by the rising generation': on which Ellis comments, '[The

contributory, are not of primary importance: it is with the general character of Chapel services in Simeon's time that we are here concerned.

In 1834—two years before Simeon's death—the academic dovecotes were thrown into a flutter by Connop Thirlwall's *Letter to the Rev. Thomas Turton, D.D., Regius Professor of Divinity in the University of Cambridge, and Dean of Peterborough, on the Admission of Dissenters to Academical Degrees.*

The circumstances were as follows. In 1833, the year after the passage of the Great Reform Bill, Professor Pryme, M.P. for Cambridge borough, and Professor of Political Economy in the University, had reopened the old controversy about Subscription. By this date, the question was no longer complicated by the side-issue of Socinianism. That wave had spent its force. 'There are no avowed Socinians now at Cambridge', wrote Sedgwick in 1834. 'During the latter half of the last century there was a considerable number of this party in the University; a few of them were left after I came up to College [in 1804]; and whatever errors there may have been in their creed, they were respected for their age, their great simplicity of character, and their deep learning: and one of them,[1] in founding our Hebrew Scholarships, greatly assisted in promoting the study of sacred literature. But they are all gone, and have not left one apostle of their opinions.'[2] It was therefore now a perfectly straightforward issue as to whether or not Dissenters should be permitted to receive degrees.

Professor Turton took up the challenge in a very able pam-

practice of bowing to the Altar, the Editor believes, is now entirely left off at Oxford. That of turning to it for the Creed is pretty generally retained: and certainly has its use, in contributing very often to recall the wandering thoughts of those who attend the Chapel Service.]'—Cf. *Four Years in France...; preceded by some account of the Conversion of the Author to the Catholic Faith, in 1798* [by Henry Digby Beste] (1826), pp. 8–9: at Magdalen, 'the president [Dr Horne] even bowed to the altar on leaving the chapel.... Here we all turned towards the altar during the recital of the Creed; at Lincoln this point of etiquette was rather disputed among the congregation....'—At Brasenose, the custom of bowing to the altar, together with several other 'peculiar little ceremonies' described by A. C. Benson in his *Walter Pater* (English Men of Letters, 1906, p. 85), would seem to have persisted without interruption.

[1] Tyrwhitt.
[2] *Four Letters*, p. 46.

phlet,[1] in which he claimed for members of the Church of England the same privilege as was enjoyed by the Dissenters, namely, the possession of their own seminaries of education in which, 'to youths of their own communion, those principles of Religion alone are taught, which are in agreement with their own peculiar views. For the Members of the Church of England I claim the privilege of teaching the Religion of that Church, as established by the Laws of England.'[2] And, among the advantages bestowed by the Universities as at present constituted, he enumerated the relation of pupil to Tutor, the Chapel services, and the College lectures.

The daily service—the occasional Sacrament—the Lectures—the intercourse with those to whom is entrusted the government of the Society to which [the young man] belongs—all conspire to impress upon his mind the reflection that, in common with those around him, he is a Member of the Church of England. To him, at his youthful time of life, religion is communicated, not in general terms—not through the turbid medium of controversy—but as it was understood by the Fathers of the Protestant Church of England:—a Church by which, in maturer years—when he shall have fully ascertained the foundations on which it rests—we trust that he will be content to stand or fall. It is for this end that, for a season, he is committed to our keeping; and for this we hold it to be our duty to provide.[3]

Thirlwall, who was an Assistant Tutor at Trinity, expressed himself as more than doubtful 'whether the ordinary service of our college chapels, or our college lectures, can properly be numbered among the aids to religion which this place furnishes'.[4] He was opposed on principle to 'compulsory religion'.[5] His own opinion was 'that it would be a great benefit to religion, if our daily services were discontinued, and if in their stead there was established a weekly service, which should remind the young men of that to which they have most of them been accustomed at home', and which 'would afford the best opportunity of

---

[1] *Thoughts on the Admission of persons without regard to their religious opinions to certain Degrees in the Universities of England* (1834). 2nd ed. enlarged (1835) with new title: *A Review of the principal Dissenting Colleges in England during the last century.*
[2] *Op. cit.* (2nd ed.), pp. 30–1.　　　[3] *Ibid.* pp. 31–2.
[4] *Letter to Turton*, p. 19.　　　[5] *Ibid.* p. 20.

affording instruction of a really religious kind...which should apply itself to their situation and prospects, and address itself to their feelings. I need hardly say, that in my opinion this weekly service ought to be purely voluntary....'[1]

My reason for thinking that our daily services might be omitted altogether, without any material detriment to religion, is simply that, as far as my means of observation extend, with an immense majority of our congregation it is not a religious service at all, and that to the remaining few it is the least impressive and edifying that can well be conceived. No one could reasonably expect the case to be otherwise with a compulsory service exacted from a body of young men under such circumstances....[2]

As to any other purposes, foreign to those of religion, which may be answered by these services, I have here no concern with them. I know that it is sometimes said that the attendance at chapel is essential to discipline: but I have never been able to understand what kind of discipline is meant: whether it is a discipline of the body, or of the mind, or of the heart and affections. As to the first, I am very sensible of the advantage of early rising: but I should think this end might be attained by a much less circuitous process: and I suppose that it will hardly be reckoned among the uses of our evening service, that it sometimes proves a seasonable interruption to intemperate gaiety.[3] But I confess that the word discipline, applied to this subject, conveys to my mind no notions which I would not wish to banish: it reminds me either of a military parade, or of the age when we were taught to be *good* at church.[4]

Cambridge was not yet ripe for sentiments so liberal as these, and Thirlwall paid the price of his imprudence. His pamphlet had been published on May 21, 1834; on May 25 there appeared an answer from Whewell, as Tutor of the College; on May 26 the Master, Dr Wordsworth, invited him to resign his Assistant

[1] *Ibid.* p. 33.　　　　　[2] *Ibid.* p. 20.
[3] 'I cannot but deeply regret, that...Mr Stanley...is reported to have spoken with scorn of the notion that our students should be summoned immediately from their convivial meetings to their religious services.* [*Lord Palmerston is reported to have expressed a similar opinion.]...I must beg him to recollect, that the observances do not come in a capricious and unexpected manner; that the interruption not only may be looked for, but must be foreseen as a matter of course....'—W. Whewell, *Remarks on some parts of Mr Thirlwall's Letter* (1834), pp. 13–15.
[4] *Letter to Turton*, p. 22.

RELIGION IN THE UNIVERSITY

Tutorship. Thirlwall complied, under protest. The story has been told in J. Willis Clark's *Old Friends at Cambridge and elsewhere* (1900), pp. 109–27, and in chapter v of J. C. Thirlwall's *Connop Thirlwall: Historian and Theologian* (1936). But for us the really interesting feature of Thirlwall's pamphlet is that it attacked the compulsory Chapel service only because it was compulsory, and not because it was indecorous. '...My opinion on this subject does not at all depend on the degree of outward decorum with which these ceremonies are conducted. In this respect there is, as far as my own observation goes, very little to complain of: indeed scarcely anything to amend. But if this decorum were to be carried to the highest perfection, as it might easily be, if it should ever become a mode and a point of honour with the young men themselves, the thing itself would not rise one step in my estimation. I should still think, that the best which could be said of it, would be, that at the end it leaves everyone as it found him, and that the utmost religion could hope from it, would be to suffer no incurable wounds.'[1]

Thirlwall here admitted that this outward decorum was not yet 'a mode and a point of honour with the young men themselves', and ample corroboration of this point will be found in. vol. i of *Alma Mater, or Seven Years at the University of Cambridge*, by a Trinity-Man (1827).[2] Yet 'as a general rule', wrote J. Willis Clark, looking back on his own undergraduate days at Trinity (1851–56), 'everybody behaved with propriety. "Iniquity Corner", as the space at the east end on each side of the altar was called, may occasionally have effectually sheltered card-playing; but when a young snob went so far as to light a

[1] *Letter to Turton*, p. 21.
[2] By J. M. F. Wright.—'As things now go, there is not one man who goes to *pray*—not even amongst the saints or Simeonites. In the morning they muster, with all the reluctance of a man going to be hanged; and in the evening, although now awake, and enlivened with the convivialities of the bottle, there is much the same feeling. They contrive, however, when once assembled, not only to lose sight of the ostensible object for which they are called together, but also of the disagreeable necessity of thus congregating. Table-talk is much more abundant here than "at table"—there being no other occupation, and the wine having by this time sufficiently (in many cases overmuch) warmed the imagination....' (*Alma Mater*, vol. i, p. 33.)—Wright was admitted to Trinity as a sizar, Sept. 1813: matriculated 1814: scholar 1818: B.A. 1819. He was thus a contemporary of Beverley.

cigar thoro he had the pleasure of finishing it in the country, for he was rusticated. It was on a cognate occasion in Jesus College, in which cobblers' wax played a prominent part, that Dr Corrie dismissed the culprit, after a severe lecture, with these admirable words: "Your conduct, sir, is what a Christian would call profane, and a gentleman vulgar."[1] But there was still room for improvement in respect of the attendance of the Fellows. On February 7, 1838, the Master and Seniors of Trinity College published an order, requiring all undergraduates to 'attend Chapel eight times at the least in every week, that is twice on Sunday and once every other day', and breathing threats of rustication. The undergraduates were very angry, and a deputation of scholars waited on Carus, the Senior Dean, who incautiously employed the highly dangerous argument that attendance at Chapel was not so much a duty as a privilege, which was valued the most by those who were oldest and therefore best qualified to form an opinion on the subject. Accordingly the young men retaliated by forming a Society for the Prevention of Cruelty to Undergraduates, which tabulated the weekly attendance of the Fellows at Chapel during the remainder of the Lent Term, and finally published a list, in which the Fellows were arranged in four classes, after the manner of a College Examination: two were not classed at all: Whewell himself was placed in the middle of the Second Class, having obtained only 34 marks: the Deans, being obliged, in virtue of their office, to attend twice daily, were disqualified from obtaining 'the Prize Medal for regular attendance at Chapel and good conduct when there', which was therefore awarded to Mr Perry, afterwards Bishop of Melbourne, who, with 66 attendances to his credit, 'was only 18 marks below the highest number which he could possibly have gained. It is, therefore, to be hoped Mr P. will be more regular and do still better next term.' The 'Prize Medal' took the form of a large family Bible, bound in calf, stamped with the arms and supporters assumed by the Society (the arms of the College supported by two undergraduates in knee breeches waving their caps, and with the motto *Nemo me*

[1] '*J*', by A. E. Shipley, p. 38.

impune lacessit), and suitably inscribed: 'From the Undergraduates of Trinity College to the Rev. Charles Perry, M.A., as a mark of affection and esteem for the good example which he set them and the *rest* of the College by his constant attendance at Chapel.' It was secured for the College Library in 1906.[1] But, obviously, the whole atmosphere was entirely different from what it had been thirty years before, when the writer in *The Satirist* penned his malignant, and no doubt distorted, picture of the religious exercises of a Cambridge College:

> The chapel itself exhibits a scene of the most disgusting and disgraceful indecency. The Dean generally goes through the first part of the service to a single auditor. Towards the beginning of the first lesson 'the students come in right frisky'; some running, some laughing, and some staggering. The lessons are not unfrequently read by a drunken scholar, who is either too blind to read what is before him, or too much inclined to v-m-t to pronounce what he can read. The rest of the men are, perhaps, in the mean time, employed in tossing the candles at each other, in talking obscenity, or in d-mn-ng the Dean, the chapel, and the Master. Those who are not engaged in any of these amusements, and who are neither asleep nor *catting* in a corner, are usually employed in reading F[anny] H[ill], the Age of Reason, the Barouche Driver and his Wife, or some other *delicate* and *fashionable* production.[2]

And in his biographical memoir, written in 1813, Simeon himself declared: 'The service in our chapel has almost at all times been very irreverently performed.'[3] He himself apparently

---

[1] The fullest account of this episode is in W. W. Rouse Ball's *Cambridge Papers* (1918), ch. iv. Cf. also '*J*', pp. 36–8. On Bishop Perry, *vide* George Goodman, *The Church in Victoria during the episcopate of Bishop Perry* (1892), p. 33 ff.: W. J. Conybeare, *Essays Ecclesiastical and Social* (1855), pp. 71–3.
[2] *The Satirist*, May 1808, vol. ii, pp. 248–9.
[3] Carus, p. 10.—Cf. *Strictures upon the Discipline of the University of Cambridge* (1792), p. 12: 'The service is frequently performed in that slovenly manner, which reflects equal disgrace upon the minister, and upon those, who, by their absence, may be said to connive at it.'—Cf. also *Remarks on Dr Vincent's Defence of Public Education*, by a Layman (1802), p. 39: 'Though piety, whim, or affectation, might make a few casual exceptions, the usual manner of performing the service, was, from all I have observed and heard, calculated to produce the worst effects; to alienate the young from pious attendance on public worship, and to teach them to contemn their Superiors, who so openly made a mock of their holy profession. For children will notice the actions of the full grown, and the profligate object to clergymen the neglect of the clerical character.'

seldom if ever went near the place as a Fellow;[1] although he knew enough about the fabric to be able to explain it to Mr Joseph Farington, R.A., and to impart to him some curious and interesting information. 'He told me he had lately compared the size of it with the dimensions of Noah's Ark as given in the Scripture, and found that the Ark was twice the length, and twice the breadth, and two-thirds the height of the Chapel.'[2]

The services in King's Chapel when he came up as a freshman were as follows:

On every day throughout the year (excepting the Sabbath and holy days) divine service is performed in the Chapel three times. In the morning twice. Early prayers are read at a quarter before seven, intended chiefly for the Scholars. There is likewise cathedral service at ten; and cathedral service at five in the afternoon. On Sundays and Saints days, there is only cathedral service in the morning at eight: and at four in the afternoon. On the eves too of these days the service is at four in the afternoon. But if on Sunday or other holy day the sacrament is to be administered, there is cathedral service and a sermon at ten.

On the twenty-fifth day of March, at eleven in the morning, (which is a grand feast in honour of the Virgin Mary, to whom the Chapel is dedicated) a sermon is preached in the Chapel by one of the Fellows of the College; which the whole University, instead of going to St Mary's church, as usual, on that day attends.[3]

There does not in general appear to have been much preaching in the College Chapels. Sermons appear to have been delivered regularly on Sacrament Days: Hall, in his *Letter to R. M. Beverley, Esq.* (1834), states that 'the sacrament is always preceded by the prayers and a sermon. The sermon is usually one peculiarly adapted to the occasion':[4] and in some cases—at

---

[1] 'He never attends the *College Chapel*.' (*Farington Diary*, vol. vii, Oct. 7, 1814, p. 280.) Cf. *Life in the Old Court, King's College, Cambridge, 1822–25* [by W. H. Tucker], printed in *Etoniana*, Nos. 32–5 (March–Nov., 1923), p. 514: 'I never once saw him in our Chapel.'—Cf. also Simeon to the Rev. E. Edwards (Oct. 24, 1798): '...my attention to my work is so unintermitted as to leave me no time to see a friend, to write a letter, to go into Chapel twice a week as Dean [of Divinity], or scarcely to eat my dinner. I scarcely ever go to hall, and I intend to give up my office, and take a Bursarship instead' (Carus, p. 165).

[2] *Farington Diary*, ed. James Greig, vol. iii, Sept. 13, 1805, p. 107.

[3] *An Account of King's College-Chapel, in Cambridge....* By Henry Malden, Chapel-Clerk (1769), p. 62. [4] *Op. cit.* p. 27.

Sidney Sussex, for example—this was demanded by the statutes. Milner at Queens' preached regularly on Good Friday.[1] But the evidence is very scanty. Romilly's diary speaks of the introduction of a Sunday sermon, twice a term, in Trinity College Chapel: that was in 1856, and he says that this was already in operation 'at Corpus, King's, Queens', Jesus and Clare, I think'.[2] The experiment had been tried at Trinity earlier in the century, but had proved such a dismal failure that it was given up after two terms. Assuming Romilly to be correct, the custom seems also to have lapsed at King's, for it was revived 'after long years of silence' when Austen Leigh was Dean (1871–73).[3]

In Simeon's time, however, it was assumed that members of the University would attend the University Sermon at Great St Mary's. The assumption does not appear to have borne any very close relation to the facts. 'It is not reckoned fashionable', wrote the author of *Ten Minutes Advice to Freshmen* (1785), 'to go to *St Mary's*, on a Sunday.—But I know no harm in going, nor that it is any reproach to a man's understanding to be seen publickly in the same place with the most dignified and respectable persons of the University.—To say nothing about the regularity of the thing, and its being approved of by people whose good opinion you may be desirous to obtain.'[4] Attendance had at one time been compulsory, and enforced by the not inconsiderable fine of sixpence.[5] But now the anonymous author of *Remarks on the Enormous Expence in the Education of Young Men in the University of Cambridge* (1788) could very properly

[1] *Life of Milner*, p. 658. [2] *Vide* Appendix A.
[3] *Augustus Austen Leigh: A Record of College Reform*, by W. Austen Leigh (1906), pp. 121, 188.
[4] *Op. cit.* pp. 32–3.—Cf. *Remarks on the Rev. Dr Vincent's Defence of Public Education*, by a Layman (1802), p. 39: 'Those went who liked it. I speak largely if I say I heard there five sermons, that I could wish to hear again.'
[5] 'We can scarcely be surprised to find that the less well-disposed took occasion to manifest their impatience of such compulsion by inattention and levity. A manifesto on the part of the authorities in the year 1602, directed against the prevailing license, animadverts upon the "uncumly hemminge and hawkinge at holie exercises and at the preaching of God's word".'— J. B. Mullinger, *The University of Cambridge from the Royal Injunctions of 1535 to the accession of Charles I* (=vol. ii: 1884), pp. 428–9.

complain that 'Another shameful Piece of Neglect in the University is, its not compelling its Undergraduates, of what Rank or Description soever, to attend the public Sermon at Saint Mary's, Morning and Afternoon. The Neglect shown to this public Duty of the Sabbath is highly offensive in the Eye of Decency: Derogatory from the Honour of the University, and what is of infinitely greater Consequence, from the Honour of God. Nor would I have the Attendance on the Sunday Sermon alone insisted on, but that of the Holydays also, and with equal Strictness: Which, independent of every Motive of Piety, would, as being at Eleven o'Clock, so divide the Morning, as to render the going out on Horseback less possible, and the going to Hunt utterly impracticable.'[1]

The University Church can seldom have been so deserted on a Sunday morning as when Gray wrote to Mason (April 23, 1757): 'the D: of Bedford has brought his Son [to settle him at Trinity], ay, & Mr Rigby too. they were at Church on Sunday morning, and Mr Sturgeon preach'd to them & the Heads, for no body else was present.'[2] Yet it is notable that Wakefield's 'friend M R. TYRWHITT once proposed a *grace*, either that the *Undergraduates* should be compelled to attend the sermons at *St Mary's*, or that those sermons should be abolished': he did not succeed, however, in finding 'more than *six* or *seven* abettors', although these included the Provost of King's (Dr Cooke) and Dr Hey.[3] And Wakefield also pertinently enquires: 'Now what can be conceived more disgraceful to the *University*, than for strangers to go into the church on a *Saint's* day, and see the preacher exhibiting only to the *Vice-Chancellor*, the *beadle*, *Mr Blue-Coat*,[4] and the WALLS?'[5] On Sundays the attendance was doubtless not so bad, even although 'the common ex-

[1] *Op. cit.* pp. 20–1.
[2] *Correspondence of Thomas Gray*, ed. W. Paget Toynbee and Leonard Whibley (1935), vol. ii, p. 500.—Roger Sturgeon, a former Fellow of Caius, was Master of the Perse School, 1751–9.
[3] Wakefield, pp. 145–6.
[4] The University Marshal.—'...that worthy Magistrate, the Man-in-Blew', Gray to Wharton, Dec. 27, 1743 (*Correspondence of Thomas Gray*, vol. i, p. 220: cf. 'Blew-Coat', *ibid.* vol. i, p. 323). *Vide* art. '*The Man-in-Blew*', by Dr H. P. Stokes, in the *Cambridge Review*, May 6, 1927.
[5] Wakefield, p. 146.

hibitioners...were the *hack* preachers, employed in the service of defaulters and absentees. A piteous unedifying tribe!

"From eloquence and learning far remov'd
As from the centre thrice to th' utmost pole."[1]

Yet it is also clear that certain names would always draw a congregation. There was, for example, the Rev. James Scott, D.D., Fellow of Trinity, who 'frequently occupied the University pulpit' between 1761 and 1771, 'and whenever he preached', says his biographer, 'St Mary's was crowded; the parts of the Church appropriated to the University were filled. Noblemen, bishops, heads of houses, professors, tutors, masters of arts, undergraduates, all attended St Mary's to hear this celebrated preacher. The inhabitants of the town expressed the same eagerness; for in hearing Mr Scott, their understandings were informed, and their affections captivated. The discourses addressed to the University are in general uninteresting, the matter studiously abstruse, and the delivery of it unimpassioned and lifeless. Mr Scott, therefore, deviated altogether from the usual mode of preaching: the subjects of his discourses attracted attention, the discussion of them awakened the feelings, and the elocution of the preacher delighted and fascinated the hoary sage, the ingenuous youth, and the unlettered Christian.'[2] At a slightly later period, it is obvious that Professor Marsh was also a great draw; and so was Simeon, in the latter half of his life.[3]

Indeed, at the turn of the century a great improvement appears to have set in.[4] 'Let [the reader] enter the University Church at the hour of service', wrote Sedgwick in 1834, 'and he may sometimes see six or seven hundred Undergraduates in the performance of a voluntary worship, and hanging with deep

[1] Wakefield, p. 97.
[2] *A Sketch of the Life of the Author*, by S. Clapham, in *Sermons on Interesting Subjects*, by the late Rev. James Scott, D.D. (1816), pp. v–vi.
[3] '...at this moment *there is not a more popular man in the whole* University, than the Venerable Minister of Trinity Church; and when he preaches before the University, there is not a master of a college, nor a master of arts, nor a professor, nor an undergraduate absent, who can possibly be present.' F. R. Hall, *Letter to R. M. Beverley*, p. 36. Cf. Moule, pp. 95, 168, 240.
[4] Except, however, as regards the saints'-day sermons, which continued to be preached to empty benches. Hall, *op. cit.* p. 22.

attention on the accents of the preacher.'[1] The Rector of Fulbourn was even more emphatic. '*The more impressive the preacher is, the more he is attended.* When a clergyman preaches, whose sermons are more searching than sermons sometimes are, St Mary's is crowded from one end to the other, and frequently half an hour before the time; and many an undergraduate goes away, not finding room to stand in. And though two thousand persons are in the church, you might hear a pin fall.'[2] 'Of the afternoon preachers at St Mary's, since the halcyon days of Benson,' writes Appleyard in 1828, 'Rose, Le Bas, and Graham, are decidedly the most popular.'[3] Other lists speak of Benson, Chevallier, Blunt, and Rose;[4] of Bishops Marsh, Kay, Maltby, and of Simeon, Benson, Musgrave, Rose, Le Bas, Lee, Scholefield, Chevallier, Blunt, Evans, Thorp, Whewell, Melvill.[5]

The congregation, if large, was not uncritical. '*There is very great attention paid by the undergraduates to the style of preaching. None but the modern school of preachers are tolerated by them.* Should a preacher, at all resembling those you [Beverley] describe,[6] be known to be about to preach at the University church, they would go in crowds to the other churches.'[7] There was also a more traditional, if a less courteous, method of

---

[1] Sedgwick, *Four Letters*, p. 47. The *Letter to R. M. Beverley* by an Undergraduate also speaks of 'the crowded galleries of St Mary's' (p. 15).
[2] F. R. Hall, *Letter to R. M. Beverley*, p. 24 *n.*
[3] *Letters from Cambridge*, p. 115.
[4] *Letter to H. R. H. Frederick, Duke of Gloucester*, p. 15: duplicated in *Letter to R. M. Beverley...*, by an Undergraduate, p. 13.
[5] Sedgwick, *Four Letters*, p. 46.—Of these, Benson, Chevallier, J. J. Blunt, and Henry John Rose had all discharged the office of Hulsean Lecturer, or Christian Preacher. On the Rev. John Hulse's benefaction, *vide* Christopher Benson's *Hulsean Lectures for 1820* (the first to be delivered upon this foundation), pp. i–ii, 10–53; *Memoir of Hulse, with extracts from his will,* prefixed to Richard Parkinson's *Rationalism and Revelation* (Hulsean Lectures for 1837), pp. xv–xlvii; *Admissions to the College of St John the Evangelist, Cambridge*, pt. iii, ed. R. F. Scott, pp. 374–6; *Endowments of the University*, ed. J. Willis Clark (1904), pp. 117–21.
[6] 'The general style of preaching, excepting always the sermons of the Evangelical party, is dry, profitless, dull, and anti-Christian. The Gospel is quite unknown, and indeed is rarely ever alluded to. They preach about virtue and justification by good works, a little against enthusiasm, a good deal about subordination and the duty of being a Tory....There is, however, nothing like eloquence to recommend their bad doctrine. Their heathenism is too insipid to be palatable.' R. M. Beverley, *Letter to H.R.H. the Duke of Gloucester*, pp. 21–2.
[7] F. R. Hall, *Letter to R. M. Beverley*, p. 24 *n.*

registering disapproval, and it is one that still survives in the Universities of North Britain: namely, *scraping*. This is defined in Grose's *Classical Dictionary of the Vulgar Tongue* (3rd ed. 1796) as 'A mode of expressing dislike to a person, or sermon, practised at Oxford by the students, in scraping their feet against the ground during the preachment; frequently done to testify their disapprobation of a proctor who has been, as they think, too rigorous'. The custom was not, however, peculiar to Oxford, for there is mention of it in the *Gradus ad Cantabrigiam* (1803 and 1824), accompanied by the interesting note: 'SCRAPING seems to have been of great antiquity. In one of Hugh Latimer's sermons, preached before King Edward the Sixth, is the following passage: "Et loquentem eum audierunt in silentio, et seriem lectionis non interrumpentes. They heard him, saith hee, (Chrysostom,) in silence; not interrupting the order of his preaching. He meanes, they heard him quietly, without any SHOVELING feete." (*Fruitful Sermons*, 4to, 1635. B.L.).'[1]

The last recorded application of this mode of protest in Great St Mary's would appear to have been on Advent Sunday, Nov. 30, 1828, when Julius C. Hare 'disregarded the usual limits of time' and preached for an hour and twenty minutes on 'The Children of Light'. It may however have been some consolation to him that more than two hundred undergraduates petitioned him afterwards to print his sermon.[2] No such consolation was administered to the Rev. John Wilgress, Fellow of Pembroke, who in November 1773, at the height of the Subscription controversy, preached what Jebb described as 'a most papistical sermon....He attacked the latitudinarians vehemently, and maintained that the liberty of private opinions rent the church of Christ, and made as many creeds as persons....The young men were offended at him for his behaviour as proctor, and therefore SCRAPED him. When the sermon was over, the

[1] *Op. cit.* ['by a Brace of Cantabs'] (ed. 1803), p. 118.
[2] Todhunter's *Whewell*, vol. i, p. 40; *Life, Journals and Letters of Henry Alford, D.D., Dean of Canterbury*, 3rd ed. 1874 ('...tremendous long sermon, one hour twenty minutes, men scraped with their feet'), p. 36; 'T.S.' in the *Guardian*, March 22, 1882, p. 429.

vice-chancellor, called (to the) proctors, to take the names of all the gentlemen in one of the galleries. On this, there was a general hiss, and many rushed out before the door could be secured. At length, the bishop of Peterborough, the two proctors, and the vice-chancellor, arrived at the foot of the stair-case. The young men made a push, and broke the door off its hinges, and multitudes escaped. The names of the rest were taken, and a meeting of the heads followed; but, as all were guilty, all escaped unpunished. Such indecency was never seen, and they will have riots upon riots, unless some scheme is thought of to employ the active spirits of young men.'[1]

Even the Rev. James Scott, for all his popularity, had had a taste of the same medicine on June 21, 1767, when he preached a powerful sermon against gaming which was very much resented by the undergraduates: but he retorted by preaching on the following Sunday from Eccles. v. 1: '*Keep thy foot, when thou goest to the house of God....*'

No sooner was the text pronounced, than the galleries were in an uproar; but Mr Scott, so far from being either overcome by affright, or rouzed to indignation, calmly requested the Vice-chancellor to preserve silence. This, by the interposition of the Proctors, was at length effected, when the preacher delivered a discourse so eloquent, appropriate, and impressive, as to excite universal admiration.'[2]

Thirlwall in his *Letter to Turton* observes significantly that among the principal means by which religion was communicated to the undergraduates he ranked 'the social worship, not of our chapels, but of our churches'.[3] For this assertion there was plenty of corroborative evidence. 'To whichever party the clergy may belong, their churches are well filled.'[4] 'The number of Bachelors and Undergraduates resident at Cambridge during full term may be estimated between fourteen and fifteen hundred,

---

[1] *Memoirs of the life of the Author*, by John Disney, D.D., F.S.A., in Jebb's *Works* (1787), vol. i, pp. 57–8: cf. Wakefield's *Memoirs*, pp. 111–13 ('I myself was one of the offending gallery; but whether an offender or not, I will not say, for I do not recollect; though too prone to mischiefs of that nature').

[2] Clapham's *Sketch of the Life of the Author* in Scott's *Sermons on Interesting Subjects*, pp. vi–vii. The sermon against gaming is included in this selection (Sermon xi, pp. 181–96).

[3] *Op. cit.* p. 18.   [4] Hall, p. 25.

and at most of the Colleges they are expected to be present at the chapel service twice on the Sunday. Nevertheless the usual number of men of these two orders who voluntarily give their attendance at the University Church is about seven hundred, and often amounts to above a thousand; while those who attend at the various parish churches in the town may be reckoned beyond the larger number, though here it must be remembered that the same individual often enters into both calculations.'[1] Even more impressive, because utterly impartial, is the testimony afforded by Appleyard's *Letters from Cambridge* (1828): 'the churches...are very numerous, and extremely well attended, both morning and afternoon, which is the more creditable to the feelings of the students, as, with the exception of the afternoon preacher at St Marys, Mr Chevalier (*sic*) at St Andrews, and perhaps the eccentric, but pious, Simeon, there is no minister effective enough to attract hearers for his own sake alone. I had forgotten—there is one more who would not suffer in comparison with the most brilliant of his contemporaries,—Mr Professor Scholefield....' (To these names, an editorial footnote adds that of 'Mr Melville of Peter-house, occasional preacher at Little St. Mary's, very eloquent, very impressive, and very sensible.') '...There is a night service at two or three of the churches. This is best attended, particularly at little St Mary's (*sic!*), where Mr Simeon holds forth extempore to an attentive auditory.... These are all that are worth while noticing; but if you have a taste for sound divinity, and like the vigorous reasoning of Tillotson and others of the old school, you may be sure to meet with them, a little masqueraded perhaps, at any of the other churches which you are disposed to visit....'[2]

Certainly in the Town, the Evangelicals dominated the situation. According to J. F. Russell,[3] 'of the *twelve* parish

---

[1] Letter signed 'An Undergraduate', *Leeds Mercury*, April 26, 1834.
[2] *Op. cit.* pp. 112–18.
[3] *Letter to the Rt. Hon. Henry Goulburn*, p. 13.—Of these six churches, five are readily identified, viz. Holy Trinity (Simeon: instituted 1782, St Giles' with St Peter's (Farish, 1800), St Bene't's (John Lamb, D.D., Master of Corpus, 1824), St Michael's (Prof. Scholefield, 1823), and St Sepulchre's (R. R. Faulkner, 1825: plaintiff in the celebrated Stone Altar Case, 1845). In the following year (1834) Thomas Webster, a son-in-law of Scott of Aston Sandford, succeeded a scandalous old ruffian as Rector of St Botolph's.

INTERIOR OF TRINITY CHURCH, CAMBRIDGE, IN 1830

From J. and H. S. Storer, *Illustrations of the University of Cambridge*,
second series

churches in which regular duty is performed, *six* ' were at their entire disposal, while the pulpit of a seventh (Great St Mary's) was occupied in the evening by the curate of the parish [William Carus], who was also lecturer at Trinity Church. ('Of the remaining five, one [St Andrew the Great] is hallowed by the graceful and sacred eloquence of the classical CHEVALLIER; another [St Edward's], by the soul-subduing pathos of the present Hulsean lecturer [Henry John Rose], who well deserves to rank among our modern Herberts—and...in *no* place of the same size are the parochial duties so ably and completely performed as in the...town of Cambridge.') But as yet, if Beverley may be believed—and on this point he was not contradicted—the Evangelicals, or serious Christians, although 'a powerful party', did not predominate in the University: there the High Church party was still 'the most numerous of all'.[1]

But on all hands a most remarkable improvement had taken place in the past thirty years, and a great deal of it may be attributed, directly or indirectly, to the influence of Simeon's fervour and persistence. Before his time, 'only *Dr Ogden*, the minister of the Round Church, and *a few others*, preached in the style that is now deservedly *popular* in the University'.[2] To-day Samuel Ogden is perhaps remembered chiefly as the author of the classic observation on a goose—'The goose is a silly bird,— too much for one, and not enough for two'—and of a memorable letter to the Prime Minister, soliciting some piece of ecclesiastical patronage, which began as follows: 'The great are always liable to importunity; those who are both good and great are liable to a double portion.'[3] 'However, he was always unsuccessful in his applications for preferment. It was only his

—Cf. with this Wesley's *Journal*, Monday, Dec. 20, 1784: 'I went to Hinxworth, where I had the satisfaction of meeting Mr Simeon, Fellow of King's College, in Cambridge.... He gave me the pleasing information that there are three parish churches in Cambridge wherein true scriptural religion is preached, and several young gentlemen who are happy partakers of it' (vol. vii, pp. 39–40): the three churches were presumably Holy Trinity (Simeon), St Edward's (Atkinson), and St Sepulchre's (Coulthurst: not St Giles', as stated by Moule, p. 102). Cf. Berridge to Benjamin Mills, Nov. 20, 1784 (*Congreg. Mag.* March, 1838, p. 163).
[1] *Letter to H.R.H. the Duke of Gloucester*, pp. 21, 28.
[2] F. R. Hall, p. 35.   [3] Gunning, vol. i, pp. 215, 216.

reputed wealth that made him a *produceable* man, for he was singularly uncouth in his manner, and spoke his mind very freely upon all occasions.'[1] But as a preacher he excelled.[2]

His person, manner, and character of composition, were exactly suited to each other. He exhibited a large black, scowling, *grizly* figure, a ponderous body with a lowering visage, embrowned by the horrors of a *sable periwig*. His voice was growling, and morose; and his sentences desultory, tart, and snappish.

His sermons are interspersed with remarks, eminently brilliant and acute, but too epigrammatic in their close. They display that perfect propriety and purity of English diction, that chastized terseness of composition, which have scarcely been equalled by any writer. Like *Cicero* he wants nothing to *complete* his meaning; like *Demosthenes* he can suffer no *deduction* without essential injury to the sentence. He was a good scholar, a liberal-minded Christian, and an honest man.[3]

Gunning records that 'from the singularity of Dr Ogden's manner, as well as of his matter, he was very popular in the pulpit: he preached at the Round Church, which was always crowded.'[4] His tenure of the pulpit at St Sepulchre's lasted from 1753 to 1778.[5] 'When his stock of sermons became large, he did not hesitate to preach them over again periodically; nevertheless, he is said to have adhered constantly to the rule of composing a new one, to be delivered on the first Sunday of every month.'[6]

His published sermons, especially the famous course on *Prayer*,[7] were much admired by Dr Johnson: and the recovery of the original manuscript of Boswell's *Journal of a Tour to the Hebrides* has restored to history that memorable scene at Iona

[1] Gunning, vol. i, p. 216.
[2] He is stated to have been the favourite preacher of King George III. (*D.N.B.*)   [3] Wakefield, *Memoirs* (2nd ed. 1804), vol. i, pp. 95–6.
[4] Gunning, vol. i, pp. 218–19.—He 'was constantly attended by a numerous audience, consisting principally of the younger members of the University' (Samuel Hallifax, preface to Ogden's *Sermons*, 5th ed. 1814, p. iv).
[5] He also held the livings of Stansfield, Suffolk, and Lawford, Essex, in addition to the Woodwardian Professorship of Geology, to which he was appointed in 1764.
[6] *Sermons by the Rev. Samuel Ogden, D.D.*, ed. T. S. Hughes (1832), p. v.
[7] *On the Efficacy of Prayer and Intercession.*—Cf. Boswell's *Life of Johnson* (ed. G. Birkbeck Hill, revised by L. F. Powell, 1934, vol. iii, p. 248): *Tuesday 7 April* 1778.—BOSWELL. 'I like Ogden's Sermons on Prayer very much, both for neatness of style and subtilty of reasoning.' JOHNSON. 'I should like to read all that Ogden has written.

on Wednesday, Oct 20, 1773, when Boswell stole away before breakfast into the ruined cathedral, and, after offering up his adorations to God and invoking the heavenly intercessions of 'Saint Columbus', 'read with an audible voice the fifth chapter of St James, and Dr Ogden's tenth sermon. I suppose there has not been a sermon preached in this church since the Reformation. I had a serious joy in hearing my voice, while it was filled with Ogden's admirable eloquence, resounding in the ancient cathedral of Icolmkill.'[1]

Yet it may well be doubted whether the piety of Dr Ogden would have proved entirely satisfying or congenial to the young Charles Simeon. Ogden was a divine of the old school, and too much conformed to this world. 'One of his singularities was a fondness for good cheer, with an excessive appetite; and his failing, an immoderate indulgence of it.'[2] Upon such a failing, Simeon's judgment was likely to have been severe.[3] In any case, Ogden died on March 22, 1778, ten months before Simeon came up. He was succeeded in his pulpit by his friend and admirer, Dr Hallifax, afterwards Bishop of St Asaph, who 'affected his tone and manner of delivery, but did not succeed in attracting so numerous a congregation'.[4]

Of the other preachers of the town, apart from Robinson, the Baptist minister, then at his prime, I find no record: but it can hardly be without significance that it was long before Charles Simeon succeeded in finding a spiritual anchorage. 'I had endeavoured to find out some minister who preached those truths which I loved and delighted in; and I attended at St Mary's for a long time but to little purpose. At last I heard Mr A[tkinson] at St Edward's; and he came nearer to the truth than anyone else that I could hear. I therefore, from the time that I became a Fellow of King's, attended regularly at his church.'[5]

---

[1] *Boswell's Journal of A Tour to the Hebrides with Samuel Johnson, LL.D.* Now first published from the original manuscript, ed. F. A. Pottle and C. H. Bennett (1936), p. 336.
[2] Wakefield, p. 97 n.
[3] Although Simeon himself, according to W. H. Tucker, had 'one weakness—openly confessed and deplored by his disciples—a tendency towards the pleasures of the table'. (*Life in the Old Court, King's College, Cambridge, 1822–25,* in *Etoniana,* No. 33, pp. 514–15.)
[4] Gunning, vol. i, p. 219. [5] Carus, p. 21.

Christopher Atkinson, Tutor of Trinity Hall and Curate of St Edward's (1781–5), was brother to the more famous Miles Atkinson of Leeds, and son of the Rev. Christopher Atkinson, who had been one of the original Methodists at Oxford, and a correspondent of Whitefield, the Wesleys, Ingham, Hervey, and the rest.[1] He seems, however, to have been a rather colourless personality, and cuts only a very minor figure in the records of the Evangelical Revival in Cambridge. What Simeon was looking for was a good pastoral clergyman to whom he might turn as guide, philosopher, and friend. This is exceedingly significant, because it explains so much of his subsequent career. As Vicar of Holy Trinity, it was his object to supply to undergraduates what he himself, in his own undergraduate days, had sought in vain: and to successive generations of young men he played precisely that role of guide, philosopher, and friend, which he had so long since envisaged. But this was not the role for which Providence had cast the Rev. Christopher Atkinson.

Being the only gownsman that attended there, I rather wondered that he did not take any notice of me; I thought that if I were a minister, and saw a young gownsman attending as regularly and devoutly as I did, I should invite him to come and see me; and I determined, if he should do so, I would avail myself of the opportunity to get acquainted with him. I longed exceedingly to know some spiritual person who had the same views and feelings with myself; and I had serious thoughts of putting into the papers, as soon as I should be ordained, an advertisement to the following effect: 'That a young Clergyman who felt himself an undone sinner, and looked to the Lord Jesus alone for salvation, and desired to live only to make known that Saviour unto others, was persuaded that there must be some persons in the world whose views and feelings on this subject accorded with his own, though he had now lived three years without finding so much as one; and that if there were any *minister* of that description he would gladly become his curate, and serve him gratis.' At last he did invite me to come and drink tea with him; and invited a Mr D., an artist, to come and meet me. The conversation did not take a useful turn, for Mr D. was not what I should call a religious man; and we parted without any profitable communication of our sentiments.[2]

[1] *Countess of Huntingdon*, vol. i, p. 303.
[2] Carus, p. 22.

However, this was the last of Simeon's disappointments. A few days later he invited Mr Atkinson to sup with him, and (with the curious social unimaginativeness of the eternal undergraduate) asked Mr D. to meet him: but providentially Mr D. could not come,

so that Mr. A. and I were tête-à-tête. I soon dropped some expressions which conveyed the idea of my feeling myself a poor, guilty, helpless sinner; and Mr A. was quite surprized, for he had set it down as a matter of course that I must be a staunch pharisee; he had, even for the whole space of time that I had been at college, noticed my solemn and reverent behaviour at St Mary's, so different from that which is generally observed in that place, and concluded, as three of his pious friends had also done, that I was actuated by a proud pharisaical spirit: when therefore he found that I was of a very different complexion, he manifested an union of heart with me, and introduced me the very next day to an excellent man, my dear friend, Mr John Venn.... Here I found a man after my own heart, a man for whom I have retained the most unfeigned love to his last moments, and of whom I ever shall retain the most affectionate remembrance....[1]

John Venn was two years senior to Simeon, having come up to Sidney as a scholar in 1777. His father, Henry Venn, the great Evangelical vicar of Huddersfield, had intended to enter him at Trinity, but found that 'the tutor and master were disinclined to admit him through fear of Methodism'.[2] He took his Bachelor's degree in January 1781, and stayed on in College with a view to preparing himself for ordination. In May he was unexpectedly passed over for a Fellowship: but he was assured that he would be elected in the following year. On May 29, 1782, he came up again for election: but this time a violent quarrel broke out between two of the Fellows, and the election was deferred. On June 1, while his fate was still hanging in the balance, he and his friend Jowett of Magdalene were invited to drink tea at Mr Atkinson's to meet Mr Simeon of King's, who had been ordained deacon the previous Sunday (Trinity Sunday, May 26), and had volunteered to take charge at St Edward's during the Long Vacation. (The suddenness of this arrangement is a little startling.)

[1] Carus, pp. 22–3.   [2] *Venn Family Annals*, p. 114.

Venn and Simeon took to each other at once, and their new-found friendship ripened with a phenomenal rapidity, even allowing for the fact that Venn was just on the point of going down. Their acquaintance commeneed at Christopher Atkinson's tea-party on Saturday, June 1. From that moment it seemed almost impossible for them to see too much of each other. On June 2, Simeon preached his first sermon at St Edward's, and the same party—Venn, Jowett, Simeon, and Atkinson—again drank tea together. On June 3, Venn called on Simeon and walked with him to Trumpington, and supped with him and Atkinson. On June 4, Simeon and Atkinson drank tea with Venn. On June 6, Venn called on Simeon and walked to Grantchester: it was the same day on which he was notified that the Fellowship election was postponed *sine die*.[1] On June 7, Venn went down for the vacation.

Happily, his home was not far away: for his father had retired from Huddersfield on grounds of health in 1771 and had taken a country living at Yelling, Hunts., some fourteen miles from Cambridge. On June 13 Simeon walked over to visit him, and on the following day Venn rode with Simeon to Everton, a few miles distant, to introduce him to old John Berridge.[2] Young Venn was alone at the Rectory, for his father and the rest of the family were away. This was unfortunate, for Simeon had long been anxious to meet the Rector. Another visit was therefore arranged: and on Tuesday, July 16, 1782, Simeon rode over to Yelling from Cambridge for the day, arriving at 8 o'clock in the morning and not leaving until after 8 o'clock at night.[3]

To resume the thread of Simeon's narrative:

He, Mr J. Venn, soon took me over to Yelling, and introduced me to a man of no ordinary character, his own dear and honoured Father. O what an acquisition was this! In this aged minister I found a father, an instructor, and a most bright example: and I shall have reason to adore my God to all eternity for the benefit of his acquaintance.[4]

[1] *Venn Family Annals*, pp. 120–1.
[2] Carus, pp. 23–4 *n*. (Extract from the Diary of Mr J. Venn.)
[3] Carus, p. 24 *n*.   [4] Carus, p. 23.

so terminated his quest. At last God had led him to the man for whom he had been seeking during the past three years and more.

The pleasure was reciprocal, for on Oct. 9—John Venn had been ordained on the previous Sept. 22,[1] as curate to his father—Henry Venn wrote to his old friend, the Rev. James Stillingfleet: 'He has been over to see me six times within the last three months: he is calculated for great usefulness, and is full of faith and love. My soul is always the better for his visits. Oh to flame, as he does, with zeal, and yet be beautified with meekness!'[2] But the lesson of meekness was one that Simeon had still to learn.

[1] He left Cambridge finally on Dec. 21 (*Venn Family Annals*, p. 121).
[2] Venn, p. 345.

APPENDICES TO CHAPTER III

Appendix A

[Extracts[1] from the Diaries of the Rev. Joseph Romilly (1791–1864): admitted to Trinity College, Cambridge, as a pensioner, 1808: scholar 1810: B.A. 1813: Fellow 1815: M.A. 1816: Registrary of the University, 1832–62. (Cambridge University Library MSS.)]

[1843.] *Sunday the 5th of March.* (Last Sunday we began at Trinity to have the Terminal Sac^t on Sunday;—it used to be on the Th^y after Division.—We have now imitated the rest of the Univ^y in having it on Sunday.—We have a compulsory chapel service at the usual hour of 8, without the Communion:—then at 11 the service begins with the Communion, is followed by a Sermon & concludes with the Sacrament—)....

[1856.] *Wednesday the 3^d of December.*

...Two hours Seniority about various matters:—there is an agitation made about a Sermon in the College Chapel (as they have at Corp, Kings, Queens, Jesus & Clare—I think): we tried the experiment some years ago: it was a failure & broke down after 2 terms:—we have agreed now to try again—on the reduced scale of 2 Sermons per term, one on 1st Sunday at beg^g of term, the other on the Sunday before Sacr^t:—the Dean & Tutors are to be responsible for these sermons:—the Sermon is to be separate from the usual morning service & to be at 11:—so 3 services on these 2 Sundays:— attend^{ce} at 2 out of the 3 compulsory.—...

[1856.] *Thursday the 4th of Dec^r.*

...The College Audit from 10 to ¼ to 2.—After it was over & the Auditor (Denman) gone we discussed...'College Sermons':—2 Seniors (Sedgwick & Mathison) were present who were not at the meeting yesterday....We heard Mathison's very stout objections to the 'Sermon' scheme & abandoned it: Mathison boldly said that he thought it would be very difficult to provide College-Sermons w̄ch would do the youngsters good:—Sedgwick thought that there could be no more hopeful congr^n except the sick in a hospital.—...

---

[1] I am indebted for these references to the Vice-Master of Trinity, Mr D. A. Winstanley.

RELIGION IN THE UNIVERSITY

[1859.] 1^d *Sunday a. Easter—*8th *of May.*

...—Yesterday (at the Seniority) I got the following details concerning the new exper^t (wch began last Term) of having a sermon (with the Communion Service) on Sundays in Chapel at 10½

	Feb. 6	Feb. 13	Feb. 20	Feb. 27	Mar. 6
Preacher	Tayler	Master	Luard	Blore	Lightf^t
1st Morning	250	278	256	227	224
2^d Morning	170	201	200	224	235
Both Serv^s	64	111	62	57	59
Total	356	368	394	394	400

	Mar. 13	Mar. 20	Mar. 27	Apr. 3	Apr. 10
Preacher	Tayler	Ellis	Grote	Clark	Jeremie
1st Morning	276	213	216	195	162
2^d Morning	158	215	219	213	188
Both Serv^s	93	56	56	51	37
Total	341	372	379	357	313

—In the above table Tayler & Ellis were the Senr & Junr Dean: there were 2 Sacr^t Sundays (viz. Feb. 13 & Mar. 13): the Master & the 2 Deans preached 4 of the Sermons: the 3 Tutors (Mathison, Clark & Lightfoot) were to be answerable for the other 6: Mathison had 2 deputies:—the fullest attend^{ce} was on the 6th of March when 400 were present at one or other of the services & 235 heard the Sermon: —the smallest n° who came to the Sermon was on the 6th Sund (Mar. 13) when there were only 158 present.—...

[1859.] *Tuesday the* 11th *of Oct^r.*

...At 10 to Chapel to swear in the new fellows.—We afterwards had a long Seniority....At this Sen^{ty} we agreed to go on with the experiment of Sunday sermons: we also agreed to accept the bust of Tennyson & to place it in the staircase of the Library.—A sealing afterwards in the Chapel, but profitless.—...

RELIGION IN THE UNIVERSITY

From the *Windsor Castle Archives:*

Dr Philpott to General Grey, 23 February 1860.

'Another Grace (No. 3) was opposed, but carried by a large majority. By this Grace the Sunday morning service before the University will be discontinued; and only the afternoon sermon at 2 o'clock will be preached.

It has been thought better to substitute a Sunday morning sermon in every College Chapel where the Students are obliged to attend, instead of the University Sermon which, in point of fact, very few students attended.

Each College will now have a complete morning service in its own Chapel, the sermons being taken by the Master and Fellows in turn.'

Appendix B

[Extract from the MS. notebooks of the late Canon Christopher Wordsworth, sometime Chancellor of Salisbury Cathedral, author of *Social Life at the English Universities in the Eighteenth Century* (1874) and *Scholae Academicae* (1877).]

In May 1868 (?) another noticeable petition was drawn up and presented to the Master and Seniors to the following effect:—

'We, the undersigned Bachelors and Undergraduates of Trinity College, most earnestly desire that there should be a Celebration of the Holy Communion every Sunday morning, and on Ascension Day, before the usual early service, at which all Communicants may receive the Holy Sacrament, kneeling at the Altar-rails, instead of at their seats as at present.

'We also respectfully desire that the present custom of Communicants leaving their names with the Deans should be discontinued.'[1]

The regulation mentioned in the last paragraph of the foregoing petition refers to a custom which had been established, I believe, not as a general Communion Test in the spirit of the seventeenth century, but for the convenience of the College authorities when called upon to give a testimonial to candidates for Holy Orders on behalf of former members of the College. By the time that the graduate

---

[1] This petition lay for signature at the rooms of
   A. Pretor, M.A. (27, Green Street)—M.A. Trin. 1868. Fellow of St
      Catharine's.
   G. F. R. Barker (P, Master's Court).
   C. Hankey (Combination Staircase).
   H. W. S. Kynnersley (O, Master's Court).
At this period the additional court, on the other side of Trinity Street, founded in memory of Dr Whewell, was sometimes called 'Whewell's', sometimes 'The Master's' Court.

required such a document his dean and his tutor might have gone out of residence; regularity at the ordinary services (being then *de rigueur*) was no criterion. The authorities therefore could find nothing better on which to base their opinion of the young man's religious character in his earlier years than this record of regular or irregular communion.

As to another detail mentioned in the same petition I remember when I was a lad, not yet matriculated, visiting Trinity Chapel on Feb. 11, 1866. It happened to be the Quinquagesima Sunday on which Dr Whewell preached that vigorous sermon, on Rev. i. 8, which proved to be his last before his fatal illness.[1] It struck me as a strange custom, that, after administering the Sacrament to those who were kneeling at the massive oaken rails, which enclosed three sides of a square or oblong in front of the lofty baldacchino (which was then flanked by paintings of the Blessed Virgin and St John the Baptist, of whom later frescoes now adorn the western end of the Chapel enclosure), the Master and his assistants, instead of waiting for other communicants to approach, had the sacrarium-doors opened, and went round with paten and chalice, passing among the benches, to the students kneeling at intervals in the long chapel seats. I cannot say with certainty whether this was a relic of the puritan custom, or whether it may not have been the usage from the time of the Royal Founders. . . .

[1] Passages from the Sermon were quoted by (Bp.) J. B. Lightfoot in a memorial sermon on I Cor. xv. 32, which he was too deeply affected to preach beyond the description of Dr Whewell having the blinds raised because 'the sky always seemed to him brighter, when framed by the walls and turrets of our Great Court...that he might look once more on this familiar scene, so fair and pleasant to his eyes'. It was subsequently printed by request.

IV

BERRIDGE OF EVERTON

✠

Sunday, May 31 [1789. At Biggleswade].

... The Doctor now comes Mounted to attend me; and we rode first to see the Doctors Stud, a Brood Mare, a Colt, and a Hackney, and his two Cows; thence over the Sandy Hills to near Everden Church (whence were many people returning from the Evening-Service) where a famous Preacher has been renowned in his Pulpit for many years. His Face appears to me abundant of Honesty, Zeal, and good works: tho' no Disciple of Lavaters there seems as if much useful knowledge were to be acquired from the studying of Physiognomy.—To his Church does the County flock for Instructions, and Consolation: But He is generally term'd a Methodist: and as such held out by the Clergy, as a stumbling Block, and a dangerous Character.

Now what the Title of Methodist is meant to signify I know not; but if these Preachers do restore attention, and congregations within the Churches, and do preach the Word of God, They appear to me as Men most commendable; and as useful to the Nation, by their Opposition to the Church Ministry, as in an opposition of The Minister of the Country, in Parliament; Active Orators keeping Vigilant Observation, and Preventing any Idleness in, or abuse of their authority: and so tending as effactually to the Preservation of our Rights, as these Methodistical Preachers do to the conservation of Religion. They are like military Martinets, who are scoff'd at by the Ignorant, and Indolent, but who preserve the Army from Ruin.

The Torrington Diaries: containing the Tours through England and Wales of the Hon. John Byng (later fifth Viscount Torrington) between the years 1781 and 1794, vol. iv, p. 105.

Chapter Four

BERRIDGE OF EVERTON

IN Pastor Moritz's *Travels, chiefly on foot, through several parts of England, in 1782, described in letters to a friend*,[1] there is an unforgettable description of the writer's introduction to a certain side of academic life. It was a Sunday evening towards the end of June: and Moritz, who had spent the previous night at Nettlebed, a village eighteen miles from Oxford, had counted on breaking his journey at either Dorchester or Nuneham and walking the remaining five or six miles to 'that seat of the muses' on the Monday morning. But Dorchester looked to be 'too fine a place' for him, so he pushed on to Nuneham, only to be treated with what he calls 'unparallelled inhospitality' by the inn-keeper, who refused to give him lodging or even to serve him food, and told him that as he had come so far, he might as well walk on to Oxford.

By this time it was dark, and Moritz was almost dropping with hunger and physical exhaustion. Indeed, in sheer desperation, he was looking for a field in which to sleep, when he heard footsteps behind him, following at a quick pace, by which he was not a little alarmed. His pursuer, however, turned out to be no footpad, but a respectable clergyman of the Church of England, who was returning from his curacy at Dorchester, where he had just been taking duty, and who invited Moritz to accept his company. They conversed agreeably along the road, and finally reached Oxford close on midnight, when Moritz's companion

stopped to take leave of me, and said, he should now go to his college.

And I, said I, will seat myself for the night on this stone-bench, and await the morning, as it will be in vain for me, I imagine, to look for shelter in an house at this time of night.

[1] *Reisen eines Deutschen in England im Jahr 1782. In Briefen an Herrn Oberkonsistorialrath Gedike von Carl Philip Moritz* (Berlin, 1783). Engl. tr. 1795, 'by a Lady': ed. P. E. Matheson (1926), pp. 139–58.

Seat yourself on a stone, said my companion, and shook his head: No! no! come along with me to a neighbouring ale-house, where, it is possible, they mayn't be gone to bed, and we may yet find company. We went on, a few houses further, and knocked at a door....They readily let us in; but how great was my astonishment, when, on our being shown into a room on the left, I saw a great number of clergymen, all with their gowns and bands on, each with his pot of beer before him. My travelling companion

who proved to be a Mr Modd, a Chorister of Magdalen, and subsequently Chaplain of Corpus

introduced me to them, as a German clergyman, whom he could not sufficiently praise, for my correct pronunciation of Latin, my orthodoxy, and my good walking.

I now saw myself, in a moment as it were, all at once transported into the midst of a company, all apparently, very respectable men, but all strangers to me. And it appeared to me extraordinary, that I should, thus at midnight, be in Oxford, in a large company of Oxonian clergy, without well knowing how I had got there. Meanwhile, however, I took all the pains in my power to recommend myself to my company, and, in the course of conversation, I gave them as good an account as I could of our German Universities, neither denying, nor concealing, that, now and then, we had riots and disturbances. 'O we are very unruly here too', said one of the clergymen, and he took a hearty draught out of his pot of beer, and knocked on the table with his hand. The conversation now became louder, more general, and a little confused....

It was indeed a memorable company. There was Mr Modd, and Mr Clerk, who was very facetious, and kept on 'telling us, again and again, that he should still be, at least, a *Clerk*, even though he should never become a *clergyman*', and another Divine, a Mr Caern, who in all emergencies invoked the authority of 'his absent brother, who had already been forty years in the church'. Mr Clerk, whose facetiousness was not always in the best of taste, kept 'starting sundry objections to the Bible'. He began by informing Mr Modd 'that it was said, in the Bible, that God was a *wine-bibber*, and a *drunkard*': at which Mr Modd 'fell into a violent passion, and maintained that it was utterly impossible that any such passage should be found in the Bible', and Mr Caern referred the company to 'his absent brother, who had already been forty years in the church, and must certainly know something of such a passage, if it were in the Bible, but he would venture to lay any wager his brother knew nothing of it.'

Waiter! fetch a Bible! called out Mr Clerk, and a great family Bible was immediately brought in, and opened on the table, among all the beer jugs.

Mr Clerk turned over a few leaves, and in the Book of Judges, 9th chapter, verse xiii, he read, 'Should I leave my wine, which cheareth God and man?'

At this the whole company sat dumb-founded for several minutes, until little Pastor Moritz had an inspiration, and cried out, 'Why, gentlemen! you must be sensible, that is but an allegorical expression!...' 'Why, yes, to be sure,' said Mr Modd and Mr Caern, 'it is an allegorical expression; nothing can be more clear; it is a metaphor, and therefore it is absurd to understand it in a literal sense': and, flushed with their triumph, they drank Pastor Moritz's health in copious tankards.

But Mr Clerk was not done for yet: for he next 'desired them to explain to him a passage in the Prophecy of Isaiah, where it is said, in express terms, that *God is a barber*'. Mr Modd was so enraged at this, that he called *Clerk* an impudent fellow; and Mr *Caern* again still more earnestly referred us to his brother, who had been forty years in the church; and who, therefore, he doubted not, would also consider Mr Clerk an impudent fellow, if he maintained any such abominable notions. Mr Clerk, all this while, sat perfectly composed, without either a smile or a frown; but turning to a passage in Isaiah, chapter vii, v. 20, he read these words:—'In the same day, the Lord shall shave with a razor—the head, and the hair of the feet; and it shall also consume the beard.'

Once more, Mr Modd and Mr Caern sat stunned and confounded; and once more little Pastor Moritz plunged into the breach, observing: 'Why, gentlemen, this is also metaphorical, and it is equally just, strong, and beautiful.' 'Why to be sure it is', rejoined Mr Modd and Mr Caern, both in one breath, at the same time rapping the table with their knuckles: and Pastor Moritz went on to explain the Oriental custom of shaving the beards of one's captives; 'the plain import, then, of this re-markable expression, is nothing more, than that God would deliver the rebellious Jews to be prisoners to a foreign people, who would shave their beards! Aye to be sure it is; any body may see it is; why it is as clear as the day! so it is, rejoined Mr Caern; and my brother, who has been forty years in the church, explains it just as this gentleman does.' The satisfaction was general: Mr Clerk relapsed into a moody silence: and Pastor Moritz's health 'was again *encored*, and drank in strong ale', which he himself did not care for: 'it either intoxicated, or stupefied me; and I do think it overpowers one much sooner than so much wine would'. By this time everybody was a little drunk. At last, when dawn was almost breaking, Mr Modd suddenly exclaimed, 'Damn me, I must read prayers this morning at All-Soul's!' He invited Pastor Moritz to come and see him in the morning, and very politely offered to show the curiosities of Oxford: and so took his leave, whereupon the company broke up: and the good people of the inn—it was, of course, *The Mitre*—with great civility showed Pastor Moritz to 'a very decent bed-chamber'.

It is sad to have to record that he woke next morning with 'so dreadful an head-ach, from the copious and numerous toasts of my jolly and reverend friends, that I could not possibly get up'. However, in the afternoon he was able to make a little promenade: but, probably on account of his 'head-ach', he did not find Oxford 'nearly so beautiful and magnificent' as Mr Modd had led him to expect: indeed, it seemed to him to have 'but a dull and gloomy look'. The only comfort was that his bill was 'not unreasonable'. It is also sad to know that Mr Modd, when he had been appointed Chaplain of Corpus, needed to be admonished by the President and Fellows on the score of drunkenness and other failings.[1]

Such were the sort of men who, in the eighteenth century, discharged the pastoral office in the country villages in the

[1] 'April 8, 1779. Mr Modd, Chaplain of the College, convened before the President, Seniors and Officers, and admonished for his misbehaviour, drunkenness, extravagance, and other irregularities.'—Thomas Fowler, *Corpus Christi* (Oxford College Histories), p. 190.

neighbourhood of either University: good-natured, convivial, and not unlearned men, kindly and conscientious according to their lights—Mr Modd was putting himself to a great deal of trouble to secure provision for the necessitous family of his late parish clerk—yet men who cannot, by the more exacting standards of a later age, be regarded as particularly edifying specimens of their profession: while their conception of a pleasant Sunday evening went far beyond the bounds of that 'holy cheerfulness' (unmarred by any 'spirit of idle jesting or frivolous merriment') which Dr Vaughan regarded as appropriate to 'the Sunday evening of the Clergyman'.[1]

At Cambridge there were several Colleges where supper was served in hall on Sundays: Trinity, until the middle of the nineteenth century, was one of them. In those Colleges where there was no supper, the officiating clergy formed Sunday-evening Clubs, each Club being restricted to the members of that College, who supped together, often in the Combination Room. At St John's there was 'The Curates' Club': at King's, where necks of mutton, cut into chops, composed the only dish provided, the Club was called 'The Neck or Nothing'; under the slightly more decorous title of 'The Samaritan Club' it survived into the 'seventies of last century. At Christ's, the Club was called 'The Apostolic'; the supper was always tripe, dressed in various ways.[2] Apart from Gunning's statement that 'as many of the curates had dined early, and fared but scantily, they enjoyed their supper prodigiously',[3] there appears to be no evidence forthcoming as to the measure of decorum preserved, or lost, on these occasions.

Of the quality of their pastoral ministrations it is possible to speak with more assurance. Dr Edmund Keene, a former Master of Peterhouse, who was translated from the see of Chester to that of Ely in 1771, 'remarked it in a printed charge

---

[1] *Addresses to Young Clergymen*, by C. J. Vaughan, D.D., Master of the Temple (1875), pp. 76–7.
[2] *Reminiscences of the University, Town, and County of Cambridge from the year 1780*, by Henry Gunning, Senior Esquire Bedell (2nd ed. 1855), vol. i, p. 165; Christopher Wordsworth, *Social Life at the English Universities in the XVIIIth Century* (1874), p. 129.
[3] Gunning, vol. i, p. 165.

to his clergy at his first visitation at Cambridge, that the people
round Cambridge have less knowledge of religion than is to be
found in any other part of the kingdom, the other university
adjacencies excepted'.[1] 'The truth is', says Gunning, 'that most
of the churches within ten miles of Cambridge were served by
Fellows of colleges. In some cases the curate hastened back
[after the morning service] to dine in hall; there were others who
undertook two or three services',[2] probably in different parishes,
for, as Bishop Moule explains, 'to expedite the process, a signal
was sometimes concerted between the parson and the clerk; the
hoisting of a flag assured the rider that there was no congregation, and that he might pass on in peace...'.[3] To quote Gunning
again: 'A large portion of Simeon's congregation consisted of
the peasantry from the neighbouring villages, where, with but
few exceptions, the services were performed in a careless
manner; the comfort and ease of the ministers appearing to be
their first consideration. If the Sunday proved wet, Dr Drop
(a cant phrase signifying there was no service) did the duty.'[4]

Some were more scrupulous than others: Gunning is justified
in claiming that Dr Farmer, who had the curacy of Swavesey
until he became Master of Emmanuel, was exemplary, at least in
comparison with most of his contemporaries: for he made a
point of attending in all weathers, began the service punctually,
gave a plain practical sermon, chatted most affably with his
congregation after service, and never failed to send some small
present to such of his poor parishioners as had been kept from
church through illness. He then repaired to the public-house,
where he dined expeditiously on a mutton chop and potatoes.

[1] *Select Works of the Rev. Robert Robinson, of Cambridge*, ed. W. Robinson
(1861), (Memoir) p. xli. *n.*—In 1813, of 140 livings in the diocese of Ely, 45
had resident incumbents (as compared with 70 in 1728); another 17 incumbents (as compared with 34) resided near and performed the duty. There were
also 35 curates, some of whom resided eight, ten, or twelve miles from their
churches. Meanwhile the population had risen from 56,944 to 82,176, and
the values of the livings had increased from £12,719 to £61,474 per annum.
Vide *The Black Book; or, Corruption Unmasked!* (1820), p. 290.
[2] Gunning, vol. i, pp. 164–5.
[3] Moule, p. 10: cf. P. H. Ditchfield, *The Parish Clerk* (1907), p. 15 [Hauxton,
Newton, and Barrington].
[4] Gunning, vol. ii, p. 140. Cf. Alfred Leedes Hunt, *David Simpson and the
Evangelical Revival* (1927), pp. 141–2.

Immediately after the removal of the cloth, his Churchwarden and one or two of the principal farmers made their appearance, to whom he invariably said, 'I am going to read prayers, but shall be back by the time you have made the punch'. Occasionally another farmer accompanied him from church, when pipes and tobacco were in requisition until six o'clock. His horse was then led to the door, and conveyed its master to his rooms by half-past seven. Farmer then put on his slippers and night-cap and went to sleep in his elbow-chair until nine o'clock, when he was woken by his bed-maker, and, resuming his wig, started for the Parlour, where the Fellows were in the habit of assembling on a Sunday evening.[1] Comberton, again, was doubly fortunate in the ministry, first of William Unwin, the friend of Cowper, and then, in succession to him, of William Bennet, Fellow and Tutor of Emmanuel,[2] of whom Wakefield writes that when he first entered upon his curacy, the place was 'overrun with *methodists*. His discernment readily pointed out the principal cause of the emptiness of the *church*, whilst the neighbouring barn teemed with *catechumens*: namely, the *humdrum* method of fixing the eye immoveably upon the book; where nothing distinguishes the exhibitioner from a statue of wood or stone, but the droning whine and the mumbling lip. He adopted instantly the extemporaneous mode of preaching, and soon transferred the swarm into his own hive.'[3] It was less,

[1] Gunning, vol. i, p. 163.—'He gained the respect of his congregation, rather by his affability and social manners, than by the solemnity of his carriage, or the rigour of his doctrines' (*Literary Anecdotes of the 18th Century*, by John Nichols, F.S.A., 1812, vol. i., p 621).—'"Swavesey was at that time frequented by Methodists; occasioned by the Rev. Mr Venn, then Rector of Yelling..., and by the Rev. Mr Berridge, then vicar of Everton....Between these gentlemen and Farmer there existed no great cordiality; for Farmer was no friend to their doctrines, which appeared to him irrational and gloomy. He classed them with Presbyterians; and both Presbyterians and Methodists he considered as Puritans and Roundheads. Farmer was a greater adept at cracking a joke, than in unhinging a Calvinist's creed, or in quieting a gloomy conscience. He, however, possessed a spirit of benevolence; and knew how to perform a generous action to a distressed family...." *Annual Necrology.*' (*Ibid*. p. 621 *n*.)

[2] Unwin (a Chancellor's Medallist and a graduate of Christ's) and Bennet had both been members of Rowland Hill's 'Methodist Club' (A. L. Hunt, *David Simpson*, p. 117 and passim). Their rector, the Rev. Richard Oakley, was an absentee (*ibid*. p. 167).

[3] Wakefield, *Memoirs*, p. 184.

however, his pastoral efficiency, than the happy circumstance that the Earl of Westmorland (appointed Lord Lieutenant of Ireland in 1790) had been his pupil, that carried him in 1790 to the Irish bishopric of Cork and Ross, and thence in 1794 to the more lucrative see of Cloyne. Henry Venn, as Fellow of Queens', served for about six months the curacy of Barton, 'where he distributed religious tracts, and conversed with the poor in a manner that several of them affectionately remembered after an interval of above thirty years'.[1] Thomas Robinson, Fellow of Trinity, afterwards Vicar of St Mary's, Leicester, was for two years curate at Witcham and Witchford, near Ely, where he drew a large congregation from the surrounding villages, some coming even from Cambridge: but 'some controversy accompanied with much warmth and malice was excited in his parish, by a professed dislike to the singing of hymns in the church service': his own incumbent was the leader of the opposition: and he therefore judged it expedient to withdraw.[2] The simple village church of Lolworth is hallowed by the memory of Henry Martyn, Fellow of St John's, who preached his first sermon there after his ordination (Oct. 29, 1803):[3] besides being curate of Lolworth, he was also curate to Mr Simeon at Holy Trinity, until his departure for India in April 1805 as a Chaplain in the service of the East India Company. And it is interesting to note that in 1794 Simeon himself obtained the curacy of Stapleford, in addition to his other duties, 'as I thought it unprofitable for one minister to labour three times a day in the same Church':[4] for Stapleford was the village where, forty years earlier, the Rev. John Berridge, Fellow of Clare, had exercised his ministry with an unusual diligence.

John Berridge was born at Kingston, Notts., on March 1, 1716. He was the eldest son of a prosperous farmer and grazier,

---

[1] *Venn Family Annals*, p. 72.

[2] E. T. Vaughan, *Some Account of the Rev. Thomas Robinson, M.A., late Vicar of St Mary's, Leicester* (1816), pp. 39–54.

[3] John Sargent, *Memoir of the Rev. Henry Martyn, B.D.* (2nd ed. 1819), p. 38; *Journals and Letters of the Rev. Henry Martyn*, ed. S. Wilberforce (1837), vol. i, pp. 66–245 passim, esp. pp. 66, 67–8, 173, 245; Constance E. Padwick, *Henry Martyn, Confessor of the Faith* (1922), ch. v.

[4] Carus, p. 137: he used to take the afternoon, and Thomason (his curate) the morning duty. Cf. *ibid.* pp. 171–4: Preston, pp. 35, 37.

in whose steps he was designed to follow. But an utter in-
capacity to think in terms of fat stock prices, coupled with a
precocious and alarming predilection for reading and religion,
obliged his relatives to decide instead, reluctantly enough, to
send him to the University. In this decision, 'which was
perfectly congenial with his own inclinations, he most readily
concurred; and after previous preparation, was entered at Clare
Hall, October 28th, 1734, in the Nineteenth year of his age....
A neighbour soon after meeting his father, and inquiring for his
son, he jocosely replied, "He is gone to be a light to lighten the
Gentiles"....'[1]

Berridge at Cambridge was in his element. He applied himself
to his studies with an uncommon assiduity: nor was his thirst
for knowledge slaked by the acquisition of a Fellowship. 'In
learning he was inferior to very few of the most celebrated sons
of science and literature at the University. His masculine ability,
his uniform sobriety, and long residence at College were favourable to improvement; and so insatiable was his thirst for knowledge, that from his entrance at Clare Hall, to his acceptance of
the Vicarage at Everton [twenty-one years later], he regularly
studied fifteen hours a day. A Clergyman [Henry Venn], with
whom he had been in habits of friendship about fifty years, said
of him, that he was as familiar with the learned languages, as he
was with his mother tongue....'[2] Once, at least, he was appointed Moderator in the schools: a very real distinction, and
one by which George Whitefield was very properly impressed.[3]
But it was his wit, rather than his learning, that most endeared
him to his colleagues. 'Favoured with a good understanding,
improved by literature, and possessing a natural vein of humour,
which was extremely fascinating, he rose in respect; and his
acquaintance at the University was courted by ecclesiastics of
superior rank, though of wider principles, and less rigid morals.
Being of a witty turn of mind, he cultivated an acquaintance
with works of wit. Hudibras was so familiar to him, that he was

---

[1] Whittingham's *Memoir of the Rev. John Berridge* in Berridge's *Works*
(1838), p. 4.
[2] *Ibid.* pp. 19–20.
[3] Tyerman's *Whitefield*, vol. ii, p. 441: cf. Brown, p. 200.

at no loss in using any part of it on any occasion. While he was at college, if it was known that he would be present at any public dinner, the table was crowded with company, who were highly delighted with the singularity of his conversation and witty sayings.'[1] In short, he was a studious, clever, fat and jolly don: the best company in the world.

But it was not so well with his soul's health. '*As evil communications corrupt good manners,* he caught the contagion [of his environment], and drank into the Socinian scheme to such a degree, as to lose all serious impressions, and discontinue private prayer for the space of ten years, a few intervals excepted. In these intervals he would weep bitterly, reflecting on the sad state of his mind, compared with what it was when he came to the University; and would frequently say to a fellow student, afterwards an eminent Minister in the Establishment, *O that it were with me as in years past!* '[2] This period would seem to have lasted from about 1738, when he took his B.A. degree, to 1748.

Commenting on this phase of Berridge's development, Bishop Ryle, in his *Christian Leaders of the Last Century*, observes, perhaps a thought unkindly: 'No earthly condition appears to be so deadening to a man's soul as the position of a resident Fellow of a college, and the society of a Common room at Oxford or Cambridge. If Berridge fell for a season before the influences brought to bear upon his soul at Clare Hall, we must in justice remember that he was exposed to extraordinary temptations. How hardly shall resident Fellows of colleges enter the kingdom of God! It was a miracle of grace that he was not cast away for ever, and did not sink beneath the waters, never to rise again.'[3]

But Berridge, after all, humanly speaking, was saved by the fact that he had a particularly acute intelligence of the academic pattern: he perceived that from Socinianism he was insensibly lapsing into mere infidelity: and, being sufficiently impartial in

---

[1] Whittingham, p. 4.
[2] *Ibid.* p. 5: cf. however (*Works*) p. 350 ('In this manner [reading, praying, and watching] I went on, though not always with the same diligence, till about a year ago': Berridge's *Letter to a Clergyman*, 3 July 1758).
[3] *The Christian Leaders of the last century; or England a Hundred Years Ago*, by J. C. Ryle, D.D., Lord Bishop of Liverpool (2nd ed. 1899).

his scepticism to be sceptical of unbelief itself, he fought his way back to orthodoxy and renounced his former errors. At the same time 'he returned to the regular exercises of devotional religion'.[1] His vocation to the pastoral ministry was stirring within him, and he began to feel strong inclinations to exercise it. Accordingly in 1749 he accepted the curacy of Stapleford, which for the next six years he regularly served from College. His parishioners were ignorant and dissolute, but he laboured conscientiously for their improvement. 'During this time I was thought a Methodist by some People, only because I was a little more grave, and took a little more Pains in my Ministry than some others of my Brethren....'[2] His preaching was acceptable because his language was simple and his delivery impressive. But he did not see those fruits of his ministry for which he looked among his people. 'Tho' I took some extraordinary Pains, and pressed Sanctification upon them very earnestly, yet they continued as unsanctified as before, and not one Soul was brought to Christ. There was indeed a little more of the Form of Religion in the parish, but not a *Whit* more of the *Power*.'[3]

Baffled at Stapleford, he broke away, and in July 1755 was instituted to a College living at Everton, on the borders of Cambridgeshire, Bedfordshire, and Huntingdonshire, where he resided to the end of his life. Here at the outset his labours were equally exemplary, judged by the standards of the time, but equally barren of results. 'Here again I pressed Sanctification and Regeneration as vigorously as I could; but finding no Success, after two Years preaching in this Manner, I began to be discouraged; and now some secret Misgivings arose in my Mind, that I was not right myself. (This happened about Christmas last [1757].) These Misgivings grew stronger, and at last very painful. Being then under great Doubts, I cried unto the Lord very earnestly. The constant Language of my Heart was this,—"Lord, if I am right, keep me so; if I am not right,

---

[1] Whittingham, p. 5.
[2] *A Letter from the Rev. Mr Berridge to a Friend, giving an Account of his Life, Study, and Conversion: together with the Great Work of God among his People* [dated Everton, July 3, 1758], p. 21: *Works*, p. 359.
[3] *A Letter* etc. p. 10: *Works*, p. 350.

make me so. Lead me to the Knowledge of the Truth, as it is in Jesus." After about ten Days crying unto the Lord, he was pleased to return an Answer to my Prayers, and in the following wonderful Manner. As I was sitting in my House one Morning, and musing upon a Text of Scripture, the following Words were darted into my Mind with wonderful Power, and seemed indeed like a Voice from Heaven, (*viz.*) "*Cease from thine own Works*". Before I heard these Words, my Mind was in a very unusual Calm; but as soon as I heard them, my Soul was in a Tempest directly, and the tears flowed from my Eyes like a Torrent. The Scales fell from my Eyes immediately, and I now clearly saw the Rock I had been splitting on for near thirty Years.'[1]

The rock of which he spoke was what, in a later work (*The Christian World Unmasked: Pray Come and Peep*, 1773), he described so aptly as 'the mixed covenant' of man's corrupt invention, 'consisting *partly* of works, and *partly* of grace'.[2] Hitherto he had 'despised the Doctrine of Justification by Faith alone, looking on it as a foolish and a dangerous Doctrine': he had gone about to establish a righteousness of his own: he had imagined that sanctification was the way to justification, not knowing that it follows after it: therefore he had not sought after righteousness through faith, but as it were by the works of the Law. '—In short, to use a homely Similitude, I put the Justice of God into one Scale, and as many good Works of my own as I could into the other, and when I found, as I always did, my own good Works not to be a Ballance to the Divine Justice, I then threw in Christ as a Make-weight. And this every one really does who hopes for Salvation, partly by doing what he can for himself, and relying on Christ for the rest.'[3] And this was the doctrine which he had been preaching for the past eight years.

'But, dear Sir, Christ will either be a whole Saviour or none at all. And if you think you have any good Service of your own to recommend you unto God, you are certainly without any

---

[1] *A Letter* etc. pp. 10–11: *Works*, pp. 350–1. He was then in the forty-second year of his age.
[2] *Works*, pp. 209, 208.
[3] *A Letter* etc. pp. 16, 12, 16: *Works*, pp. 354, 351, 354–5.

Interest in Christ: Be you ever so sober, serious, just and devout, you are still under the Curse of God, as I was, and know it not, provided you have any allowed Reliance on your own Works, and think they are to do something for you, and Christ to do the rest.'[1]

' From this day forward he began to preach a very different gospel from that of the mixed covenant, telling his flock 'very plainly, that they were Children of wrath, and under the Curse of God, though they knew it not;...labouring to beat down Self-Righteousness: labouring to shew them that they were all in a lost and perishing State, and that nothing could recover them out of this State, and make them Children of God, but Faith in the Lord Jesus Christ. And now see the Consequence. This was strange Doctrine to my Hearers. They were surprised, alarmed, and vexed. The old Man, the carnal Nature, was stirred up, and railed, and opposed the Truth. However, the Minds of most were seized with some Convictions....'[2] It was after he had preached for two or three Sundays in this strain, without any visible result, and was beginning to wonder whether he was right after all, that one of his parishioners came to see him. 'Being introduced, "Well, Sarah", said he.—She replied, "Well, not so well, I fear". "Why, what is the matter, Sarah?"— "Matter, why I don't know what's the matter. These *new Sermons*. I find we are all to be lost now. I can neither eat, drink, nor sleep. I don't know what's to become of me." The same week came two or three more on a like errand.'[3] Others began to follow. 'The Hearts of some were truly broken for Sin, so that they came to me, as those mentioned in the Acts, thoroughly pricked to the Heart, and crying out with strong and bitter Cries, What must I do to be saved? I then laid the Promises before them, and told them, if they found themselves under the Curse, Christ was ready to deliver them from it; if they were really weary and heavy laden, Christ would give them Rest; if their Hearts were broken for Sin, and they would look unto Christ, he would heal them. I exhorted them also to

---

[1] *A Letter* etc. pp. 16–17: *Works*, p. 355.
[2] *A Letter* etc. pp. 17, 18: *Works*, pp. 355–6.
[3] Whittingham, p. 11.

thank God for these Convictions, assuring them it was a Token of
Good to their souls. For God must first smite the Heart, before
he can heal it, Isa. xix. 22. I generally found that they received
Comfort from the Promises; and tho' they complained much
of the Burden of Sin, and of an Evil Heart of Unbelief, yet they
always went away refreshed and comforted. Many have come
to me in this Manner, and more are continually coming; and
tho' some fall off from their first Convictions, yet others cleave
stedfastly unto the Lord. They begin to rejoice in him, and to
love him; they love his Word, and meditate much upon it; they
exercise themselves in Prayer, and adorn their Profession by a
suitable Life and Conversation.

'And now let me make one Reflection. I preached of Sanctification very earnestly for six Years in a former Parish, and
never brought one Soul to Christ. I did the same at this Parish
for two Years, without any Success at all; but as soon as ever I
preached Jesus Christ, and Faith in his Blood, then Believers
were added to the Church continually; then People flocked
from all Parts to hear the glorious Sound of the Gospel, some
coming six Miles, others eight, and others ten, and that constantly.'[1]

The first that Wesley heard of these developments was
probably from Madan, who wrote (April 29, 1758):[2]

By a letter from Everton, to Mr Daw, from Mr Berridge, the
Rector of that place, we receive the blessed news of another Gospel
Minister's being raised up in that dry desart; his words are these:
'GOD has been pleased to bless and prosper my labours, in a very
extraordinary manner, for these last three months. Since I preached
the real Gospel of Christ, seven people in my own parish have now
received the Gospel in the appointed way of repentance towards GOD,
and faith towards our Lord JESUS CHRIST. Nine or ten from Potton
are in a very hopeful way, two at Gamlingay, and two at Eaton. There
is now such a storm arising that I know not how it will end, or when.
I bless God, my mind is easy and quiet. Thou, O GOD, will keep him
in perfect peace, whose mind is stayed on thee! The tempest is now

[1] *A Letter* etc. pp. 18–19: *Works*, pp. 356–7.
[2] *Arminian Magazine*, vol. xx (1797), pp. 612–13: *Evangelical Magazine*,
vol. xx (1812), pp. 460–2.

whistling about my ears, but it does not ruffle or discompose my heart. Some time ago, I was told by several hands, that twelve Clergymen had combined together, in order to oppose and prosecute me, if they could. My 'Squire swears he will do my business; and last Lord's-day evening, when I came from church, he stopped me, and called me the usual names of Enthusiast, &c. &c. To-day, I hear the 'Squire has sent for such of his tenants as are disposed to hear the word of GOD, and has given them warning to leave their farms directly. He tells all what things he will do, against me; and to shew he is in earnest, swears by his Maker, *he will do it.*' Thus far are Mr Berridge's own words; he adds a desire of being remembered at the Throne of Grace by all our Christian friends: And I trust, dear Sir, that you amongst the rest won't forget him....

The Evangelical Revival in Cambridgeshire dates from the conversion of John Berridge, and Everton was its first centre. Rumours of strange occurrences in that country parish came to the ears of the Methodists, and on June 2, 1758, John Walsh,[1] the converted Deist, rode over from Bedford to explore: he afterwards sent a report to John Wesley, telling him about Berridge, 'who had read several of your works, and greatly longs to see you.... He meets little companies of his Converts from several towns and villages, at his own house. He was once ashamed of the word Methodist, but takes it to himself now as freely as I do. The country seems to kindle round him.'[2] Towards the end of July, George Whitefield passed through Everton, and preached there, on his way to Scotland: 'Mr Berridge,' he wrote, 'who was lately awakened...promises to be a burning and a shining light.'[3] On Nov. 10, Wesley himself paid his first visit to Everton at Berridge's urgent invitation, and preached at six in the evening and again at five in the morning. 'For many years', he recorded in his *Journal*, 'he was seeking to be justified by his works; but a few months ago he was thoroughly convinced that "by grace" we "are saved through faith."' Immediately he began to proclaim aloud the redemption

---

[1] *An Extract of the Life and Death of Thomas Walsh* will be found in *The Works of the Rev. John Wesley, M.A., Late Fellow of Lincoln College, Oxford* (Bristol, 1771–4), vol. xi, p. 307–vol. xii, p. 26.
[2] *Arminian Magazine*, vol. iii (1780), pp. 104–5.
[3] Tyerman's *Whitefield*, vol. ii, p. 410.

that is in Jesus, and God confirmed His own word exactly as He did at Bristol, in the beginning, by working repentance and faith in the hearers, and with the same violent outward symptoms.'[1]

It is these 'violent outward symptoms' that now demand our attention.

'For a season', writes Southey in his *Life of Wesley*,[2] 'this man produced a more violent influenza of fanaticism than had ever followed upon either Whitefield's or Wesley's preachings.' The symptoms were not slow in making their appearance. Berridge's new style of preaching was frankly terrifying to his fascinated auditory. Crowds thronged to hear him from all the surrounding countryside, and many of his hearers were moved to cry out with tears and groans under the power of his oratory and under the conviction of sin. On June 22 he began for the first time to preach outside his own parish,[3] in barns and farm-houses and cottages. On Sept. 17[4] he was joined by a neighbouring clergyman, the Rev. William Hicks, Vicar of Wrestlingworth, four miles from Everton, who had hitherto been hostile, even to the extent of refusing the sacrament to those of his parishioners who went to hear Mr Berridge,[5] but who now became his regular assistant. The physical effects of strong religious emotion began to manifest themselves among their hearers. When Wesley preached at Wrestlingworth on his way to Everton (Nov. 9–10, 1758), 'in a large church, well filled with serious hearers', on each occasion, evening and morning, in the middle of his sermon a woman fainted, and 'dropped down as dead': and at Everton, twenty-four hours later, 'some were struck, just as at Wrestlingworth. One of these was brought into the house, with whom we spent a considerable time in prayer.'[6] On his next visit (Dec. 18), many of his hearers 'were not able to contain themselves, but cried aloud for mercy.'[7]

---

[1] Wesley's *Journal* (standard edition), ed. N. Curnock, vol. iv, p. 291.
[2] *Op. cit.* (ed. M. H. Fitzgerald, 1925), vol. ii, p. 170.
[3] Whittingham, p. 13.
[4] Hicks was first convinced of sin on Aug. 1, and, finding peace in about six weeks, first preached the gospel on Sept. 17.—*Journal* (Walsh's narrative), vol. iv, p. 335: Whittingham, p. 12.
[5] *Journal* (Mrs Blackwell's narrative), vol. iv, p. 321: cf. p. 291.
[6] *Journal*, vol. iv, pp. 291–2.   [7] *Ibid.* p. 295.

BERRIDGE OF EVERTON

On the other hand, when he came again on March 1, 1759, nothing out of the ordinary seems to have taken place: there is no mention of any swooning or crying out.[1]

But the epidemic had not yet spent its force: on the contrary, it was now about to display itself upon a more extensive scale.

On Monday, May 14, 1759, Berridge, standing on a table in a farmyard on the way to Meldreth, preached for the first time in the open air, to about 150 people. The same evening he preached in a field at Meldreth to about 4000 people, and on the following morning, at five o'clock, Hicks preached in the same field to about a thousand. 'And now', writes Berridge,[2] 'the presence of the Lord was wonderfully among us. There was abundance of weeping and strong crying, and, I trust, beside many that were slightly wounded, near thirty received true heartfelt conviction. At ten we returned and called again at the farmer's house. Seeing about a dozen people in the brewhouse, I spoke a few words. Immediately the farmer's daughter dropped down in strong convictions. Another also was miserably torn by Satan, but set at liberty before I had done prayer. At four I preached in my own house, and God gave the Spirit of adoption to another mourner....' This 'tearing by Satan' appears to mark the beginning of those extraordinary physical convulsions, so scandalous alike to the sober piety of Southey in 1820 and to the fastidious rationalism of Lecky in 1878,[3] which now began to break out among the hearers of the new preaching, and spread like wildfire.

Luther says: 'Repentance which is occupied with thoughts of

[1] Wesley's *Journal*, vol. iv, p. 300.—It was after this visit that Wesley wrote to Lady Huntingdon (March 10, 1759): 'Mr Berridge appears to be one of the most simple as well as most sensible men of all whom it has pleased God to employ in reviving primitive Christianity.... They come now twelve or fourteen miles to hear him; and very few come in vain. His word is with power; he speaks as plain and home as John Nelson, but with all the propriety of Mr Romaine and tenderness of Mr Hervey.' (*Letters*, ed. Telford, vol. iv, p. 58.)

[2] [To Mrs Blackwell,] quoted in Wesley's *Journal*, pp. 321–2.

[3] Southey's *Life of Wesley* (ed. Fitzgerald, 1925), vol. ii, pp. 166–76; Lecky, *History of England in the Eighteenth Century* (4th ed. 1888), vol. ii, pp. 582 ff.— Southey calls Berridge 'buffoon as well as fanatic' (vol. ii, p. 203); Lecky says 'he was eccentric almost to insanity' (vol. ii, p. 620), but pays tribute to his earnestness and to his power.

peace is hypocrioy. There must be a great earnestness about it and a deep hurt if the old man is to be put off. When lightning strikes a tree or a man, it does two things at once,—it rends the tree and slays the man, but it also turns the face of the dead man and the broken branches of the dead tree to itself, toward heaven. So the grace of God terrifies and pursues and drives a man, but turns him at the same time to Himself.'

But here the external and visible effects of conversion passed far beyond all ordinary measure. On the following Sunday (May 20) amazing scenes were witnessed at Everton. In the morning, several fainted and cried out while Berridge was preaching. Children, in particular, were thrown into violent contortions. 'The church was equally crowded in the afternoon, the windows being filled within and without, and even the outside of the pulpit to the very top; so that Mr B[erridg]e seemed almost stifled by their breath. Yet, feeble and sickly as he is, he was continually strengthened, and his voice for the most part distinguishable, in the midst of all the outcries. I believe there were present three times more men than women, a great part of whom came from far; thirty of them having set out, at two in the morning, from a place thirteen miles off. The text was, "Having a form of godliness, but denying the power thereof". When the power of religion began to be spoke of, the presence of God really filled the place. And while poor sinners felt the sentence of death in their souls, what sounds of distress did I hear! The greatest number of those who cried or fell were men; but some women, and several children, felt the power of the same almighty Spirit, and seemed just sinking into hell. This occasioned a mixture of various sounds, some shrieking, some roaring aloud. The most general was a loud breathing, like that of people half strangled and gasping for life. And indeed almost all the cries were like those of human creatures dying in bitter anguish. Great numbers wept without any noise; others fell down as dead; some sinking in silence, some with extreme noise and violent agitation. I stood on the pew-seat, as did a young man in the opposite pew, an able-bodied, fresh, healthy countryman. But in a moment, while he seemed to think of nothing less, down he dropped, with a violence inconceivable. The adjoining pews seemed shook with his fall. I heard afterward the stamping of his feet, ready to break the boards, as he lay in strong convulsions at the bottom of the pew.... When he fell, B[lackwe]ll and I felt our souls thrilled with a momentary dread; as when one man is killed by a cannon-ball, another often feels the wind of it.'[1]

Such is the narrative of an eye-witness, which Wesley transcribed into his *Journal*. After service, the people crowded into the vicarage. 'We continued praising God with all our might, and His work went on as when Mr Berridge was exhorting.' A well-dressed stranger, who had come forty miles to hear Mr Berridge, suddenly 'fell backward to the wall, then forward on his knees, wringing his hands and roaring like a bull. His face at first turned quite red, then almost black. He rose and ran against the wall, till Mr Keeling and another held him. He screamed out, "Oh what shall I do? what shall I do? Oh for one drop of the blood of Christ!" As he spoke, God set his soul at liberty; he knew his sins were blotted out, and the rapture he was in seemed too great for human nature to bear.'[2] But not all who were thus stricken received the immediate sense of pardon and release. Some indeed received consolation, and wept for joy; others remained in deep sorrow of heart; John Keeling, of Potton, above-mentioned, fell into an agony for about a quarter of an hour, after which he became calm, although he received no clear sense of pardon until ten days later, at which time his sister also, who was in great distress, was set at liberty.[3] 'And indeed I have observed of the people in general who hear Mr B., their convictions are not only deep and violent, but last a long time. Wherefore those that are offended at them who rejoice should consider how terrible a cup they received first. Now they

---

[1] Wesley's *Journal*, vol. iv, p. 318.—The *Journal* contains two eye-witness narratives of the Everton Revival: (*A*.) May 20–24 (pp. 317–22), and 'a farther account' (*B*.) July 9–23 (pp. 333–43). The writers have been identified by H. J. Foster as (*A*.) Mrs Elizabeth Blackwell, of Lewisham, and (*B*.) John Walsh (*ibid*. pp. 317 *n*., 333 *n*.). The style of Mrs Blackwell's narrative, in its direct simplicity, is strongly reminiscent of George Fox's *Journals*.
[2] *Ibid*. pp. 318–19 (*A*.).
[3] *Ibid*. p. 319 (*A*.), p. 334 (*B*.).

are all light, but they well remember the darkness and misery, the wormwood and the gall.'[1]

On the next day (Monday, May 21) Berridge preached in the evening on Shelford Common to 'near ten thousand people... among whom were many gownsmen from Cambridge': but he states only that 'the audience behaved with great decency'.[2] He gave notice that on the following Monday he would preach at Grantchester. On Thursday, May 24, at Wrestlingworth when Hicks was preaching, there was much crying and struggling as at Everton on the previous Sunday. 'The violent struggling of many in the above-mentioned churches has broke several pews and benches. Yet it is common for people to remain unaffected there, and afterward drop down in their way home. Some have been found lying as dead in the road; others, in Mr Berridge's garden, not being able to walk from the church to his house, though it is not two hundred yards.'[3]

Throughout the summer these phenomena continued. Berridge and Hicks agreed to go into Hertfordshire together: 'afterwards to separate, and go round the neighbourhood, preaching in the fields, wherever a door is opened, three or four days in every week'.[4] The area covered extended into Cambridgeshire to within a mile of Cambridge, and about as far into Huntingdonshire: but it was in the eastern and northern parts of Bedfordshire that the work flourished most of all.[5]

Dear Sir,[6]

Mr H. and myself have been preaching in the fields for this month past, and the power of the Lord is wonderfully present with the word. We have been casting the gospel-net in the neighbourhood; but success at present only, or chiefly attends us in the Eastern parts: and there we now direct the whole of our endeavours. Near twenty

---

[1] *Ibid.* p. 334 (*B.*).
[2] Berridge to [Mrs Blackwell], *ibid.* p. 322 (*A.*).—Cf. *Congregational Magazine*, 1819 (supplement), vol. ii, p. 813.
[3] *Journal*, vol. iv, p. 321 (*A.*).
[4] Berridge to [Mrs Blackwell], n.d., quoted in *Journal*, vol. iv, pp. 321–2 (*A.*).
[5] *Ibid.* p. 321 (*A.*).
[6] Berridge to Wesley, July 16, 1759: *Arminian Magazine*, vol. iii (1780), pp. 611–13.

towns have received the gospel in a greater or less degree; and we continually receive fresh invitations, whenever we go out. The word is every where like a hammer, breaking the rocks in pieces. People fall down, cry out most bitterly, and struggle so vehemently, that five or six men can scarcely hold them. It is wonderful to see how the fear of the Lord falls even upon unawakened sinners. When we enter a new village, the people stare, and laugh, and rail abundantly; but when we have preached night and morning, and they have heard the outcries of wounded sinners, they seem as much alarmed and terrified, as if the *French* were at their doors. ...

Of late, there has been a wonderful out-pouring of the spirit of love amongst Believers. Insomuch that they have fainted under it, fallen down, and lain upon the ground, as dead, for some hours. And their bodies have been so weakened by these transports of joy, that they were not able to endure hard labour for some days afterwards. ...

But it is apparent that the reports which had found their way to London were giving rise to a good deal of uneasiness in official Methodist circles.

I would not have you publish the account of A[nn] T[horn] which Mr W[alsh] has sent you.[1] It might only prejudice people against the Lord's work in this place: and I find our friends in town begin to be in great pain about the work. They are very slow of heart to believe what they do not see with their own eyes. Indeed these things seem only designed for the spot on which they are wrought. What men see or hear they will be brought to credit. Men's attention is raised, and their prejudices against what is called a new doctrine removed by them. And thus the design of God is answered. But where people lie out of the reach of the doctrine, you will find them lie out of the reach of conviction. These signs are not for them, and so are disregarded by them. Give my love to Mr Grimshaw, and John Nelson, and believe me your affectionate Servant for Christ's sake.

J.B.

Mysterious and alarming portents accompanied the casting of the Gospel-net. 'There were three farmers, in three several

---

[1] '...I discoursed also with Ann Thorn, who told me of much heaviness following the visions with which she had been favoured; but said she was at intervals visited still with such overpowering love and joy, especially at the Lord's Supper, that she often lay in a trance for many hours. She is twenty-one years old' (*Journal*, vol. iv, p. 334 (*A.*)). Wesley himself interrogated her 'and two others who had been several times in trances' on Aug. 6: *ibid*. p. 344.

villages, who violently oot themselves to oppose it, and for a time they kept many from going to hear; but all three died in about a month. One of them owned the hand of the Lord was upon him, and besought Him, in the bitterness of his soul, to prolong his life, vowing to hear Mr Berridge himself. But the Lord would not be entreated.'[1] Yet it was observed that on the whole 'few ancient people experience anything of this work of God; and scarce any of the rich. These generally show either an utter contempt of or enmity to it'.[2]

It was further remarked, with regard to Berridge and Hicks themselves, that 'neither of these gentlemen have much eloquence, but seem rather weak in speech, the Lord hereby more clearly showing that this is His own work'.[3] Berridge, moreover, was physically far from strong, and often in great bodily weakness: for example, on July 17 'he was greatly fatigued and dejected, and said, "I am now so weak, I must leave off field-preaching". Nevertheless, he cast himself on the Lord, and stood up to preach, having near three thousand hearers.' This was at Harston. 'He was very weak at first, and scarce able to speak; but God soon performed His promise, imparting new strength to him, and causing him to speak with mighty power. A great shaking was among the dry bones. Incessant were the cries, groans, wringing of hands, and prayers of sinners, now first convinced of their deplorable state. After preaching he was lively and strong, so that the closeness of a crowded room neither affected his breath nor hindered his rejoicing over two children, one about eight, and the other about six years old, who were crying aloud to God for mercy.'[4] 'When he is weakest, God so strengthens him that it is surprising to what a distance his voice reaches. I have heard Mr Whitefield speak as loud, but not with such a continued, strong, unbroken tenor.'[5] Despite his weariness, he did not spare himself, preach-

---

[1] *Journal*, vol. iv, p. 321 (*A*.).
[2] *Ibid.* p. 321 (*A*.); cf. p. 319 ('Mr B. about this time retired, and the Duke of M[anchester], with Mr A[stell], came in. They seemed inclined to make a disturbance, but were restrained, and in a short time quietly retired').
[3] *Ibid.* p. 321 (*A*.).   [4] *Ibid.* p. 337 (*B*.).
[5] *Ibid.* p. 342 (*B*.).

ing four times a Sunday, at 7.0, at 10.30, at 2.30, and again in the evening,[1] to the multitudes who thronged to hear him.

The watchful Lady Huntingdon despatched two of her chaplains to investigate, Romaine and Madan. Both when they arrived were 'in doubt concerning the work of God here', but were convinced by the artless testimony of two little girls aged fifteen and eleven.[2] On the following day (Saturday, July 14), continues the author of the 'farther account' incorporated by Wesley in his *Journal*, 'Mr B., being ill, desired me to exhort a few people in his house, which the Lord enabled me to do with such ease and power that I was quite amazed. The next morning, at seven, his servant, Caleb Price, spoke to about two hundred people. The Lord was wonderfully present, more than twenty persons feeling the arrows of conviction. Several fell to the ground, some of whom seemed dead, others in the agonies of death, the violence of their bodily convulsions exceeding all description. There was also great crying and agonizing in prayer, mixed with deep and deadly groans on every side.

'When sermon was ended, one brought good tidings to Mr B. from Grantchester, that God had there broken down seventeen persons last week by the singing of hymns only;[3] and that a child, seven years old, sees many visions and astonishes the neighbours with her innocent, awful manner of declaring them.

'While Mr B. preached in the church, I stood with many in the churchyard, to make room for those who came from far; therefore I *saw* little, but *heard* the agonizing of many, panting and gasping after eternal life. In the afternoon Mr B. was constrained, by the multitude of people, to come out of the church and preach in his own close. Some of those who were

---

[1] Whittingham, p. 30.　　　[2] *Journal*, vol. iv, 335 (*B*.).
[3] '...As soon as three or four receive convictions in a village, they are desired to meet together two or three nights a week, which they readily comply with. At first they only sing; afterwards they join reading, and prayer to singing; and the presence of the Lord is greatly with them. Let me mention only two instances. At *Orwell* two people were broken down in one night, only by hearing a few people sing hymns. At *Grandchester*, a mile from *Cambridge*, seventeen people were seized with strong convictions last week, only by hearing hymns sung. When Societies get a little strength and courage, they begin to read and pray, and then the Lord magnifies his love as well as power amongst them by releasing souls out of bondage.'—Berridge to Wesley, July 16, 1759 (*Arminian Magazine*, vol. iii (1780), p. 612).

here pricked to the heart were affected in an astonishing manner
The first man I saw wounded would have dropped, but others,
catching him in their arms, did, indeed, prop him up, but were so
far from keeping him still that he caused all of them to totter
and tremble. His own shaking exceeded that of a cloth in a wind.
It seemed as if the Lord came upon him like a giant, taking him
by the neck and shaking all his bones in pieces. One woman tore
up the ground with her hands, filling them with dust and with
the hard-trodden grass, on which I saw her lie, with her hands
clinched, as one dead, when the multitude dispersed. Another
roared and screamed in a more dreadful agony than ever I heard
before. I omitted the rejoicing of believers, because of their
number, and the frequency thereof, though the manner was
strange; some of them being quite overpowered with divine
love, and only showing enough of natural life to let us know
they were overwhelmed with joy and life eternal. Some continued long as if they were dead, but with a calm sweetness in
their looks. I saw one who lay two or three hours in the open
air, and, being then carried into the house, continued insensible
another hour, as if actually dead. The first sign of life she
showed was a rapture of praise intermixed with a small, joyous
laughter.'[1]

There was an astonishing scene at Stapleford on Wednesday,
July 18. Berridge's 'heart was particularly set on this people,
because he was curate here five or six years; but never preached
a gospel sermon among them till this evening. About one
thousand five hundred persons met in a close to hear him, great
part of whom were laughers and mockers. The work of God,
however, quickly began among them that were serious, while
not a few endeavoured to make sport by mimicking the gestures
of them that were wounded. Both these and those who rejoiced
in God gave great offence to some stern-looking men, who
vehemently demanded to have those wretches horse-whipped
out of the close.... However, in a while, many of the scoffers
were weary, and went away; the rest continued as insensible as
before. I had long been walking round the multitude, feeling a

[1] *Journal*, vol. iv, p. 336 (*B*.).

jealousy for my God, and praying Him to make the place of His feet glorious. My patience at last began to fail, and I prayed, "O King of glory, break some of them in pieces; but let it be to the saving of their souls!" I had but just spoke when I heard a dreadful noise on the farther side of the congregation, and turning thither, saw one Thomas Skinner'—the ringleader of the scoffers—'coming forward, the most horrible human figure I ever saw. His large wig and hair were coal black; his face distorted beyond all description. He roared incessantly, throwing and clapping his hands together with his whole force. Several were terrified, and hasted out of his way.' After a while, he began to pray aloud, and then 'fell to the earth, crying, "My burden! My burden! I cannot bear it!" Some of his brother scoffers were calling for horse-whips, till they saw him extended on his back at full length. They then said he was dead. And, indeed, the only sign of life was the working of his breast and the distortions of his face, while the veins of his neck were swelled as if ready to burst....His agonies lasted some hours; then his body and soul were eased.

'When Mr B. had refreshed himself a little he returned to the close and bid the multitude take warning by Skinner, who still lay roaring and tormented on the ground. All the people were now deeply serious, and several hundreds, instead of going when Mr B. dismissed them, stayed in Mr Jenning's yard. Many of these, especially men, were truly broken in heart. Mr B. talked with as many as could come into the house, and, seeing what numbers stood hungering without, sent me word to pray with them....

'It was late when I went to lodge about half a mile off, where I found a young woman reading hymns, and the power of the Lord falling on the hearers, especially one young man, who cried aloud in...bitter anguish....'[1]

On the following morning (Thursday, July 19) Berridge preached at Grantchester to 'about one thousand persons, among whom the Lord was wonderfully present, convincing a far greater number now than even last night...'.[2]

[1] *Journal*, vol. iv, pp. 338–40 (*B*.).   [2] *Ibid.* p. 340 (*B*.).

BERRIDGE OF EVERTON

But the Rev. John Green,[1] D.D., Master of Corpus Christi (or Bene't) College, and Dean (hereafter shortly to be Bishop) of Lincoln, late Regius Professor of Divinity in the University of Cambridge, declined to be impressed by the 'constant number of groaners, sighers, tumblers, and convulsionists' who attended Mr Berridge's itinerant ministrations, and doubted 'whether to ascribe those sudden explosions to the catching nature of enthusiasm, or the unusual power of methodistical oratory', accompanied as it was 'with a loud tone of voice, vehement gesture, wild looks, and that terrible relievo which is sometimes given to the cheeks and eyes of a field-preacher'; a combination which 'must strongly operate on weak minds, and strike terror into an ignorant and inexperienced multitude'.[2] His attitude was evidently not peculiar to himself: although whether Berridge was ever guilty of such strange expressions as 'Fall! *won't you fall! why don't you fall! better fall here, than fall into hell!*' seems much more doubtful. Dr Green states that these particular words had been related to him by one of Berridge's hearers:[3] but it is impossible to accept that as conclusive evidence.

In any case, by the beginning of August,[4] when Wesley visited Everton again, the violence of this religious hysteria seems to have much abated: a few persons cried aloud during the prayers, as also during the sermon and the administration of the sacrament, but it was from love and joy, and not from sorrow or fear. He also preached at Wrestlingworth: there two or three

---

[1] Vide *Memoirs of the Life of the late Bishop of Lincoln* in the *Gentleman's Magazine*, vol. xlix (1779), pp. 234–6; Masters' *History of Corpus Christi College*, ed. John Lamb (1831), pp. 240–50; Baker's *History of St John's College*, ed. J. E. B. Mayor (1869), pt. ii, pp. 710–13; *Memoirs of a Royal Chaplain*, 1729–1763, ed. Albert Hartshorne (1905), pp. 271, 278–9. A number of personal references will also be found in *The Blecheley Diary of the Rev. William Cole, 1765–67*, ed. F. G. Stokes (1931): e.g. to Green's 'want of Behaviour & Manners', his 'ungain, awkward, splay-footed Carriage & Yorkshire Dialect' (p. 35), his confirmation 'more like a Bear bating, than any Religious Institution' (p. 22), his nepotism (p. 39), his Cambridge nickname of 'Jockey Green' (p. 40).

[2] *The Principles and Practices of the Methodists considered, in some Letters to the Leaders of that Sect. The first addressed to the Reverend Mr B—E.* [Signed 'ACADEMICUS.'] 2nd ed. (1761), pp. 28–9.

[3] *Ibid.* p. 28 *n.*

[4] Aug. 5–6, 1759; *Journal*, vol. iv, pp. 344–7.

175

fell to the ground, and were extremely convulsed; but none cried out. He noted in his *Journal*: 'I have generally observed more or less of these outward symptoms to attend the beginning of a general work of God. So it was in New England, Scotland, Holland, Ireland, and many parts of England; but, after a time, they gradually decrease, and the work goes on more quietly and silently.'[1] There was a slightly ominous note in his next sentence: 'Those whom it pleases God to employ in His work ought to be quite passive in this respect; they should choose nothing, but leave entirely to Him all the circumstances of His own work.'

He came again on Aug. 28,[2] and for the week-end of Nov. 24–27.[3] On the last occasion Berridge was away, preaching, surprisingly enough, before the University of Cambridge. He returned, however, before Wesley left, and reported that 'in the midst of the sermon...one person cried out aloud, but was silent in a few moments. Several dropped down, but made no noise, and the whole congregation, young and old, behaved with seriousness.' Wesley comments: 'God is strong as well as wise: who knows what work He may have to do here also?'[4]

It appears that it was not one isolated sermon, but, as was

---

[1] Wesley's *Journal*, vol. iv, 347–8. For Wesley's considered judgement regarding these 'extraordinary circumstances', *ibid*. 359–60.—It is significant that Henry Martyn was seriously perturbed when, at a week-day cottage prayer meeting at Lolworth (Wednesday, Oct. 17, 1804), one of his hearers fell into a fit. 'We sung a hymn, and I then explained the parable of the barren fig-tree. In the midst of the prayer, a man fell down and was carried out, and our meeting ended; the man was young and of a dull disposition, and had never a fit of any kind before, and the room was by no means warm; I did not much like the event, instantly recollecting the Methodist accounts' (*Journals and Letters of the Rev. Henry Martyn*, vol. i, p. 173).

[2] *Journal*, vol. iv, p. 349–50.

[3] *Ibid*. p. 359. 'In the afternoon God was eminently present with us, though rather to comfort than convince. But I observed a remarkable difference since I was here before as to the manner of the work. None now were in trances, none cried out, none fell down or were convulsed; only some trembled exceedingly, a low murmur was heard, and many were refreshed with the multitude of peace.' Cf. p. 434 (Feb. 3, 1761): 'Few of them are now affected as at first, the greater part having found peace with God. But there is a gradual increasing of the work in the souls of many believers': also p. 483 (Jan. 3, 1762): 'I found the people in general were more settled than when I was here before, but they were in danger of running from east to west. Instead of thinking, as many then did, that none can possibly have true faith but those that have trances or visions, they were now ready to think that whoever had anything of this kind had no faith.'

[4] *Ibid*. p. 360.

then the custom, for four consecutive Sunday afternoons,[1] that Berridge was invited to preach before the University. The Master of Corpus, a hostile witness, says that 'the lenity and moderation of that learned body, though there was something offensive enough in your manner of treating *them*, suffered' these sermons 'to pass without any reprehension'. Dyer, more bluntly, declares that Berridge's preaching 'gave great offence to the University'.[2]

On some, no doubt, these sermons in Great St Mary's made a more favourable impression: but Berridge 'formed no party at the time, which openly countenanced him in the University'.[3] In any case, the mere geographical remoteness of Everton from Cambridge militated against the possibility of his exerting a continuous influence upon the undergraduates. It is known that many of them used to come to Grantchester whenever he preached there: but Grantchester was at the outer limit of his circuit. Had it been his base of operations, things might have been very different. Nevertheless, his periodic visits to a village within a mile of Cambridge gave him some point of contact with members of the University. Thus, on Dec. 18, 1764, he sent a note to Rowland Hill, a freshman at St John's, saying that he had been asked to get into touch with him; that he was staying at the Mill at Grantchester, where he had preached that morning and on the previous night, and that he would not be leaving until 3 p.m.: would Mr Hill take a walk over? ('The weather is frosty, which makes it pleasant under foot.')[4] Rowland Hill accepted the invitation, with the result that he spent the Christmas recess at Everton vicarage. His sister and his elder brother, Richard, distinctly approved, but at the same time thought it proper to give him a caution 'how you go too frequently to Mr B. for should that be discovered, I need not tell you the storm it would raise'.[5] Undaunted by their warnings,

[1] Cf. Moule, p. 77.
[2] [John Green,] *The Principles and Practices of the Methodists considered* [in a letter to] *the Reverend Mr B—E.* (2nd ed. 1761), p. 75. George Dyer, *History of the University and Colleges of Cambridge* (1814), vol. i, p. 122.
[3] Dyer, p. 123.
[4] Sidney, *Rowland Hill*, p. 21; *Congregational Magazine*, Sept. 1841, vol. v, n.s., p. 599.
[5] Sidney, *Rowland Hill*, p. 22.

he regularly attended Berridge's ministry, riding over to Everton almost every Sunday, and returning in time for College Chapel.[1] As at Eton, so also at St John's, Hill formed around himself a small religious society. He and his fellow Johnian, David Simpson, used to read together 'the Greek Testament, and other evangelical publications; these meetings we always concluded with prayer.... Others soon joined us, to the number of ten or twelve.'[2] Of these, the most notable in after life were two undergraduates from Pembroke, who had been contemporaries at Christ's Hospital: Thomas Pentycross and Charles De Coetlogon.[3] Through Rowland Hill, Berridge was brought into some contact with this circle: he describes, for instance, Pentycross coming to his house with 'two pockets full of doubts and scruples relating to the Articles and Liturgy', and talking somewhat wildly of becoming a field preacher like Mr Whitefield, and of going to Lady Huntingdon's college at Trevecca.[4] But, again from the point of view of distance, Berridge stood at a disadvantage compared with the Rev. Robert Robinson, minister of the Particular Baptist chapel in St Andrew's Street and a good popular preacher, whose Sunday evening lectures were generally crowded by both Town and Gown. With Berridge's warm approval and encouragement, Robinson began to itinerate through the villages in the neighbourhood of Cambridge,[5]

[1] Sidney, *Rowland Hill*, p. 21.
[2] 'The University then', he adds, 'was almost in total darkness' (*Journal through the North of England and parts of Scotland* by Rowland Hill, 1799, p. 4).
[3] For the Rev. Thomas Pentycross (1748–1808), vide *Evangelical Magazine*, vol. xvi (1808–9), pp. 453–8, 497–504, vol. xvii, pp. 265–6; J. I. Wilson, *The History of Christ's Hospital* (1821), pp. 200–9; Funeral Sermon by the Rev. Thomas Scott (*The Duty and Advantage of remembering Deceased Ministers*) in Scott's *Works*, vol. vi, pp. 433–65; *Countess of Huntingdon, passim; Congregational Magazine*, Oct. 1826 (vol. ii, n.s., pp. 505–11), Dec. 1842 (vol. vi, n.s., pp. 825–6); *Proc. Wesley Hist. Soc.*, vol. ix (1914), pp. 73–4.—For the Rev. Charles De Coetlogon († 1820) vide *The New Spiritual Magazine, or Evangelical Treasury*, vol. v [1783], pp. 1385–8; J. I. Wilson, *History of Christ's Hospital*, pp. 209–15; William Trollope, *A History of the Royal Foundation of Christ's Hospital* (1834), p. 302 n.; [Benjamin Flower,] *Memoirs of the life and writings of the author*, prefixed to Robert Robinson's *Miscellaneous Works* (1807), vol. i, p. xxiv; Brown, p. 106.
[4] *Countess of Huntingdon*, vol. ii, p. 59 n.
[5] Including Dry Drayton, Duxford, Fowlmere, Foxton, Fulbourn, Grantchester, Harston, Haslingfield, Hauxton, Ickleton, Sawston, Fen Stanton, Stapleford, Swavesey, Whittlesford, and Wickhambrook.

preaching and catechising: in these activities he had the assist-ance of Hill, De Coetlogon, and Pentycross.[1] Hill also did a good deal of preaching on his own account, chiefly to the prisoners in the Castle and in a private house at Chesterton,[2] 'and particularly in a barn at Waterbeche, where was a numerous seminary of the disciples of Mr Berridge of Clare Hall, called from him *Berridges*, and who to this day send out preachers, gardeners, collar-makers, shop-keepers, &c. into many of the adjacent villages. It was for this irregularity, perhaps, that the Master [of St John's] thought proper to refuse a testimonial...'.[3]

But by the end of 1771 all the members of this society had gone down, and some of them at least were busily engaged in endeavouring to persuade wary Bishops that their irregularities had not disqualified them for holy orders in the Church of England: Pentycross had a very trying and unfruitful interview with the Archbishop of York,[4] and Rowland Hill was turned down by six Bishops before he could find one to admit him to the diaconate, beyond which he was never suffered to proceed.[5] 'During my residence at this seat of learning', he wrote, not altogether fairly, in 1799, 'even drunkenness and whoredom were deemed less exceptionable practices in a candidate for the Ministry than visiting the sick and imprisoned, and expounding the Scriptures in private houses.'[6]

Never again was Berridge to enjoy so close an intercourse with undergraduates. More and more he came to the conclusion

---

[1] *Memoirs of the Life and Writings of Robert Robinson*, by George Dyer (1796), p. 55; *Memoirs* [by B. Flower], prefixed to Robinson's *Miscellaneous Works* (1807), vol. i, p. xxiv; *Evangelical Magazine*, vol. xvi (1808), p. 455.

[2] Sidney, *Rowland Hill*, p. 23 ff.

[3] *Literary Anecdotes of the 18th century*, by John Nichols, F.S.A. (1812), vol. i, p. 574: cf. p. 573. (From the MSS. of the Rev. William Cole.)

[4] *The Substance of a Conference between the Rev. Thomas Pentycross, M.A., and the Hon. Dr Drummond, Lord Archbishop of York*: transcribed from the original documents in the possession of Mr Thornton. (*Congregational Magazine*, Oct. 1826, vol. ii, n.s., pp. 505–11.)

[5] Sidney, *Rowland Hill*, pp. 48, 88, 93.—He was thus, as he used jocularly to say, obliged to pass through life 'wearing only one ecclesiastical boot'. (*Congregational Magazine*, Dec. 1841, vol. v, n.s., p. 869.)

[6] R. Hill, *Journal through the North of England and parts of Scotland* (1799), p. 4.—Bishop Blomfield, in his primary Charge to the Clergy of the Diocese of Chester (1825), complained of the unscrupulousness and irresponsibility with which Collegiate bodies granted testimonials to candidates for holy orders: but this abuse was of long standing (p. 29 *n*. and refs.).

that they were not the type he wanted. In June 1771, when he was looking for a curate, he wrote to Lady Huntingdon: 'There are several serious students at both Universities, but I fear they are very prudent and very doctrinal, and such would not suit me.'[1] One element in his prejudice against them was, no doubt, his settled disparagement of human learning. 'I now lament the many years I spent in Cambridge in learning useless lumber —that wisdom of the world which is foolishness with God.'[2] 'P.S. Why did you put A.M. on the back of your letter? It makes me seem a coxcomb, got into my dotage.'[3]

Meanwhile he had been called, from time to time, to exercise his preaching upon a wider auditory. Towards the end of the original Everton Revival, that Mother in Israel, Lady Huntingdon, swooped down upon the village, attended by her preachers, Venn, Fletcher, and Madan, to the amazement of the neighbourhood. Vast crowds collected to hear the preaching: nine sermons were delivered in three days: at the end of which, leaving Madan in charge at Everton, her Ladyship carried Berridge off to London to introduce him 'to the religious circles of the metropolis, with a view to his spiritual improvement. During his stay he preached two or three times in the city churches, assisted by Mr Whitefield and the Messrs Wesley, and expounded almost every morning and evening at Lady Huntingdon's, besides his occasional lectures at Lady Gertrude Hotham's, in New Norfolk-street, Grosvenor-square, and Lady Fanny Shirley's, in South Audley-street.'[4] His ministrations were so far acceptable, that henceforward he used regularly to assist at Whitefield's Tabernacle and at Tottenham Court Chapel, usually going up to London after Christmas and returning to Everton before Easter.[5] Until he acquired a whole-time curate, his duty was ordinarily taken by a clergyman supplied by Lady Huntingdon; on one occasion, by the Rev. the Hon. Walter Shirley, for whom he left the following paper of instructions, which throws a flood of light upon his mode of living.

---

[1] Berridge's *Works*, p. 513: cf. p. 461.
[2] *Ibid.* p. 468: cf. p. 358. [3] *Ibid.* p. 463.
[4] *Countess of Huntingdon*, vol. i, pp. 399–400.
[5] Whittingham, p. 41.

THE REVEREND JOHN BERRIDGE PREACHING AT
WHITEFIELD'S TABERNACLE

From a contemporary engraving

(Not dated.)

FAMILY.

Prayers at nine in the morning, and nine in the evening; first reading a chapter, and singing a hymn, the hymns always sung standing. On Saturday evenings, the serious people of the parish come to my house about seven. I first sing a hymn, then expound a chapter, then sing another hymn, then pray, and conclude with singing on my knees, Praise God from whom, &c.

DIET.

You must eat what is set before you, and be thankful. I get hot victuals but once a week for myself, viz. on Saturday:[1] but because you are an Honourable man, I have ordered two hot joints to be got each week for you, with a pudding each day at noon, some pies and a cold ham; so that you will fare bravely; much better than your Master with barley bread, and dry fish. There is also ale, port, mountain, and a little madeira to drink: the liquor suits a coronet. Use what I have, just as your own. I make no feasts, but save all I can, to give all I can. I have never yet been worth a groat at the year's end, nor desire it.

I hope you will like your expedition: the people are simple-hearted. They want bread and not venison: and can eat their meat without sauce, or a french cook. The week-day preachings are in the evening at half an hour past six. If you can preach in a house, the method with us, is, first to sing a hymn, then pray, then preach, then sing another hymn, then pray again, then conclude with Praise God from whom, &c.

The Lord bless you, and make your journey prosperous! Your affectionate servant,   J. B.[2]

To this may be appended the advice given by Berridge to a country clergyman: 'Keep a barrel of ale in your house; and when a man comes to you with a message, or on other business, give him some refreshment, that his ears may be more open to your religious instructions.'[3] The old man lived plainly and

---

[1] Cf. '...I am glad to hear you write of a visit to Everton: we have always plenty of horse provender at hand, but unless you send me notice beforehand of your coming, you will have a cold and scanty meal, for we roast only twice in the week; let me have a line, and I will give you the same treat I always gave to Mr Whitefield, an eighteen-penny barn-door fowl; this will neither burst you, nor ruin me. Half you shall have at noon with a pudding, and the rest at night' (Berridge to John Thornton, Esq., Nov. 1, 1786, *Congregational Magazine*, vol. ix, n.s., 1845, p. 741: *Works*, p. 466).

[2] Berridge's *Works*, p. 491.   [3] Whittingham, p. 79.

frugally, but not austerely: like most of the early Evangelicals, he would have found himself sadly at a loss amid a generation of teetotallers and vegetarians.

The sympathy with and understanding of his people which underlay these memoranda, moulded the form and idiom of his preaching, as surely as his reading of the Scriptures supplied its content. His style was plain; the points in his argument boldly underlined; the language simple,[1] colloquial, and sometimes jocular, but never trifling. The sermon on II Cor. iii. 2,[2] printed by Whittingham among his *Works*, is a particularly good example, and illustrates how Berridge stands within that great tradition of English popular preaching which looks back to Bishop Latimer and forward to that grand old man of Cornish Methodism, the Rev. Mark Guy Pearse, with whom it seems, at least for the time being, to have become extinct. For the truest type of popular preaching is that which has about it a certain rustic homeliness: whereas most modern popular preaching appears to be indelibly suburban.

Furthermore, although few men have had more reason to know the power and efficacy of a preaching ministry, Berridge was always sensible of its limitations. 'Crowded and attentive congregations are reviving sights; yet perhaps this is rather an age of much hearing, than much praying. The old puritan spirit of devotion is not kindling and breathing among us.'[3] 'Much preaching and hearing is among the Methodists, and plenty of ordinances is a great blessing, but if they do not bring us much upon our knees, they suckle the head without nourishing the heart. We shall never obtain the old puritan spirit of holiness, till we obtain their spirit of prayer.'[4]

---

[1] Whittingham, p. 69: 'On an occasion when the Rev. Mr R—— had been preaching at his church, after the service, the good Vicar said, "Brother R——, your sermon was good, but my people cannot understand your language." Mr R——, whose style was remarkably simple, could not recollect any expression in his sermon, that could be above their comprehension; and, therefore, requested him to mention it. Mr Berridge said, "You have endeavoured to prove that God is omniscient and omnipotent; but if you had said, that God was almighty, and knew everything, they would have understood you."'
[2] *Vide* Appendix.
[3] Berridge's *Works*, p. 405. (To John Thornton, Esq., Feb. 11, 1779.)
[4] *Ibid.* p. 424. (To John Thornton, Esq., July 2, 1785.)

The reference to the Methodists is not without significance, for Berridge was no longer, if he had ever been, a simple follower of John Wesley: nor could any study of his life and influence pretend to be complete, or even honest, if it failed to mention his ill-starred participation in the Calvinistic controversy of 1771–77, which for a time divided the forces of the Evangelical Revival into two hostile camps.

The detailed history of that controversy may be read elsewhere.[1] It was, in effect, a civil war between Calvinistic and Arminian Methodists; the ground of conflict being the ageless and unfathomable problem of Predestination and Free Will. On the one hand, Whitefield had embraced, and held inflexibly, 'the doctrine of election and final perseverance of those who are in Christ': on the other, Wesley was not only apprehensive of the antinomian implications of this doctrine, but was also sceptical about the doctrine itself. The rift between the leaders first became apparent in 1739, upon the publication of Wesley's sermon on Free Grace: but such was their mutual regard that it was patched up within the decade, although neither of the two protagonists receded an inch from his declared opinions. Another ominous crack was caused in 1755 by the publication of Hervey's *Theron and Aspasio*, of Wesley's answer to it, and of Hervey's reply to Wesley. But not until 1771, the year after Whitefield's death, did the division of opinion widen into an open breach.

At the Annual Conference of his Itinerant Preachers in August 1770, Wesley took up the subject at the point at which it had been left at the first Conference, twenty-six years before: 'We said in 1744, We have leaned too much toward Calvinism.' Lady Huntingdon was pleased to describe herself, in her humility, as 'a poor worm', but few worms have ever turned more fiercely or more often; and she now retaliated by dismissing Joseph Benson from her College at Trevecca, whereupon Fletcher promptly severed his connection with it. In November,

---

[1] There is a very full account in Tyerman's *Wesley's Designated Successor: The Life, Letters, and Literary Labours of the Rev. John William Fletcher, Vicar of Madeley, Shropshire* (1882). Cf. also Abbey and Overton, *The English Church in the Eighteenth Century* (1878), vol. ii, pp. 144–66.

Wesley preached what was intended as an eirenic sermon on the death of Whitefield: six weeks later, this was respectfully attacked in the *Gospel Magazine* for January, 1771. Then followed the publication of the Minutes of the Conference of 1770, and the long impending storm broke out with extraordinary fury.

Wesley himself deliberately stood aloof from the controversy, and left it to his subalterns to handle. Fletcher contributed a Vindication of the offending Minutes, which drew an answering fire from Lady Huntingdon's detachment. He followed it up with his *Second, Third, Fourth,* and *Fifth Checks to Antinomianism.* Toplady, the ablest writer on the opposing side, produced a bitter rejoinder in his *More Work for John Wesley.* As the controversy proceeded, the pamphlets on both sides became increasingly scurrilous and abusive: Toplady, in particular, displayed a quite remarkable talent for invective. 'The Calvinistic controversy', writes Overton, 'exceeded all other controversies of the century in bitterness. It will be remembered that the Deistical controversy was conducted with considerable acrimony on both sides: but the Deistical and anti-Deistical literature is amenity itself when compared with the bitterness and scurrility with which the Calvinistic controversy was carried on.'[1] But he also points out that if those who took part in it gave and asked no quarter, it was because they believed the fundamental doctrines of Christianity to be at stake.

To us, the idiom and the presuppositions of the controversy, like those of the Baptismal Controversy of 1847–50, seem not so much archaic as, rather, almost inconceivably remote. It might be equally true to say that they have become so utterly familiar that we are oblivious of their controversial bearing. The issue is no longer, at this moment, a living issue: and, since the original italics are no longer there to guide us, we miss the note of protest and polemic in such a hymn as Toplady's *Rock of Ages—*

> *Nothing* in my hand I bring,
> Simply to Thy Cross I cling—

[1] Abbey and Overton, vol. ii, pp. 166, 157.

or in Charles Wesley's

> Father, Whose *everlasting love*
> Thy only Son for sinners gave,
> Whose grace to *all* did *freely* move,
> And sent Him down *a world to save*;
>
> Help us Thy mercy to extol,
> Immense, unfathom'd, unconfined;
> To praise the Lamb who *died for all*,
> The *general Saviour of mankind*.[1]

It may be that for this, as Bishop Moule suggests, we are in some degree indebted to Charles Simeon, who, in his celebrated interview with John Wesley at Hinxworth, Herts., on Monday, Dec. 20, 1784, rejoiced to know that the differences between them were differences rather of expression than of opinion.[2] To Simeon belongs the grand discovery, so naturally disconcerting to the English mind, that 'the truth is *not in the middle*, and *not in one extreme; but in both extremes*':[3] and he enforced it in the Preface to his *Horæ Homileticæ* (1819).[4] The fires of the Calvinistic controversy, which had blazed out so fiercely fifty years before, had died down almost abruptly in 1777: but the embers were still smouldering well into the nineteenth century. 'It was Simeon, more than any other man, who was able to reduce to order, and largely to pacify and harmonize, the predestinarian controversy of the previous generation; pointing out how much (not all, but much) of the conflict was over the two sides of one shield.'[5]

Berridge's contribution to the controversy consisted of a reply to Fletcher's *Checks to Antinomianism*, entitled *The Christian*

---

[1] Cf. Henry Bett, *The Spirit of Methodism* (1937), pp. 147–56.
[2] *Vide* Preface to *Horæ Homileticæ*, standard edn. (1832–3), vol. i, p. xvii n., quoted in Moule, pp. 100–1; cf. Wesley's *Journal*, vol. vii, p. 39.
[3] Simeon to the Rev. Mr T—— on 'the golden mean', July 9, 1825: Carus, p. 600.
[4] Quoted in Carus, pp. 528–34: cf. pp. 566 n., 599–600. Cf. Brown, ch. xiii, *Notes on Calvinism and Arminianism* ('Both of them are right in all they affirm, and wrong in all they deny,' p. 267), and *passim*. Cf. also the Rev. C. M. Chavasse on *Simeon and his love for the Bible*, in *Charles Simeon: an Interpretation* (1936), esp. pp. 51–3.
[5] H. C. G. Moule, *The Evangelical School in the Church of England* (1901), p. 12.

World Unmasked: Pray Come and Peep (1773), to which Fletcher replied conclusively in the Second Part of his *Fifth Check to Antinomianism* (1774). Berridge's pamphlet was a singularly temperate performance, in so far as he never mentions either Wesley or Fletcher by name, although their tenets are of course attacked and ridiculed. 'The Vicar of Madeley has sent me word', he wrote to the Rev. John Newton (Sept. 20, 1773), 'that my prattle in my pamphlet of sincere obedience "is the core of Antinomianism, has exposed St James, and touched the apple of God's eye", and that he intends to put my head in the pillory, and my nose in the barnacles for so doing. How fierce a tiger is zeal without knowledge! and I have been that tiger myself. And what utter destruction the Lord's own servants would make in.his vineyard, if the Lord himself did not hold the vines in his right hand! Oh, for that world, where all will say, I am of Christ; and oh, for more of Christ, while we live in this world!'[1]

Southey, upon the internal evidence alone, opines that Berridge was also the writer of some lamentable verses, signed 'Auscultator', in *The Gospel Magazine*: '*The Serpent and the Fox; or, an Interview between old Nick and old John.*'

> There's a fox who resideth hard by,
> The most perfect, and holy, and sly,
> That e'er turned a coat, or could pilfer and lie....[2]

But the internal evidence is very inconclusive; and the external evidence makes this identification exceedingly improbable, for Berridge plainly deplored the controversy, and would have been the last man deliberately to inflame it. 'I have written to Mr Fletcher', he told John Thornton (Sept. 25, 1773), 'and... acquainted him, that I am an enemy to controversy, and that if his tract is published, I shall not rise up to fight with him, but will be a dead man before he kills me. I further told him, I was afraid that Mr Toplady and himself were setting the christian world on fire, and the carnal world in laughter, and wished they

[1] Berridge, *Works*, p. 386.
[2] Southey's *Life of Wesley*, vol. ii, pp. 397–400 (note xxvi).

could both desist from controversy.'[1] It is true, however, that his personal relations with John Wesley had been somewhat awkward ever since the spring of 1760, when Wesley, whose polite but autocratic temper was affronted by Berridge's rustic independence, had felt it expedient to unburden his mind of a few home truths.

Dublin, April 18, 1760.

Dear Sir,

Disce, docendus adhuc quae censet amiculus; and take in good part, my mentioning some particulars which have been long on my mind: and yet I know not how to speak them. I was afraid, it might look like taking too much upon me, or assuming some superiority over you. But love casts out, or at least over-rules that fear. So I will speak simply, and leave you to judge.

It seems to me, That of all the persons I ever knew (save one) you are the *hardest to be convinced.* I have occasionally spoken to you on many heads; some of a speculative, others of a practical nature: but I do not know that you was ever convinced of one, whether of great importance or small. I believe you retained your own opinion in every one and did not vary a hair's breadth. I have likewise doubted whether you was not full as *hard to be persuaded,* as to be convinced: whether your will do not adhere to its first bias, right or wrong, as strongly as your understanding. I mean with regard to any impression which another may make upon them. For perhaps you readily, too readily change of your own mere motion: (as I have frequently observed, great *fickleness* and great stubbornness meet in the same mind.) So that it is not easy to please you long; but exceeding *easy to offend* you. Does not this imply the *thinking* very *highly* of *yourself?* Particularly of your own understanding? Does it not imply (what is always connected therewith) something of *self-sufficiency?* 'You can stand alone; you care for no man. You need help from no man.' It was not so with my brother and me, when we were first employed in this great work. We were deeply conscious of our insufficiency: and though (in one sense) we trusted in God alone, yet we sought his help from all his children, and were glad to be taught by any man. And this, although we were really alone in the work: for there were

---

[1] Berridge, *Works,* p. 387.—Cf. p. 384: 'Whatever Mr Fletcher may write against my pamphlet, I am determined to make no reply. I dare not trust my own wicked heart in a controversy. If my pamphlet is faulty, let it be overthrown; if sound, it will rise up above any learned rubbish that is cast upon it. Indeed, what signifies my pamphlet or its author? While it was publishing, I was heartily weary of it, and have really been sick of it since....'

none that had gone before us therein. There were none then in England, who had trod that path, wherein God was leading us. Whereas *you* have the advantage which we had not; you tread in a beaten path. Others have gone before you, and are going now in the same way, to the same point. Yet it seems you *chuse* to stand alone: what was necessity with *us*, is choice with *you*. You like to be unconnected with any, thereby tacitly condemning all. But possibly you go farther yet: do not you explicitly condemn all your fellow labourers, blaming one in one instance, one in another, so as to be thoroughly pleased with the conduct of none? Does not this argue a vehement proneness to condemn? A very high degree of *censoriousness*? Do you not censure even peritos in suâ Arte? Permit me to relate a little circumstance to illustrate this. After we had once been singing a hymn at Everton, I was just going to say, ' I wish Mr Whitfield would not try to *mend* my brother's hymns. He cannot do it. How vilely he has murdered that hymn? *Weakening* the sense, as well *as marring* the poetry?' But how was I afterwards surprized to hear it was not Mr Whitfield but Mr B.!¹ In very deed it is not easy to *mend* his hymns, any more than to imitate them. Has not this aptness to find fault frequently shewn itself, in abundance of other instances? Sometimes with regard to Mr Parker,² or Mr Hicks:³ sometimes with regard to me. And this may be one reason why you take one step which was scarce ever before taken in christendom: I mean the discouraging the new converts from reading: at least from reading any thing but the bible. Nay, but get off the consequence who can: if they ought to *read* nothing but the bible, they ought to *hear* nothing but the bible, so away with sermons, whether spoken or written! I can hardly imagine, that you discourage reading even our little Tracts out of jealousy, lest we should undermine you, or take away the affections of the people. I think you cannot easily suspect this, I myself did not desire to come among them: but you desired me to come. I should not have obtruded myself either upon them or you: for I have really work enough: full as much as either my body or mind is able to go through, and I have (blessed be God) friends enough:

¹ Cf. art. *The Rev. John Berridge and his Hymn-Book, 1760 and 1785*, by R. Butterworth, in *Proc. Wesley Hist. Soc.* vol. xi (1918), pp. 169–74.
² William Parker, the Methodist mayor of Bedford, and a local preacher. The first Methodist preaching-place in Bedford was his corn-loft, which was over a hog-stye: Wesley speaks of the stench as 'scarce supportable', and adds 'Surely they love the gospel who come to hear it in such a place.' (*Journal*, vol. iv, pp. 84–6, 201, 248, 358–9, vol. v, p. 485, vol. vii, p. 35 *n*.)
³ The Rev. William Hicks, vicar of Wrestlingworth.—Cf. *Journal*, vol. iv, p. 344 (Aug. 6, 1759): 'I soon found Satan was labouring to create misunderstandings between Mr Berridge and Mr Hicks. But on Monday they talked freely together, and the snare was broken.'

BERRIDGE OF EVERTON

I mean, as many as I have time to converse with; nevertheless I never repented of that I spent at Everton: and I trust it was not spent in vain. I have not time to throw these notes into a smoother form: so I give you them just as they occur. May the God whom you serve give you to form a right judgment concerning them, and give a blessing to the rough sincerity of,

Dear Sir,

Your affectionate servant,

JOHN WESLEY.[1]

If Berridge was as '*easy to offend*' as Wesley thought, his answer to this letter did him considerable credit:

Everton, Nov. 22, 1760.

Dear Sir,

I received your letter from Ireland, and purposely delayed my answer till your return to England, that I might not write in a spirit unbecoming the Gospel. I wish that all who love the Lord Jesus Christ, were perfectly agreed in their religious sentiments: But this, I find, is a matter rather to be wished than expected. And perhaps a little disagreement in non-essentials, may be designed as one part of our trial, for the exercise of our candor and patience. I discourage the reading of any books, except the Bible and the Homilies, not because of the jealousy mentioned by you, but because I find that they who read many books, usually neglect the Bible, and soon become eager disputants, and in the end turn out Predestinarians. At least 'this has happened so with me. If my sentiments do not yet altogether harmonize with yours, they differ the least from yours of any others. And as there is nothing catching or cankering in those sentiments of yours which are contrary to mine, I am not only willing but desirous you should preach at Everton, as often as you can favour us with your company. Last week I was at Bedford, and preached to your society; from whom I heard, that you was returned out of the West, and purposed to come amongst us soon. Will you call at Everton, as you go to, or return from Bedford? You will be welcome. My invitation is sincere and friendly: accept of it.

I send my love to your Brother, and to all that labour among you. May grace, mercy, and peace be multiplied on you, and your affectionate servant,

JOHN BERRIDGE.[2]

---

[1] *Arminian Magazine*, vol. iii (1780), pp. 499–501 ('Letter cxxx [From the Rev. J. Wesley, to ——]'): Wesley's *Letters*, ed. J. Telford, vol. iv, pp. 91–3.
[2] *Arminian Magazine*, vol. xx (1799), pp. 305–6.

This letter may have reassured John Wesley, for he accepted the proffered invitation, and preached at Everton on Ash Wednesday, Feb. 4, 1761, and again (when Berridge was absent) on Jan. 3, 1762.[1] But these were his last visits to Everton, although the *Journal* shows that he preached for Hicks at Wrestlingworth on Dec. 4, 1783, Oct. 17, 1786, and Oct. 31, 1787.[2] A letter to him from Berridge, dated Everton, Jan. 1, 1768,[3] seems to indicate a growing estrangement, at least on Wesley's part.

Dear Sir,

I see no reason why we should keep at a distance, whilst we continue servants of the same Master; and especially when Lot's herdsmen are so ready to lay their staves on our shoulders. Though my hand has been mute, my heart is kindly affected toward you. I trust we agree in Essentials, and therefore should leave each other at rest with his Circumstantials. I am weary of all disputes, and desire to know nothing but Jesus; to love him, trust in him, and serve him; to chuse and find him my only portion: I would have him my meat, my drink, my clothing, my sun, my shield, my Lord, my God, my All. Amen.

When I saw you in town, I gave you an invitation to Everton; and I now repeat it, offering you very kindly the use of my house and church. The Lord accompany you in all your journies. Kind love to your Brother. Adieu.

JOHN BERRIDGE.

But by this date Berridge was definitely coming over to the Calvinist side.[4] 'Being of an ardent constitution', says Whittingham, 'he was led to embrace, in the most prompt and avowed manner, that system of religion which appeared to him to be

---

[1] *Journal*, vol. iv, pp. 433–4, 483.
[2] *Ibid.* vol. vi, p. 464, vol. vii, pp. 216, 338.—On June 14, 1780, Wesley wrote to the Rev. Brian Bury Collins, who was taking duty for Berridge during his annual visit to the Tabernacle: 'A few years ago the people at and around Everton were deeply alive to God and as simple as little Children. It is well if you *find* them so now. Perhaps you may by the help of God *make* them so now. Mr Hicks, in particular, *was* a burning and shining light, full of Love and Zeal for GOD. I hope you will see him as often as you can, and (if need be) lift up the hands that hands that (*sic*) hang down; and encourage him to set out anew in ye great Work, and to spend and be spent therein.' (*Proc. Wesley Hist. Soc.*, vol. ix, p. 31: Wesley's *Letters*, ed. Telford, vol. vii, pp. 22–4.)
[3] *Arminian Magazine*, vol. vi (1783), p. 616.
[4] He seems to have adopted Calvinist opinions in 1768–69 (G. J. Gorham, cited in Whittingham, p. 61). Venn in Nov. 1771 found him 'a true Calvinist' (*Life of H. Venn*, p. 185).

most consonant with the sacred Scriptures When first brought
to discover how erroneously he had been building his hope of
eternal felicity, or that he had not been simply depending on
the merits of Christ for Salvation, but had been trusting in
part in his own doctrine for that purpose, he strongly leaned to
the side of Arminianism as held and inculcated by the leaders
of Methodism. He warmly opposed the opposite tenets, and
regarded all those who maintained them as being egregiously
deficient in their views of the true doctrine of the Scriptures.
It was while he was under the influence of the doctrine,
which he at first believed to be founded on the word of God,
that he was most successful in alarming the ungodly, and
inducing them to forsake the destructive paths of sin, and to
flee from the wrath to come to Christ for refuge. He was indeed
a Boanerges, causing, as it were, the lightenings of Mount Sinai
to flash with awful vividness, and her thunders to roll in sounds
appalling to the hearts of the wicked.... Some years afterwards
he imbibed the peculiar sentiments of Calvinism, which he
maintained and strenuously inculcated for several years....'[1]

His literary duel with Fletcher took place in 1773–74.[2]
Berridge was completely outmatched by his opponent: but
Fletcher, both in the Introduction and in the Conclusion to his
answer, paid a magnanimous tribute to his vital piety and
indefatigable labours.

Before I mention Mr Berridge's mistakes, I must do justice to his
person.... His conduct as a Christian is exemplary; his labours as a
minister are great; and I am persuaded that the wrong touches which
he gives to the ark of godliness are not only undesigned, but *intended*
to do God service....
Were I to conclude these strictures upon the dangerous tenets,
inadvertently advanced and happily contradicted, in *The Christian
World Unmasked*, without professing my brotherly love and sincere
respect for the ingenious and pious author, I should wrong him,

[1] Whittingham, pp. 16–7. Cf. Berridge to Mr Adams, June 9, 1773: 'Pray
tell Mrs Adams...that I am become a Moderate Calvinist' (*Life of the Rev.
Robert Housman* (1841), p. lxiii).
[2] 'My...preaching at Bedford seems to be foreclosed by the stench which
my pamphlet has occasioned....' (Berridge to the Rev. John Newton, Sept.
20, 1773: *Works*, p. 386.)

myself, and the cause which I defend. I only do him justice when I say that few, very few, of our elders equal him in devotedness to Christ, zeal, diligence, and ministerial success.... A sharp pen may be guided by a kind heart; and such, I am persuaded, is that of my much-esteemed antagonist, whom I publicly invite to my pulpit; protesting that I should be edified and overjoyed to hear him enforce there the *guarded* substance of his book, which, notwithstanding the vein of solifidianism I have taken the liberty to open, contains many great and glorious truths.[1]

The two antagonists met again in December 1776, when Fletcher visited Berridge at Everton. Sixteen years had passed since his first visit there,[2] and much water had flowed beneath the bridges. 'They embraced each other with tears of affection, at first meeting, and saluted by the endearing name of brother: surely never did two more kindred spirits meet....After the first expressions of regard, they naturally adverted to their last meeting; and thence began to trace the circumstances of the intervening years.—Myself and two other friends then purposely left them together for full two hours. On our return they told us they had been having a great deal of conversation; but we perceived with great satisfaction, that the spirit with which they met, had not evaporated: they were still consulting how they might be most useful to the Church of Christ. They were now to part, and as Mr F. was in such an ill state of health, that he did not expect even [? ever] to see Mr B. again, it was the more solemn. They invited us who were present, and also called in Mr Berridge's servants to join them in a parting address to the throne of grace. Mr F..prayed fervently and affectionately; and having concluded, all were about to rise from their knees, when Mr B. began to pray in language equally warm and loving with that of his dear brother. Their parting was such as might be expected after such a meeting....Indeed the behaviour of these two friendly opponents, was worthy of their high calling, and truly ornamental to their holy profession: the savour of it has remained very forcibly on my mind to this day.

'In the spring of 1777, Mr Berridge being in London, had a desire to return Mr Fletcher's visit; and I therefore accompanied

---

[1] Quoted in Tyerman's *Fletcher*, pp. 297–8. [2] March 1760. (*Ibid.* pp. 51–2.)

him to Stoke Newington, where Mr F. then was, having an increase of his disorder. They met and parted, as they did at Everton, in the true spirit of Christian love; and I believe saw each other no more in the body.'[1]

Indeed, the spirit of controversy was not natural to John Berridge, nor was the practice of it congenial to him. After describing his adoption of the Calvinist position, Whittingham continues:

At length, however, through reading various works on theological subjects, and much thinking on them, his views of different Systems of Religion become moderate. The Editor well recollects his conversation with him on the points in debate between certain controversialists at that time. He frankly owned, that he saw such difficulties attending the Systems of Arminianism and Calvinism, as defied the reason of man to solve, or to show which was most agreeable to the counsels of the Most High.... Hence he came to the determination of adhering steadily to one leading and important Maxim, viz., *That Salvation is of God, and Man's Destruction of himself.*

Influenced by this maxim during the remaining part of his life, he became indifferent to the reading of controversial works. He wanted his mind to be kept at ease, and not to be disturbed by the opposing sentiments of different writers. His chief desire was to have his thoughts employed, without interruption, about the subjects of religion which are essentially necessary to salvation....

When therefore an eminent Minister, paying him a visit, inquired whether he had read certain works on the controverted points relating to Arminianism and Calvinism, he replied, 'I have them on my shelves in my Library, where they are very quiet; if I take them down, and look into them, they will begin to quarrel and disagree.' He regarded controversy, being often conducted with acrimony, with no favourable opinion, regarding it as injurious to heavenly-mindedness, as well as to a peaceful state of mind....[2]

There is little else to record in Berridge's ministry at Everton beyond the normal ebb and flow in the life of a parish. 'Church-work goes on heavily here', he wrote to Newton in 1782: 'many of the old sheep are called home, and few lambs drop into the

---

[1] G. J. Gorham, quoted by Whittingham, pp. 61–3. Cf. Tyerman's *Fletcher*, pp. 371–2. But Fletcher did not die until 1785, and Simeon records a later (and slightly comic) meeting of old friends at Everton (Brown, p. 201).
[2] Whittingham, pp. 17–18.

fold. The wealthier sort seem to be growing downward into the earth.... Sometimes I am ready to be offended at them, but this is stifled by finding more cause to be offended with myself.'[1] To Benjamin Mills he expressed himself with greater freedom. 'My church at present is in a decline, and seems consumptive. Mr Hicks supplied my church from September last till the following Easter; and fairly drove away half my congregation. My present curate is a stop-gap, but no assistant. He cannot preach without notes, nor read handsomely with notes; so my hearers are dwindling away, and transporting from Everton Church to Gamgay Meeting....'[2] But in 1785 we find him writing in a more cheerful vein. 'My church is usually very full in afternoons, and the people are awake and attentive, but the congregation is almost a new one. Many old sheep are housed in the upper fold; and many, who live at a distance, are dropped into neighbouring meetings, and only pay occasional visits to Everton. I shall meet them all by and by, and a blessed meeting it will be, when sheep and shepherds will give to Jesus all the glory of it.'[3]

In the winter of 1771 he was greatly cheered by the coming of Henry Venn from Huddersfield to the neighbouring vicarage of Yelling, nine miles away. Venn wrote of him to Stillingfleet (Nov. 22, 1771): 'Last Wednesday Mr Berridge was here, and gave us a most excellent sermon. He is a blessed man, a true Calvinist; not hot in doctrine, nor wise above what is written, but practical and experimental. Summer differs not more from winter, than this dear man from what he was ten years ago: he is now broken in heart, yet fervent in spirit.'[4] 'He is often telling me, that he is sick of all he does, and loathes himself for the inexpressible corruption he feels within: yet is his life a pattern to us all, and an incitement to love and serve the Lord with all our strength.'[5] Berridge conceived a great affection for

---

[1] Berridge to the Rev. John Newton, Sept. 17, 1782: *Works*, p. 419.
[2] Berridge to Benjamin Mills, Esq., Sept. 24, 1782: *Congregational Magazine*, April 1845, vol. ix, n.s., p. 273. 'Gamgay Meeting'—the Baptist meeting-house at Gamlingay.
[3] Berridge to John Thornton, Esq., July 13, 1785: *Works*, p. 447.
[4] *Life of H. Venn*, p. 185.—'Dear Mr Berridge preaches for me every month' (Dec. 7, 1773), *ibid.* p. 200.
[5] *Ibid.* (Venn to Stillingfleet, Aug. 12, 1776), p. 226.

BERRIDGE OF EVERTON

Venn's son, John, 'a very gracious youth',[1] who entered Sidney as a scholar in 1777. 'Jacky is the top branch of the tree, highest and humblest. His abilities seem equal to anything he undertakes, and his modesty is pleasing to all that behold him. He has daily hours of retirement for waiting secretly on God, as have his sisters, father, and mother; and he is so recollected in his talk, that I seldom hear him speak a trifling thing. His behaviour in College has turned the hearts of the Master and Fellows entirely to him, who were very averse, and even injurious for a season, on account of his being the son of a Methodist Clergyman. There seems not a doubt but he will be elected Fellow next Easter....'[2] A fortnight after the final disappointment of that hope, on June 14, 1782, John Venn rode over to Everton with his new friend, the Rev. Charles Simeon, 'to introduce him to Mr Berridge'.[3] There was a historic significance in that meeting: yet it was not John Berridge, but Henry Venn, who was to play in Simeon's life the role of guide, philosopher, and friend, which Berridge, eighteen years before, had played in the life of Rowland Hill.[4] In the concluding lecture we shall see how Berridge tried to draw Simeon into an itinerant course, and how Venn firmly put a stop to it. Yet not even this produced a rupture in their personal relations: and to the end of Berridge's life, Charles Simeon and Henry Venn used to go over and dine with him every Tuesday.[5]

Berridge had always been somewhat eccentric, and as he grew older he began to suffer from delusions, as, that he was

[1] Berridge to the Rev. John Newton (Sept. 17, 1782): *Works*, p. 418.
[2] *Ibid.* (Berridge to Henry Thornton, Nov. 24, 1781), p. 415.
[3] Carus, p. 24 *n.*
[4] In the *Congregational Magazine*, vol. v, n.s. (1841), will be found eight letters from Berridge to Rowland Hill, 1764–76 (pp. 597–602, 867–71). Cf. p. 601, 'I feel my heart go out towards you whilst I am writing, and can embrace you as my second self' (May 8, 1771); p. 870, 'My dear Rowly,—I need not say that I love you, because all who are acquainted with the old and young ass, know it well, and I would have them know it, and the more scandalous you grow, I mean evangelically scandalous, the more I must love you' (June 7, 1776).—'Mr Hill used to say, "many a mile have I rode, many a storm have I faced, many a snow have I gone through, to hear good old Mr Berridge; for I felt his ministry, when in my troubles at Cambridge, a comfort and blessing to my soul. Dear affectionate old man. I loved him to my heart."' (Sidney, *Rowland Hill*, p. 173.)
[5] Brown, p. 201.

made of glass, or that his body had swelled up to a monstrous size and was about to burst: on one occasion there was an alarming scene when he had inadvertently put on somebody else's greatcoat, which was several sizes too small for him.[1] At no time had he been very robust,[2] and in old age he became very feeble. 'What a poor Do-little I am', he wrote to Benjamin Mills (Oct. 9, 1788), 'next to a cumber-ground! Twenty-one good meals in a week, with a bever besides, and one sermon chiefly. Sure no lazy servant was ever so fed.... Solomon's account of old age suits me well. The windows are dark; the daughters of music are low; the grinders cease, for all are gone; and the grasshopper is a burden. Well, thanks be to God thro' Jesus Christ for the prospect of a better world.'[3] Two years later we find him writing: 'Our years are rolling away fast, and will quickly roll us into eternity. How needful that admonition: Prepare to meet thy God!... The windows of my house grow dimmer, scarce give a straight line, or spell a word right, and dislike a pen much. Yet thanks to the Lord, my health is better, my ears pretty stout, and my legs keep mending, are peaceable in a chair, though fretful in bed. I purpose, with the good leave and help of my Master, to set off for Tabernacle on Tuesday the 28th of December, unless a fall of snow then happen, which would delay me until the roads are tracked. The Lord afford his presence, protection, and blessing!... My eyes cry for quarter, so with affectionate respects to your partner, the Trustees, and preachers, I remain your much obliged servant, John Berridge.'[4] Venn came to visit him in the winter of 1791, and found him slowly breaking up. 'His sight is very dim, his ears can scarcely hear, and his faculties are fast decaying; so that if he continues any time, he may outlive the use of them. But in the ruin of his earthly tabernacle, it is surprising to see the joy in his counten-

---

[1] Brown, pp. 202–3.
[2] In 1768, he was laid aside by illness, and unable to itinerate for five years. (*Congregational Magazine*, vol. vi, n.s. (1842), pp. 218, 821; *Works*, pp. 378–9.)—Cf. John Gadsby, *Memoirs of the Principal Hymn-Writers and Compilers of the 17th and 18th centuries* (2nd ed. 1855), p. 24.
[3] *Works*, pp. 466–7.
[4] To Benjamin Mills, Nov. 23, 1790: *ibid.* pp. 467–8: *Congregational Magazine*, Oct. 1845, vol. ix, n.s., p. 742.

ance, and the lively hope with which he looks forward to his dissolution. In his prayer with me and my children...we were much affected by his commending himself to the Lord, as quite alone, not able to read, or hear, or do anything;—"but if I have, Lord," said he, "Thy presence and love, *that* sufficeth!"'[1]

In January 1793, in the seventy-sixth year of his age, he was for the first time obliged to forego his annual visit to the London Tabernacle. On the very morning appointed for his setting out (Jan. 12), he was seized with a violent asthma, and his life was despaired of. He rallied, however, and lingered for ten days. He spoke but seldom, yet what he did say was in terms of gratitude for the presence and love of his adorable Redeemer, and of his full assurance of being with Him for ever. 'What should I do now', he asked, 'if I had no better foundation to rest upon than what Dr Priestley points out?' He expressed himself as alarmed at the growing infidelity of the country; yet pleased that a Spirit was stirred up against it. 'Have you burned Tom Paine yet at St Neots?' he demanded. On being told that they had, he seemed much pleased. His former curate, and biographer, Richard Whittingham, the Vicar of Potton, was with him at the end. 'Sir,' said Whittingham, '—the Lord has enabled you to fight a good fight, and to finish a truly glorious course.' He answered, 'Blessed be His holy Name for it'. There was a pause. Then Whittingham said, 'Jesus will soon call you up higher.' The old man replied: 'Ay, Ay, Ay, higher, higher, higher.' Then he added: 'Yes, and my children too will shout and sing, "*Here comes our father*".' Immediately he sank beneath the mortal stroke.[2]

They buried him the following Sunday, in the presence of a vast concourse of people from all the surrounding countryside. Six neighbouring clergymen acted as pall-bearers, and the funeral sermon, on II Tim. iv. 7, 8, was preached by Charles Simeon, in the place of Venn, who was prevented by illness.[3] In

---

[1] *Life of H. Venn*, pp. 493–4.
[2] Whittingham, pp. 42–3, 65: *Life of H. Venn*, pp. 511–12: John Gadsby, *Memoirs of the Principal Hymn-Writers and Compilers of the 17th and 18th centuries* (2nd ed. 1855), p. 28.
[3] *Life of H. Venn*, pp. 511–12.

obedience to Berridge's express instructions, his body was interred on the north-east side of the churchyard, in a part hitherto reserved for criminals and suicides.[1] The epitaph on his tomb, which may still be read, was of his own composition:

> Here lay the earthly Remains of JOHN BERRIDGE
> late *Vicar* of *Everton*, and an itinerant Servant
> of JESUS CHRIST who loved his Master and his Work,
> and after running on his Errands many Years was called
> up to wait on him above. Reader art thou born again
> No Salvation without a new Birth.
> > I was born in Sin Feb. 1716
> > Remained ignorant of my fallen State till 1730,
> > Lived proudly on Faith & Works for Salvation till 1754
> > Admitted to Everton Vicarage 1755.
> > Fled to JESUS alone for Refuge 1756.
> > Fell asleep in Christ Jan.ʸ 22ᵈ 1793.

Canon Overton comments: 'It is a very characteristic example of the Evangelical way of looking at the religious life. There is no mention of Baptism or Confirmation as marking actual steps, but all is concentrated upon the consciousness of saving grace and the necessity of being born again.'[2]

---

[1] Whittingham, p. 66.
[2] Overton and Relton, *The English Church from the Accession of George I to the End of the Eighteenth Century* (1906), p. 150.

APPENDIX TO CHAPTER IV

From *The Evangelical Magazine* for July, 1796 (vol. iv, pp. 291–2). Berridge's *Works*, ed. Whittingham, pp. 118–121.

BRIEF OUTLINES OF A DISCOURSE
BY THE LATE REV. MR BERRIDGE

"Ye are our Epistles."

THIS was the language of the great Apostle Paul (who, in his own eyes, was less than the least of all saints) in an address to the Corinthian church, the members of which had been some of the most abandoned characters; and to whatever place the Apostle went, where letters of commendation were required of the visiting ministers, he pointed to those conspicuous converts who were living epistles, and so eminent as to be known and read of all men. The change in them was so great as to render it evident to every one: the drunkards were become sober; the dishonest, just; the miser, liberal; the prodigal, frugal; the libertine, chaste; and the proud, humble. To these the Apostle appealed, for himself and fellow-labourers, as letters of commendation, who were living epistles at Corinth, and as lights in the world.

In an epistle then must be *paper*, or *parchment*, a *pen*, *ink*, a *writer*, and *somewhat written*.

1st. The paper, or parchment, we may consider, in these divine epistles, as the *human heart*; which, some people say, is as clean as a white sheet of paper; but if it be so on one side, it is as black as sin can make it on the other. It may appear clean like a whited sepulchre *without*, but it is full of all uncleanness and defilement *within*.

2d. The *pen* may be well compared to the *ministers* of the Gospel, who are used in those living epistles as such, and many of them are willing to acknowledge themselves very *bad* pens, scarcely fit to write with, or any way to be employed in so great a work.

It seems that they have been trying for many years to make good pens at the universities; but after all the ingenuity and pains taken, the pens which are made there *are good for nothing till God has nibbed them*. When they are made, it is well known the best of pens want *mending*. I find that the poor old one that has been in use now for a long while, and is yet employed in scribbling, needs to be mended two or three times in a sermon.

3d. The *ink* used in these divine epistles I compare to the influences of divine grace on the heart; and this flows freely from the pen when it has a good supply from the fountain-head, which we constantly stand in need of; but sometimes you perceive the pen is exhausted, and almost dry. Whenever any of you find it so, either at *Tabernacle*, *St Ann's*, or Tottenham-court Chapel, and are ready to say, 'O what a poor creature this is, I could preach as well myself'; that may be true; but instead of these sad complaints, lift up your hearts in prayer for the poor pen, and say, '*Lord, give him a little more ink*'.

But if a pen is made well, and quite fit for use, it cannot move of itself; there must be an agent to put it into motion, and,

4th. The *writer* of these glorious and living epistles is the Lord Jesus Christ. Some people talk about, and are very curious in fine writing; but there is something in the penmanship of these epistles, which exceeds all that was ever written in the world; for, as the Lord Jesus spake, so he writes, as no man ever spoke or wrote. One superior excellency in these epistles is, that they are all so plain and intelligible, as to be known and read of all men, and the strokes will never be obliterated.

As pens cannot move of themselves, so we profess, when we take on this sacred character, to be moved thereunto by the Holy Spirit, nor can we move to any *good purpose* without his divine assistance.

Lastly. In all epistles there must be *somewhat written*. Many things might be said here, but I shall include the divine inscription of these epistles in *repentance*, *faith*, and *holiness*. Repentance is written with a *broad-nibbed pen*, in the *old black* letter of the *law*, at the foot of mount Sinai. Faith is written with a crow-quill pen, in finè and gentle strokes, at the foot of mount Calvary. Holiness is gradually and progressively written; and when *this* character is *completely* inscribed, the epistle is finished, and sent to glory.

TIMOTHEUS.

V

CADOGAN OF READING

✠

The object is of incalculable importance. The securing of a
faithful Ministry in influential places would justify any outlay
of money that could be expended on it.

The Rev. CHARLES SIMEON to the Rev. Mr I —, Aug. 8, 1836.
(Carus, p. 780.)

Chapter Five

CADOGAN OF READING

WITH an unholy relish, and with the comment '[This letter well merits preservation.—ED.]', the Editor of *The British Magazine* for May 1836 favoured his readers with the following 'Copy of a letter from the Rev. Charles Simeon, of Cambridge, on the subject of purchasing livings with a view to secure a *gospel* ministry in the respective churches:—'

'I had got to the length of my tether, as you will readily imagine with 21 livings in my possession. But being strongly urged to purchase the living of Bridlington with 6,000 souls, I broke my tether and bought it.... *After having purchased it,* five of those who had urged me to it, knowing how ill able I was to bear the expense, sent me 100 *l.* each, and two 50 *l.* each, and one anonymously 40 *l.*, and left me not above 140 *l.* to pay. I felt this a call from God to *know nothing of tethers,* but to go to the utmost extent of my power, now that the corporation livings are on sale.... Accordingly I devote to this blessed work 2,500 *l.* and I send to a variety of places this proposal: —Collect amongst you one-half, and I will give the other half—or, if three persons will subscribe three-fourths, I will give one fourth, and the *first presentation.* Thus on the first plan my pittance will go as far as 5,000 *l.*, and on the second plan, as far as 10,000 *l.* And then I say to any persons, Help *me* to enlarge my pittance; because every 100 *l.* will, on the first plan, be equal to 200 *l.*, and on the second plan to 400 *l.* If I could get from others 1,000 *l.*, it would not spare *me* one penny, but would enlarge my efforts to the amount of 4,000 *l.* But behold, I have begun with Derby, and, (with the exception of Mr Evans, who wishes to enlarge my sphere of operation,) I have got but 100 *l.*, and that is from Mr Cope. So that I shall have to sacrifice for that one place nearly one-half of my pittance, whereas I expected that the religious people there would gladly meet me half way. On receiving his letter I was almost ready to weep. Truly, for the most magnificent church in the county, there is only one person found to meet my offer of fixing the gospel there in perpetuity, or to give a shilling towards it, and thus all my glorious plans and prospects are defeated.... I had *pledged myself* to purchase the great living at

Northampton at any price. But the vicar has written me word that the corporation intend to get, *if they can*, an act of Parliament to enable the bishop of Lincoln to add to it a valuable sinecure in the town; and in return for *that*, to have the nomination vested in him. Whether this will go forward I do not know. If it do, my intentions with regard to *it* will be frustrated. But should that be the case, I have my eye upon *all the provincial towns*, to spend all I can in securing the gospel to them.... I have actually sent to *Bath* my proposals, and if they be accepted, (Bath will sell for at least 5,000 *l.*, having five churches under it,) I shall have my poor pittance swallowed up by that alone. I wrote thither under the full persuasion that the people of Derby would meet me half way, instead of only giving one solitary hundred towards it.... What to do I know not. (All that I purchase will be committed to my trustees, as all my twenty-two livings are.) I think I *must* secure Derby, because of the immense importance of it. I will have four or five other places if I can get them, and get the means of fulfilling my engagements. Pray do for me all you can with any of your friends who are able to assist in this good cause. Any sum may be placed to my account at Smith, Payne, and Smith's, London. Oh that there were amongst religious people more zeal for God, and more love to immortal souls! In all my livings I have no *personal* interest *whatever*. If I had never done more than purchase Cheltenham, I should be already well repaid for all the pains I have taken, and all the labours I have expended.'[1]

Now the purport of this document may easily be misapprehended by a generation that has had experience of other and more recent Party Trusts, more negative in purpose, more polemical in spirit, and less honourable in method.[2] Simeon's policy may have been unfortunate in its ultimate consequences, but at least its motive was 'love to immortal souls'[3] and not

[1] *The British Magazine*, vol. ix (Jan.–June 1836), pp. 549–50.—This 'letter' was in fact, as might have been suspected, composed of extracts unscrupulously pieced together from various letters of a confidential nature which Simeon had written to persons who had liberally aided him with their contributions. Simeon had no idea how the editor had access to these letters, 'but it was a grievous act of treachery in those who delivered them up to him'. He recognised that the publication of the 'letter' had made an 'evil impression on the public', although, 'through the goodness of God', it also brought him in some more donations. (Simeon to the Rev. Mr I——, Aug. 8, 1836: Carus, pp. 779–80. Cf. *The Christian Examiner* (Dublin), Jan. 1837, pp. 14–17.)
[2] Cf. *Sibbes and Simeon: An Essay on Patronage Trusts*. By Herbert Hensley Henson, Lord Bishop of Durham. 1932.
[3] Cf. Simeon's Solemn Charge to his Trustees, *ibid*. pp. 38–40: or, in A. J. Tait, *Charles Simeon and his Trust* (1936), pp. 39–40.

hatred of Anglo-Catholicism. He sought to secure the gospel to all the provincial towns: which is at least a wider aim than that of prohibiting the Eastward position and taking the cross and candles off the altar. And when he bought a living, it was not with the object of stopping an Anglo-Catholic earth with Protestant money, but of 'fixing the gospel there in perpetuity'. That is the significant phrase: and a cursory examination of the fortunes of the Evangelical Revival in his own native town of Reading may serve to elucidate its meaning.

The Rev. the Hon. William Bromley Cadogan was Vicar of St Giles', Reading, from 1774 until his death in 1797. The manner of his entrance upon his ecclesiastical career, though not in any way exceptional or remarkable according to the standards of the time, affords a sardonic illustration of the continuity of the Church of England: for the administrative system of the Hanoverian Church, which we are apt to judge so harshly and, as it were, in isolation from its context, was, as Professor Sykes has demonstrated, essentially a survival from the Middle Ages. That pure and reformed part of the One Holy Catholic and Apostolic Church established in this realm is, in the form in which we know it, the product of a double Reformation; namely, of a doctrinal Reformation which may be said to have begun in 1535 and to have been completed by 1662, and of an administrative Reformation which began in 1835 and is still in progress. Three centuries were suffered to elapse between the year in which the majestic lord first broke the bonds of Rome, and that in which the conscientious baronet first cracked the cake of custom. But Sir Robert Peel was not yet born when Earl Bathurst, the Lord Chancellor, very good-naturedly paid a morning call at the town residence of the Cadogan family in Bruton Street, and disclosed 'his intention of presenting Mr Cadogan's son, who he had heard was intended for orders, to the living of St Giles's, as being near the family seat' at Caversham Park.[1] His conduct in this matter was as generous as it

---

[1] *Memoirs of the Hon. and Rev. W. B. Cadogan* by the Rev. Richard Cecil, prefixed to Cadogan's *Discourses* (1798), pp. xviii–xix: reprinted, with a few alterations, in Cecil's *Works*, ed. Josiah Pratt, vol. i (2nd ed. 1816). *Evangelical Magazine*, vol. vi (1798), pp. 5–6.

was unsolicited, for St Giles', Reading, was one of the most valuable livings in the gift of the Crown: and the technical impediment that young Mr Cadogan was still at Oxford, and could not be ordained until the following year, was fortunately immaterial, for the living could be sequestrated for the interval, during which period the spiritual necessities of his parishioners might be satisfied by his predecessor's curate, Mr Hallward. Not long after, Lord Cadogan himself was able to add to this provision the family living of St Luke's, Chelsea, of which Mr Cadogan became Rector in May 1775, at the promising age of twenty-four. Here again there was a slight technical impediment, inasmuch as Mr Cadogan was not legally capable of holding two livings without being a Master of Arts: but, for the cadet of noble family, Archbishop Cornwallis proved no less accommodating than the Lord Chancellor, and willingly conferred on him a Lambeth degree to tide over the interval until he should be of sufficient standing to proceed to his M.A. at Oxford, which he was able to do in the following year.[1]

Having been duly ordained to the sacred ministry, Mr Cadogan was instituted to the living of St Giles', Reading, early in 1775. It was a parish with an Evangelical tradition, established by his predecessor, the Rev. William Talbot, who had been presented to the living by Lord Camden, as Lord Chancellor, in 1768.

There is, I think, a tendency to exaggerate the extent to which the pioneers of the Evangelical Revival, clergy and laity alike, were men of humble origin. Nevertheless, the Evangelicals of the latter part of the eighteenth century do unmistakably appear to have laboured under a sense of social inferiority which betrays itself, for instance, in the well-known lines of Cowper:

> Envy, ye great, the dull unletter'd small:
> Ye have much cause for envy—but not all.
> We boast some rich ones whom the gospel sways;
> And one who wears a coronet, and prays;

[1] *The History and Antiquities of Reading*, by the Rev. Charles Coates (1802), p. 361.

Like gleanings of an olive-tree, they show
Here and there one upon the topmost bough.[1]

Yet when Cowper composed his poem, *Truth*, in 1791, Lord Dartmouth's was by no means the only coronet that bowed at its devotions: and the Evangelical *regulars* and the Methodist field preachers came, for the most part, from two distinct strata of the population, even allowing for the fact that social strata were not then quite so carefully distinguished as they afterwards became.

For example, the Rev. William Talbot neither was, nor was regarded as, a social portent in the early stages of the Movement. Yet he was the eldest son of Major-General Sir Sherington Talbot, Kt., the nephew of a Lord Chancellor, and the grandson of a Bishop of the princely see of Durham. None the less, as Vicar of Kineton, in Warwickshire, he did not disdain to go itinerating under the general orders of Lady Huntingdon: Hervey of Weston Favell, in Northamptonshire, the gentle author of *Theron and Aspasio* and *Meditations among the Tombs*, records a visit from him and Madan in 1757: 'both were like men baptized with the Holy Ghost and with fire—fervent in spirit, and setting their faces as a flint':[2] and Lady Huntingdon's biographer records how, when she was induced to enlarge the sphere of her labours and to erect and open chapels at Brighton, Bath, and elsewhere, he united with Whitefield, Venn, Romaine, and other faithful witnesses of God, in 'sounding the gospel trumpet in these highly favoured places'.[3] He removed to

---

[1] Cowper's *Poetical Works*, ed. H. S. Milford (3rd ed. 1926), p. 39.—The Evangelicals (and, more particularly, the Evangelical Dissenters) appear to have been a little obsessed with coronets: cf. such titles as *A Coronet laid at the Feet of Jesus, as illustrated by the conversion of the late Lord Bloomfield*, by the Rev. George Scott (1836); *The Coronet and the Cross, or, Memorials of Selina, Countess of Huntingdon*, by Alfred H. New (1857). On the other hand it is to be remembered that the Movement owed a very great deal to aristocratic patrons, and that the Evangelicals themselves were singularly free from social snobbery (cf. Sir G. G. Scott, *Personal and Professional Recollections*, 1879, p. 28).
[2] *Countess of Huntingdon*, vol. i, p. 431.—There is a touching story of Mr Talbot at the death-bed of Archbishop Secker, *ibid.* vol. i, p. 19 *n.*, taken from Thomas Haweis, *An Impartial and Succinct History of the Rise, Declension, and Revival of the Church of Christ* (1800), vol. iii, pp. 244–5.
[3] *Countess of Huntingdon*, vol. ii, p. 396.

Reading in the hope of finding a more extensive sphere of influence than in his country parish: nor was he disappointed: his faithful labours were greatly blessed in the awakening of sinners: his piety and generosity were alike exemplary: and his ministry was attended by a large and devout congregation. After a five years' pastorate, which left its mark, he died of a putrid fever contracted in the course of his parochial visiting. He left behind him a curate and a widow who survived him by eleven memorable years.

The news of Mr Cadogan's appointment was received with consternation by his flock. 'Their only hope was, that the new vicar, being a young gentleman of noble family, would feel no disposition to do the duties himself; and that Mr Hallward might be continued in the curacy.'[1] But, in case that hope should be disappointed, Lady Huntingdon came on a special visit to Mrs Talbot in order to discuss with her and with Mr Hallward what would be the best means of providing for the spiritual wants of the congregation in the event of Mr Hallward's being dismissed.[2] Then Mr Cadogan arrived to take possession, and Mr Hallward *was* dismissed. In vain the churchwardens presented to the incoming vicar a petition signed by a considerable number of the most respectable of his parishioners, desiring that Mr Hallward's services should be retained: for he refused even to look at it, declaring that he would not comply with it, had it been signed by every individual in the parish; and that Mr Hallward should never again preach in his pulpit upon any consideration.[3] He also rebuked his parish clerk for going to hear a visiting Evangelical preacher, the Rev. Philip Gurdon, curate of Cookham in the neighbourhood of Reading: 'Mr Baylis, if you expect to remain clerk in my church, you must cease to make one of a mob who run after preachers of a certain description, like Mr Gurdon.' 'Indeed sir,' replied Mr B., 'I know not of any *mob*; a few of us who had received benefit from Mr Gurdon's ministry in your church during Mr Talbot's life, were glad to hear him preach when he came so near us, and

[1] *Evangelical Magazine* (1798), p. 6.
[2] *Countess of Huntingdon*, vol. ii, p. 399.
[3] Cecil, *Memoirs*, p. xxix: *Evangelical Magazine* (1798), p. 6.

had no apprehension of giving you offence.' '*Mr Baylis, I utterly disapprove of this step; if I myself were to throw about my arms, and make a great noise, I could be popular too.*'[1] The dismissal of a curate, even under circumstances such as these, could not be regarded to-day, and was still less likely to be regarded in the eighteenth century, as a matter of more than local interest and local scandal. But the Rev. John Hallward was a curate with a history. Although only twenty-six at the time of his dismissal, he was almost a veteran of the Evangelical Revival, and might claim to be numbered among its confessors during the period of persecution. As such, he was a marked man, if not to those who opposed the Movement, at least to those who favoured and promoted it.

In the words of his friend and neighbour, the Vicar of Acton, Suffolk, who preached his Funeral Sermon, 'his religious impressions were first fixed (like Josiah's) in his sixteenth year'.[2] Previous to that date, what he himself styled 'his sinful infancy' had been spent at two or three different schools, and 'in the same vain foolish way, common to school boys'. But in March 1763 he was removed to the care of the Rev. Mr Davies, at Evesham,[3] under whose tuition and ministry, as he records in a brief autobiographical fragment, 'it pleased God to incline my heart to attend to the things of my everlasting peace. I was led to read my Bible, and to pray in secret, and to see that this was the way to heaven, and to desire to walk in it'.[4] The impressions thus received became the governing principle of his life.

In his seventeenth year he was entered as a commoner at Worcester College, Oxford. He was elected a scholar on the foundation in 1769; admitted B.A. 1770; M.A. 1773; elected to a Fellowship, 1775.[5] But his career at Oxford was more than the regular *cursus honorum* that these particulars might suggest. The fires of Methodism were still smouldering in the University of its origin. Haweis, who was a disciple of Walker of Truro,

[1] Cecil, *Memoirs*, p. liii.
[2] *Mortality swallowed up of Life. A Memorial of the Rev. John Hallward, Vicar of Assington, and Rector of Milden, Suffolk, and formerly Fellow of Worcester College, Oxford....* By John Bickersteth, M.A., Vicar of Acton, Suffolk (1827), p. 14.
[3] *Ibid.* p. 22.   [4] *Ibid.* p. 14.   [5] *Ibid.* p. 22.

CADOGAN OF READING

had come to St Mary Magdalene's as curate. There he had laboured under exceptional difficulties, for his church was placed out of bounds for undergraduates and was visited spasmodically by the proctors:[1] but his influence was felt. In 1762 the Bishop of Oxford (Dr John Hume) arbitrarily revoked his license. Haweis appealed to Archbishop Secker, offering to submit 300 of his sermons as evidence of his doctrinal orthodoxy: but his Grace of Canterbury replied, 'Sir, whether *you gave the offence, or they took it, I cannot take upon myself to determine.* I am no longer your Bishop and cannot interfere.'[2] Mr Talbot, at that time Rector of Kineton, promptly offered himself to Bishop Hume for a license to succeed Haweis in his curacy, and was as promptly refused: there was some talk of legal proceedings, or at least of publication, but the matter was allowed to drop.[3] It was evident that there was a storm brewing over Oxford: and in 1768 it broke.

A humble saddler of the town, a certain Durbridge, had been converted by George Whitefield, and had lately made an edifying death: and a small group of pious undergraduates had formed the habit of meeting regularly in his widow's drawing-room on Sunday evenings for prayer and mutual encouragement in religion. Six of them came from St Edmund Hall: James Matthews, Thomas Jones, Joseph Shipman, Benjamin Kay, Erasmus Middleton, and Thomas Grove. The others included Hallward of Worcester, Foster of Queen's, Pugh of Hertford, Gurdon of Magdalen, and Clark of St John's: but their president was a Fellow of Merton, the Rev. James Stillingfleet, a friend of Lady Huntingdon, and afterwards Prebendary of Worcester.[4] These prayer meetings, or, as the authorities preferred to regard them, illicit conventicles, do not appear to have been strictly confined to members of the University, for there is some mention in the subsequent proceedings of extempore prayer being offered

[1] [Richard Hill,] *A Letter to the Reverend Dr Nowell* (1769), p. 11 *n.*
[2] Thomas Haweis, *An Impartial and Succinct History of the Rise, Declension, and Revival of the Church of Christ* (1800), vol. iii, p. 247 *n.*; *Countess of Huntingdon*, vol. i, p. 414 *n.*
[3] Edwin Sidney, *Life of Sir Richard Hill, Bart.* (1839), pp. 83-5.
[4] *Countess of Huntingdon*, vol. i, p. 422; Edwin Sidney, *Life of the Rev. Rowland Hill* (1834), p. 31.

up by one Hewett, a stay-maker.[1] There was also a society of pious undergraduates at Cambridge, in which the guiding spirit was Rowland Hill, an undergraduate of St John's: and the two societies kept in touch, chiefly by means of correspondence between Hallward and the Hills, although there is also record of a personal visit from Rowland Hill, accompanied by two pious Danes, in July 1767, and of another a few weeks later by his elder brother, Richard, a graduate of Magdalen College, Oxford, who delivered 'a very sweet and excellent sermon'.[2] At Oxford, as at Cambridge, there seems to have been a certain amount of irregular preaching on the part of members of the society: for example, Jones had conducted an assembly for public worship at Wheaton Aston, Staffs., in which he himself, though not in holy orders, had publicly expounded the Scriptures to a mixed congregation; and offered up extempore prayers,[3] and Grove had preached to an assembly of people called Methodists in a barn;[4] and there appear to have been similar activities at Nuneham, which became known, and created a considerable stir, 'so that the people of Oxford, both Gown and Town, begin now more than ever to cry out and make a great noise'. Thus Hallward reported to Rowland Hill (Aug. 18, 1767).[5] He had himself, as Sidney puts it, 'begun preaching prematurely'[6] under the auspices of Richard Hill at Hodnet, Shropshire, which seems to have been a family living of the Hills.

Whitefield watched the experiment with a lively interest. 'The good news from Oxford is encouraging', he wrote to Rowland Hill (July 14, 1767). 'Say what they will, preaching should be one part of the education of a student in divinity—*Usus promptos facit.*'[7] Eight months later, the blow fell. The Rev. John Higson, Vice-Principal and Tutor of St Edmund Hall, went to the Principal, Dr Dixon, with a complaint 'That there were several

---

[1] Thomas Nowell, D.D., *An Answer to a Pamphlet, entitled Pietas Oxoniensis* (1768), p. 25.
[2] Edwin Sidney, *Life of Sir Richard Hill, Bart.* (1839), pp. 100–2: the same author's *Life of the Rev. Rowland Hill*, p. 31.
[3] Cf. [R. Hill], *Pietas Oxoniensis* (1768), p. 6.
[4] This he denied.—*Ibid.* p. 17. But cf. Nowell's *Answer*, p. 142.
[5] Sidney, *Richard Hill*, p. 102.
[6] *Ibid.* p. 100.   [7] Sidney, *Rowland Hill*, p. 33.

Enthusiasts in that society, who talked of regeneration, inspiration, and drawing nigh unto GOD'.[1] But, seeing that Mr Higson had the misfortune to be subject to recurring fits of insanity, and had previously been under restraint, Dr Dixon 'thought that the less he argued the case with him the better, and only observed, that these were all scriptural phrases or apostolical expressions, and the use of them authorised by the offices of the Church of *England*, [and] that therefore he could see no cause to look upon the Gentlemen as enthusiasts for having adopted these terms'.[2] As he afterwards confided to Richard Hill, he 'never remembered in his own, or in any other College, six students whose lives were so exemplary, and who behaved themselves in a more humble, regular, peaceable manner' than the accused.[3] But Mr Higson was not satisfied. He made private enquiries, and then, having collected a good deal of evidence from various quarters,[4] adopted the extreme measure of appealing to the Vice-Chancellor, Dr Durell, in his capacity as Visitor of St Edmund Hall.

The Vice-Chancellor encouraged him to present formal articles of accusation against the offending students, and himself meanwhile consulted with the Heads of Houses as to what measures to adopt. The Heads were not at first disposed to take the matter very seriously. It was felt that discipline would be sufficiently asserted if the young men were reprimanded and asked to promise not to repeat their offences, a promise which they were quite prepared to make.[5] But 'certain intimations of what was wished to be done were received from a certain quarter',[6] 'yea even from a Right Reverend quarter, which much changed the face of the young men's affairs, and caused it to wear a blacker aspect'.[7] It was accordingly decided to make a public example

[1] *Pietas Oxoniensis*, p. 2. [2] *Ibid.* p. 3.
[3] Sidney, *Richard Hill*, p. 106.
[4] *Ibid.* p. 105 (Sidney had access to Mr Higson's papers, and quotes from this correspondence).
[5] S. L. Ollard, *The Six Students of St Edmund Hall expelled from the University of Oxford in 1768* (the best and fullest account), 1911, p. 9.
[6] *Goliath Slain*, p. 16.
[7] *Letter to Dr Nowell*, p. 9.—Hill evidently suspected the intervention of Bishop Hume, translated from Oxford to Salisbury in 1766, and an ardent anti-Methodist (Ollard, p. 9). He also speaks of Higson being made 'the tool or cat's-paw' of others, 'to perpetrate what, thro' shame or fear, they durst not undertake themselves' (*Pietas Oxoniensis*, p. 4).

of the accused: and Matthews, Jones, Shipman, Kay, Middleton, and Grove were duly summoned to appear before the Vice-Chancellor and his four Assessors[1] (Dr Randolph, President of Corpus and Lady Margaret Professor; Dr Fothergill, Provost of Queen's; Dr Nowell, Principal of St Mary Hall, and Public Orator; and Mr Atterbury, of Christ Church, the Senior Proctor). All six were accused of being 'enemies to the doctrine and discipline of the Church of *England*'; Matthews, Middleton, Jones, and Shipman were further accused of being 'destitute of such a knowledge in the learned languages as is necessary for performing the usual exercises of the said Hall and of the University',[2] and the two former of having also behaved indecently towards their Tutor, 'either by neglecting to attend his lectures, or misbehaving themselves, when at them';[3] and Matthews, Jones, and Shipman were in addition accused of being 'bred to trades'. There was also a separate accusation against Middleton, of having officiated 'as a minister in holy orders, altho' a layman, in the parish Church of *Cheveley*, or in one of the Chapels of Ease belonging and appertaining unto the said Church of *Cheveley* in the county of *Berks*, and diocese of *Salisbury*'.[4] On March 11, 1768, the Vice-Chancellor pronounced that all the accused be expelled from St Edmund Hall, and expressed the thanks of the whole University to Mr Higson for that day's work.[5]

[1] It was intended originally to have only three, and Dr Dixon was permitted to nominate two of them; 'the fourth was added afterwards at the request of Mr *Higson*, who had ungenerously expressed some apprehensions of partiality in the other assessors to the cause of the Principal' (Nowell's *Answer*, p. 8). Mr Higson did not at first make at all a good impression on the Assessors (*ibid.* p. 7).—Dr Dixon denied to Hill that he had the appointment of any of the Assessors (*Letter to Dr Nowell*, p. 6).

[2] A seventh undergraduate, one Benjamin Blatch, was also included in this accusation, and in that of neglecting Mr Higson's lectures: but, since he was no Methodist, and 'was represented to be a man of fortune, and declared that he was not designed for holy orders' (Nowell's *Answer*, 2nd ed. p. 55), the charges against him were dropped (Ollard, p. 13).

[3] Cf. Ollard, pp. 5–6, for the true explanation of this charge.

[4] Hill did not attempt to defend what he admitted to be 'a very high indiscretion, and a flagrant violation of the Twenty-third Article': but he pointed out that the offence had been committed (and repented) 'a long time before he was a member of the University', and that Middleton had ever since behaved with the greatest regularity (*Pietas Oxoniensis*, pp. 23–4).

[5] *A Letter to the Reverend Dr Durell, Vicechancellor of the University of Oxford....* by George Whitefield, M.A., late of Pembroke College, Oxford; and Chaplain to the Countess of Huntingdon (1768), p. 20.

There was a good deal in the proceedings that invited criticism. For example, part of the evidence against Jones was a letter from a gentleman in Shropshire, who testified that the accused had made him a periwig:[1] and another witness for the prosecution, a commoner of St Edmund Hall, John Welling, known to his fellow-undergraduates as 'the Infidel',[2] was not only notoriously more illiterate and of even lower social extraction than any of the accused, but was also proved to have delivered it as his opinion ' "that whosoever believed the miracles of our SAVIOUR or of MOSES, must be a knave or a fool", or words to the like import'.[3] It is true that some notice was taken of this, and Mr Welling was obliged, before being allowed to proceed to holy orders, to read a public apology, to the effect that when he uttered those expressions he was disguised in liquor at the St John's Gaudy.[4] But the animus of the Court throughout the proceedings was so obvious as to be indecent; and even the President of Magdalen, Dr Horne, the future Bishop of Norwich, commented mildly that 'if these six gentlemen were expelled for having too much religion, it would be very proper to enquire into the conduct of some who had too little'.[5]

Inevitably the verdict was followed by a war of pamphlets.[6] Whitefield addressed an open letter to the Vice-Chancellor, admirable, restrained, and trenchant, but dealing only with the general aspects of the case and with the principles at stake. Richard Hill published anonymously his *Pietas Oxoniensis*,[7] the best and fullest defence of the Six Students, based presumably on information received from Hallward, among others. To this the Public Orator, Dr Nowell, who had been one of the Vice-

[1] Sidney, *Richard Hill*, p. 116.—This allegation was afterwards declared to be untrue.
[2] *Pietas Oxoniensis*, p. 22.   [3] *Ibid.* p. 22.
[4] Nowell's *Answer*, pp. 56–63. 'An acquaintance of his asking this Gentleman why he went into Orders, as he did not believe the Bible? He answered (as I am very credibly informed) "that he might as well be paid for reading that Book as any other".' (*Pietas Oxoniensis*, p. 79 *n.*, where also a merciless exposure of 'the sordid and disgraceful records of his past': Ollard, pp. 25–6.)
[5] Sidney's *Rowland Hill*, p. 41.
[6] *Vide* Ollard, pp. 51–6.
[7] 'By a Master of Arts of the University of Oxford.' Dedication to the Rt. Hon. the Earl of Lichfield, Chancellor of the University.

Chancellor's Assessors, felt it necessary to reply. He adopted a tone of magisterial scorn, and claimed that 'it was no injury but rather a kindness to send them from a place, where they were mis-employing their time, and abusing the ill-placed kindness of their friends, who supported them here in idleness, that they might follow their respective trades elsewhere, and get their livelihood in an honest, and reputable manner. Mr *J—s* makes a good periwig; he need not starve, he may get his bread by his proper profession. Mr *M—s* and Mr *S—n* may maintain themselves and serve their country better at the loom, or at the tap, or behind the counter, than they were likely to do in the pulpit —tractent fabrilia fabri.—'[1] Hill retorted with *Goliath Slain*. Nowell brought out a second edition (1769) of his *Answer*, fuller and longer than the first. Hill returned to the attack with *A Letter to the Reverend Dr Nowell: containing some Remarks on certain Alterations and Additions in the Second Edition of his Answer to Pietas Oxoniensis*. A writer, who simply signed himself 'No Methodist', supported him with *Strictures on an Answer to Pietas Oxoniensis*. These were the most important pamphlets in the controversy: there were many others, of which the most scurrilous was contributed by a Baptist minister in London, John Macgowan, formerly a Methodist local preacher: '*Priestcraft Defended: a Sermon, occasioned by the Expulsion of Six Young Gentlemen from the University of Oxford*. By the Shaver.'

But the true significance of the verdict was disclosed by Dr Nowell, who expressed his satisfaction that the unscrupulous designs of the Methodist leaders 'of filling the church with their votaries have by this seasonable interposition been disappointed; and the plan, which they have for some time been labouring to accomplish, is at present disconcerted at least, if not entirely defeated'.[2] Similarly, the Countess of Huntingdon found herself accused in the public journals of 'seducing' young men from their trades and sending them to the University, that they

[1] Nowell's *Answer*, p. 55.—On 'the absurdity and indecency of the usage of extempore prayers', *ibid.* pp. 133–5.
[2] *Ibid.* p. 1.

214

might 'SKULK INTO ORDERS';[1] an accusation to which her Ladyship did not deign to reply. The University of Whitefield and the Wesleys had openly declared itself against the Evangelical Revival. The warning was too rude to be mistaken: henceforward Cambridge was to be the University at which Evangelical clergy must receive their training.[2]

The expulsion had its repercussions, and a few more undergraduates were sent down, or induced to take their names off the books of their respective colleges. So implacable were the University authorities, that Grove, who had petitioned the Archbishop of Canterbury (Secker), was denied readmission to St Edmund Hall despite his willingness to make submission for irregularity, and even despite the fact that he was supported by the Chancellor, the Earl of Lichfield. But Hallward himself was not molested: and in 1773 he was ordained deacon, and

[1] *Countess of Huntingdon*, vol. i, p. 425: *Pietas Oxoniensis*, p. 22: Tyerman's *Whitefield*, vol. ii, p. 542.—This charge was widely circulated and widely believed, both in the University and outside it. Cf. the letters of a contemporary undergraduate of University College, Walter Stanhope, who speaks of 'a Herd of Methodistical Handicraftsmen', and of 'Eight Methodistical Mechanics... entered at St Edmund Hall with a view to procure Orders, by means of a recommendation, as was supposed, from Lady Huntingdon to the Principal; and five of them (*proh pudor*), Gentlemen Commoners, in sooth a barber, a grocer, a soap-boiler, a tallow-chandler, and a blacksmith' (*Annals of a Yorkshire House*, 1911, vol. i, pp. 227, 228). Cf. also Dr Johnson's observations about a cow in a garden (Boswell's *Life of Johnson*, ed. G. Birkbeck Hill, vol. ii, p. 187).

[2] Magdalene, where Farish became Tutor in 1782, was their first asylum, and the Elland Society sent its ordinands there. 'Forty years ago I had none but Magdalen men at my parties' ('Mr Simeon's personal reminiscences', Brown, p. 191): Magdalene in 1786 'the general resort of young men seriously impressed with a sense of religion' (*Memoirs of the Rev. Thomas Dykes* by the Rev. John King, 1849, p. 6): cf. *Gradus ad Cantabrigiam* (1803), s.v. SIMEONITES (p. 119): Rev. R. Polwhele's Introduction to Bishop Lavington's *The Enthusiasm of Methodists and Papists compared* (1820), p. cclxxxviii. (Section xx.—Universities—Seeds of Sectarism sown there.—'That the seeds of Sectarism are sown even in our universities, is a notorious fact. There are colleges both at Oxford and Cambridge, that pay particular attention to the education of Gospel ministers. In Cambridge, Magdalen-college is reported to pour forth Evangelical students more copiously than Edmund-hall in Oxford. It is highly necessary, therefore, that the heads of the universities watch over such societies, and that they check the slightest tendency in their youth to Evangelical irregularities.')—Later the balance shifted towards Queens' under the energetic rule of Isaac Milner (George Dyer, *Privileges of the University of Cambridge*, vol. ii (1824), Supplement (*Cambridge Fragments*), p. 23).—Also from 1783 to 1854 St Edmund Hall again became the Evangelical centre in Oxford: Ollard, p. 47; *Memoir of the Rev. William Marsh, D.D.* (1867), p. 15: *Christian Observer*, June 1837, p. 411.

licensed to Mr Talbot at St Giles', Reading. His vicar died during the period of his diaconate, but, under the sequestration caused by Mr Cadogan's minority, he was continued in his curacy by the churchwardens, and was ordained priest on the same title, which was readily accepted by the Bishop.[1] A few months later, the new Vicar of St Giles' notified his predecessor's curate that his services would no longer be required. As Hallward himself bore witness, he did it like a gentleman, as he did everything else:[2] but he did it all the same.

The ejected curate had at least one consolation: he did not have to worry how he was to support himself. The Evangelical Party in the Church of England may have been numerically weak, but it had a remarkable solidarity and cohesion: and, among other things, it possessed something of the character of a society for mutual protection and assistance. Towards the close of 1775, Hallward, who in the previous May had been elected to a Fellowship at his old College, was presented by Mr Richard Hill to the living of Shawbury, Salop, which he resigned four years later on being presented by the Rev. Philip Gurdon of Assington Hall, Suffolk, to the adjacent benefices of Assington and Milden in that county. Mr Gurdon has already been mentioned as curate of Cookham, Berks., and an old friend of Mr Talbot. But his acquaintance with John Hallward was of even longer standing, for it went back to the days when 'Mr Hallward of Worcester' and 'Mr Gurdon of Magdalen'[3] had been fellow-members of that small society of pious undergraduates which used to meet for prayers and mutual encouragement in Mrs Durbridge's drawing-room on Sunday evenings.

Hallward died in harness on Dec. 21, 1826, at the age of seventy-seven. His piety, from the time of his commencing his religious course sixty-two years before, had been remarkably even and consistent, and old age had merely added an increased

[1] Cecil, *Mem.* p. xxvii.—Ironically enough, this was none other than Bishop Hume: but the prelate who had deprived Haweis of his license was no doubt unconscious of Hallward's connection with the Six Students of St Edmund Hall.
[2] Cecil, *Mem.* p. lvi.
[3] Demy of Magdalen College, 1765–8: B.A. 1768, M.A. 1770: Fellow, 1770–8: † 7 May 1817.

solemnity and earnestness to his ministry His last sermon to his parishioners, delivered on the Sunday before his death, was an exhortation 'more than usually affecting, copious, impressive, and tender' to celebrate the Feast of Christmas at the Lord's Table, alluring them to compliance, anticipating and answering their objections, reproving their delay, and reminding them how many had been, how soon they themselves might be, by the hand of death, arrested and beguiled of another opportunity.[1] Before that week was out, he who had made it the subject of his repeated prayers that in dying he might have nothing to do but to die,[2] was taken suddenly, as he had wished.

Upon the dismissal of their curate, the congregation of St Giles' soon dispersed. 'It would be the foolishness of folly', writes Mr Seymour, 'to suppose that those who have ever experimentally been taught the truth as it is in Jesus, and tasted indeed that the Lord is gracious, would be confined to the walls of a parish church, when *Ichabod* is written upon them; and neither the same gospel preached, nor the same exemplary conduct or zeal and labour pursued by the successor.[3] Many naturally repaired to those places where the gospel was preached in their vicinity, where they could hear to edification; others, not satisfied with the new doctrines preached by the vicar, nor the form and discipline of the dissenting meetings, applied to the Countess of Huntingdon, and, having taken a place which would contain several hundred people, opened it as a chapel according to the forms of the Established Church, where they might worship God in their own customary way, and sit again under the refreshing sound of Jesus Christ and his salvation.'[4]

Mr Hallward had himself written immediately to her Ladyship to notify her that the blow had fallen, and had received in reply a vague epistle steeped in pious casuistry. '...The wisdom from above is as free from partiality as it is from hypocrisy.... The present Reformation has been owned by the Lord under

[1] Bickersteth, *Mortality swallowed up of Life*, pp. 17–18.
[2] *Ibid.* p. 18.
[3] This sentence is lifted (as usual, without acknowledgement) from Thomas Haweis' *Life of the Rev. William Romaine* (1797), pp. 200–1.
[4] *Countess of Huntingdon*, vol. ii, pp. 401–2.

the general idea of *irregularity*; but I humbly think his orders
are more regularly observed by this conduct than by any other
means....The express word of God orders and directs his
servants, as messengers of peace to the whole world....Simple,
childlike obedience, while the heart is led by the spirit of God,
and consistently disposed and united with the precepts, never
can, or ever did, essentially err....My point is, I fairly own,
for myself a universal devotedness through all, and such as
would make me, by disposition, and not by plausible appearance,
the honest and simple disciple of Jesus Christ; neither formality
nor legal bondages having any part of my care, but the pure
truth, according to the Bible, verified and understood, by being
actually possessed and experienced, and as by this only God is
glorified. When this becomes the real state of the heart, whether
in the Church or out of it, is no material matter....'[1]

There was prejudice on both sides: but it is clear that Mr
Cadogan was never even given a fair trial. Long before his
arrival, his congregation had quite made up their minds that he
was an enemy of 'vital godliness', and at his arrival they rapidly
dispersed. The Baptist minister, Mr Thomas Davis, being by
far the most lively preacher in the town, attracted the greatest
number, 'who, desiring full communion, where they profited
most, successively joined his church, till it became, in point of
numbers, one of the largest societies in the kingdom of the
Baptist denomination'.[2] Others, retaining a prejudice for
Anglican forms of worship, supported Lady Huntingdon's
chapel. Those who remained loyal to St Giles' did so in a highly
critical frame of mind: they remarked upon Mr Cadogan's
mistakes 'without modesty or respect; and some even presumed
to admonish him in his way from church'. The sons of noblemen
are not accustomed to be treated in that manner: and, as the
pious Cecil judiciously observes, 'persons who, like Mr C., have
acquired from their education a quick sense of what belongs to
decorum and good manners, receive a shock at conduct like that
above mentioned, which others can scarcely conceive'. Hitherto

---

[1] *Countess of Huntingdon*, vol. ii, pp. 399–401.
[2] *Ev. Mag.* (1798), p. 6.

Mr Cadogan, 'like too many more, had associated with his idea of...evangelical religion, that of the vulgar habits and fanatical weaknesses of some who profess (and sometimes do no more than profess) to embrace it': and the behaviour of these zealous and well-meaning individuals, who were 'utterly unfit to treat a case like his', merely intensified his prejudices by affronting his pride.[1]

There were other aggravating circumstances. In November 1775, Mr Hallward published a Charity Commemoration Sermon, which he had preached the previous December, entitled *The doctrine of Faith and Good Works stated and considered*, prefaced by a brief tribute to the memory and character of Mr Talbot. This was indeed to turn the knife in the wound.[2] But still more aggravating was the fact that Mrs Talbot not only considered it her duty not to remove from the spot where her late husband's labours had been so richly blessed, but actually opened her own house for religious exercises: 'Lady Huntingdon's chaplains, Mr Romaine, Mr Shirley, and Mr Glascott, united with Mr Newton, Mr Venn, and Mr [Rowland] Hill, and other ministers who visited her, in expounding the Scriptures to the people; and prayer was continually offered up under her roof for the conversion of Mr Cadogan.'[3] Even those who are most willing to be prayed for are seldom willing to be prayed for publicly in that way. Mr Cadogan was highly annoyed, and remonstrated vehemently; and various letters passed between them.

It was no wonder, therefore, that he decided to fix his principal residence at Chelsea, rather than at Reading. He expended over £800 upon repairing the parsonage house, which was extremely dilapidated, no Rector having resided there for the

---

[1] Cecil, *Mem.* pp. xxxix–xli, xlv.

[2] The sermon was bitterly assailed in the *Reading Mercury* by an anonymous writer, subsequently revealed to be the Rev. William Wainhouse, a former curate of St Giles', who described Mr Hallward as an 'inconsistent, damning, harsh, uncouth, flighty, rhapsodical, odious, uncharitable preacher'. Thereupon Richard Hill, whose appetite for religious controversy was growing with its exercise, rushed to the defence of his old friend and client with a pamphlet entitled *Pietas Redingensis*, which contains a noted passage on the character of 'a *moderate divine*'. (Sidney, *Richard Hill*, pp. 248–52.)

[3] *Countess of Huntingdon*, vol. ii, p. 402.

past ten years: and he went into occupation in the following year (1776).[1] At once he plunged with unexpected zeal and energy into the work of his parochial cure. 'Mr C.', writes one who knew him intimately at this period, 'not only laboured hard to instruct and reform his parish, but wished to know every person in it: the most miserable cottage was not neglected. He exhorted them all to come to church, and live like Christians.' He visited assiduously: he sought out unbaptised children: he became principal manager of the charity schools, and distributed Bibles and Prayer Books to the pupils: he delivered extemporary lectures on the Catechism on Wednesdays and Fridays: in winter, he doled out meat and broth to the poor, 'and, to prevent their continuing in total ignorance of religion, he insisted upon their first saying the Lord's Prayer, or engaging to learn it against the next time they came'.[2] A strict Sabbatarian, he set his face resolutely against Sunday trading, and used to rise at five o'clock and go round the parish with his servant, entering any shops that he found open, remonstrating with the proprietors, and threatening them with prosecution if they continued. 'Several, disregarding his admonitions, were fined; and some of them theatened to murder him, but he pursued his course without fear.... By such perseverance this scandalous custom was in a considerable degree repressed.'[3] 'His zeal also appears from his conduct towards a set of ringers, who used to begin their entertainment early on a Sunday morning. He took his Bible, went up into the belfry, and told them that as some *serious* and some *sick* persons in the parish might find their ringing at such an unseasonable time a great disturbance, he was come to make their early rising more profitable: then opening the Bible, he expounded some suitable scripture for a considerable time. Both the ringing, however, and the expounding ended on that occasion, for the ringers came no more.'[4] He even proposed to rebuild and enlarge his church, which, besides being decayed, was small and inconvenient: but he failed to arouse any enthusiasm for this project among his parishioners.[5]

[1] Cecil, *Mem.* p. xix.   [2] Quoted by Cecil, *Mem.* pp. xx–xxi.
[3] *Ibid.* pp. xxi–xxii.   [4] *Ibid.* p. xxii.   [5] *Ibid.* p. xxii.

Indeed, by this time the novelty of his coming as the son of Lord Cadogan had worn off, and his popularity was at an end. 'The train of coaches that first attended his church soon drew off, and the parish in general did not choose to be disturbed.'[1]

Baffled at Chelsea, he turned back again to Reading. The irony of the situation was that his unpopularity in the former parish was due to the fact that he was held to be, and in the latter parish to the fact that he was held not to be, a favourer of what its enemies described as 'Methodism' and its friends as 'vital godliness'.[2] Actually, as Cecil says, 'he had been brought up, and certainly remained to the last, what many would call a high churchman'.[3] Here, as so often, the precise significance of that term is not entirely clear: and his biographer himself hastens immediately to add that he was not bigoted against evangelical Dissenters, and that he was a decided Calvinist in his theological opinions. But, whatever may be implied here by the words 'High Churchman', it is evident that Mr Cadogan at the outset of his ministry was a sincere and conscientious clergyman with a strong pastoral instinct, if of a somewhat autocratic cast; and also that he was violently prejudiced against the 'Methodists'. In Evangelical language, he was 'perfectly legal'.[4] When John Wesley, hearing of his zeal and his integrity, sent him a complete collection of his works, the recipient with considerable indignation burnt the whole lot upon his kitchen fire, declaring that 'he was determined to form his opinions from the Bible alone. We cannot but commend his zeal for the Scriptures', observes Mr Cecil, 'and also his refusing to take Mr Wesley as their interpreter' (Cecil was a staunch Calvinist): 'but surely his immediately consigning so many volumes, without distinction, to the flames, savoured of rashness'.[5]

Rashness apart, it was men of his stamp, although admittedly seldom of his station, who were the salt of the Hanoverian Church; the salt that kept it from corruption. As the second son of an heir to a peerage, he had, like Samuel, been early

---

[1] Cecil, *Mem.* p. xxiv.
[2] *Ibid.* p. xxxii.
[3] *Ibid.* p. xcviii.
[4] *Ev. Mag.* (1798), p. 8.
[5] Cecil, *Mem.* pp. xxxvii–xxxviii.

destined to the sacred ministry, although from very different motives. The eldest son was naturally intended for the Army: provision for the second could be afforded by the ecclesiastical Establishment. As it happened, his own youthful inclinations coincided with the more worldly outlook of his relatives: but there was always the danger lest the latter should become predominant, and the young Cadogan settle down to the comfortable, unexacting life of a negligent and wealthy pluralist. It was, however, his good fortune to have a mother and a grandmother who were both piously disposed, and who instructed him from his infancy in the Holy Scriptures. At Westminster, where he became a King's Scholar and Captain of the School, his early religious impressions were strengthened by his sometimes attending, with one of his school-fellows, the ministry of a zealous clergyman at the west end of the town. There was also a Mr Bakewell who kept a school in Palace Yard, and who, though often interrupted by the rudeness of the Westminster scholars, preached in the evenings to such of his neighbours as wished to attend. The young Cadogan not infrequently resorted there to jeer with his companions, but often he found himself impressed against his will: and Cecil states that he received many friendly attentions from Mr and Mrs Bakewell, who endeavoured to impress upon his mind the nature and importance of vital godliness.[1]

From Westminster he entered Christ Church, Oxford, in 1769. There he distinguished himself in the academic line: but at the same time his religious impressions became deeper and more lasting. He felt acutely the tension between his own convictions and the tone of the undergraduate set in which he moved: and though he kept pious books upon his shelves, he had a shameful care to have them in plain bindings and not lettered on the backs.[2] Now at Reading, after these bitter disappointments, that tension was once more renewed. 'He had at this time the strongest conflicts between the dictates of his conscience and the influence of his habits and circumstances.'[3]

[1] Cecil, *Mem.* pp. xii–xiii, xv; *Ev. Mag.* (1798), p. 4.
[2] Cecil, *Mem.* p. xvi.   [3] Cecil, *Mem.* p. xl.

His father had just succeeded to the peerage, and was Master of the Mint and in high favour at court. It would have been extraordinarily easy for him to have abandoned the pastoral struggle, and to have drifted lazily in the direction of a bishopric. About this time, he used to pass many hours at his family seat at Caversham, but principally in the library, where he abandoned himself to religious exercises, to writing sermons, and, in particular, to reading the Scriptures on his knees. At a much later date he showed to one of his curates a Bible in that library, covered with his annotations, and said: 'Thus I spent my time here, while I was despised both by the world and by the church.'[1]

But, in the words of Mr Cecil, 'Providence, which never wants instruments suited to its purposes, had prepared for him the *Friend*, the *Guide*, and the *Example* he so much needed.'[2] When he first came to Reading, Mrs Talbot, with perfect courtesy, had invited him to select any books that suited him from her late husband's library. At that first meeting, she saw at once that he was not all that she had hoped and prayed for: but she saw also that at least he was of a very different character 'from such as have no other notion of their ministry than that of a mere *profession*, which, like the Physician's or Lawyer's, should be turned to the greatest worldly advantage. She observed in him a serious *aim* to do good, though he had but a very imperfect knowledge of the *means*': and from that moment she formed the resolution 'to bear with his defects, and endeavour to draw out and cultivate his excellencies'.[3] From this first acquaintance, their relations passed through an acrimonious correspondence— acrimonious on his side, at least—into a deeper intimacy, founded on mutual respect. Her elegant manners and perfect sensibility afforded both a contrast and an antidote to the rudeness he had suffered at the hands of others: he recognized her absolute sincerity, admired her piety, and finally yielded to her influence. In the sermon which he preached on the occasion of her funeral (Dec. 4, 1785), he spoke of her 'not only as the best friend I ever had in my life, but as a Mother to me in love, in every good office, and in continual prayers for my person and

[1] Cecil, *Mem.* p. xxviii.   [2] *Ibid.* p. xli.   [3] *Ibid.* p. xliv.

ministry', and 'as the common friend and parent of the church of G O D in this place committed to my care'.[1]

The alteration in his sentiments became manifest to his parishioners: and in the spring of 1780, he requested Mrs Talbot to forward a letter which he had written to Lady Huntingdon asking her advice about his preaching, and to which in due course he received a long and rambling answer exhorting him chiefly to cry aloud, and spare not.[2] In September of the same year he wrote very humbly to Mr Hallward, inviting him to return to his old curacy: but Mr Hallward had been otherwise provided for, although he readily consented to desert his own parishes for six months in order to come and minister the Word again at Reading.[3] By this date Mr Cadogan's conversion to Evangelical principles was decided: and he paid the price of it a little after by being passed over for a canonry at Westminster which, from his aristocratic connections, he might otherwise have secured.[4]

It is true, however, that in the following year (1781) he suffered a short and violent reaction which assailed him when he least expected it. This is, of course, a perfectly normal phenomenon of the spiritual life. The truth is that he badly needed a holiday after six years of intense psychological and spiritual strain. His own account of this episode is contained in a letter to the Rev. John Newton (Nov. 16, 1782).[5] 'I was enticed from the care of souls into Suffolk, with my worldly friends; got into their habits—entered into their spirit—and found how timely it was said of the faithful, "that if they had been mindful of that country from whence they came, they might have had opportunity to have returned". I was received, caressed, and I may say, that I had almost been even as they; my treadings had well nigh slipped.' But a severe illness, which laid him at death's door, brought him to recollection and repentance: and from that

---

[1] *The Love of Christ the Portion and Principle of the Children of God.* Reprinted in Cadogan's *Discourses* (1798), p. 32.—There is a short account of Mrs Talbot in Samuel Burder's *Memoirs of Eminently Pious Women of the British Empire* (ed. 1815), vol. ii, pp. 272–80.

[2] *Countess of Huntingdon*, vol. ii, pp. 407–9.

[3] Cecil, *Mem.* pp. lvii–lix; *Ev. Mag.* (1798), p. 9.

[4] Cecil, *Mem.* p. lx. [5] Cadogan's *Discourses*, pp. 335–9.

THE REVEREND THE HONOURABLE WILLIAM BROMLEY CADOGAN

From an engraving by J. Collyer after a miniature

day forward, he sought no more the friendship of the world. It may also have been providential that he temporarily alienated his family by what they considered an imprudent marriage with the widow of a military officer of undistinguished rank.[1]

As a parish priest he was exemplary, judged by the standards of the age. For several years, he resided at Chelsea from January to June, coming over to Reading on the first Sunday of each month, and resided at Reading from July to December, returning to Chelsea on the last Sunday of each month to administer the Sacrament.[2] This arrangement must, however, have been somewhat modified after his marriage in December 1782, for, Mrs Cadogan being something of an invalid, he endeavoured to procure her relief by travelling: and in 1785, 1786, and 1788 they toured in Scotland, in Wales, and in the Isle of Wight.[3] Later, having allowed himself to be persuaded by his family to let the parsonage at Chelsea, and finding lodgings inconvenient, he left his London parish almost entirely in the hands of his curate, Mr Middleton, except during Lent and on the last Sunday of each month, when he generally went up to preach and to administer the Lord's Supper.[4] But there is evidence of a genuine effort to satisfy the needs of both parishes: nor would it have occurred to anybody at that date that he ought to have resigned one or other of them.

It was his habit, both in summer and in winter, to retire at 11.0 p.m. or after, and to rise at 6.0 a.m. Excepting his attendance at breakfast and family prayers, he worked in his study until noon: he then went out on horseback for about two hours, visiting his outlying parishioners in the country: after dinner, he used to visit those in the town. He disliked mere social visiting, and, apart from a few select friends, confined his visits to the sick, the afflicted, and the poor. His charity was liberal, and not discreet: on Saturdays he used to go out visiting with his pocket full of silver: 'nor could any of his congregation mention an object of distress, but he was always ready to give what they required'. During the three winter months he supplied the

[1] Cecil, *Mem.* p. lxvi; *Ev. Mag.* (1798), p. 11.
[2] Cecil, *Mem.* p. xciv.   [3] *Ibid.* p. lxxii.
[4] *Ev. Mag.* (1798), p. 10.

poor of the parish with meat and broth, 'for which purpose', recorded his widow, 'we had thirty pounds of beef every week'.[1]

His conversation was serious and earnest. 'He neither debilitated his mind by idleness and gossiping, nor by gorging it with too much study.'[2] His mornings were chiefly spent in studying the Hebrew Bible or the Greek Testament, 'so that he acquired a knowledge of the bible beyond most men, and expressed himself in the pulpit, and upon all other occasions, with incredible facility'.[3] Of human authors, he gave the preference to Archbishop Leighton: 'but you might have found him remarking with delight on the works of Fenelon or Quesnel, of Baxter or Erskine, of Bishop Horne, or his biographer Jones; though on some points he could not but wish that they had expressed themselves otherwise'.[4]

On Sundays he held three services in church, transferring Evensong from the usual hour ('immediately after dinner, when both preacher and hearer are generally heavy'[5]) and turning it into an evening service: in the afternoon, prayers were read at 3.0, and either he or his curate catechised the children. In addition, he generally managed to find time to visit the Sunday-schools, which were his great concern, and cost him at least £30 a year.[6] He himself preached morning and evening, and sometimes (the curate being ill or absent) in the afternoon:[7] he also preached a Thursday evening lecture, and on Tuesday evenings admitted his parishioners to his family worship—reading of Scripture with exposition and prayer—in his own parlour, until pressure of numbers necessitated a removal to the chancel of St Giles'.[8] The Lord's Supper was administered every month, and so numerous were the communicants, certainly at Chelsea, that he obtained permission from the Bishop (Lowth) to pro-

---

[1] Cecil, *Mem.* pp. xc–xcii; *Ev. Mag.* (1798), pp. 12–13.
[2] *Ev. Mag.* (1798), p. 12.
[3] *Ibid.* p. 12; Cecil, *Mem.* p. cxv: 'His mind was a concordance and harmony of Scripture'.
[4] Cecil, *Mem.* p. c.
[5] Cadogan to Hallward, Sept. 3, 1780: Cecil, *Mem.* p. lviii.
[6] Cecil, *Mem.* p. xci; *Ev. Mag.* (1798), p. 11.
[7] *Ev. Mag.* (1798), p. 10.　　　　　　　[8] *Ibid.* p. 11.

nounce the words of administration to more than one communicant at a time.[1]

His preaching, which was extempore, was plain, and very scriptural. His delivery was not good. He had at all times 'a scowling sort of aspect':[2] his voice was deep-toned and rough, and his utterance in the pulpit 'rather indistinct, and at times unpleasantly monotonous.... His memory indeed was remarkably strong, his mind firm and vigorous, and his discourses studied; but he had little Imagination, Taste, or Ear.'[3] The power of his sermons came from the passionate sincerity and urgency with which they were delivered.[4] 'He had', says Cecil, 'such a conviction of the reality and importance of divine Revelation, that he did not treat of it as some do, who seem to doubt whether it would bear them out should they go all lengths with it.... In treating of his grand theme, the glory of the Redeemer, I know not that he has left his equal upon earth.'[5] He was essentially a parochial preacher, and, even on holiday, was never happy preaching away from either of his parishes. 'He often said when he was absent, that "*he feared he was not in the path of duty, and for that reason did not preach so comfortably abroad*". He used to wonder at the taste of those who love running from house to house.'[6]

At Chelsea, 'where few of the inhabitants had been used to the gospel',[7] his ministry was not perhaps very generally appreciated. But at Reading he quickly refilled St Giles': indeed, such multitudes flocked to hear him from all parts of the town and from the surrounding villages, that in 1784 an enormous

[1] Cecil, *Mem.* p. lxxvii.—Cf. J. H. Overton, *The English Church in the 19th century*, p. 129.
[2] *Ibid.* p. cxiii.
[3] *Ibid.* p. cxvii.—This passage was slightly toned down in the final version (Cecil's *Works*, vol. i, pp. 263–4).
[4] Cf. the characterisation of various preachers of the time of John Bacon, R.A., the eminent sculptor, and a lay-member of the Eclectic Society, at a meeting of the Society on Jan. 21, 1799. 'Cadogan:—had no variety, tone, or dash; but perception of subject: determination: sawing through: energy: reality: he took by force; the one object he kept in view.' [Josiah Pratt's] *Eclectic Notes; or, Notes of Discussions on Religious Topics at the Meetings of the Eclectic Society, London, during the years 1798–1814*, ed. John H. Pratt (2nd ed. 1865), p. 92.
[5] Cecil, *Mem.* pp. cxviii–cxix.
[6] Cecil, *Mem.* p. xciii.   [7] *Ev. Mag.* (1798), p. 10.

gallery had to be put in, and five years later, the congregation still increasing, Mr Cadogan offered to enlarge the church at his own expense. But the Vestry prudently declined his offer, on the ground that after his death the additional room might not be wanted.[1]

Their prudence was entirely justified by the event. That was indeed the fatal limitation which attended such a ministry as this, so rich in its immediate blossoms, but so uncertain of abiding fruits. Too much was allowed to depend upon the personality of a single individual, upon the maintenance of a particular brand of doctrine, upon the ministry of preaching as a thing in isolation from the Common Prayer. The Evangelical preachers were men very much in earnest: they were also, on the whole, peculiarly selfless and free from the personal vanity which is the besetting temptation of the popular preacher: but they set an exaggerated and distorted value, not upon their preaching, but on preaching itself:[2] and when preaching becomes concreted in a sermon, to attach importance to that sermon at the expense of, and without regard to, the act of common worship to which it is intended to be ancillary, is to turn a congregation of humble worshippers into an audience of captious critics. Needless to say, the silly affectation, sometimes to be observed in Anglo-Catholic churches of the 'advanced' type, of pretending not to listen to the sermon but rather busying oneself with a rosary or a St Swithun's Prayer Book or some manual of private devotion, is equally obnoxious, because it savours equally of spiritual pride, and because it is equally a negation of the whole principle of corporate worship. We do not come to church in order to hear sermons, but neither do we come to church in order not to hear sermons. It is a part of the duty both of the priest and of the people to attach neither too little nor too much importance to the sermon, but rather to be careful that their

---

[1] Cecil, *Mem.* p. lxv.
[2] Although it has also to be remembered that it was the Evangelicals who restored frequent communion: cf. Shane Leslie, *Henry Edward Manning*, p. 478; G. W. E. Russell, *Short History of the Evangelical Movement*, p. 19, and *Household of Faith*, pp. 318 ff.; Overton, *The English Church in the 19th century*, p. 129.

common worship shall be of such a quality as to take the sermon in its stride.

Now, it is this sense of liturgical prayer that Evangelicalism largely lost, and that Anglo-Catholicism, which is the child of Evangelicalism, has lost again, if it has ever really had it. The earlier Evangelicals valued the Prayer Book only less than the Articles, which they regarded as their charter. What they distrusted, and rightly distrusted, was the dry and barren formalism with which the liturgy was generally ministered. Not unpardonably, therefore, they were to a large extent unconscious that the liturgy has a life of its own, and they looked to the ministry of preaching to give it life, or at least a sort of artificial respiration. One of the most significant incidents in Mr Cadogan's ministry at Chelsea arose out of his decision to substitute a Tuesday evening lecture in place of the daily reading of the offices, which he restricted to Wednesdays and Fridays. Some of his parishioners complained to the Bishop, and appealed to him to interfere.

He did. Mr Cadogan replied,—That the substitution of the lecture proved the frequency of reading prayers was not abolished through idleness or inattention—That he must be allowed to judge what would be the best method of promoting the spiritual welfare of the people of his parish—That the reading of prayers every day took up too much of a minister's time, which could be better employed—That very few ever attended the prayers—That they who did might as well read the scripture and pray at home, if they had the spirit of prayer—That if they had not, but did it as a matter of form, on which they placed dependance, they might have reason hereafter to rejoice that their false props were removed, and a course of instruction substituted, that would lead them to Christ the only true and sure foundation.[1]

This string of specious and irrelevant arguments, in which there is none the less so much to command the respect and almost the approval of the reader, appears to have satisfied the Bishop: at any rate, Mr Cadogan heard no more from his Lordship on the subject, and construed the episcopal silence as tantamount to permission to continue to violate the rubric. 'The discontented were not so easily appeased, nor could they, for a long time to come, be reconciled to his proceedings.'[2]

[1] *Ev. Mag.* (1798), p. 10.   [2] *Ibid.* p. 10.

Mr Cadogan's letter to his diocesan may justly be regarded as one of the most illuminating documents of the Evangelical Revival. It did not mean that he intended to disparage the liturgy or the ordinances of the Church, but that he honestly regarded a Tuesday evening lecture as more vital than daily matins and daily evensong. So it might be, at that particular moment, and so long as he himself was there to preach it. But the point was that, whereas it mattered very little, if at all, who read matins or evensong in church, it did matter very considerably who was to preach the Tuesday evening lecture. The Evangelicals, in their shortsighted zeal, made the personal factor carry a far heavier weight than it was ever meant to carry.

Again, the personal factor, precisely because it is personal, lays itself open to personal criticism, whether friendly or unfriendly. Even at Reading there were ominous signs of trouble in store. True, the particular cave of Adullam which had been established under the auspices of Lady Huntingdon was languishing as St Giles' revived, and at the end of 1781 the managers gave her Ladyship a great deal of annoyance by complaining of the ministers she had provided, and by expressing their desire to be organised on the plan of what she called '*a mere Dissenting church*'.[1] On the other hand, in 1790 the appearance in Reading of what Cecil calls 'an antinomian preacher' was the signal for many of the St Giles' flock to stray from their lawful fold. Mr Cadogan boldly stood his ground and redoubled his eloquence: and after six years 'the false Apostle', being unable to pick up a satisfactory livelihood, removed elsewhere, and his meeting-house was afterwards shut up.[2] But the whole episode was disturbing. Furthermore, in spite of Mr Cadogan's remarkable prestige, and in spite also of his decidedly autocratic manner, his testiness and his abruptness, he had had not infrequently to contend with individual members of his congregation who, in forming their various schemes for the promotion of religion, had presumed to dictate to him 'the part which he, as a Minister of Christ, was *bound* to take in them; and who had

[1] *Countess of Huntingdon*, vol. ii, p. 404.
[2] Cecil, *Mem.* pp. lxxxi–lxxxviii.

not only been offended at his sometimes refusing to concur, but also had passed illiberal reflections upon such refusals'.[1] The congregation as a whole remained unshaken in their attachment to him: but there was, as so often happens, a hostile faction which occasioned him a good deal of uneasiness towards the very end of his life. 'After a long and successful ministry at Reading', says Cecil, 'the mind of my Friend was grieved at observing a disposition in a few of his hearers to separate from him....He also feared the effects of a secession....Though no substantial reason could be urged for such a step at that time: yet the case was easily understood by those among us, who had been witnesses to similar separations....'[2]

In short, his people were getting out of hand, and needed a strong curb if they were to be kept together. Indeed, in view of all the changes and chances which to this very day, and much more in the eighteenth century, must govern the succession to a benefice, the situation, despite its superficial aspect of security, was fraught with unknown perils. For it was to be remembered that Mr Cadogan's conversion was itself an uncovenanted mercy, and one, moreover, that had not been vouchsafed for some six years; and the circumstances, which were exceptional on both sides, were most unlikely to be repeated.

Having laboured zealously for more than twenty years as Vicar of St Giles', Reading, the Rev. the Hon. W. B. Cadogan finished his earthly course on Jan. 18, 1797. His Funeral Sermon was preached by the Rev. Charles Simeon, and was reviewed with studied insolence in the *Gentleman's Magazine* for April. 'Mr S. is one of the *evangelical* preachers of the University of Cambridge; but this discourse, from Heb. iii. 8. tells us nothing that we have not read in such discourses before, and, perhaps, its only merit may have been the manner of delivering it to the people of Reading. All it says of Mr C. is, that he died, in his 46th year, of an inflammation in his bowels, with texts of scripture in his mouth.'[3]

The phenomena which had marked the death of Mr Talbot

---

[1] Cecil, *Mem.* p. lxix. [2] *Ibid.* pp. civ-cvii.
[3] *Gent. Mag.* vol. xlvii, p. 316.

were reproduced upon the death of his successor. Mr Cadogan left a deeper impress upon the character of Reading:[1] and, in Simeon's words, 'The multitudes who attended his funeral with their sighs and tears, yielded a far more real honour to his memory, than all the empty pageantry of this world could possibly afford.'[2] But the loyalty of his followers was still essentially personal, and not institutional. Application was made immediately to secure the living for a successor of the same principles: but it had already been offered, through the instrumentality of a gentleman of consequence, resident in the neighbourhood of Reading, to a Mr Allcock. Mr Allcock would probably have been acceptable, for he is described as 'a clergyman whose modesty can never be too much admired nor too much regretted':[3] but that fatal modesty led him to the conclusion that he would not be able 'to fill with advantage a pulpit constantly occupied for so many years by so great a man as Mr Cadogan'.[4] The same gentleman who had offered him the living, continuing deliberately to ignore the general wishes of the people, then procured as Mr Cadogan's successor the Rev. Joseph Eyre, Vicar of Ambrosden, in Oxfordshire (a benefice which he continued to retain), who signalised his ecclesiastical prejudices by preaching in the parish church of St Mary's, Reading, on July 30, 1798, at the visitation of John [Douglas], Lord Bishop of Salisbury, a sermon entitled *A Dispassionate Enquiry into the Probable Causes and Consequences of Enthusiasm*, in which, with insufferable condescension, he alluded to the 'well-meant piety' of his predecessor.[5] His preaching is otherwise described, admittedly by a hostile critic, as 'a miserable farago of Pelagian and Socinian errors, undisguised by ingenuity and unembellished by elocution'.[6]

Three possible alternatives lay open to the congregation of St Giles', and they are discussed in a clever pamphlet entitled *Five Letters to a Friend, occasioned by the death of the Rev.*

[1] 'His influence was wide and deep, and yet lingers.'—W. M. Childs, *The Town of Reading during the Early Part of the Nineteenth Century* (1910), p. 49.
[2] Cecil, *Mem.* p. cxii.   [3] *Ev. Mag.* (1789), p. 13.
[4] *Ibid.* p. 13.   [5] *Ibid.* p. 392.
[6] *Countess of Huntingdon*, vol. ii, p. 411.

CADOGAN OF READING

William Bromley Cadogan, late Minister of the Gospel at Reading, Berks. (1797). The author, John Cooke, of Maidenhead, was himself an evangelical Dissenter who had left the Church of England from disgust with the parochial ministrations of a formal and worldly clergyman,[1] and he naturally harped upon the privilege enjoyed by the Dissenters of *'choosing their own teachers'*, instead of having some 'mere "hireling" *imposed* upon them'.[2] 'I own to you, that it shocks my understanding, it shocks my sensibility, to think of *a lay-chancellor* appointing a minister to *a church of Christ!* I cannot express to you my feelings, when with my Bible in my hand, I think of a successor to Cadogan...being chosen by political friendships, and regulated by state reasons.'[3] It was a strong point, and he made the most of it, long before any such appointment had in fact been made.

The expectation that Mr Cadogan would be succeeded by a Vicar of a very different type and temper was not, of course, peculiar to Mr Cooke. Indeed, it appears that several serious and evangelical clergymen and private individuals used their influence to persuade the congregation of St Giles' to be loyal, at all costs, to their church.[4] To Mr Cooke, this was extremely shocking. 'When clergymen advise members of the establishment to prefer the ministry of an erroneous and unconverted teacher among them to a gospel ministry among the Dissenters...I call it BIGOTRY; as it betrays an unreasonable attachment to a party, not supported by the blessed scriptures. I consider it as contrary to the dictates of the Bible,—and as in direct opposition to the duty of churchmen, as it would be to that of dissenters to hear Arianism at a dissenting meeting, rather than the pure gospel in the established church.'[5] His own advice was naturally the reverse of theirs. 'Reading is abundantly favoured with the gospel, and if your fears should be realized, and "the truth" should not continue at St Giles's, you may hear the gospel, and enjoy all "the ordinances of the Lord", among

---

[1] *Op. cit.* pp. 32–5.
[3] *Ibid.* p. 12.
[5] *Ibid.* p. v. Cf. pp. 20–1.

[2] *Ibid.* pp. iv, 12, 13.
[4] *Ibid.* pp. iii, 19, 27, 35.

the dissenters.'[1] He recognised that there was a third alternative
—'to build a chapel, and use the church prayers'[2]—but he did
not propose it, from a belief in the superior advantages of
extemporary prayer.

It was, however, this third alternative that was in fact adopted.
After applying in vain for permission to appoint a lecturer, whose
salary they naturally undertook to provide, a considerable
section of the St Giles' congregation left their parish church and,
under the auspices of the Rev. Rowland Hill and of the Rev.
John Eyre, of Hackney, who had at one time been curate to
Mr Cadogan at Chelsea, built themselves a chapel on the site of
the old County Gaol in Castle Street and procured the services
of a minister from Lady Huntingdon's Connexion. The seceders
retained the liturgy of the Church of England; the chapel was
not used for baptisms; and its trust deeds envisaged a possible
surrender to episcopal authority at some future time.[3] Their
first settled minister (1798–1805) was the Rev. William Green,
who had been trained at Lady Huntingdon's College at Trevecca,
and had been ordained in 1783 at the first ordination in Lady
Huntingdon's Connexion on the plan of secession.[4] He was
succeeded for a short time by the Rev. Henry Gauntlett, a dis-
gruntled curate of the Church of England with scruples respecting the doctrine of baptismal regeneration, to whom the appointment was suggested by Sir Richard Hill in the following terms:
'The congregation consists of the late Mr Cadogan's hearers,
and they are, for the most part, zealous for the church, and
therefore if they cannot hear the gospel in it, they are resolved
to keep as near to it as they can.'[5] But Mr Gauntlett was not
happy in his new sphere of work: he 'found himself surrounded
with greater difficulties than had hitherto attended the exercise
of his ministry; especially with regard to that freedom which he

[1] Cooke, p. 37.   [2] Ibid. p. 40.
[3] W. M. Childs, The Town of Reading, p. 50; Memoir of the Rev. James
Sherman, by Henry Allon (1863), pp. 164, 167; Reminiscences of Reading, by
an Octogenarian [W. S. Darter], 1888, p. 11.—It was apparently designed to
name this chapel 'Cadogan Chapel': cf. Gent. Mag. July 1798, vol. lxviii,
pt. ii, p. 555.
[4] Countess of Huntingdon, vol. ii, pp. 412, 436–50.
[5] Memoir of the Author, in Sermons by the late Rev. Henry Gauntlett,
Vicar of Olney, Bucks. (1835), vol. i, p. xlix.

considered indispensable to usefulness'·[1] and, having reconsidered with increased attention the baptismal formularies of the Church of England and become perfectly convinced of their entire conformity with Holy Scripture, he resigned his situation after having held it for two years, and accepted the curacy of two villages in Oxfordshire which he served from Reading. A few months later, a new secession took place (1808): the malcontents bought an old Presbyterian meeting-house and reopened it under the name of Salem Chapel.[2] It is also noteworthy that, although the Rev. Joseph Eyre continued to occupy St Giles' until his death in 1816,[3] the Evangelical cause had found a new champion in the Rev. William Marsh, a disciple and friend of Mr Cadogan, who as curate of St Lawrence's, Reading, from 1800 to 1811, wielded over vast congregations power scarcely inferior to that of his exemplar.[4]

Meanwhile the Castle Street Chapel struggled on without a settled pastor, being supplied by ministers of various denominations, chiefly from Lady Huntingdon's Connexion, until 1821, when the Rev. James Sherman, himself a minister of that Connexion, accepted the pastorate. Under his powerful preaching, the congregation revived in numbers: but, although Dissenters in practice, they remained Churchmen in theory; and in 1831 they made overtures to the Bishop (Burgess), praying him to license the chapel and to give Mr Sherman episcopal ordination. However, the Rev. H. H. Milman, afterwards Dean of St Paul's, but at that time Vicar of St Mary's, Reading, in which parish the chapel was situated, made certain stipulations with which the trustees were unwilling to comply, and the plan fell through.[5] In 1836, when Sherman left Reading to pick up the somewhat tattered mantle of Rowland Hill at the Surrey Chapel, the surrender was finally effected, and the chapel was licensed as the Episcopal Chapel of St Mary. But it was then too late: 'the building went one way, and the congregation another,'[6] for most of the latter had by now become

---

[1] *Ibid.* p. lii.   [2] *Countess of Huntingdon*, vol. ii, p. 412.
[3] *Reminiscences of Reading*, by an Octogenarian [W. S. Darter], p. 83.
[4] Childs, p. 50; *Life of the Rev. William Marsh, D.D.* (1867), pp. 23 ff.
[5] Allon's *Sherman*, p. 216.   [6] *Ibid.* p. 164.

CADOGAN OF READING

'Nonconformists on conviction and principle'; and they proceeded to raise on the opposite side of the street 'a most splendid erection' which was opened as a Congregational Chapel in 1839.[1] Moreover, the dependent village chapels, established by Sherman 'in harmony, so far as was possible, with the Episcopalian sympathies' of his trustees, threw in their lot with the seceders.[2]

Thus Mr Cadogan's Reading congregation, rent by successive schisms, was almost entirely dissipated within the space of forty years.[3]

At Chelsea also the situation was far from satisfactory. His curate there was the Rev. Erasmus Middleton, who almost exactly thirty years before had been one of the six students expelled from St Edmund Hall. His principal offence had been the 'daring impiety' of officiating in a chapel of ease belonging to the parish of Cheveley, Berks., not being in holy orders: the fact that this offence had been committed three years[4] before he entered the University was regarded as wholly immaterial. After his expulsion he entered himself at King's College, Cambridge, where he was maintained by a Dissenting banker of the name of Fuller: but he does not appear to have graduated there. He procured ordination in Ireland from the Bishop of Down, and was for some years minister at Dalkeith, where he became Chaplain to the Countess of Crawford and Lindsay, and married into a branch of the ducal family of Gordon.[5] Migrating southward, he became curate to Mr Cadogan at St Luke's, Chelsea, where his ministry proved so acceptable that, when the vacancy occurred, the principal inhabitants interested themselves on his behalf. But the living was bestowed upon the Rev. Charles Sturges,[6] Vicar of St Mary's, Reading, and also of Ealing, Middlesex, a very estimable clergyman, but one whose religious

[1] Childs, p. 50. [2] Allon's *Sherman*, p. 207.
[3] Cf. also J. J. Cooper, *Some Worthies of Reading* (1923), pp. 109–13.
[4] *Countess of Huntingdon*, vol. i, p. 425 *n*. [5] Ollard, pp. 42–3; *D.N.B.*
[6] Rev. Charles Sturges (1738–1805), Fellow of King's College, Cambridge, 1761–3: Vicar of St Mary's, Reading, 1763–1805: Vicar of Ealing, Middlesex, 1775–97: Rector of St Luke's, Chelsea, 1797–1805: Prebendary of Salisbury: chaplain to Earl Cadogan (to whom he was related): Prebendary of St Paul's. (Cf. *Registers of St Mary's, Reading*, 1538–1812, ed. G. P. Crawfurd, vol. i, introd.; *Eton College Register*, 1753–90, ed. R. A. Austen Leigh; Nichols, *Lit. Anecd.* vol. ix, pp. 109–11 *n*.)

sentiments were not those of his predecessor. At first things went tolerably well: the new Rector showed Mr Middleton much respect, and exhibited no disposition to dismiss him from his curacy. But he gradually changed his conduct, and finally insisted on his curate's making such an alteration, respecting his future sermons, as he could not conscientiously comply with. The parishioners opened a subscription to support him and his family, until he could be otherwise provided for: to which the Bishop of London himself subscribed £50.[1] (It might be remembered that, although the Hanoverian Bishops were no doubt grossly overpaid, they were expected to, and generally did, employ a considerable portion of their revenues in such charitable purposes: and this is also true of many of the richer pluralists.) The learned and unfortunate Middleton after knocking around in various London lectureships and curacies, and supplementing an exiguous income by the labours of his pen, at length, in 1804, when he was sixty-five, was given the country living of Turvey, in Bedfordshire, by the Fuller family. The parish had been neglected for a considerable period. He died there in the following year.[2] Meanwhile, at Chelsea, as at Reading, the fruits of Mr Cadogan's ministry were thrown away by the appointment of a successor of radically different temper and opinions.

Here, then, was one of the major problems by which the leaders of the Evangelical Revival in its later stages found themselves confronted. It could be further illustrated from the history of St Mary's, Wallingford, where the Rev. Thomas Pentycross, one of the veterans of the Revival in the University of Cambridge, was Rector from 1774 until his death in 1808.[3]

---

[1] *Ev. Mag.* (1798), p. 14.—But cf. the spirited vindication of '*The present Rector of* Chelsea's *Conduct to his Curate*', by E. J. in *The Gentleman's Magazine*, April 1798, vol. lxviii, pt. i, pp. 288–90, and the letter signed 'Vindex' (*ibid.* June 1798, p. 461): also *Gent. Mag.* vol. lviii (1788), pt. i, p. 110, and Nichols, *Lit. Anecd.* vol. ix, 109–11 *n.*

[2] Ollard, pp. 43–4: T. S. Grimshawe, *Memoir of the Rev. Legh Richmond, A.M.* (5th ed. 1829), pp. 112–13.

[3] '...—dined at Reading with Mr Cadogan—then on my return stayed a day with Pentecross (*sic*) at Wallingford, and preached for him....'—Simeon to the Rev. John Venn, Sept. 22, 1783 (Carus, p. 56). Cf. Pentycross to John Thornton, July 28, 1783 (*Congregational Magazine*, Dec. 1842, vol. vi, n.s., p. 826).

Here also there was a somewhat captious and enthusiastic congregation which, having been held together only by the strong hand of a pious Evangelical incumbent, fell into fragments as soon as his place was taken by a man of contrary opinions.[1] The Visitation Sermon preached by Cadogan's successor at St Giles', Reading, in 1798—*A Dispassionate Enquiry into the Probable Causes and Consequences of Enthusiasm*—is matched exactly, both in its temper and in its results, by the Visitation Sermon preached by Pentycross' successor at St Mary's, Wallingford, precisely ten years later—*The friendly Call of Truth and Reason to a new Species of Dissenters*.[2] Under such circumstances, it was difficult to maintain any real continuity in the pastoral sphere.

That was the problem: and all the Evangelical leaders were acutely conscious of it. On the one hand, there was the tendency to schism to which their congregations were peculiarly liable. On the other hand, there was the difficulty, under the existing system of patronage, of preserving that continuity in doctrine by which alone schism could be averted on the removal or demise of an incumbent. 'You say, the Lord is sending many gospel labourers into the church', wrote Berridge to Lady Huntingdon (April 26, 1777). 'True; and with a view, I think, of calling his people out of it; because, when such ministers are removed by death, or transported to another vineyard, I see no fresh gospel labourer succeed them, which obliges the forsaken flocks to fly to a meeting. And what else can they do? If they have tasted of manna, and hunger for it, they cannot feed on heathen chaff, nor yet on legal crusts, though baked by some staunch Pharisee quite up to perfection. What has become of Mr Venn's Yorkshire flock?—what will become of his Yelling flock, or of my flocks, at our decease? Or what will become of your students at your removal? They are virtual Dissenters now, and will be settled

---

[1] Vide *Memoir of the late Thomas Pentycross, A.M., Rector of St Mary's, Wallingford, Berks.*, in the *Evangelical Magazine*, vol. xvi (1808), pp. 453–8, 497–504.
[2] *Countess of Huntingdon*, vol. ii, p. 62 *n.*—The new Rector, the Rev. Edward Barry, M.D., had been a student at Trevecca and a minister in Lady Huntingdon's Connexion: but, on obtaining orders from the Bishop of Sodor and Man, he turned against his former associates.

Dissenters then. And the same will happen to many, perhaps most, of Mr Wesley's preachers at his death...."But", you reply, "some of my best preachers leave me in my life-time." Perhaps they may; and if I may judge of your feelings by my own, on such occasions, this must grieve you, on the first view at least; but wait and see whether the Lord's hand be not in it....Some years ago, two of my lay-preachers deserted their ranks, and joined the Dissenters. This threw me into a violent fit of the spleen, and set me a coughing and barking exceedingly; but when the phlegm was come up, and leisure allowed for calm thought, I did humbly conceive the Lord Jesus might be wiser than the old Vicar; and did well in sending some preachers from the Methodist mint among the Dissenters, to revive a drooping cause, and set old crippled pilgrims on their legs again. Nay, it is certain that some of these deserting preachers have not only quickened the Chelsea invalids, but raised up new and vigorous recruits for the King's service. Be glad, therefore, my Lady, to promote the Lord's cause in any way—in your own line, if it may be; in another line, if it must be.'[1]

There was therefore little consolation, although there was a little, in the argument of William Hey, 'that the present system of presentation in the Church of England, with all its unavoidable disadvantages, was still to be preferred before the method followed by Dissenters'. He admitted that whenever an Evangelical clergyman died, or removed elsewhere, and was succeeded by one of a different temper or persuasion, 'it sometimes happens that a partial dissent occurs; some of the congregation leave the Church, and place themselves under dissenting teachers, where they conceive the truth to be faithfully preached'. Yet 'in the course of time a vacancy occurs; new trustees, or a new patron, may succeed; and in answer to the unwearied prayers of a faithful few who remained in the bosom of the Church, a pious and zealous minister, one after their own heart, may be mercifully granted to them. A revival of religion may take place, and much good be again effected. Thus, by this mode of presentation, there is at least a prospect, a remote hope,

[1] Berridge's *Works*, pp. 517–8; *Countess of Huntingdon*, vol. ii, pp. 423–4.

of seeing the gospel light return into places from which it has departed for a season.' Whereas in Dissenting congregations the minister is normally elected by the people, and they are unlikely to choose anyone whose standard in divinity is different from their own. This answers very well so long as they themselves are truly pious and orthodox; in such a case, 'they will admit no teachers but men of sound principles and exemplary conduct': but when they hold High Calvinist or extreme Arminian opinions, or when they are tainted with Arian or Socinian errors, 'there seems to be little or no prospect of their restoration to the pure and primitive doctrines of Christianity, as abundant experience painfully testifies'.[1] But the argument cuts both ways: and 'a remote hope' which may, or may not, be fulfilled 'in the course of time' in answer to 'unwearied prayers', is cold consolation to men who are looking for an immediate remedy in an extremely distressing condition of affairs.

Moreover, it was far easier to lose 'serious hearers' to Dissent than to reclaim them from it. When 'T'owd Trumpet', Henry Venn, decided to resign from Huddersfield, he wrote at once to Lady Huntingdon imploring her to press for the nomination of his successor, and urging particularly the claims of his curate, Mr Riland.[2] But these precautions were ineffective: the patron bestowed the living upon a clergyman of very different sentiments. 'When he arrived the bell was ringing for the Thursday evening lecture; and his first act of dominion was to silence the bell, and to suppress the service. His subsequent course corresponded in all respects with this commencement....'[3]
the people who had profited by [Venn's] preaching were repelled from the parish church, by discourses which formed a marked contrast to those they had lately heard within the same walls; so that they were dispersed in various directions, some to neighbouring churches, some to dissenting chapels.[4] Several of them at length

---

[1] Pearson's *Life of Hey*, pt. ii, pp. 85–8.
[2] *Countess of Huntingdon*, vol. ii, p. 45 *n*.
[3] *Memoirs of the Rev. Joseph Cockin, late Minister of the Gospel, at Halifax* (2nd ed. 1841), p. 80.
[4] 'Those who lived on one side of the town went to Slaithwaite Church, to hear Mr Powley; a few on the other side went to Elland Church, to hear Mr Burnet; and those who were indifferent to Churchism went to Hopton Chapel, to hear Mr Toothill. Sometimes they went to Heckmondwike to tell

determined upon building a chapel, in the hope that they might be united together in one body, under a pastor of their own choice. Mr Venn gave his sanction and assistance to this plan, and advised the people to attend the chapel after it was built.[1]

Such liberality is described as 'very uncommon',[2] as no doubt it was. But Venn went further. Not only did he himself subscribe to the building fund,[3] but he collected £170 towards it among his friends in London:[4] and when the chapel was opened on New Year's day, 1772, he even went so far as to print 'an affectionate pastoral Letter to the people',[5] dated Jan. 3, 1772, in which he said: 'Your meeting is built upon principles truly christian. It is your high value for the sum and substance of the christian faith as it hath been taught you by us, and the efficacy of which you experienced, which led you to separate from the parish church, the beloved place of your stated worship.'[6] It is true that the minister elected by the separatists (after a strenuous canvass, and by the precarious majority of a casting vote) was a personal friend and admirer, a Calvinistic Methodist named William Moorhouse, who as a young man had been a frequent attendant at Venn's church, walking over to Huddersfield from his home—a journey of twenty-five miles there and back—for the privilege of sitting under him; and whom he himself had recommended to them for their minister.[7] Venn had long since detected in him 'the presages of future eminence and usefulness':[8] and there is extant a letter which he addressed to him, dated 'Yelling, Sept. 26th, 1772', full of valuable counsel regarding the work of the ministry, and concluding as follows:

their sorrows to Mr Scott, and to ask his advice.' (*Ibid.* p. 81.)—Powley and Burnet had both been Venn's curates (*ibid.* p. 70): the Rev. James Scott conducted an orthodox Dissenting Academy at Heckmondwike.—It is not irrelevant that many of Venn's congregation had not been brought up as members of the Church of England: his powerful ministry had steadily drained the Dissenting meetings, and his departure meant the returning of the tide. Cf. D. F. E. Sykes, *Huddersfield and its Vicinity* (1898), p. 342.
[1] *Life of Venn*, p. 168.
[2] *Memoir of the late Rev. W. Moorhouse, of Huddersfield, Yorkshire*, in the *Evangelical Magazine and Missionary Chronicle*, vol. ii, n.s. (Jan.–Feb. 1824), p. 2.
[3] Sykes, *Huddersfield and its Vicinity*, p. 346.
[4] Cockin, pp. 87–8.   [5] *Ev. Mag.* Jan. 1824, p. 2.
[6] Cockin, p. 86.   [7] *Ev. Mag.* Jan. 1824, p. 2.
[8] *Ibid.* p. 1.

'God be praised that your church is in a flourishing condition. It has my daily prayers. Remember us also at the throne of grace. I shall be glad to hear from you as my successor to a people whom I shall always love, and hope to meet one day in glory. From your affectionate fellow-labourer in the Gospel, H. VENN.'[1]

His conduct did not pass without much criticism. Even the curate whom he left behind him, Mr Riland, strove to exert a countervailing influence. His advice and exhortation to the people was, 'Stick to the Church; by all means stick to the Church; and pray for the conversion of your minister; and if you cannot approve of his preaching, remember you have the gospel in the prayers.'[2] Another of Venn's former curates, Mr Powley, whom he had presented to a chapelry in the parish, also remonstrated with him faithfully upon his conduct. To him Venn replied, protesting his utmost veneration for the Prayer Book and his loyalty to the authentic principles of the Church of England:

How often in your hearing, how often in the church, [have I] declared the superior excellency, in my judgment, of the Liturgy to every mode of worship, not only amongst the Dissenters, but that had ever been in the Church of Christ, as far as I had knowledge: nay, more than once have I said, I never was present at any meeting where I perceived the power of godliness, as amongst the congregations of our Church, where the Gospel is preached. Now, after all this, I think, in justice, you ought to have supposed me as much a friend to the Church of England as yourself.—I have long, you know, had to combat with the senseless prejudices against our Form; and see plainly the advantage Satan makes of these prejudices, and lament it. But this evil, compared with the sort of religion taught now by some of the clergy, appears to me but small. One lays waste the grand fundamental truth; the other only exhibits it in a less edifying manner.—[3]

It is also fair to add that Venn had hoped that the Prayer Book

---

[1] *Ev. Mag.* Jan. 1824, pp. 3–4.
[2] Cockin, p. 80.—For an answer to this argument, cf. John Cooke, *Five Letters to a Friend, occasioned by the death of the Rev. W. B. Cadogan* (1797), pp. 35–6.
[3] *Life of Venn*, p. 160.

would bo uood in the new chapel 'But in this, and in many more important respects, his expectations were disappointed.'[1]

A few months later he was made to see even more forcibly the folly and disaster of his policy. His successor, the Rev. Harcar Crook, died almost within two years of his appointment, and 'another Vicar came to the living, from whose instructions he would never have wished his people to secede: but few, comparatively, returned to the parish church'.[2] The schism, thus impatiently contrived, naturally persisted: Mr Moorhouse retained his charge until his death in 1823: and the new congregation at Highfield Chapel, although not free from schisms of its own, gradually developed into a permanent Dissenting community, which it still remains. 'Such was the beginning of the Independent interest at Huddersfield.'[3]

The problem, therefore, which confronted the leaders of the Evangelical Party in the Church of England at the beginning of the nineteenth century was not primarily the problem of recruiting and training a supply of Evangelical clergy. Since March 19, 1777, the Elland Clerical Society (founded ten years earlier at Huddersfield by Henry Venn) had furnished an Evangelical ordination candidates' fund, to which Wilberforce and the Thorntons and other wealthy laymen were generous contributors,[4] and had been able to send a steady trickle of

[1] *Ibid.* p. 159.   [2] *Ibid.* p. 159.
[3] Cockin, p. 86.
[4] Vide *A Review of the Origin and History of the Elland Clerical Society* [by Canon Hulbert], 1868, pp. 5–9, 25 ff.: also art. *The Elland Clerical Society*, by T. Alfred Stowell, in the *Churchman*, May 1896, reprinted as a pamphlet, pp. 4–5 and *n*.—'The following is a brief description of the qualifications required in candidates applying for help from the Society, extracted from the early Journals:
1. Sound and unaffected Christian piety.
2. A sound and inquiring mind, capable of the benefit which a literary education is calculated to afford.
3. A thorough persuasion of the truth and importance of the principles expressed in the Liturgy, Articles and Homilies of the Church as established in these dominions; and of the value of her services as a means of public religious instruction and edification.
4. A conviction of the necessity of order and union in the Church of Christ.
5. A decided attachment to the doctrine, sacraments, and discipline of Christ, " as this Church and Realm have received the same ".' (Hulbert, p. 6.)
Among the more notable of the earlier pensioners of the Society were Samuel Marsden, Thomas Thomason, Charles Jerram, William Mandell, and Kirke White. Cf. *Letters and Journals of Samuel Marsden, the Apostle of*

ordinands to Magdalene and, at a slightly later period, to Queens'. In 1793, according to Charles Jerram, 'there were not fewer than eight or ten on the Society's books at Cambridge',[1] where Mr Simeon's Conversation Parties and classes in sermon composition and delivery, and the pastoral oversight of Farish of Magdalene and Sowerby of Queens',[2] more than made up for the deficiencies of the unreformed curriculum. Similar work was done by the Bristol Clerical Education Society (founded by Biddulph in 1795) and by the London Clerical Education Society (founded by Simeon in 1816), and by others.[3] Furthermore, over and above those Evangelical clergymen who, from the very beginning of the Movement, had supplemented their exiguous stipends by taking pupils, several Evangelical private schools were coming into being, such as the Rev. Mr Rawson's, at Seaforth, which numbered Mr Gladstone and Dean Stanley among its pupils, or Mr Newcome's, at Hackney, which had the peculiar honour of educating Stratford Canning and Mr Creevey, or the Rev. Mr Preston's,[4] at Little Shelford, where the precocious intellect of Thomas Babington Macaulay was gravely nurtured; and these were the forerunners of the Evangelical public schools established later in the century.[5]

New Zealand, ed. J. R. Elder (1932), pp. 19–21; John Sargent, *Life of the Rev. T. T. Thomason, M.A., late Chaplain to the Honourable East India Company* (1833), ch. ii; *Memoirs of the Rev. Charles Jerram* (1855), ch. iv; Southey's *Memoir* prefixed to Kirke White's *Remains* (1807). Marsden entered Magdalene in 1790, Thomason and Jerram in 1792 and 1793 respectively, after some months' preliminary tuition from the Rev. Thomas Clark, the venerable Rector of Chesham Bois, Bucks., who regularly performed this office for Elland men without remuneration, the Society paying simply for their board: cf. Sargent's *Thomason*, p. 21; *Jerram*, pp. 68–9; *Ev. Mag.* vol. ii (1794), pp. 133–43.—The Elland Society still flourishes, and continues to assist Evangelical ordination candidates to obtain a University education, with the proviso that they must be prepared to spend at least the first two years of their ministry in the Northern Province.

[1] *Memoirs of the Rev. Charles Jerram*, p. 58.

[2] Hulbert, p. 8.

[3] Charles Hole, *Manual of English Church History*, p. 384; Overton, *The English Church in the 19th century (1800–1833)*, p. 285; Carus, pp. 404, 432.

[4] The Rev. M. M. Preston, who succeeded Thomason as curate of Stapleford, was a Fellow of Trinity and a close friend of Simeon. He removed his school to Aspeden Hall, Herts., in 1814.

[5] Trent College, Derbyshire (1866); the South Eastern (now St Lawrence) College, Ramsgate (1879); Dean Close Memorial School, Cheltenham (1886). —Balleine, *History of the Evangelical Party* (ed. 1933), p. 275.

Nor was the problem that of finding Bishops willing to ordain their candidates. This was becoming easier with every year: in case of emergency, Simeon could generally count upon the friendly offices of Bishop Mansel of Bristol (Master of Trinity College, Cambridge) or Bishop Burgess of St David's:[1] and when in 1820 his old opponent, Bishop Marsh of Peterborough, attempted to exclude Evangelicals from his diocese by requiring all candidates for holy orders to answer an examination paper—the celebrated 'Trap to catch Calvinists'—consisting of eighty-seven carefully constructed questions, he was badly mauled by Sydney Smith in the *Edinburgh Review*[2] in an article entitled 'Persecuting Bishops', and not one of his episcopal colleagues came forward to defend him in the House of Lords.

Nor was the crucial problem that of finding curacies and benefices for clergy of the Evangelical persuasion. This problem generally solved itself: indeed, by 1814 the demand for pious curates had outstripped the supply:[3] besides, a man's friends could usually find him something sooner or later, and not infrequently an individual patron, such as Mr Gladstone's father,[4] would apply to Mr Simeon and ask him to recommend a suitable person for some living. It is true, however, that Evangelicals were seldom advanced to offices of higher dignity until the halcyon days of Palmerston's appointments.[5]

---

[1] Cf. Carus, pp. 427–8, 432, 497–500.

[2] Nov. 1822: the article is reprinted in *Works of the Rev. Sydney Smith* (ed. 1850), pp. 356–67.—The literature of the controversy is summarised in Baker's *History of St John's College, Cambridge*, ed. J. E. B. Mayor, vol. ii, pp. 871–87.

[3] 'Our demand for pious Curates is so great, that the Societies of Elland and Bristol cannot furnish a tenth of the number wanted. I am therefore engaged in establishing a Society in London on a similar plan, for the education of young men at the University. I hope this will be the means of procuring many labourers for the Lord's vineyard.'—Simeon to the Rev. Thomas Thomason, Dec. 29, 1814 (Carus, p. 404).

[4] Morley's *Life of Gladstone* (pop. ed., 1908), vol. i, p. 9.

[5] 'They can number no bishop, nor scarcely a dignitary among them' (Haweis, *Impartial History of the Church of Christ*, 1800, vol. iii, p. 266).—Cf. Gladstone, *Gleanings of Past Years*, vol. vii, pp. 210–11 (*The Evangelical Movement: its Parentage, Progress, and Issue*: reprinted from the *British Quarterly Review*, July 1879): 'The first and, until the days of the Sumners, the only bishop who was reckoned with the party was Dr Ryder, of Lichfield. His piety, dignity, kindliness, and moderation of mind rendered him well worthy of the honours of the prelacy; but possibly these did not contribute

But the real and urgent problem was that of securing continuity of teaching in any given parish. No congregation could ever thrive if subjected to violent alternations of religious guidance or misguidance. And to this problem, Patronage was the only key. Already Mr John Thornton (1720–90), a philanthropic Russia merchant, the Nuffield of the Evangelical Revival, had sporadically 'devoted a large amount of money to the purchase of advowsons, which gave him the opportunity of presenting church livings to some eminently holy and devoted ministers of Christ'.[1] His policy was continued on a more systematic basis by his son, Mr Henry Thornton (1760–1815), who, when he died, designated three Trustees, of whom Simeon was one, to administer his livings.[2] The advantages accruing from investments of this character were not lost upon the Vicar of Holy Trinity, who appears to have begun to purchase advowsons on his own account in 1816, devoting to this object 'a great part of the principal, and all the interest' from the legacy of £15,000 bequeathed to him by his brother Edward, and being assisted by contributions from like-minded individuals.[3] Simeon, in fact, inherited the Thornton policy and applied it, no doubt

more to lift him over the bar than his noble birth, and his being the brother of a Cabinet Minister. Any deans, canons, or heads of houses of that epoch, who were held to wear the same colours, might readily be counted on the fingers.' (Gladstone is here controverting Lecky's view that 'before the close of the [18th] century, the Evangelical movement became dominant in England', and 'completely altered the whole tone and tendency of the preaching' of the Anglican clergy.)—Cf. also W. L. Mathieson, *English Church Reform: 1815–1840* (1932), p. 3: Hole, pp. 381, 389: Balleine, pp. 192–6, 265–9.
  [1] *Incidents in the life of John Thornton, Esq., the Philanthropist*, in *Congreg. Mag.* Dec. 1842, vol. vi, n.s., p. 825.
  [2] Carus, pp. 368, 379, 380–3.
  [3] Hole, p. 385: Carus, p. 590. The same idea had occurred, perhaps not altogether independently, to Simeon's friend, William Marsh, whom he had just put into the living of St Peter's, Colchester (*Life of the Rev. W. Marsh, D.D.*, pp. 112–13). The Simeon Trust was constituted in 1817: by the time of its founder's death, it controlled 21 advowsons: it now controls 150. Cf. Prebendary E. Murphy, Chairman of Simeon's Trustees, on *Simeon and Patronage*, in *Charles Simeon: an Interpretation* (1936), pp. 90–6. The text of Simeon's Solemn Charge to his Trustees (1833) is printed in Henson's *Sibbes and Simeon*, pp. 38–40: also in Canon A. J. Tait's *Charles Simeon and his Trust* (1936), pp. 39–40, which otherwise is little to the point, except that the appendix contains some useful notes by Prebendary Murphy on the administration of the Trust (pp. 61–4).

with keener strategy,[1] but to the same entirely honourable end 'There is this difference', he wrote, 'between myself and others: they purchase *incomes*—I purchase *spheres*, wherein the prosperity of the Established Church, and the kingdom of our blessed Lord, may be advanced; and not for a season only, but if it please God, in perpetuity also.'[2] In short, it is the history of such a parish as St Giles', Reading, that explains the Simeon Trust.

In the light of that history, it was natural enough for Mr Simeon to speak of 'my blessed work of purchasing Livings'.[3] Yet whether it was altogether salutary for a Church Party thus early in its course to discover the power of Money to prescribe and regulate the ordinances of the sanctuary and to control the ministry of the Word and Sacraments, is, indeed, another question.[4]

[1] Simeon concentrated his efforts on securing key positions in large towns and cities. Cf. Sir James Stephen, *Essays in Ecclesiastical Biography* (ed. 1875), p. 578: Gladstone, *Gleanings*, vol. vii, p. 212.
[2] Carus, p. 780.—On the normal traffic in advowsons, cf. Élie Halévy, *Histoire du Peuple Anglais au XIXᵉ siècle*, vol. i (1912), p. 372 (in the English tr., 1924, Simeon is carelessly described as 'vicar of Christ Church', p. 380): Thomas Timpson, *Church History through all Ages* (1832), p. 428 *n.*, and *British Ecclesiastical History* (1838), pp. 499–501.
[3] Carus, p. 604.
[4] Cf. H. Hensley Henson, *Sibbes and Simeon: An Essay on Patronage Trusts* (1932).

VI

SIMEON AND CHURCH ORDER

✪

...If you are invited to go out, and feel yourself inclined to do so, take a lover's leap, neck or nothing, and commit yourself to Jesus. Ask no man's leave to preach Christ; that is unevangelical and shameful. Seek not much advice about it; that is dangerous. Such advice, I found, generally, comes the wrong way—heels uppermost. Most preachers love a snug church, and a whole skin; and what they love they will prescribe. If you are determined to be evangelically regular, *i.e.* secularly irregular; then expect, wherever you go, a storm will follow you, which may fright you, but will bring no real harm. Make the Lord your *whole* trust, and all will be well. Remember this, brother David! for if your heart is resting upon some human arm for support, or if your eye is squinting at it for protection, Jesus Christ will let you fall, and roll you soundly in a kennel, to teach you better manners. If you become a recruiting serjeant, you must go out—*duce et auspice Christo.* The Lord direct, assist, and prosper you...

> Rev. JOHN BERRIDGE to the Rev. DAVID SIMPSON,
> of Macclesfield, Aug. 8, 1775.
>
> Sir J. B. Williams, *Life of David Simpson*, prefixed to Simpson's *A Plea for Religion and the Sacred Writings*, ed. 1837, pp. xxiv–xxv.

...we have the character of Methodism complete: *it is christian godliness without christian order.*

> Jones' *Life of Bishop Horne.* (*Theological and Miscellaneous Works of the Rev. William Jones, M.A., F.R.S.*, ed. 1810, vol. vi, p. 146.)

Chapter Six

SIMEON AND CHURCH ORDER

IN my first lecture, I suggested that the quality of genius in the ecclesiastical statesmanship of Charles Simeon resided in his ability to solve the problems by which he found himself confronted. For Simeon's problems were problems which confronted not himself alone, but the whole Evangelical Party within the Church of England: and of these problems the two most critical were those which are so clearly illustrated in the ministries of two men with whom Simeon had intimate acquaintance, Cadogan of Reading and Berridge of Everton; namely, the problem of Continuity, and the problem of Church Order.

No Anglican incumbent of his day defied Church Order more violently than John Berridge, or with as much impunity. 'And sure there is a cause', he wrote, 'when souls are perishing for lack of knowledge. Must salvation give place to a fanciful decency, and sinners go flocking to hell through our dread of irregularity?'[1] That was his defence. Yet his impatience of church order rested, in the last analysis, upon an impatience, a pessimism, a scepticism regarding the Church of England which is, perhaps, less easily defended. It was precisely at this point that Simeon rallied the wavering Evangelicals and confirmed them in their faith and loyalty. For it was Simeon, more than any other single individual, who taught the Evangelicals to believe in the Church of England and to steer clear, not only of the Scylla of academic latitudinarianism, but also of the Charybdis of that pastoral enthusiasm which walks disorderly in its indiscriminate and unthinking zeal. 'My mind was wholly unbiassed', wrote Bishop Watson, recounting how he had discharged his office, and his conscience, as Regius Professor of Divinity in the University of Cambridge; 'I had no prejudice against, no predilection for the Church of England; but a sincere

---

[1] Berridge to John Thornton, Esq., Aug. 10, 1774 (*Works*, p. 394).

regard for the *Church of Christ*, and an insuperable objection to every degree of dogmatical intolerance.'[1] At the opposite end of the Anglican scale we find John Berridge using identically the same language.

> I regard neither high church, nor low church, nor any church, but the Church of Christ, which is not built with hands, nor circumscribed within peculiar walls, nor confined to a singular denomination.[2] I cordially approve the doctrines and liturgy of the Church of England, and have cause to bless God for a church-house to preach in, and a church revenue to live upon. And I could wish the Gospel might not only be preached in all the British Churches, but established therein by Christ's Spirit, as well as by a national statute; but from the principles of the clergy and the leading men in the nation, which are growing continually more unscriptural and licentious, I do fear our defence is departing, and the glory is removing from our Israel....
>
> When I consider that the doctrines of grace are a common offence to the Clergy, and the Bible itself a fulsome nuisance to the great vulgar; that powerful efforts have been made to eject the Gospel doctrines out of the Church; and the likelihood there is, from the nation's infidelity, of a future attempt succeeding; there is room to fear, when the Church doctrines are banished the Church by a national act, Jesus will utterly remove the candlestick, and take away his Church-bread from those hirelings who eat it and lift up the heel against him....
>
> ...Perhaps, *in less than one hundred years to come, the church-lands may be seized on to hedge up Government gaps, as the abbey-lands were two hundred and fifty years ago.* 'But', you say, 'the Lord is sending many Gospel labourers into his church.' True; and with a view, I think, of calling his people out of it; because, when such ministers are removed by death, or transported to another vineyard, I see no fresh

---

[1] Watson's *Anecdotes* (1817), p. 39.

[2] Cf. Berridge to John Thornton, Nov. 17, 1784: 'By birth and education I am both a churchman and a dissenter—I love both, and could be either, and wish real Gospel ministers of every denomination could embrace one another. And though I do think the best Christianity was found before establishments began; and that usually there are more true ministers out of an establishment than in it; and that establishments are commonly of an intolerant spirit, and draw in shoals of hirelings by their loaves and fishes; yet I am very thankful for an establishment which affords me a preaching-house and an eating-house, without clapping a padlock on my lips, or a fetter on my foot.' (*Congregational Magazine*, April 1845, vol. ix, n.s., p. 275.)— Cf. [B. Flower,] *Memoirs of the life and writings of the author*, prefixed to Robert Robinson's *Misc. Works*, vol. i, p. xxiv.

gospel labourer succeed them, which obliges the forsaken flocks to
fly to a meeting. And what else can they do? If they have tasted of
manna, and hunger for it, they cannot feed on heathen chaff, nor yet
on legal crusts, though baked by some staunch Pharisee quite up to
perfection....[1]

There was something ominous in this differentiation between
'gospel labourers' on the one hand, and the main body of the
clergy on the other. The point was very temperately put by the
author of *Zeal without Innovation* (1808) in his enumeration of
'some justly censurable things found among the class of clergymen, called evangelical ministers'. 'I am constrained to admit',
he wrote, 'that there is a great deal of truth in what has been
often alledged by their opponents, namely, that under their
preaching there has arisen an unfavourable opinion of the body
of the clergy.... [Among the more illiterate of their followers,]
the clergy, as a body, are considered...as men who do not
preach the Gospel; an imputation which, in their account,
implies the forfeiture of all that reverence and support which is
due to Christian instructors. Nor can it be maintained, that
their favourite preachers are universally innocent of being, in
some degree, the cause of so ill an opinion respecting the clergy.
Some of them are not content with enforcing what they believe
to be necessary to salvation, and shewing the evil tendency of
the contrary doctrine; but mingle therewith such intimations
of a general departure from the truths of the Gospel, as their

[1] Berridge to Lady Huntingdon, April 26, 1777 (*Works*, pp. 516–19;
Countess of Huntingdon, vol. ii, pp. 422–4).—Cf. Berridge to Benjamin Mills,
Nov. 20, 1784: 'I believe the Lord Jesus, in half a century, will shut up
church-doors, by directing Government to seize on church lands, as Harry
the Eighth did on the abbey lands; such seizure may lessen the national debt,
and a churchman, you know, cannot preach without his tythes—the fleece
makes his flock; in the mean time the Lord is sending his ministers into the
church, to awaken and call but his elect; and wherever a gospel clergyman
comes, and meets with success, at his removal, I never see a gospel clergyman
succeed him, and of course his flock must become dissenters to get food, for
awakened sinners cannot live upon chaff....P.S.—You are young, and may
live to see government first nibbling on the deaneries and prebends, then on
the church livings and bishopricks, and no outcry will now be raised, so little
regard is paid for the church, especially since the plunder is to pay off the
debt. And well may Jesus give up the church-lands, since church ministers
eat his bread, and lift up the heel against him.' (*Congregational Magazine*,
March 1838, vol. ii, n.s., pp. 163–4.)

hearers naturally apply to the persons really meant by the preacher to be included in the censure; that is to say, the clergy in general. In reply to this, the ministers in question may with great truth affirm, that *they* have suffered much in the public opinion from a like treatment. But they are to remember, that a retort is not an exculpation.

'Of a piece with the conduct here noticed, is the language which some included in this class of clergymen use, in reference to those parishes in which their own views of Christianity are not inculcated. Of such places, though the ordinances of Christian worship be regularly administered in them, they speak in terms similar to those in which the antient prophets expressed themselves, when describing the state of heathenism. Thus leading the unthinking, to blend appointments ordained for the honour of the living and true God, with idolatrous institutions: as if there were no difference between diminished light and absolute darkness; between sinking below the level of completely evangelical instruction, and the entire absence of Christianity.'[1]

Indeed, once granted this distinction, it was difficult not to be impatient of Church Order, and it was difficult not to despair of preserving continuity of gospel-teaching in any parish. The two problems were intimately connected. Secession was a possible solution: Lady Huntingdon's following were already virtual Dissenters. Yet was it possible to discover an alternative solution which might enable the Evangelicals to remain within the Church of England?

Individual secessions there were bound to be, although less numerous and generally less sensational than those which

---

[1] *Zeal without Innovation: or the present state of Religion and Morals considered; with a view to the dispositions and measures required for its improvement. To which is subjoined, an Address to Young Clergymen; intended to guard them against some prevalent errors.* [By the Rev. James Bean] (1808), pp. 152–4.—Cf., e.g. *An Impartial History of the Church of Christ*, by the Rev. Thomas Haweis, Chaplain to the late Countess of Huntingdon, and Rector of All Saints, Aldwincle, Northamptonshire (1800), vol. iii, p. 271: 'Different itinerant societies have been established, in order to send instruction to the poor in the villages where the gospel is not preached.... Probably not less than five hundred places for divine worship have been opened within the last three years.'—Cf. also *Countess of Huntingdon*, vol. i, p. 363: 'In the beginning of the year 1765 the Countess of Huntingdon, ever active in well doing, began to concert measures for introducing the Gospel into the town of Lewes....'

marked the course, and more especially the crises, of the Oxford Movement. The most noteworthy was the so-called 'Western Schism', which began in 1815: 'it was fortunately limited in extent, and ended after a short period. The seceders were Evangelical clergymen....Their stumbling-block was infant baptism, though some of them also wandered in doctrinal divinity.'[1] The Rev. Peter Hall, in an appendix to his *Congregational Reform* (1835), enumerates thirteen 'pious and honest clergymen, sound in faith and attachment to the good cause', and six of them beneficed, who had left the Church of England on conscientious grounds during the past fifteen years, the majority between 1832 and 1834.[2] In 1837 the Rev. Henry Battiscombe, Fellow of King's, and Farish's curate at St Giles', Cambridge, where he had done exceptionally good work, resigned his fellowship and his curacy on joining with the Baptist denomination, and founded Zion Chapel, where he ministered for seven or eight years; at the end of which time, however, he returned to the Church of England, and after a proper interval became a curate at Lowestoft, and subsequently minister of St German's Chapel, Charlton, near Blackheath.[3] I have not succeeded in discovering a similar list for the earlier period: but, of the handful of Cambridge undergraduates who had come under Berridge's influence, the Rev. Rowland Hill (who had never been allowed

---

[1] Charles Hole, *A Manual of English Church History* (1910), pp. 391-2.

[2] *Congregational Reform, according to the Liturgy of the Church of England: in four sermons...by the Rev. Peter Hall, M.A., Rector of Milston, Wilts., and Curate of St Luke's, Chelsea* (1835), App. L, pp. 209-13.—Of these seceders, the most notable was the Rev. H. B. Bulteel, curate of St Ebbe's, Oxford, and formerly Fellow of Exeter, whose diocesan Bishop revoked his license (Aug. 10, 1831) on account of his preaching in the open air and in Dissenting chapels. Bulteel pronounced the Bishop's action to be 'that of an officer of the Church of Antichrist', and, with the financial assistance of his friends, built himself a large chapel behind Pembroke College, to which he for some years attracted a numerous congregation, who were called 'Bulteelers'. Cf. the scandalous reference (Jan. 29, 1832) in Hurrell Froude's *Remains*, vol. i, p. 252: 'But I really do feel sceptical whether Latimer was not something in the Bulteel line.' Gladstone had been a constant attendant at St Ebbe's before the catastrophe (Morley, popular ed., vol. i, p. 44). Bulteel's anonymous skit on the Tractarians—'*The Oxford Argo*, by an Oxford Divine' (1845)—is still deservedly remembered: it is printed, e.g., in S. F. Hulton's *The Clerk of Oxford in Fiction* (1909), pp. 351-6.

[3] Cf. art. *The Founder of Zion Chapel*, in *Mems and Gems of Old Cambridge Lore*, by Urbs Camboritum [W. R. Brown]; *Register of Admissions to King's College, Cambridge, 1797-1925*, ed. John J. Withers, p. 22.

SIMEON AND CHURCH ORDER

to proceed beyond deacon's orders) exercised to the end of his life a very irregular ministry at Surrey Chapel: and the secession of the Rev. David Simpson,[1] Minister of Christ Church, Macclesfield, was averted only by his death in March 1799.[2] Yet I think we may confidently say that, without the steadying influence of Simeon at Cambridge, there would have been many more secessions than in fact occurred.

The fundamental divergence between Evangelicals and Methodists came over the problem of Church Order. Men such as Hervey of Weston Favell, Walker of Truro, Adams of Wintringham, while in complete, or almost complete, agreement with Methodist doctrines, yet 'thoroughly disapproved of the Methodist practice of itinerancy, which they regarded as a mark of insubordination, a breach of Church order, and an unwarrantable interference with the parochial system'.[3] It was on this ground that Hervey and Walker and Adams had expostulated with Wesley on his irregularities: it was on this ground also that Simeon was directly critical of John Berridge. '—He was, perhaps, right in preaching from place to place as he did. But I, who knew him well, was hardly satisfied that he was doing right.... He lived when few Ministers cared about the Gospel, and when disorder was almost needful. I don't think he would

[1] Yet Simpson as an undergraduate of St John's had been 'shackled more with ecclesiastical trammels' than most of the other members of Rowland Hill's society, and had declined to have any part in the field-preaching in which Hill and Pentycross and De Coetlogon, with Berridge's encouragement and full approval, assisted Robert Robinson, the Baptist minister of Cambridge.—Cf. Jones, *R. Hill*, p. 17; Sidney, *R. Hill*, p. 45.

[2] To these names may be added that of Rev. Brian Bury Collins, a Johnian of the next generation, who, while still a deacon, indulged himself with a roving commission and, in consequence, found difficulty in procuring full orders: he was finally ordained priest by Bishop Porteus of Chester in 1781 on Simpson's granting him a title. But he was too restless and too independent to remain long at Macclesfield, and he ended rather as a Wesleyan Methodist preacher than as a minister of the Established Church. During his five years' diaconate, he had supplied at Everton in 1780 during Berridge's annual visit to the Tabernacle. Wesley found him difficult.—Cf. *Correspondence of the Rev. B. B. Collins*, ed. A. M. Broadley, in *Proc. Wesley Hist. Soc.*, vol. ix (1914), pp. 25–35, 49–58, 73–86; *Admissions to St John's College, Cambridge*, pt. iv, ed. R. F. Scott, pp. 198–9; G. Dyer, *Life of Robert Robinson*, p. 125.

[3] C. J. Abbey and J. H. Overton, *The English Church in the Eighteenth Century*, vol. ii, p. 190.—Cf. J. Wesley to the Rev. James Rouquet, March 30, 1761: 'The grand breach is now between the irregular and regular clergy' (*Letters*, ed. Telford, vol. iv, p. 143).

255

do now as he did then; for there are so many means of hearing the Gospel, and a much greater spread of it; a much greater call for order, and much less need of disorder. To do *now* as he did *then* would do much harm.'[1]

Yet Berridge's case was plain enough. To him, the one urgent need was for the preaching of the Gospel to men who were perishing: there was no time for scruples about Church Order. He might have echoed the very words which Wesley had addressed to Bishop Secker of Oxford: 'Methinks I would go deeper. I would inquire what is the end of all ecclesiastical order? Is it not to bring souls from the power of Satan to God and to build them up in fear and love? Order, then, is so far valuable as it answers these ends; and if it answers them not, it is nothing worth.'[2] So far as might be possible, let the new wine of evangelical religion be poured into the old bottles of the parochial system: yet let no man quibble if it overflowed them. As Wesley told the Bishop of London, 'Church or no Church, we must attend to the work of saving souls'.[3]

One consequence of that attitude was the supersession of the traditional ecclesiastico-political divisions into Churchmen and Dissenters, or into High Churchmen and Low Churchmen, by this new and radical distinction between the enemies and the professors of 'vital godliness', and between those clergymen and ministers who did, and those who did not, preach 'the Gospel'. The division of mankind into the two categories of 'evangelical' and 'formal' cut right across the old divisions and, in effect, ignored them. As Troeltsch has pointed out, the Church of Methodist theory and doctrine was a Church of the sect type, a community of the elect, a *societas perfectorum*. This is seen very clearly in Wesley's answer to the question, 'But do you not weaken the Church?' 'Do not they who ask this, by the Church

[1] Brown, p. 200.
[2] Letter dated June 25, 1746: quoted in Henry Bett, *The Spirit of Methodism* (1937), p. 79.
[3] *Ibid.* p. 79.—Cf. J. Wesley to the Rev. George Downing, April 6, 1761: 'I had an agreeable conversation with Mr Venn.... I think, he is exactly as regular as he ought to be. I would observe every punctilio of order, except where the salvation of souls is at stake. There I prefer the end before the means.' (*Arminian Magazine*, Dec. 1780, vol. iii, p. 672; Wesley's *Letters*, ed. Telford, vol. iv, p. 146.)

mean themselves? We do not purposely weaken any man's hands, but accidentally we may thus far—they who come to know the truth by us, will esteem such as deny it less than they did before. But *the Church, in the proper sense, the congregation of English believers*, we do not weaken at all.'[1]

Paradoxically, the breaking down of traditional barriers in the name of a larger liberty and a wider comprehension tended, as it always does, to issue in a jealous and censorious exclusiveness of outlook. Charles Simeon himself was tinged with it: witness his conversation with Arthur Young in 1804. 'I mentioned Fry's calculation of three millions of Christians [in England], but he very properly thought it very erroneous. He thinks Cambridge a fair average, and in 10,000 people knows but of 110 certainly vital Christians—more than 150 can scarcely be from a seventy-fifth to a hundredth part therefore! There are, I am rejoiced to hear it, many very pious young men in the colleges.'[2] Yet the Church on earth, as Cranmer taught, following St Augustine, is a wide field in which tares and wheat grow side by side: and it is a perilous thing for fallible men, however single-minded, to presume to anticipate the task of the angels at the Day of Judgment. 'It is obvious', writes Mr Warre Cornish, 'that the familiarity with God's presence which accompanies continual prayer may easily lead to that kind of spiritual self-satisfaction which is repulsive to the unreligious mind, and which was perfectly understood by Thomas à Kempis. Christians of the traditional schools are restrained by authority, by formularies, and by the confessional, from over-estimating the value of their own convictions and emotions. The besetting sin of the Evangelicals, and Puritans in general, is not spiritual pride, but spiritual vanity. When a man seeks divine guidance on every occasion, and is convinced of his own integrity, it is difficult for him to avoid the belief that he is inspired. Even Wilberforce, "at all times in good humour and in charity with all men", is gently reminded by Southey that "poor creature"

[1] H. Bett, *The Spirit of Methodism*, p. 76.
[2] Sunday, June 24, 1804.—*Autobiography of Arthur Young*, ed. M. Betham-Edwards, p. 398.

is his name for those who have the misfortune to differ from him.'[1]

Thus Berridge, with his implicit teaching that admission into the True Church is not by baptism, but by conversion, was scandalised by the language of the Catechism. 'I do not much prize our Church Catechism', he wrote; 'it begins so very ill, calling baptism our new birth, and making us thereby members of Christ, children of God, and heirs of the kingdom of heaven. Mr Stillingfleet should have spoken more fully and pointedly about this weighty matter; for all carnal churchmen fancy they are new born, because baptized, and quote the Catechism as a proof of it, and the carnal clergy preach accordingly, and quote the same authority. The acting as sponsors is now become a mere farce, and a gossipping business; and the promising for infants, what they cannot engage for themselves, may suit a covenant of works, but not a covenant of grace.'[2]

All these considerations, explicit or inarticulate, underlay Berridge's activities as an itinerant preacher, or, as he sometimes put it, 'a recruiting serjeant' or 'a riding pedlar'.[3] Whittingham states that, when on circuit, 'he preached, upon an average, from *ten to twelve sermons a-week*, and frequently rode a hundred miles. Nor were these extraordinary exertions the hasty fruit of intermitting zeal, but were regularly continued during the long succession of more than twenty years.'[4] The hardships to be faced in an itinerant ministry were considerable. 'I fear', wrote Berridge to Lady Huntingdon (Dec. 26, 1767), 'my weekly circuits would not suit

[1] F. Warre Cornish, *The English Church in the Nineteenth Century*, vol. i, p. 19.
[2] Berridge to John Thornton, Oct. 27, 1767: *Works*, p. 457.—Similarly the Rev. John Riland, in *The British Liturgy; an attempt towards an Analysis, Arrangement, and Compression, of the Book of Common Prayer* (1833), complains of 'the indiscriminate and gregarious manner in which the members of a *national* church—gathering, as a matter of course, within its fold the very dregs and refuse of mankind, both socially and spiritually—are addressed in our services. *All* sponsors are believers; *all* the baptised are regenerate; *all* the confirmed, forgiven; *all* the catechumens, elect; *all* kings, religious; *all* the dead, subjects of thankfulness; to the total oblivion of the present and eternal distinction between the saved and the lost' (p. 209).—Cf. also the Appendices to the Rev. Peter Hall's *Congregational Reform* (1835).
[3] Berridge's *Works*, pp. 512, 367, and passim.—'He called himself a "Riding Pedlar", because his master, as he used to express himself, employed him to serve near forty shops in the country, besides his own parish' (G. Dyer, *Memoirs of Robert Robinson*, 1796, p. 54).
[4] Whittingham, p. 29.

a London or a Bath divine, nor any tender evangelist that is environed with prunello. Long rides and miry roads in sharp weather! Cold houses to sit in, with very moderate fuel, and three or four children roaring or rocking about you! Coarse food and meagre liquor; lumpy beds to lie on, and too short for the feet; stiff blankets, like boards, for a covering; and live cattle in plenty to feed upon you! Rise at five in the morning to preach; at seven, breakfast on tea that smells very sickly; at eight, mount a horse with boots never cleaned; and then ride home, praising God for all mercies!'[1] Yet it was characteristic of the man that 'cottagers were always gainers by his company. He invariably left half-a-crown for the homely provision of the day, and during his itineracy it actually cost him *five hundred pounds* in this single article of expenditure.'[2]

Perhaps it is not altogether surprising that he did not find it easy to get curates. 'I do not want a helper merely to stand up in my pulpit, but to ride round my district.'[1] 'I am now daily calling on my heavenly Counsellor to provide me a Curate; telling him, I am unable to find or to choose one; but he is able to do both; and I am running much to his door on this errand. ...On Saturday I wrote to Mr ** acquainting him with my speedy want of a Curate, and desiring him to inquire among his Cambridge friends about Mr ** or any other that might seem suitable. But indeed I am not very fond of College youths; they are apt to be lofty and lazy and delicate, and few of them might like to unite with such an offensive character as mine. I should think a young man from the Hull academies might suit better....'[3] 'Unmarried: not afraid of work' were to his mind the primary qualifications. 'No trap so mischievous for the field-preacher as wedlock, and it is laid for him at every hedge corner. Matrimony has quite maimed poor Charles [Wesley], and might have spoiled John [Wesley] and George [Whitefield], if a wise Master had not graciously sent them a brace of ferrets. Dear George has now got his liberty again, and he will scape well if he is not caught by another tenter-hook.'[4] And, quite in

---

[1] Berridge's *Works*, p. 503.   [2] Whittingham, p. 34.
[3] To John Thornton, Esq., Dec. 30, 1788: Berridge's *Works*, p. 461.
[4] To Lady Huntingdon, March 23, 1770: *ibid.* p. 508: *Countess of Huntingdon*, vol. i, pp. 388–9.

the spirit, though not precisely in the language, of Lord Halifax and Mr Athelstan Riley,[1] he expressed the strongest disapproval of 'candidates for the ministry...preparing to get into petticoats, before they get into orders'.[2] 'Before I parted with honest Glascott, I cautioned him much against petticoat snares. He had burnt his wings already; sure he will not imitate a foolish gnat, and hover again about the candle. If he should fall into a sleeping-lap, he will soon need a flannel night-cap, and a rusty chain to fix him down, like a church-bible to the reading-desk....Eight or nine years ago, having been grievously tormented with housekeepers, I truly had thoughts of looking out for a Jezebel for myself. But it seemed highly needful to ask advice of the Lord; so falling down on my knees before a table, with a Bible between my hands, I besought the Lord to give me a direction; then, letting the Bible fall open of itself, I fixed my eyes immediately on these words, "When my son was entered into his wedding chamber, he fell down and died": II Esdras, x. 1. This frightened me heartily, you may easily think; but Satan, who stood peeping at my elbow, not liking the heavenly caution, presently suggested a scruple, that the book was Apocryphal, and the words not to be heeded. Well, after a short pause, I fell on my knees again, and prayed the Lord not to be angry with me whilst, like Gideon, I requested a second sign, and from the Canonical scripture; then letting my Bible fall open as before, I fixed my eyes directly on this passage, "Thou shalt not take thee a wife, neither shalt thou have sons or daughters in this place": Jer. xvi. 2. I was now completely satisfied; and being thus made acquainted with my Lord's mind, I make it one part of my prayers. And I can look on these words, not only as a rule of direction, but as a promise of security, *Thou shalt not take a wife*, that is, I will keep thee from taking one.'[3] What Lady Huntingdon thought of all this is not

[1] Vide *The Times*, Monday, Dec. 13, 1937: p. 9.
[2] To John Thornton, Dec. 30, 1788: Berridge's *Works*, p. 461.
[3] To Lady Huntingdon, March 23, 1770: Berridge's *Works*, pp. 508-9.—
He goes on to defend the use of *sortes Biblicae* by means of Old Testament analogies: 'However, this oracular enquiry is not to be made on light and trifling occasions, and much less with a light and trifling spirit', etc.: *ibid.* pp. 509-11; *Countess of Huntingdon*, vol. i, pp. 388-90.

recorded. We do, however, know that her Ladyship did not, as a rule, get on so well with the wives of her clergy as she did with their husbands: she was by nature somewhat imperious and overbearing, and made them feel her superiority of rank. There were a few exceptions, such as Mrs Fletcher, Mrs Charles Wesley, and Mrs Thomas Pentycross, to whom she was always partial, and to whom she went so far as to present a silver teapot as a small token of her affectionate remembrance.[1]

Mobility and staying power were in fact prerequisite to the discharge of the duties of the sacred ministry as Berridge conceived of it. His own possession of these qualities was not so much appreciated by his brother clergy upon whose parishes he descended: and the fact that his itinerant ministry was undoubtedly heroic constitutes no proof that it was right. Efforts were made to put a stop to his activities. About a year before his death, he recounted the whole story to a friend of Mr Sutcliffe of Olney, who in turn communicated it to the *Evangelical Magazine*.[2]

'Soon after I began', said he, 'to preach the Gospel of Christ at Everton, the church was filled from the villages around us, and the neighbouring clergy felt themselves hurt at their churches being deserted. The squire of my own parish, too, was much offended. He did not like to see so many strangers, and be so incommoded. Between them both it was resolved, if possible, to turn me out of my living. For this purpose, they complained of me to the bishop of the diocese, that I had preached out of my own parish. I was soon after sent for by the bishop; I did not much like my errand, but I went.

When I arrived, the bishop accosted me in a very abrupt manner: 'Well, Berridge, they tell me you go about preaching out of your own parish. Did I institute you to the livings of A[bbotsle]y, or E[ato]n [Socon], or P[otto]n?'— 'No, my lord,' said I, 'neither do I claim any of these livings; the clergymen enjoy them undisturbed by me.'— 'Well, but you go and preach there, which you have no right to do?'— 'It is true, my lord, I was one day at E[ato]n, and there were a few poor people assembled together, and I admonished them to repent of their sins, and to believe in the Lord Jesus Christ for the salvation of their souls; and I remember seeing five or six clergymen that day,

---

[1] *Countess of Huntingdon*, vol. ii, p. 77.
[2] *Evangelical Magazine*, Feb. 1794, vol. ii, pp. 73–6.

my lord, all out of their own parishes upon E——n bowling-green.'—
'Poh!' said his lordship, 'I tell you, you have no right to preach out
of your own parish; and, if you do not desist from it, you will very
likely be sent to Huntingdon gaol.'—'As to that, my lord,' said I,
'I have no greater liking to Huntingdon gaol than other people; but I
had rather go thither with a good conscience, than live at my liberty
without one.' Here his lordship looked very hard at me, and very
gravely assured me, 'that I was beside myself, and that in a few months
time I should either be better or worse.'—'Then,' said I, 'my lord, you
may make yourself quite happy in this business; for if I should be
better, you suppose I shall desist from this practice of my own
accord; and, if worse, you need not send me to Huntingdon gaol, as
I shall be provided with an accommodation in Bedlam.'

His Lordship now changed his mode of attack. Instead of threatening, he began to entreat: 'Berridge,' said he, 'you know I have been
your friend, and I wish to be so still. I am continually teazed with
the complaints of the clergymen around you. Only assure me that
you will keep to your own parish; you may do as you please there.
I have but little time to live; do not bring down my grey hairs with
sorrow to the grave.'

At this instant, two gentlemen were announced, who desired to
speak with his lordship. 'Berridge,' said he, 'go to your inn, and
come again at such an hour, and dine with me.' I went, and on
entering a private room, fell immediately upon my knees. I could
bear threatening, but knew not how to withstand entreaty; especially
the entreaty of a respectable old man. At the appointed time I
returned. At dinner, I was treated with great respect. The two gentlemen
also dined with us. I found they had been informed who I was, as
they sometimes cast their eyes towards me in some such manner as one
would glance at a monster. After dinner, his lordship took me into
the garden. 'Well, Berridge,' said he, 'have you considered of my
request?'—'I have, my lord,' said I, 'and have been on my knees
concerning it.'—'Well, and will you promise me, that you will preach
no more out of your own parish?'—'It would afford me great pleasure',
said I, 'to comply with your lordship's request, if I could do it with
a good conscience. I am satisfied, the Lord has blessed my labours
of this kind, and I dare not desist.'—'A good conscience!' said his lordship, 'do you not know it is contrary to the canons of the church?'—
'There is one canon, my lord,' I replied, 'which saith, *Go preach the
Gospel to* EVERY CREATURE.'—'But why should you interfere with the
charge of other men? One man cannot preach the Gospel to all
men.'—'If they would preach the Gospel themselves,' said I, 'there
would be no need of my preaching it to their people; but as they do

not, I cannot desist.' His lordship then parted from me in some displeasure. I went home, not knowing what would befall me; but thankful to God that I had preserved a conscience void of offence.

I took no measures for my own preservation, but Divine Providence wrought for me in a way that I never expected. When I was at Clare Hall, I was particularly acquainted with a fellow of that college; and we were both upon terms of intimacy with Mr Pitt,[1] [*sc.* nephew to] the late Lord Chatham, who was at that time also at the university. This Fellow of Clare Hall, when I began to preach the Gospel, became my enemy, and did me some injury in some ecclesiastical privileges, which beforetime I had enjoyed. At length, however, when he heard that I was likely to come into trouble, and to be turned out of my living at Everton, his heart relented. He began to think, it seems, within himself, We shall ruin this poor fellow among us. This was just about the time that I was sent for by the bishop. Of his own accord he writes a letter to Mr Pitt, saying nothing about my methodism, but, to this effect: 'Our old friend Berridge has got a living in Bedfordshire, and, I am informed, he has a squire in his parish, that gives him a deal of trouble, has accused him to the bishop of the diocese, and, it is said, will turn him out of his living: I wish you could contrive to put a stop to these proceedings.' Mr Pitt was at that time a young man, and not chusing to apply to the bishop himself, spoke to a certain nobleman, to whom the bishop was indebted for his promotion. This nobleman within a few days made it his business to see the bishop, who was then in London. 'My lord,' said he, 'I am informed you have a very honest fellow, one Berridge, in your diocese, and that he has been ill-treated by a litigious squire who lives in his parish. He has accused him, I am told, to your lordship, and wishes to turn him out of his living. You would oblige me, my lord, if you would take no notice of that squire, and not suffer the honest man to be interrupted in his living.' The bishop was astonished, and could not imagine in what manner things could have thus got round: It would not do, however, to object; he was obliged to bow compliance, and so I continued ever after uninterrupted in my sphere of action.*

[*The squire having waited on the bishop to know the result of the summons, had the mortification to learn, that his purpose was defeated. On his return home, his partisans in this prosecution fled to know what was determined on, saying, 'Well, you have got the old Devil

---

[1] Thomas Pitt (1737–93), first Baron Camelford, politician and connoisseur of art: fellow-commoner of Clare, 1754–58, M.A. *per literas regias* 1759: M.P. for Old Sarum, Dec. 1761–March 1768 and 1774–84, and for Okehampton 1768–74: in politics, a follower of George Grenville.

out?' He replied, 'No; nor do I think the very Devil himself can get him out.']¹

It is not a wholly edifying story. But the crucial phrase is Berridge's answer to his Bishop: 'There is one canon, my lord, which saith, *Go preach the Gospel to* EVERY CREATURE.' The Bishop might fairly have retorted that he did not find it among the Canons of the Church of England. It was, however, the text to which the itinerant preachers habitually appealed to justify their violation of Church Order. 'In preaching through England, Scotland, Ireland, and Wales,' wrote Rowland Hill, 'I always conceived *I stuck close to my parish*. We are to "preach the Gospel to every creature, even to the end of the world".'²

---

¹ With this account, cf. Berridge to David Simpson, Aug. 8, 1775: '... When I began to itinerate, a multitude of dangers surrounded me, and seemed ready to ingulph me. My relations and friends were up in arms; my college was provoked; my Bishop incensed; the clergy on fire; and the church canons pointing their ghastly mouths at me. As you are now doing, so did I send letters to my friends, begging advice, but received unsatisfactory, or discouraging answers. Then I saw, if I meant to itinerate, I must not confer with flesh and blood, but cast myself wholly upon the Lord. By his help, I did so, and made a surrender of myself to Jesus, expecting to be deprived, not only of my fellowship and vicarage, but also of my liberty. At various times, complaints or presentments were carried to my college, to successive archdeacons and bishops; and my first diocesan frankly told me I should either be in Bedlam or Huntingdon gaol by and by. But, through the good blessing of my God, I am yet in possession of my senses, my tythes, and my liberty; and he who has hitherto delivered, I trust will yet deliver me from the mouth of ecclesiastical lions, and the paw of worldly bears. I have suffered from nothing, except from lapidations and pillory treats [threats?], which yet have proved more frightful than hurtful....' (*The Life of the Rev. David Simpson, M.A.*, by Sir J. B. Williams: prefixed to Simpson's *A Plea for Religion and the Sacred Writings*, ed. 1837, p. xxiv.)—From the explicit reference, in this letter, to 'my first diocesan', coupled with the other reference to Mr Thomas Pitt, it is possible to date the episode with some precision. Berridge's first diocesan, Bishop John Thomas (1691–1766), was translated from Lincoln to Salisbury in November 1761. Thomas Pitt went abroad in January 1760, and started home from Florence in July 1761. Unless the interview between Berridge and the Bishop took place in the autumn of 1761, it must have taken place before Jan. 1760.

In a letter to John Thornton (Nov. 17, 1784), Berridge describes himself as 'not indebted to the mercy of church canons or church governors for itinerant liberty, but to the secret overruling providence of Jesus, which rescued me at various times from the claws of a church commissary, an archdeacon, and a bishop.... Hitherto the Lord has delivered me, and I trust will deliver. No weapon formed against me has prospered.' (*Congregational Magazine*, April 1845, vol. ix, n.s., p. 275).

² Rowland Hill, *Journal through the North of England and parts of Scotland. With ... some Remarks on the Propriety of what is called Lay and Itinerant Preaching* (1799), p. 67.

Yet Berridge's conduct might have been less resented had he not interpreted that text to mean, not only that he had a right to preach in any parish where (in his opinion) the incumbent was not doing his job, but also that he had a special duty to preach in any parish where the incumbent had preached against him, against his doctrine, and against his mode of operation. 'Not only Harlston, but Stapleford and Triplow, to which Mr B. was now going, were places in which he had never preached the gospel, and probably never would have done had it not been for the thundering sermons made against him from their several pulpits. So does Satan frequently overshoot himself, and occasion the downfall of his own kingdom.'[1] The satisfaction here evinced by the writer of the eye-witness narrative of the Everton Revival was unlikely to be shared by the incumbents of the parishes concerned: and the Master of Corpus had reason enough for his insinuation that Berridge in his public preaching did not abstain from baiting 'the worldly-minded clergy'.[2]

Nor was this the only complication. For, granted that human beings are divisible into two classes, 'certainly vital Christians' on the one hand, and, on the other, a larger and more miscellaneous category composed, at one end, of mere formal professors, and, at the other, of libertines and infidels: it follows that men's fellowship in the Gospel cuts right across the barrier between Churchmen and Dissenters, and that the ministry of the Word must be impatient of conventional distinctions between clergy and laity.[3] If the Gospel is to be preached to every creature, it may, of necessity, having regard to the conditions of the time, be preached by any creature who has received it, whether he be cleric or layman, or even lay-woman

[1] J. Wesley, *Journal*, vol. iv, p. 337 [John Walsh's narrative (B.) of the Everton Revival].

[2] [Dr John Green,] *The Principles and Practice of the Methodists considered* [in a letter to] *the Reverend Mr B——E* (2nd ed. 1761), p. 23.

[3] 'I do think that the words *Clergy* and *Laity*, as they are generally understood, are more nearly allied to the tricks of Rome than most people are aware of; and if the people who love their Bible read the New Testament, without the presupposed distinctions of different sects and parties, they would discover uncommon simplicity in the first ages of Christianity.'—Rowland Hill, *Journal through the North of England and parts of Scotland* (1799), p. 181 *n*.

for that matter, and whether he be within or without the pale of the ecclesiastical Establishment.

Thus, co-operation with Dissenters was, in many instances, a noted feature of the Evangelical Revival. The liberality of John and Henry Thornton drew no nice sectarian distinctions:[1] Hannah More was rebuked by Dr Daubeny for her attention to unauthorised preachers, and was even alleged to have received communion 'sundry times' at the hands of Mr Jay of Bath:[2] while Newton of Olney went so far in his efforts to fraternise with Nonconformists as not merely, upon particular occasions, to attend the Baptist or the Independent Meeting, but even to suspend one of his own week-day prayer-meetings or evening lectures in order not to clash with it; for example, he recorded in his diary under Tuesday, Sept. 26, 1765—'Omitted our prayer-meeting to-night and attended Mr Bradbury, who preached a very good sermon at Mr Drake's [the Independent Meeting]. I am glad of such opportunities at times to discountenance bigotry and party spirit, and to set our Dissenting brethren an example, which I think ought to be our practice towards all who love the Lord Jesus Christ, and preach His Gospel without respect to forms or denominations.'[3] So also when Robert Robinson, the Baptist minister, began to itinerate among the villages lying to the south of Cambridge, he had not only Berridge's example, but also his encouragement:[4] while, in the county of Cambridgeshire alone, Dissenting congregations at Bassingbourn, Bottisham Lode, Croydon, Duxford, Ely, Grantchester, Haddenham, Harston, Steeple Morden, Great

---

[1] Cf. *Incidents in the life of John Thornton, Esq., the Philanthropist*, in the *Congreg. Mag.*, April and Dec. 1842, vol. vi, n.s., esp. p. 827: also *The Love of Christ the Source of Genuine Philanthropy:—Discourse occasioned by the death of John Thornton, Esq., of Clapham, Surrey, who died November 7, 1790*, in *The Works of the late Rev. Thomas Scott, Rector of Aston Sandford, Bucks.* (1824), vol. vi, p. 346.

[2] 'We cannot doubt Mr Jay's positive assertion, that Mrs M. received the sacrament at his hands sundry times—not merely once by accident, as her sister stated it.'—Rev. R. Polwhele, ed. Bishop Lavington's *The Enthusiasm of Methodists and Papists considered* (1820), Introduction, pt. ii, p. ccxxxi *n*. But cf. Dr Valpy's *Reminiscences* in *The Christian Observer*, March 1835, p. 168.

[3] Thomas Wright, *The Town of Cowper* (2nd ed. 1893), pp. 137, 135.

[4] George Dyer, *Memoirs of the Life and Writings of Robert Robinson* (1796), pp. 53–5: *Memoirs of the life and writings of the author* [by Benjamin Flower], prefixed to Robinson's *Miscellaneous Works*, vol. i, p. xxiii.

Shelford, Stretham, Swavesey, and Waterbeach, were either planted or revived by the itinerant labours of the Vicar of Everton in the parishes of his brethren of the Established Church.[1]

Berridge was also the patron and presumably the more or less acknowledged chief of a small band of itinerant lay-preachers. They were uneducated men: but this, to him, was rather a recommendation than the reverse. There are occasional references in his correspondence to money received on their behalf from London friends and mostly spent on cloth and tailors. 'Dear Sir—Your kind letter, with the enclosed, came safe to hand, for which I return you my hearty thanks; and yesterday bought a great coat for one that needed it much. Your letter not only brought seasonable advice, but made a seasonable purchase; and the Devonshire Plane will keep the wearer's back warm for some years....' '...I know not what my poor Lay-evangelists would do without some assistance received from yourself and your society. They are labouring men, whose paws maintain their jaws, and two of them have seven children, and their wives are kindling every year. They seem the only free grace preachers in the land; for they do preach free grace freely, without money, and without price, having nothing for their preaching but a plain dinner, and sometimes not even that.' 'Dear Sir,—I had bought some very strong good cloth to make two coats and breeches, for two very poor but upright preachers, and had sent it a fortnight ago, with a guinea to each to make the clothes up, with some thoughts of your bounty to eke the matter out, but I find you are no friend to eking, for you have made the whole up, with a remnant besides. On opening your letter, I gave the Lord hearty thanks for your donation, with a prayer for a blessing on the donor; and may his blessing ever rest on you and yours, Amen....P.S. Please to present my love to the

---

[1] This list is taken from the *Statistical View of Dissenters in Cambridgeshire* in the *Congreg. Mag.*, 1819–20: vol. ii, pp. 375, 437, 440, 501, 502, 630, 631, 697, 813; vol. iii, pp. 58, 112, 113.—Apart from fitting up barns at his own expense, in at least three cases Berridge assisted to raise funds for the erection of permanent meeting-houses: vol. ii, pp. 375, 437; vol. iii, p. 58.—Cf. Thompson Cooper, *New Biographical Dictionary* (1873), p. 219, quoting Cole MSS. (Waterbeach); also Nichols' *Literary Anecdotes*, vol. i, p. 574.

Trustees, and all the labourers.'[1] He himself, with his habitual consideration and benevolence, contributed liberally, both from his modest stipend and from the little capital which he had inherited from his father, to the relief of their necessities; 'even his family plate was converted into clothes' for them.[2] To John Thornton he wrote, acknowledging a donation (May 3, 1773):

I return you hearty thanks for the enclosed paper, and will now tell you what I do with my money, and how the paper will be applied. My living is £160 a-year: £100 of which defrays the expense of housekeeping, horse-keeping, servants' wages, my own raiment, and Sunday food and liquor for poor pilgrims who come to church from afar. I keep no company; pay no visits, but preaching ones; and receive no visits but from travelling Christians, who are welcomed with some hashed meat, unless they chance to come on boiling days, which are twice a-week. The work of God has extended itself from Everton, by means of field-preaching, into four counties, viz. Bedfordshire, Hertfordshire, Essex, and Cambridgeshire. Near forty towns have been evangelized, many of which lay at a great distance from each other, and two lay preachers ride from town to town, preaching morning and evening every day. These are yearly allowed £25 a piece, to provide themselves with horses and clothes, and defray turnpike expenses. There are also six Sunday preachers, who often want support, and receive it from me. By this means the Gospel is preached without charge to the hearers. No collections are made, which mightily stoppeth the world's clamour. But, Sir, besides these constant outgoings, I have a thousand other occasional demands upon me. The flocks in every place are very poor, and often distressed, on account of their religion. Labouring men have been turned out of work; and some, who are unable to work, through sickness, lameness, or old age, have been deprived of parish collection, or received a very scanty one, because they are Methodists. These you may think will apply to me for relief—true, you reply, but how are you able to relieve them? I will tell you, Sir. When I began to preach the Gospel, I was possessed of £140 in money, and a paternal inheritance of £24 a year. The money was first expended—then I sold some needless plate and books for £50—this also was expended—and, lastly, I sold my inheritance, which is not half expended. I scatter my mites about, because I am

---

[1] To Benjamin Mills, Esq., Sept. 24, 1782 (*Congreg. Mag.*, April 1845, vol. ix, n.s., p. 273); Nov. 4, 1785 (Berridge's *Works*, p. 464); Nov. 1, 1786 (*ibid.* p. 465; *Congreg. Mag.* Oct. 1845, vol. ix, n.s., p. 740).
[2] Whittingham, p. 34.

trading for another world. What silver and copper is left behind me, will profit me nothing; but what is given for Christ's sake will find a *gracious* recompense. The world would call me a fool for this traffic, but they will see and own hereafter, that I carried my goods to the best market. The walls of my house are made of plaster, and very leaky in some parts, and I fear the woodwork is decayed; they have wanted repairing for some years, but I could not find a heart to repair them, because of the expense. Some part of your donation shall now be applied to this purpose, and the rest to Christ's poor. My health, through mercy, is better, and I am able to travel two or three days in a week to preach. It would delight you to see how crowded my cathedrals are, and what abundance of hearers they contain, when the grain is threshed out. I believe more children have been born of God in any one of these despised barns, than in St Paul's Church or Westminster Abbey....[1]

The directness and the simplicity of this statement are extraordinarily moving: and yet there were two obvious and fatal weaknesses inherent in Berridge's evangelistic work. Not only did it fail to create out of itself the discipline and organisation necessary to its consolidation and continuance: it also disparaged and defied the traditional discipline and organisation which the cumulative experience of the past had provided for the maintenance and propagation of the Christian religion in this country. To this extent, John Berridge is the spiritual ancestor of those broadminded and self-opinionated persons who, in our own generation, have talked wildly about 'the unfettered guidance of the Holy Spirit'. And it was from his contact with John Berridge that Simeon learned that, although the Kingdom of Heaven is indeed taken by violence, it is not to be held by indiscipline. There was much in Berridge's ministry of which he could approve, and to which he was probably indebted: the evangelical fervour, the untiring zeal, the pastoral sympathy and understanding, symbolised by the barrel of ale kept at the vicarage and the use of homely language in the pulpit. (It was a wise saying of Roger Ascham that 'We preachers ought to think like great men, but speak like common people'.) Simeon further emulated Berridge in his pecuniary benevolence, and in his

---

[1] *Congreg. Mag.*, April 1842, vol. vi, n.s., p. 221.

celibacy, to which he seems also to have converted Henry Martyn.[1] But there was much else in Berridge's ministry against which he was obliged to set his face: his jocularity, even in his sermons—'it is a very painful style and manner':[2] his shouting and roaring in the pulpit,[3] instead of preaching in a natural voice:[4] his impatience of profane learning—yet 'College is the place for study.... If my coachman neglected my horses, or my cook my dinner, that they might read the Bible, they would be displeasing and dishonouring their God. So, if students neglect the duties (i.e. the studies) of the place for the sake of reading their Bibles, they are not in the path of duty.... Remember, secular study, as appointed by the authorities, is here your duty to God':[5] and, the most dangerous of all his errors, his impatience of Church Order.

It is therefore peculiarly appropriate that we should be able to see the battle for Church Order being fought out, like some Homeric contest, between Venn and Berridge, with Charles Simeon's future as the prize.

Here it is necessary first to recapitulate the early history of Simeon's acquaintance with these two veterans of the Revival.

Charles Simeon was ordained deacon on Trinity Sunday, May 26, 1782. On June 1, he was introduced by Christopher Atkinson to John Venn of Sidney Sussex, son of the Rector of Yelling. On June 13, Simeon walked over to Yelling to visit his new friend: the Rector and the other members of the family were unfortunately away from home, but on the following day John Venn took him to Everton and introduced him to Mr Berridge. A month later—on Tuesday, July 16—Simeon rode over from Cambridge for the day to be introduced to the Rector of Yelling, and at once recognised 'in this aged minister' the

---

[1] 'Know therefore that I rejoice in my celibacy; and am finally resolved to abide by my first determination, to be single like yourself, and for the same reason I trust, that I may care only for the things of the Lord.'—Martyn to Simeon, Dinapore, April 26, 1807: Carus, pp. 229, 230–1: cf. J. Noble, *Memoir of the Rev. Robert Turlington Noble* (1867), p. 46.

[2] Brown, p. 200.   [3] Whittingham, p. 80.
[4] Brown, pp. 186–7.
[5] Brown, pp. 193–4: Carus, p. 843.—Wesley also expressly dissociated himself from Berridge on this point: *Letter to Dr Rutherforth* (March 28, 1768), in Wesley's *Letters*, ed. J. Telford, vol. v, p. 359.—Cf. also Venn, p. 262.

THE REVEREND HENRY VENN

From a painting by Mason Chamberlain, R.A., 1770, in the possession of
Dr J. A. Venn, President of Queens' College, Cambridge

man for whom he had been seeking ever since the great spiritual crisis of his freshman year: 'a father, an instructor, and a most bright example.'[1]

The first reference to Simeon in Berridge's correspondence occurs in a letter to the Rev. John Newton (Sept. 17, 1782). Berridge states that John Venn, 'a very gracious youth', has just gone to Buckden for his ordination by the Bishop of Lincoln: 'He seems intended for a polished shaft, and has been much in the furnace of late, a good school for Christian experience.' Then he continues: 'Mr Simeon, a young Fellow of King's College, in Cambridge, has just made his appearance in the Christian hemisphere, and attracts much notice. He preaches at a church in the town, which is crowded like a theatre on the first night of a new play. A gospel Curate is also sprung up at Royston, a market town, ten miles S.E. of Everton. Thus Christ is opening many doors to spread his gospel: may he open many hearts to receive it!'[2]

It does not transpire, however, that Berridge and Simeon had met again since June 14. Yelling, not Everton, was Simeon's lodestone: we know that he had been over there six times in the course of the past three months.[3] On New Year's day, 1783, he brought with him the Rev. William Farish, the new Tutor of Magdalene, to hear Mr Robinson of Leicester: and on the following morning the whole party went over to Everton unannounced, and prayed with Berridge, and parted in fervent love.[4] But it was Henry Venn, and not John Berridge, who visited Cambridge in February and 'spent several days…with four young clergymen'—Christopher Atkinson, Fellow and Tutor of Trinity Hall, and Curate of St Edward's: Charles Simeon, the new Vicar of Holy Trinity: Dr Jowett of Trinity Hall: and Farish of Magdalene. 'All our discourse was to the purpose. I prayed with them twice a day. Their affection for me was expressed in the most overwhelming manner. They have, since I left them, been over with me….—Mr Simeon's ministry is likely to be blessed. We may indeed say, "A great door is opened!" Many gownsmen

[1] Carus, p. 23.   [2] Berridge's *Works*, p. 418.
[3] Venn, p. 345.   [4] *Ibid.* p. 349.

hear him. What follows, is as true—"there are many adversaries". He comes over, to advise with me on every occasion; but the wonderful Counsellor is with him.—'[1] A year later, Venn writes again (Jan. 19, 1784): 'I have good news to send you from Cambridge.—Mr Simeon is made for great usefulness. There are near twenty promising young students. Several of them come over, at times, to me.... They listen to my instructions with great simplicity: and I inculcate much moderation, obedience to superiors, and no breaking out to be teachers, when they are mere novices. Hard lesson to young men! Yet they observe it, and bring credit upon their seriousness.'[2] Eighteen months later, he was to find himself under the necessity of reading a similar lesson to Charles Simeon himself.

Meanwhile at Bluntisham in Huntingdonshire, a straggling village on the left bank of the river Ouse, bordering on the Cambridge Fens, a God-fearing and high-principled young farmer named Coxe Feary (1759–1822) had become a convert to Evangelical opinions.

Feary had always been serious-minded, a great reader of religious books, and a constant and regular attendant at his parish church. But, becoming 'dissatisfied with the trifling, and, as he thought, the irreligious conduct'[3] of others who attended there, he began to turn his attention to the Dissenters, in whom he thought he saw more regard for religion than among the members of the Established Church. The Baptist congregation in the neighbouring village he found to be High Calvinists, and some of them very narrow-minded and illiberal, which repelled him from joining them: but there was a congregation of the people called Quakers at Earith, a mile or two away, whose piety he found more congenial, and with whom he occasionally worshipped. So he struggled on as best he could for five or six years, until in the spring of 1784 he chanced to meet in a bookseller's shop at Huntingdon an Evangelical clergyman

---

[1] Venn, p. 352. [2] *Ibid.* pp. 375–6.
[3] *Memoirs of Mr Coxe Feary, first Pastor of the Baptist Church at Bluntisham in Huntingdonshire: with an Account of the Rise and Formation of that Church.* By John Audley. [Incorporating most of Feary's autobiographical narrative in the Church-Book of Bluntisham Baptist Church.] (1823), p. 8.

named Brock, 'who preached the Gospel at the neighbouring villages of Stukeley and Offord. After some conversation on religious publications, Mr B. very kindly invited him to take tea with him. The invitation was gladly accepted, and the interview was truly interesting, as it led him to hear Mr B. next Lord's day, where he found himself at home under the sound of the glorious Gospel of the blessed God. After the services of the day he returned home, rejoicing to think he had found a place in the Establishment where the glad tidings of salvation were proclaimed to poor sinners. He now formed the resolution of constantly attending Mr B.'s preaching, but by the persuasion of that gentleman he was induced to give up his design, and to attend the labours of Mr Venn, of Yelling, where he could enjoy the services both parts of the Lord's day. On the day called Easter Sunday, he went to hear Mr Venn, with whose lively and zealous preaching he was much delighted. This even led to an intimate acquaintance with that gentleman, which was ever after esteemed as one of the happiest circumstances of his life.'[1]

He now gave up attending at his parish church, and instead went over to Yelling every Sunday, a distance of twelve miles. This, coupled with the earnestness with which he talked of the importance and great advantage of evangelical preaching, made a considerable impression in the village, so that in the course of the summer a number of his friends and neighbours frequently accompanied him to Yelling to hear his favourite preacher, Mr Venn. In the autumn, he happened to buy 'the Life and Sermons of the famous Mr Whitefield' in three volumes for eighteen shillings, and the evening of the same day he read one of the sermons—'What think ye of Christ?'—to his shepherd, his labourers, and his intimate and bosom friend Mr Asplan, who were much delighted. The following evening, without his knowing or expecting any such thing, a number of poor people came with Mr John Kent, a gentleman of the village, to hear him read a sermon. With some embarrassment and confusion, he read them the same sermon that he had read the night before, to their general satisfaction. One of the poor women present,

---

[1] *Ibid.* pp. 16–17.

who lived in one of the alms-houses at the bottom of the village, was very anxious that he should come and read a sermon at her house on the following evening. Feary consented, on condition that she would not make it known: but, notwithstanding his precautions, when he went to the house he found it full of people, who received with profound attention and deep serious-ness the glad tidings of salvation. He continued reading to the people in the same cottage three or four evenings a week throughout the winter months: 'and such was the awakening in the place, that the people were constantly enquiring "What they must do to be saved?"'[1] In the spring of 1785, since the house was no longer able to contain his audience, they removed into the next house, which was larger: and here, for the first time, he found courage to pray with the people after he had finished reading. Soon they were obliged to open a still larger house in the village. 'Being still a constant attendant at Mr Venn's church on the Lord's day, he acquainted him with what was going on. Mr Venn encouraged him, pressed him to keep on, saying, that "he believed God had a great work to do at Bluntisham; and that in the course of the summer he would come over and help them".'[2] Feary also 'went twice to see the eminently pious Mr Berridge, and was much encouraged by that venerable man'.[3]

Venn kept his promise; and, for his accommodation (continues Feary) 'Mr John Kent opened his barn.[4] Mr Venn preached to a very large, serious, and deeply attentive congregation. The scene was truly affecting, and Mr Venn declared, that he never but once in his life enjoyed such a season of refreshment from the presence of the Lord, in preaching to any people.'[5]

Unfortunately Venn had then to go down to London for a season, to preach for Rowland Hill at Surrey Chapel,[6] having

[1] Feary, p. 20.   [2] Ibid. p. 20.   [3] Ibid. p. 21 n.
[4] 'This barn stood a little back from the road on the opposite side to the site of the present chapel, and a few yards further up the road, but was taken down some years ago, and a new one built on the spot.'—A Century of Village Nonconformity at Bluntisham, Hunts., 1787 to 1887, by R. W. Dixon (1887), p. 147.
[5] Feary, p. 21.
[6] Venn Family Annals, p. 103. Cf. Countess of Huntingdon, vol. i, p. 292.

previously arranged for Simeon to ride over from Cambridge and take Sunday afternoon duty at Yelling in his absence. The sequel is narrated in a letter from Berridge to John Thornton, dated 'Everton, July 2, 1785'.

Yelling church is well attended under Mr Simeon's afternoon ministry. A brave Christian Serjeant he is, having the true spirit of an Evangelist, but his feet are often put into the stocks by the Archdeacon of Yelling [*i.e.* Venn], who is doubtless become a vagabond preacher as well as myself, a right gospel hawker and pedlar, but seems desirous of having the trade to himself. Through mercy he is grown as scandalous as I could wish him, yet he wants to fasten the shackle on Simeon, which he has dropped from himself. O worldly prudence, what a prudish foe thou art to grace!

Some little time before Mr Venn went to London, he preached at Bluntisham, a village in the Fens, and finding great power and success, he promised to preach there once a fortnight in some barn at his return. In the mean time I desired Simeon to strike whilst the iron was hot, and to visit Bluntisham as well as Yelling. He consented: accordingly after preaching at Cambridge on a Sunday morning, he preached at Yelling in the afternoon, and at Bluntisham in the evening; and finding a very crowded and attentive audience, he preached early on Monday morning, leaving off before six. This he did for three weeks, and then acquaints his principal with what he had done, expecting a letter of congratulation; but lo! a funeral answer comes, declaring Mr Venn is grieved at his conduct, grieved at Simeon for doing what himself had done, and intended to do. This surely is grief of all griefs, too deep even for tragedy. Pray, Sir, lay your cane smartly on the Archdeacon's back, when you see him, and brush off this heathen grief, else it may spoil a Christian Serjeant.[1]

Berridge implies quite clearly that Simeon preached at Bluntisham on three occasions, although Feary's biographer says only that 'Mr S. of C.' was one of three pious clergymen—the others being Mr Brock and Mr Venn—who favoured Feary with their friendship, and that he 'preached a sermon in Mr Feary's house, at five o'clock in the morning. The room was crowded to excess, and several persons were out of doors':[2] Dixon adds that 'tradition says many collected at the back of the house, so that Mr Simeon, standing outside near a pump which

---

[1] Berridge's *Works*, pp. 445-6.   [2] Feary, p. 20.

still remains, addressed his hearers through open door and window'.[1] 'This', continues Audley, 'was a season long remembered with peculiar pleasure, on account of the evident tokens by which God gave testimony to the word of his grace.'[2] The discrepancy between the two accounts is not significant: and, of the two, Berridge's statement is the more likely to be correct.

There is yet another document of unique interest and importance which must surely be assigned to the same episode. This is a letter, not dated, and printed by Whittingham in Berridge's correspondence with the discreetly reticent address, 'TO THE REV. MR —'.[3] In the *Evangelical Magazine* for May 1794,[4] from which Whittingham appears to have taken it, it is headed: 'COPY *of a* LETTER *of the late Rev.* JOHN BERRIDGE, *of Everton, Bedfordshire, to the Rev. Mr —, a Gospel Clergyman at C—.*' Finally, a more primitive text, unexpurgated and unpolished, and therefore presumably original, may be found in the *Arminian Magazine* for September, 1794,[5] where it is boldly headed, 'From the Rev. Mr Berridge, to the Rev. Mr Simeon'. Here, then, is this latter text, collated with the slightly bowdlerised version in the *Evangelical Magazine*.

From the Rev. Mr Berridge, to the Rev. Mr Simeon.

If every Parish Church were blessed with a Gospel Minister, there would[6] be little need of Itinerant Preaching; but since those Ministers are thinly scattered about the Country, and neighbouring Pulpits are usually locked up against them; it behoves them to take advantage of fields, or barns, or houses,[7] to cast abroad the Gospel Seed. But all are not designed to be Rural Deans. How are we to judge who are? If you are enabled to preach without Notes;—feel an abiding desire to be useful in spreading[8] the Gospel;—meet with Calls for that purpose,—comply with the Calls,—find the Word sealed;—and if persecuted and threatened, have a[9] word given for support: Where these concur, (and these are just my own experience) I have no doubt but such a Minister is designed for a Rural Dean, or a rambling Bishop.

---

[1] *A Century of Village Nonconformity*, p. 147.
[2] Feary, p. 21.   [3] Berridge's *Works*, pp. 475–8.
[4] *Ev. Mag.*, May 1794, vol. ii, pp. 198–200.
[5] *Arminian Magazine*, Sept. 1794, vol. xvii, pp. 496–8.
[6] could (*E.M.* = *W.*)   [7] *E.M. omits* or houses
[8] to spread   [9] the

SIMEON AND CHURCH ORDER

When you open your Commission, begin with ripping up the Audience, and[1] Moses will lend you a Carving Knife,[2] which may be often whetted at his Grind-Stone. Lay open the universal sinfulness of nature, the darkness of the mind, the frowardness of the tempers,[3] —the earthliness and sensuality of the affections:—Speak of the evil of sin in its Nature, its rebellion against God as our Benefactor, and contempt of[4] his authority and Love:—Declare the evil of Sin in its effects, bringing all our sickness, pains, and sorrows, all the evils we feel, and all the evils we fear:—All inundations, fires, famines, pestilences, brawls, quarrels, fightings, Wars,[5]—with Death, [to close[6]] these present sorrows,—and Hell[7] to receive all that die in sin.

Lay open the spirituality of the Law, and its extent, reaching to every thought, word and action, and declaring every transgression whether of[8] omission or commission, deserving of Death. Declare Man's utter helplessness to change his nature, or to make his peace. Pardon and Holiness must come from the Saviour. Acquaint them with the searching Eye of God, watching us continually, spying out every thought, word, and action, noting them down in the Book of his Remembrance; bringing every secret work[9] into judgment, whether it be good or evil.

When your Hearers have been well harrowed, and the clumps begin to fall,[10] (which is seen by their hanging down the head) then bring out your CHRIST, and bring him out from the heart, thro' the lips, and tasting of his Grace while you publish it.[11] Now lay open[12] the Saviour's Almighty Power to soften the heart,[13] and give it true repentance;[14] to bring Pardon to the broken heart, and the Spirit[15] of Prayer to the prayerless heart; Holiness to the filthy heart; and Faith to the unbelieving heart. Let them know that all the Treasures of Grace are lodged in Jesus Christ, for the use of poor needy sinners;[16] and that he is full of Love as well as Power; that he turns no Beggars away from[17] his Gate, but receives all Comers kindly,—loves to bless them, and bestows all his Blessings *Tythe-free*; Farmers and Country People chop at that. Here you must wave the Gospel Flag, and

[1] begin with laying open the innumerable corruptions of the hearts of your audience:
[2] a knife   [3] frowardness of the will, the fretfulness of the temper, and
[4] —its rebellion against God as our sovereign—ingratitude to God as our benefactor—and contempt both of
[5] all inundations, and fires, and famines, and pestilences—all brawls, and quarrels, and fighting, and wars,
[6] [*Supplied from E.M.*]   [7] hell afterwards   [8] by   [9] thing
[10] When your hearers are deeply affected with these things
[11] by the hanging down of their heads), preach Christ.
[12] Lay open   [13] the hard heart,   [14] give it repentance—   [15] a spirit
[16] the poor needy sinner   [17] —turns no beggars from

magnify the Saviour proudly;[1] speak with a full mouth,[2] that his Blood can wash away the foulest stains,[3] and his Grace subdue the stoutest corruptions. Exhort the people to seek his Grace directly, constantly, and diligently;[4] and acquaint them that all who thus seek, shall find[5] the Salvation of God.

Never preach in working hours: that would raise a clamour. Where you preach at night, preach also in the morning; but be not longer than an hour in the whole service,[6] and conclude before six. Morning Preaching will show whether the evening's[7] took effect, by raising them up early to hear.

Expect plain fare, and plain lodging where you preach, yet perhaps better than your Master had. Suffer no treats to be made for you, but live as your Host usually lives, else he may grow weary of entertaining you. 'Go not[8] from house to house', Luke x. 7. If the Clergy rail at you where you go, say not one word,[9] good or bad, Matt. xv. 14. If you dare be zealous for the Lord of Hosts, expect persecution and threats; but heed them not. Bind that Word[10] to your Heart, Jer. i. 19 and xv. 20. The Promise is doubled for your encouragement. The chief Block[11] in your way, will be from prudent *Peters*,[12] who will beg and entreat[13] you to avoid irregularity: Give them the same answer that Christ gave Peter, Matt. xvi. 23. They savour not the things of God, hear them not.[14] Where[15] you preach at night, go to bed as soon as possible, that the family be not kept up, and that you may rise early. When breakfast and morning family prayer are over, go away directly, that the house may be at liberty. Don't dine where you preach, if you can avoid it: it will save expence,[16] and please the people. If you could[17] do Work for the Lord, as you seem designed, you must venture for the Lord. The Christian's Motto is, '*Trust, and go forward*', though a[18] Sea is before you, Ex. xiv. 15. Do then as Paul did, give up thyself to the Lord's Work,[19] and confer not with flesh and blood. Go, and the Lord be with thee![20] Thine, &c.　　　J. BERRIDGE.[21]

One could not wish for a better or a more succinct account of Berridge's methods as a mission preacher.

---

[1] supremely
[2] Speak it with a full mouth, (*ore rotundo*),　　　　　　　[3] sins
[4] to seek his grace, to seek it directly, seek it diligently, seek it constantly,
[5] shall assuredly find　　[6] whole morning service　　[7] evening
[8] And *go not*　　　[9] a word about it,　　　[10] the Lord's word
[11] blocks　　[12] will be *the prudent Peters*,　　[13] beg, intreat, and beseech
[14] they savour of the things which be of men: Heed them not.
[15] When　　　[16] expense　　　[17] would　　　[18] the
[19] to the Lord; work,　　　[20] blood, and the Lord be with thee.
[21] Dear Brother,
　　　Your's affectionately, J.B.

'From this time', continued Feary, 'Mr Kent insisted upon the people accepting the use of the barn as often as they pleased. They thankfully embraced the offer, opened a small subscription, and fitted it up for their use. This was a new trial to their friend, C. Feary, as it looked so much like a separation from the Establishment, and of his being a Dissenting Minister; to neither of which he at that time could be reconciled. But, though this was unpleasant to his feelings, he continued meeting the people, and reading sermons, in order to keep them together, hoping to have an opportunity of procuring a Curate to preach the Gospel in the Church. For this purpose he mentioned the circumstance to the Rev. Mr S. of C., who was very desirous of accomplishing such an object, and applied to Mr H. a serious clergyman, who engaged to come, if Mr Oakes, the Rector, consented, and the people proposed a subscription towards his salary. But the proposals were rejected.'[1]

Feary also begged that Simeon himself would come and 'favour them with another sermon; but', says Audley, 'after consulting with one of his seniors, he thought proper to decline it.'[2] Venn's remonstrances had carried the day.

Yet it was true, as Berridge said, that Venn's own ministry had never been immaculate in this particular, and that he had become more reckless of irregularity since he came to Yelling. It was also true that it was Berridge himself who had taught him the use of barns as 'threshing-floors for Jesus'. In a letter to John Thornton, dated, 'Everton, Aug. 10, 1774'—three years after Venn had come to Yelling—he wrote: 'I have been recruiting for Mr Venn at Godmanchester, a very populous and wicked town near Huntingdon, and met with a patient hearing from a numerous audience. I hope he also will consecrate a few barns, and preach a little in his neighbourhood, to fill up his fold at Yelling.... Whilst irregularities in their worst shape traverse the kingdom with impunity, should not irregularity in its best shape pass without censure? I tell my brother, he need not fear being hanged for sheep-stealing, while he only whistles the flock to a better pasture, and meddles neither with flesh nor

---

[1] Feary, pp. 21–2.   [2] *Ibid.* p. 22.

fleece. And I am sure he cannot sink much lower in credit; for he has lost his character right honestly, by preaching law and gospel without mincing: The scoffing would make no other distinction between us, than between Satan and Beelzebub. We have both got tufted horns and cloven feet, only I am thought the more impudent devil of the two.'[1] Berridge's hope was realised in generous measure. Venn's grandson, who edited his *Life*, reluctantly admits that during his residence at Yelling, 'he occasionally preached in neighbouring parishes, at the houses, and, in some few instances, in the barns of the farmers'; but hastens to add the following memorandum by his father, the Rev. John Venn, of Clapham: 'Were I to deliver a panegyric agreeable to my own views of that excellent man, in whom I every day saw something new to admire and honour, I should draw a veil over what I am going to relate. But the faithfulness of an historian compels me to do violence to the feelings of a son. His mind was naturally ardent, and he was of a temper to be carried out by zeal rather than to listen to the cold calculations of prudence. Influenced by the hope of doing good, my father, in certain instances, preached in unconsecrated places. But having acknowledged this, it becomes my pleasing duty to state, that he was no advocate for irregularity in others; that when he afterwards considered it, in its distant bearings and connections, he lamented that he had given way to it, and restrained several other persons from such acts by the most cogent arguments; and that he lived long enough to observe the evils of schism so strongly, that they far outweighed in his mind the present apparent good.'[2] It is possible, as Seymour claims, that this is too highly-coloured a description of Venn's views on this important issue:[3] but, be that as it may, it leaves no room for doubt as to the attitude of two Evangelical leaders of the second and third generation towards similar irregularities.

[1] Berridge's *Works*, pp. 394-5.—Cf. *Venn Family Annals*, p. 100: 'Other clergymen in the neighbourhood we shall see none. My name is sufficient to disgust them; and if not, the preaching twice of a Sabbath is. None of the clergy in the neighbourhood, nor the gentry, come near us.'
[2] *Life of the Rev. Henry Venn, M.A.*, ed. Henry Venn (1834), pp. 170-1.
[3] *Countess of Huntingdon*, vol. i, p. 292; vol. ii, pp. 322.—But cf. Henry Venn's rejoinder in *The Christian Observer*, May 1840, pp. 261-6.

The episode of Simeon's preaching at Bluntisham may well have been the incident which forced the issue and dictated its solution. True, on the one hand, that until June 1790, when he felt no longer physically equal to the charge, Venn continued to preach for Rowland Hill at Surrey Chapel every summer:[1] true, on the other hand, that he, together with Romaine, Townshend, Jesse and others had formally withdrawn from the Countess of Huntingdon's Connexion in 1782, as a result of the decision in the Bishop of London's Consistorial Court which deprived the Connexion of its amateur status and forced it into the official position of a Dissenting sect.[2] Yet we are entitled to regard as one of the most decisive factors in the development of the Evangelical Party in the Church of England, his determination that Charles Simeon, at the outset of a ministry so full of promise, should not and must not be permitted to enter upon a course of ecclesiastical irregularity and defiance of church order. It was all very well for himself and Berridge to have preached in barns to flocks inadequately shepherded by their lawful pastors: their conduct might have been mistaken, but it was at least excusable. It was quite another thing for the young Vicar of Holy Trinity to go out of his way to borrow from them an example which it was infinitely better should die with them.

That was the real issue: and, in comparison with it, the fate of Mr Feary and his following at Bluntisham was a secondary consideration. It was perhaps inevitable that they should form themselves into a Dissenting congregation: but they did not do so immediately. At first, 'as they did not know what to do on the Lord's day, C. F. proposed to meet them in the morning before he went to Yelling, and in the evening on his return, and pray with them, and read a sermon to them. And so anxious were the people to hear the Word of God, that multitudes would be waiting on the road for his coming home. They continued this practice for some time, until the congregation became very

---

[1] *Countess of Huntingdon*, vol. i, p. 292: *Life of Henry Venn*, p. 478. His last sermon at Surrey Chapel was preached on June 13, 1790. But he had a reason for continuing to assist there: 'He [R. Hill] writes me word the people for the much greater part prefer the clergy, but if none will officiate there it must be supplied by Dissenters' (*Venn Family Annals*, p. 103).

[2] *Countess of Huntingdon*, vol. ii, p. 314.

large, not fewer than between three and four hundred. Under
these encouraging circumstances, Mr Venn advised him to stop
at home the whole of the Sabbath, which he did. Having
finished all Mr Whitefield's and Mr Hervey's sermons, he was
under the necessity of making an effort at expounding a chapter
out of the sacred Scriptures. This he did for some months; after
which he took a single passage, and endeavoured to preach from
it, which proving acceptable, he was encouraged to go on, for
"the hand of the Lord was with him, and a great number
believed and turned unto the Lord".[1] In May 1786 he began
preaching away from home, first in the Countess of Huntingdon's
Chapel at Chatteris, then in a barn at Somersham, and elsewhere
in the immediate neighbourhood. On Thursday, July 25, 1786,
the Rev. Joseph Saunders, pastor of the Independent Church in
Cambridge, came over and preached in the barn at Bluntisham,
taking as his text Phil. i. 6: 'Being confident of this very thing,
that he who hath begun a good work in you, will perform it until
the day of Jesus Christ.' In November, after long and careful
deliberation and examination of the principles of Dissent, Feary
and his friends applied to Mr Saunders for advice relative to
their forming themselves into a Christian church. On Dec. 28,
Coxe Feary and twenty-five others, twelve men and thirteen
women, publicly united themselves together to form the church.
Other members followed, and, the congregation increasing, the
barn became too small for their requirements. It was therefore
resolved to build a regular Meeting-house 'for the worship of
Almighty God according to the custom of Protestant Dissenters'.[2]
On May 9, 1787, the church met, and gave Coxe Feary a
unanimous call to the pastoral office, in which he was formally
settled on April 23, 1788: part of the ceremony was performed
by Mr Robert Robinson, the Baptist Minister at Cambridge. In
1791 Feary himself, after a careful study of Mr Robinson's
posthumous *History of Baptism*,[3] became 'dissatisfied with infant

---

[1] Feary, pp. 22–3.
[2] Dixon, p. 163.—The Meeting-house was enlarged in 1797, and a gallery
for the Sunday School children added in 1817. It was demolished in 1875
and 'replaced by the present substantial edifice' (*ibid.*).
[3] *The History of Baptism* [ed. G. Dyer] (1790.)

sprinkling, as not being the baptism of the New Testament',[1] and carried the greater part of the congregation over with him into the Baptist camp. But Robinson's was a dangerous influence, and under it he found himself developing an unhealthy appetite for political and theological controversy: his devotional exercises became formal and unprofitable, his preaching dry and flat. 'In short, I appeared to myself to be making rapid strides to *Infidelity* and *Deism*.'[2] He flung himself upon the mercy of God, and, unlike Robinson, was recovered from that ultimate catastrophe. He continued to discharge the duties of his pastorate until 1819, when ill health obliged him to retire from active work. He died on April 22, 1822, in the sixty-third year of his age, having lived to see not only the rise of a flourishing Baptist church in his own village, but also the establishment of a daughter church at Somersham and the building of a meeting-house at Woodhurst which was regularly served from Bluntisham.[3]

These were formidable inroads upon the preserves of the Established Church. Yet such a sequel would not have seemed particularly distressing to John Berridge: and although, as regards Charles Simeon, Venn's prudence had prevailed against Berridge's zeal, there was no open breach between old friends. Many years later Simeon recalled how 'old Mr Venn and I used to go over and dine with Berridge every Tuesday'.[4] But Simeon had learned his lesson: and, says Carus, 'not only in later life was he singularly attentive to order himself, but was wont particularly to enforce upon his younger brethren the importance and duty of not indulging their zeal at the expense of regularity and discretion.[5] On one occasion, a few years before his death, (in the presence of the Editor) he was good-naturedly reminded by an old friend of some of those instances of his early fervour:—"Do you remember, Mr Simeon, in former times coming very early

---

[1] Feary, p. 49. [2] *Ibid.* p. 54.
[3] Dixon, ch. xxvi. [4] Brown, p. 201.
[5] Cf. *Memoirs of the Rev. Charles Jerram* (1855), p. 126: 'I have reason to know that [in the later stages of his religious course] he not only conformed to the strictest regularity in the performance of his ministerial duties, but was the most strenuous adviser to his younger friends not to deviate from the prescribed rules of our Church in the discharge of their clerical functions.'

in the morning to my great barn, to preach to the men before they went to their work?" After a most significant look, instantly turning his face aside, and then with both hands uplifted to hide it, he exclaimed—*O spare me! spare me! I was a young man then.*[1] It was not for nothing that 'it was said in religious periodicals of his day,—"Mr Simeon is more of a *Church-man* than a *Gospel-man.*"'[2] But it is good to know that Rowland Hill, who had been Berridge's first disciple in the University, and who was himself irrevocably committed to an irregular apostolate, respected Simeon's attitude, and spoke with the sincerest delight of his invaluable labours. 'Indeed', writes Sidney, 'there is every reason to believe, that the observance of *order*, which has been so judiciously regarded by Mr Simeon and his followers at Cambridge, has tended greatly to promote the influence of numbers of the zealous clergy, who are now so vigilantly and successfully defending the best interests of the church. On one occasion, Mr Rowland Hill, with his usual delicacy of feeling, refused to preach in a dissenting place of worship at Cambridge, lest he should appear in any way to interfere with the course so wisely pursued by Mr Simeon.'[3]

One irregularity, however, Simeon continued to permit himself. It had arisen out of the unpopularity of his appointment to Holy Trinity. The parishioners had already elected his predecessor's curate, the Rev. John Hammond, to the Sunday afternoon lectureship, thereby leaving the incumbent 'only one opportunity of preaching in the whole week',[4] and that on Sunday morning, at an hour when few of the poor could easily attend.[5] Simeon therefore determined, mainly in the interest of the college servants, to establish a Sunday evening lecture, that is to say, an evening service with a sermon (extempore), at six o'clock. This he did for the first time on July 20, 1783, eight months after his institution. Such a proceeding was not quite without precedent in Cambridge, since his friend Coulthurst had initiated a similar experiment at Holy Sepulchre on the

---

[1] Carus, p. 278. Cf. Preston, p. 39.   [2] Brown, p. 11.
[3] Sidney, *Rowland Hill*, pp. 161–2.
[4] Carus, p. 44.
[5] *Ibid.* p. 87.

previous Sunday:[1] but, apart from the objection to extempore preaching, a Sunday evening service was at that date a very daring innovation, and was regarded by conservative churchmen as savouring of Methodism.[2] In any case, scarcely had Simeon established it before the churchwardens refused him access to his church. 'On one occasion the congregation was assembled, and it was found that the churchwarden had gone away with the key in his pocket. I therefore got a smith to open the doors for that time, but did not think it expedient to persist under such circumstances.'[3]

The churchwardens believed themselves to be acting within their rights, on the ground that 'the church was not a vicarage', and that the incumbent was merely a curate-in-charge.[4] Simeon privately obtained a legal opinion, which assured him that they were mistaken.[5] What was more important was that for the first time public sentiment in the parish began to veer over to his side. 'Their behaviour', he wrote to John Venn (Sept. 22, 1783), 'has been highly displeasing to the whole parish, except two or three enemies of the gospel. Nor has it been less illegal than uncivil....May God bless them with enlightening, sanctifying, and saving grace. I shall renew the lecture next summer.'[6] (On more mature consideration, however, he waited until he could secure the consent of the churchwardens before restoring it, which he finally did on July 18, 1790.[7]) But the immediate problem was to know what to do with the flock whom he had gathered to his Sunday evening lecture.

What was to be done? If those whose minds were impressed by my preaching had not some opportunity of further instruction, they would infallibly go to the dissenting meetings, and thus be gradually drawn away from the church. The only alternative I had was, to make them meet in a private room; I therefore hired a small room in my parish, and met them there, and expounded to them the Scripture, and prayed with them. In time the room was too small

---

[1] *Ibid.* p. 44 *n.*
[2] *Ibid.* p. 88.—Cf. J. H. Overton, *The English Church in the nineteenth century (1800–1833)*, pp. 141–2.
[3] Carus, p. 45.
[4] Moule, p. 46.
[5] Carus, pp. 85–6; Moule, p. 46.
[6] Carus, p. 59.
[7] *Ibid.* pp. 73, 85.

to hold us all, and I could not get one larger in my parish; I therefore got one in an adjoining parish, which had the advantage of being very spacious and very retired. Here I met my people for a considerable time.[1] I was sensible that it would be regarded by many as irregular; but what was to be done? I could not instruct them in my church; and I must of necessity have them all drawn away by the dissenters, if I did not meet them myself; I therefore committed the matter to God in earnest prayer, and entreated of Him, that if it was His will that I should continue the room, He would graciously screen me from persecution on account of it; or that if persecution should arise on account of it, He would not impute it to me as sin, if I gave up the room. He knew the real desire of my heart; He knew that I only wished to fulfil His will: I told Him a thousand times over that I did not deprecate persecution; for I considered *that* as the necessary lot of all who would 'live godly in Christ Jesus'; and more especially, of all who would preach Christ with fidelity; but I deprecated it as arising from that room.[2]

Simeon was, in fact, placing himself in an extremely vulnerable position, not only by holding an illicit conventicle, but by holding it outside his own parish; and his friends were, as he had anticipated, extremely anxious on his behalf. They finally prevailed on Henry Venn to speak to him on the subject: but, after Simeon had explained the circumstances, Venn said only, 'Go on, and God be with you',[3] and himself expounded in the room one Sunday evening in March 1786.[4] What is less generally known is that Simeon also took counsel of John Wesley on the problem, riding over to Hinxworth, Herts., to see him, on Dec. 20, 1784. It was the first of their two meetings.[5] Wesley began by talking of things in general. Simeon said: 'I am a young man come to see an old disciple. I wish you to tell me something that will do me good.' He then laid his perplexity before him. Wesley replied: 'I knew a young man who set out on a journey, and by and by he came to a difficulty. He looked at it, and went by it. Another young man set out, and when he came at it he stepped

---

[1] Apparently both on Sunday and on Thursday evenings: cf. Carus, p. 89, and *Wesleyan Methodist Magazine*, May 1914, vol. cxxxvii, p. 323.

[2] Carus, pp. 45–6.   [3] *Ibid.* p. 46.

[4] 'On Sunday last, Mr Simeon and I exchanged. There were more than twenty of the gown to hear. In the evening I spoke to eighty in a house.'— H. Venn to Rowland Hill, March 23, 1786: Sidney, *Rowland Hill*, p. 160.

[5] The second was on Oct. 30, 1787: cf. Wesley's *Journal*, vol. vii, p. 337.

over it. And a third oot out, and when he came at it he took it up and carried it on his shoulder and presently it vanished. Now I would advise you to do as the last; take up the cross and persevere.'[1] It was the advice for which Simeon had been hoping. Thirty years later, he recorded in his autobiographical Memoir: 'The persecutions in my parish continued and increased; but during the space of many years no persecution whatever arose from that room, though confessedly it was the side on which my enemies might have attacked me with most effect.'[2]

The room was still, apparently, retained for weekly prayer meetings even after 1790, when the churchwardens consented to Simeon's holding his Sunday evening lecture in the church.[3] Six years later, when he had a curate,[4] he judged it expedient to divide the people who came to these meetings—about 120 in number—into six religious societies, each of which he met regularly once a month.[5] In addition to these, there was also a weekly prayer meeting which, like others of its kind elsewhere, had been introduced on account of the War: this was now continued, 'being carried on by the people without me: for, on account of my numerous societies and engagements, I could not be present at them. This was an evil; but it was one which I could not remedy'.[6] Unfortunately, Simeon not long after became laid aside by a long illness,' the result of incessant overwork,[7] during which period the religious societies, left to themselves, got out of hand: 'several of the people became conceited and headstrong',[8] and 'an unhallowed kind of emulation'[9] arose among them. 'I saw that some of the chief stewards had lost a measure of their simplicity and tractableness; and the general rage which had recently arisen through the nation for itinerant preaching, had visibly infected some amongst them. This I

---

[1] MS. recollections of Miss Paramore (daughter of Wesley's printer), quoted in *Wesleyan Methodist Magazine*, May 1914, vol. cxxxvii, p. 323.
[2] Carus, p. 46.   [3] *Ibid.* pp. 73, 85.
[4] Simeon was elected to the lectureship at Holy Trinity in 1794, and procured the Rev. Thomas Thomason as his first curate in Oct. 1796. (Carus, p. 137; Sargent, *Life of the Rev. T. T. Thomason*, p. 75.) [5] Carus, pp. 139–40.
[6] *Ibid.* p. 141.   [7] Brown, p. 190.
[8] Carus, p. 141.   [9] *Ibid.* p. 340.

endeavoured to stop; being well convinced, that, whether it was evil in itself or not, it was not possible for me as a minister of the Established Church to countenance such proceedings amongst my people, since I should assuredly be represented by my enemies as a patron and encourager of those irregularities.[1] To a certain extent I prevailed; for I summoned the stewards to make known to them my views of the subject, and actually expelled from my societies one, who had taken out a license as a preacher.'[2] Persons had also been admitted to the weekly prayer meeting who were not members of the religious societies, thereby making the place 'really and truly a conventicle, in the eye of the law'.[3] The trouble came to a head in 1811, when Simeon found himself obliged to quell what was in fact a mutiny. It was for him a very bitter experience: 'my former trials', he wrote, 'have been nothing to this.'[4] Moreover, the undisguised hostility of the new Bishop of Ely, Dr Dampier, added to the difficulty of his situation.[5] Yet, in his final review of the whole matter, he gave it as his considered judgment that without such religious societies, 'where they can be had, a people will never be kept together; nor will they ever feel related to their Minister, as children to a parent: nor will the Minister himself take that lively interest in their welfare, which it is both his duty and his happiness to feel'.[6] He was perfectly conscious of the risks

---

[1] 'If they felt it so important to meet together as they had done, they were at liberty to do so; nor had I the least wish to abridge them of that liberty; the only thing to which I objected was, the connecting of this conduct with me. Whilst they continued to unite themselves with me as my people, I should of necessity be considered as answerable for their conduct: the world would not enquire whether I approved of their conduct or not; they would simply say, these people are connected in societies with Mr S., and they do so and so. The conclusion, that I approved of these things, would follow of course. *But was it right, that I should lay myself open to such imputations, when the cause of Religion in Cambridge depended so essentially on my conducting myself with wisdom and prudence?* [Italics mine.] Assuredly not: and therefore I told the chief of the people, that if they determined to follow their own ways, I wished them to separate entirely from me and from my ministry, that I might not be involved in their irregularities. If they chose to let off fire-works, they were at liberty to do so; only I desired they would not put them under my thatch, to burn down my house.'—Carus, pp. 335-6.

[2] *Ibid.* pp. 141-2.   [3] *Ibid.* pp. 332-3.
[4] Simeon to the Rev. T. Thomason, Jan. 22, 1812: *ibid.* p. 349.
[5] Cf. *Life of Isaac Milner*, p. 469: Carus, pp. 330-1 and *n.*—Milner protected Simeon on this occasion.   [6] Carus, p. 339.

involved, but hold that the risks involved in not having such societies was even greater: and if the Minister guard with all his might against any appearance of spiritual pride and arrogance among their leaders ('as if their taste were perfect and their judgment infallible'), 'and if he make it a rule to conduct the service in the private societies himself, he will, for the most part, keep down these evils. It was not till I was laid aside by my long indisposition, that these evils showed themselves in any considerable degree: and after all, if we will not establish such societies for fear of such consequences, we must remember that there is a Charybdis, as well as a Scylla, and that in all human institutions we have only, as it were, a choice of evils; there being nothing perfect under the sun.'[1]

The interesting point is that these religious meetings and societies were instituted by Simeon from the very first with the avowed intention of keeping his flock from 'being drawn away by the Dissenters'. 'Were the Bishops acquainted with the ministers who are called Evangelical, they would soon see the importance, yea, and the absolute necessity, of such meetings, not merely for the edification of the people, *but chiefly for the preservation of the Established Church*....Where nothing of that kind is established, the members of any church are only as a rope of sand, and may easily be scattered with every wind of doctrine, or drawn aside by any proselytising sectary. What influence can a minister maintain over his people, if he does not foster them as a brood under his wings?...Experience proves that wherever there is an efficient ministry in the Church without somewhat of a similar superintendence, the clergyman beats the bush, and the Dissenters catch the game: whereas, when such a superintendence is maintained, the people are united as an army with banners.'[2]

It is quite in character that Simeon seems to have been a pioneer in the intelligent utilisation of the laity in the pastoral, as distinct from the administrative, working of a parish. 'A Minister', he declared, 'is not the *father* of his flock; his wife is the *mother*, but he is the *Pastor*, a far higher and more important

[1] *Ibid.* pp. 340–1.   [2] *Ibid.* pp. 138–9.

office. He has more to do in the closet and study than even in the cottage. Let him nominate Elders, laymen, and laywomen, to visit the sick, to pray with them, and read to his people. I do not wholly approve of prayer meetings, nor would have these Elders help in that way, but in visiting his people. Let him meet his Elders, as a body, statedly, and hear from them the state of his parish in its minutest points. But let a Minister be careful to bear in mind that, if this engine of good be not quite under his own control, it will become sectarian, and prove so far injurious to his people.'[1] But that is a side-issue. Attention should be directed rather to Simeon's attitude in its bearing upon the problem which, as has been noted, was bound up with the problem of Church Order: namely, the problem of co-operation with Dissenters. Again, it was probably Simeon, more than any other single individual, who determined where the line was to be drawn. To him the issue was perfectly clear cut, because he did not talk loosely and vaguely about 'fellowship', neither did he confuse a tolerance of diversity of opinion with a license for ecclesiastical irregularity. 'He did not merely deem the Church preferable to Nonconformity, but honestly believed the Church right, and the principles of Dissent wrong; while yet his catholic spirit could embrace all who sincerely loved and served Jesus Christ.'[2] He regarded Dissent as an evil, and schism as a great evil:[3] he saw the weaknesses of Protestant Nonconformity, its lack of a Liturgy, its bias to disunion,[4] its 'censorious, judicial spirit'[5] evinced in the tyranny of the people over their pastors. 'Churchmen have not the spirit, have not the habit, of sitting in judgment on their Ministers; Dissenters have....It is the characteristic of Dissenting bodies....Of course, many things in the Church are faulty in some points; no human system or scheme is without its faults. But judge even our hierarchy by common earthly principles: how much better to be under one master than to have scores on the right hand

[1] Brown, pp. 217-8.
[2] *Ibid.* p. 12.
[3] *Ibid.* p. 224.
[4] 'There is in Dissent a spirit of disunion.'—*Ibid.* p. 222.
[5] *Ibid.* p. 221.

and on the left, as Dissenting Ministers have!¹ Newton well said that there were no "Independent Ministers" except in the Church, for that Dissenting teachers were "only Ministers of independent congregations". Perhaps it may be that the parishioners have too little power over the established Clergy, while Dissenters have too much over their Pastors....Many are broken-hearted by the browbeating of their people.'² 'Among the poor, we find Dissenters exhibit a more captious spirit than Churchmen: it is so even among the pious. It seems the error of their customs and views as Dissenters....It is said by those who have had means of knowing, that a good Minister among Dissenters will often receive letters on Monday, criticising and censuring his sermon of the day before, and that he not seldom goes into his pulpit nervous and fearful on account of such letters.'³ 'No Dissenter dares to preach as I do, one day Calvinist, another day Arminian, just as the text happens to be, for fear his people would take offence.'⁴

On the positive side, his devotion to the Prayer Book was unfeigned. 'He was wont to say, "The Bible first, the Prayer Book next, and all other books and doings in subordination to both". His own practice, his advice to all young Clergymen, was to deal with the Prayer Book as a reality; and he would often say, "Pray the prayers, and don't read them only; adhere sacredly to the directions of the Rubric, except where they have become obsolete, and the resumption of them would clearly do harm".'⁵ 'The finest sight short of heaven', he once declared, 'would be a whole congregation using the prayers of the Liturgy in the true spirit of them':⁶ and on his return from Scotland he always 'felt the prayers of our Church as marrow to my soul....Let any man go to all those churches where our Liturgy is not used, and also to every Dissenting chapel in town

¹ Cf. Rowland Hill, *Journal through the North of England and parts of Scotland* (1799), p. 108 *n.*: 'However I might be disposed to vote for the reduction of the Episcopacy of the English Church, yet I had much rather be under the Right Reverend Fathers in God with us, than under the jurisdiction of the Most Reverend Mothers in God, among the stricter Independents.—*Medio tutissimus Ibis*': cf. also p. 80 *n.*

² Brown, p. 221. ³ *Ibid.* p. 150.
⁴ *Ibid.* p. 221. ⁵ *Ibid.* p. 12.
⁶ *Ibid.* p. 221.

and country, and note down every prayer which is offered in
them, and then compare them with our own, and he will see the
value and excellence of ours'.[1] Indeed, he traced the characteristic
weaknesses inherent in Protestant Dissent to a liturgical source:
'The difference between the Church spirit and the sectarian spirit
is very much owing to the prayers of the Church being fixed and
commanding, and full of the things requisite for every sinner.'[2]

At the same time, he recognised that 'the Dissenters are
valuable in certain respects: one is, that without their places of
worship there would, in many populous places, be no opportunity for people to worship God at all; the church accommodation is so scanty':[3] and he admitted, not only that Dissent,
although an evil, and the result of sin in the heart, had 'mainly
arisen from a want of real religion, which was felt among the
community in consequence of the decayed state of so many of
our Clergy',[4] but even that where the Gospel truth is not declared in the pulpit, and where the Minister is one who wholly
neglects his flock, 'I dare not blame a man for going where he
thinks or feels that his soul can be fed. True, he ought to throw
his influence into the scale of the Church; but if he feel his soul
perishing, how can I say that he is wrong to go where there is a
doctor?...I would rather have a less degree of good, though
mixed with a little evil, than no good at all, where immortal souls
are at stake.'[5] 'But be cautious of separation.'[6]

He taught his young men that 'when Dissenters and Romanists
abound in a Parish, the Clergyman ought to visit them all, visit
even their Ministers, and never feel that they are Dissenters,
but try to win them back, treating them with gentleness and
delicacy, and making himself felt as their friend. They are all
his flock. I did so with success when I had [charge of] the parish
of St Edward's, in Cambridge [in the Long Vacation of 1782].'[7]

[1] Brown, p. 228. (Cf. Carus, p. 520.)   [2] *Ibid.* p. 221.
[3] *Ibid.* p. 222. (Cf. Bishop Blomfield's Charge to the Clergy of the Diocese
of London, 1843, p. 15.)   [4] *Ibid.* p. 223.
[5] *Ibid.* p. 224.   [6] *Ibid.* p. 220.
[7] *Ibid.* p. 221.— 'I visited all the parish from house to house, without
making any difference between Churchmen and Dissenters: and I remember
disputing with the Dissenting Minister (in a friendly way) about the doctrine
of Election' (Carus, p. 24: cf. p. 27).

There was a tradition that, in his younger days, he had sometimes attended Dissenting services.[1] It is true that he was not too proud to learn from the Dissenters: but the sole foundation for this particular tradition would appear to be that, when he was thinking of introducing prayer-meetings for his own congregation at Holy Trinity, he went one week-day evening into the old Meeting-house in Downing Street, and stood at the back, in the darkness, to observe how such matters were conducted there. He found about ten persons present: the only illumination was from two or three candles in the table-pew: and the whole proceeding was so utterly depressing that, when all was finished, he could not restrain himself from calling out lustily, to the astonishment of the members, who had not known that he was there, 'Let us sing, "Praise God from whom all blessings flow"!'[2] On the other hand, he befriended a well-known local character named Johnny Stittle, 'a kind of well-meaning, self-constituted City Missionary in the viler parts of Cambridge, and called by the undergraduates a Ranter'.[3] Johnny Stittle had been a hedger and thresher at Madingley when he was converted by John Berridge: he afterwards became minister of the old Green Street (Independent) Meeting-house from 1781 until his death in 1813. Simeon gave him a regular quarterly allowance, which, as he jocularly said, was 'for shepherding my stray sheep'.[4] 'In his earnest, self-denying endeavour to promote the good of souls anywhere and everywhere,' comments that staunch Churchman, Canon Abner Brown, 'he sometimes shut his eyes to irregularities,

---

[1] 'He was not so restricted, at that time, to his own pale, as to avoid religious intercourse with Christians of other communions. It is in the recollection of persons now living, that he sometimes attended the social exercises for prayer connected with our place of worship, and has been known to give out the verse of a hymn at the conclusion of the service. Some of the elder members who yet survive among us, also frequently attended similar meetings which he conducted among his own followers.'—Samuel Thodey, *The Honour attached to Eminent Piety and Usefulness: A Sermon, preached at Downing Street Meeting-House, Cambridge, November 20th, 1836, on occasion of the death of the Rev. Charles Simeon, M.A., Senior Fellow of King's College* (1836), p. 36.

[2] Williamson, p. 55.

[3] Brown, pp. 13–15. Cf. *Congreg. Mag.*, March 1819, vol. ii, p. 185. Sidney, *Rowland Hill*, p. 47.

[4] Arthur B. Gray, *Cambridge Revisited* (1921), pp. 97–9.—Byron, writing in 1811, couples Mr Simeon ('the very bully of beliefs') with John Stickles (*sic*) in a contemptuous footnote to his *Hints from Horace*.

SIMEON AND CHURCH ORDER

and looked to the desire and aim of such as were, in his opinion, working for the direct spiritual good of others, without sufficiently weighing *all* the results, remote as well as immediate, of what was going on; and thus occasionally he took a questionable step. Not a few anecdotes were current in Cambridge, which, if correct, show that his feelings sometimes went beyond his judgment in such matters.'[1]

Yet, generally speaking, his relations with the Nonconformists were as correct as they were Christian. He did not scruple to co-operate with them as far as possible: but he knew where to draw the line. On the one hand, he and Professor Farish, the Vicar of St Giles', resolutely supported the formation of an Auxiliary branch of the Bible Society in Cambridge in 1811, leaving the thunders of Professor Marsh and the indignant hosts of orthodoxy,[2] and at a later date he became a life-subscriber to a Tract Auxiliary formed on the same inter-denominational plan.[3] On the other hand, he saw that the principle of interdenominationalism could not be applied in the Mission Field: 'We cannot join the [London] Missionary Society; yet I bless God they have stood forth. We must now stand forth...Directly: not a moment to be lost':[4] and he lent his aid to the foundation, in 1799, of a Missionary Society 'in direct connexion with and under the sanction of the Church of England'—the Society for Missions to Africa and the East, which ripened into the C.M.S.[5]

[1] Brown, p. 13. Cf. *Memoirs of the Rev. Charles Jerram*, p. 126: 'It has been sometimes doubted whether Mr Simeon's prudence at all times kept pace with his zeal.'
[2] There is an extensive (but not exhaustive) survey of the literature of the controversy in J. E. B. Mayor's notes on Baker's *History of the College of St John the Evangelist, Cambridge*, vol. ii, pp. 809–64. Farish, rather than Simeon, was the real hero of the episode: cf. Brown, p. 336; S. Thodey, p. 41. (The senior members of the University, incited by the Lady Margaret Professor of Divinity, were hostile, on the grounds that the Bible Society was undenominational, and that it was undesirable for under-graduates to take the initiative in anything, especially in war-time. Farish said, 'It shall go on even if I stand on the platform alone.' 'Upon this, Mr Simeon, with his accustomed ardour, added, "You shall not stand alone, my brother, I will go with you."'—Cf. also Carus, pp. 308–20.)
[3] Thodey, pp. 41–2.   [4] Carus, p. 169.
[5] Cf. Charles Hole, *Early History of the C.M.S.* (1896), and art., *The Early Days of the C.M.S. at Cambridge*, in *The Church Missionary Intelligencer*, Sept. 1887, pp. 521–36.

With the local Nonconformist ministers he was always upon friendly terms, while at the same time remaining on his guard against any efforts to make proselytes from among his flock. 'In the thirty years that I have ministered at Trinity Church', he wrote in 1813, 'the Dissenters have not (as far as I recollect) drawn away three whom I was not glad to get rid of. It has only been the refuse, who have first lost all simplicity of mind, if not wholly departed from God, that they have been able to steal from me.'[1] This pastoral jealousy did, however, upon one occasion involve him in a brush with Robert Hall, the Baptist minister, who had a considerable following in the town. The relevant document is an open letter to Simeon from Hall, which was published in the *Cambridge Intelligencer* of Aug. 8, 1795, and subsequently reprinted as an appendix to Benjamin Flower's *National Sins considered* (1796).[2] It appears that, on the previous Sunday, Simeon had preached on behalf of the French *émigré* clergy, taking as his text Matt. vii. 15, 20—'Beware of false prophets, which come to you in sheep's clothing, but inwardly they are ravening wolves....Wherefore by their fruits ye shall know them.' In the course of the sermon it had transpired that these false prophets were the Protestant Dissenters, who employed all the arts of religious seduction in order to draw men off from the Church, especially the Baptists, who would never be satisfied until they got Mr Simeon's flock under the water. But they might be known by their fruits: for the doctrine which they preached 'had a manifest tendency to make people *factious, or disturbers of the public peace*'. From this it was an easy transition of thought to the horrors of the French Revolution, and the sufferings of the Church in France. Simeon spoke of the *émigré* clergy as his Christian brethren, comparing the difference of sentiment between himself and them 'to that which subsisted between the gentile churches and the jewish church at Jeru-

---

[1] Carus, p. 139.

[2] *A Letter, from the Rev. Robert Hall, M.A., to the Rev. Charles Simeon, A.M., Vicar and Lecturer of Trinity Church, and Fellow of King's College, Cambridge* (first printed in the *Cambridge Intelligencer*, August 8, 1795), in *National Sins considered, in Two Letters to the Rev. Thomas Robinson, Vicar of St Mary's, Leicester, on his Serious Exhortation to the Inhabitants of Great Britain with reference to the Fast,* by Benjamin Flower (1796), pp. 73–85.

salem'.[1] Alluding to recent events—the victories of the Austrian armies, and the desertion of Dumouriez—he assured them that the Lord was fighting for them, and dwelt with rapture upon the prospect of their speedy restoration. 'So transported was the preacher', adds Benjamin Flower, 'that he after sermon gave out a triumphal hymn, with the chorus at the close of each stanza—

> "The year of Jubilee is come,
> Return ye ransom'd sinners home!"'[2]

Hall, in reply, challenged Simeon to show any evidence of such proselytising efforts as he complained of: and then, at greater length, dealt with the major count in the indictment.

For myself, all who have ever heard me are witnesses that I never introduced a political topic into the pulpit on any occasion; nor have I any doubt that other dissenting ministers in this town can make the same declaration, with equal sincerity. But had our conduct been ever so remote from this moderation and reserve, modesty should unquestionably have restrained *you* from becoming our accuser; when it is well known that you are the chief, perhaps the only political preacher in the place; and that you often entertain your hearers with more politicks in one sermon, than most dissenting ministers have done during their whole lives. The doctrines of passive obedience and non-resistance, which in better times SACHEVERELL was disgraced for preaching, are familiar in your mouth....[3]

It may be doubted whether it would ever have occurred to Simeon that such doctrines could be called 'political'. It is, however, clear that his hostility to the Dissenters at this epoch (apart from his pastoral uneasiness at the extent to which Hall's splendid eloquence was drawing vast congregations, including many of his own parishioners, to the Baptist Meeting-house in St Andrew's Street) was rather political than religious. The Dissenters tended to Radicalism in politics, whereas the Evangelicals were commonly High Tories: and, in the French Revolutionary era, that division cut both sharp and deep. 'Of

---

[1] Flower, pp. 80–1.
[2] *Ibid.* p. 85 *n.*: Hymn xxviii (*The Jubilee*) in the hymn-book used at Trinity Church (*A Collection of Psalms and Hymns from Various Authors, chiefly designed for the use of public worship:* 8th ed. Cambridge, 1813, p. 88).
[3] *Loc. cit.* p. 80.

SIMEON AND CHURCH ORDER

their loyalty', wrote the author of *Zeal without Innovation* (1808),
in the course of his impartial enquiry into the character and
views of the class of clergymen, called evangelical ministers, 'I
can say, with great truth, that in this point they have not only
remained uncorrupted, but have often availed themselves of
their situation as ministers, to stem the tide of sedition. It
deserves notice, that in the most threatening periods of *Revolutionary* mania, these men spoke out very decidedly from the
pulpit, in defence of our enviable constitution. In some places,
their zeal was such, as to make many conclude, that, in the event
of an insurrection, they would be among the first that would
be sacrificed.'[1] Coulthurst, now Vicar of Halifax, preached
before the University on Oct. 25, 1796 (the anniversary of the
King's Accession) a fiercely loyal sermon which excited a good
deal of comment on its delivery, and more upon its publication.[2]
Dean Milner endeavoured to dissuade Wilberforce from going
into opposition to the Government,[3] and rejoiced over the expulsion of William Frend, for which, as Vice-Chancellor, he had
had a considerable measure of responsibility: 'It was the ruin
of the Jacobinical party as *a University thing*, so that that party
is almost entirely confined to Trinity College.'[4] Yet even Milner
was astonished at the lengths to which Miles Atkinson of St
Paul's, Leeds, was prepared to go. 'He is a worthy creature',
he wrote (June 4, 1800); 'and yet it was a strange thing to bid
his audience "Read the *Anti-Jacobin Review*", and that I heard
him say from the pulpit, last summer, myself.'[5] Henry Venn
would sometimes eagerly declare that Mr Pitt was inspired.[6]

[1] [J. Bean,] *op. cit.* pp. 165–6 *n.*
[2] *The Evils of Disobedience and Luxury. A Sermon preached before the
University of Cambridge, on Tuesday, October 25, 1796; being the Anniversary
of His Majesty's Accession.* By H. W. Coulthurst, D.D., Vicar of Halifax, and
late Fellow of Sydney Sussex College, Cambridge. *Published by request.*
1796.—Cf. *A Sermon, preached before the University of Cambridge,* by H. W.
C——t, D.D. &c. *Published by request: and now (for the sake of freshmen and
the laity,) by request translated into English Metre,* by H. W. Hopkins, A.M.
[i.e., the Rev. Alexander Geddes, LL.D.]. *Discite, terrigenæ, sacros non
spernere reges.* 1796.   [3] *Life of Isaac Milner,* pp. 106–8.
[4] *Ibid.* p. 162: but cf. Gunning, vol. i, p. 283.
[5] *Life of Isaac Milner,* p. 215.
[6] *Some Account of the Reverend Thomas Robinson, M.A., late Vicar of
St Mary's, Leicester; and sometime Fellow of Trinity College, Cambridge....*
By the Rev. Edw. Tho. Vaughan (1816), p. 148.

Robinson of Leicester did not go quite so far as that; 'but he thought him little less than an heaven-born minister, whom God had in rich mercy bestowed upon us, to meet and avert the crisis of our fate':[1] although he made no secret of his opinion, after Mr Pitt had fought a duel, on a Sunday, with Mr Tierney, that his political idol 'appeared to have declined from his former vigour and success ever after, as though he laboured under evident marks of divine displeasure for that heinous sin'.[2] Simeon seems to have been less interested in politics as such. 'I do not think Clergymen have much to do with politics', he declared in 1827. 'They had better attend more to the politics of eternity, and the care of souls. I used once to avoid all politics, for I had enough to do without them. But now I rather attend a little to them, because I have so many friends, that my opinion is often asked, and it becomes a duty to have my mind clear on subjects such as the present [*i.e.* Catholic Emancipation], that I may give my reasons. Yet I would entreat all men to avoid the acrimony that is generally mixed up with politics; and I think good men should rather support Government in this momentous crisis.'[3] Equally he disapproved of clergymen being magistrates, 'unless in very peculiar cases'; 'they must necessarily displease one party, and are likely to be ensnared into secular habits by their brother justices, or else to be hated and doubly opposed by them'.[4] Yet although he was inclined, on principle, to hold himself aloof from secular concerns, he had assisted in setting on foot the *Anti-Jacobin*:[5] and he reposed every confidence in Sir Robert Peel—'He is a man whom they may trust, and he certainly ought not to be a day out of Parliament at this conjuncture.'[6]

Simeon was, in fact, a natural Tory, and this no doubt assisted

[1] His biographer cannot refrain from adding: 'I do not think Mr Robinson always did full justice to the motives and talents of Mr Pitt's political adversaries' (*Ibid.* p. 149).
[2] *Ibid.* p. 149.
[3] Brown, p. 291.—For Simeon's views on Catholic Emancipation, cf. Carus, pp. 576, 630–3. Cf. also art., *The Protestant Revival and the Catholic Question in England, 1778–1829*, by J. H. Hexter, in *The Journal of Modern History* (Univ. of Chicago Press), Sept. 1936, vol. viii, pp. 297–319.
[4] Brown, p. 129.   [5] *Ibid.* p. 328.
[6] *Ibid.* p. 295.

to align him with the party of regularity and order in the Church.
In the generation after his death, the Evangelical Party moved
rather away from him on many points in its passionate, almost
hysterical reaction against the Oxford Movement. 'Evangelicalism had suffered a certain emaciation, it had no longer the lead,
it was forced to take up a defensive attitude. It had been
needlessly exasperated by extravagant statements. It misunder-
stood not a little. Finally, it allied itself, for the defence of
Protestantism, with the Low Church, the heirs of latitudinarians
and minimizers. Like most unions which are the product of
fear it was not a happy union.'[1] In this verdict, the present
Bishop of Chelmsford remarkably concurs. 'Unhappily, the
soul of Evangelicalism suffered in the contest. They forgot that
their tradition was based upon the preaching of a positive
Evangel of Christ's dying Love for souls. Their preaching often
became a panic anti-Roman proclamation, witnessed to by a
form of service from which dignity and beauty were rigorously
excluded.'[2] Rome was the enemy: and amid the dust and heat,
the tumult and the shouting of the conflict with the 'Roman-
ising' party within the Church of England, much that Charles
Simeon had approved and valued became either suspect or taboo.
'The evangelical party', wrote Canon Abner Brown, 'has, like
other bodies, in many respects changed with the times, not in
doctrine, but in other points, and in the relative importance
attached to one or other doctrine. Simeon, too, its then leader,
would doubtless have changed, as probably every inhabitant of
the kingdom has; but it is a question whether or not his change
would have been identical with that of the party. Some at least
of his principles, not explicitly doctrinal, were dissimilar to those
now held by many of the evangelical party—as, for instance, his
approval of Fasting; his feeling that the Priestly benediction was
more than a prayer; his deprecation of any change whatever in
the Prayer Book.'[3] To these may be added his recognition of the
priestly power of Absolution,[4] and his unconcealed repugnance

---

[1] Yngve Brilioth, *Evangelicalism and the Oxford Movement* (1934), p. 30.
[2] *The Development of Evangelicalism*, by the Rev. H. A. Wilson, in *Liberal
Evangelicalism: An Interpretation*, ed. T. Guy Rogers (1923), p. 25.
[3] Brown, pp. 64–5.   [4] *Ibid.* pp. 89, 210.

to the tone and temper of *The Record*.[1] 'It is far from improbable', continues Canon Brown, 'that were Mr Simeon now alive, he would have become, without wish or effort on his part, the leader of a very large middle party, not based upon what are called broad Church principles, but on a simply scriptural avoiding alike of the extreme Church party and the extreme evangelical party, and upon a steady opposition to both Rationalist and Roman tendencies: for the "faith once delivered to the saints", and revealed in Scripture, cannot and does not change; all Christians "must earnestly contend for it", at all periods of the world's progress; and Mr Simeon would have held it fast, and been unchanging in his adherence to it'.[2]

It is further noteworthy that even what may appear to us to be the most regrettable of his irregularities—those, namely, of which he was guilty on his Scottish tours—are not only not without parallel in the conduct even of living dignitaries of the Church of England, but seemed to him to be justified precisely by the principle of Church Order.

Herein lay the essential difference between Charles Simeon and Rowland Hill. When Rowland Hill visited Scotland in 1798 and preached in Presbyterian pulpits, he conceived himself to be exercising a general commission to 'preach the Gospel to every creature'.[3] When Simeon visited Scotland in 1796 and again in 1798, he also preached in Presbyterian pulpits and, on the former tour at least, actually received the Sacrament three times at the hands of Presbyterian ministers:[4] an Anglican may remark that he was fortunate to find so many opportunities.[5] But he justified his conduct on entirely different grounds from Rowland Hill.

Except when I preached in episcopal chapels,[6] I officiated precisely

---

[1] Brown, p. 129.   [2] *Ibid.* p. 65.

[3] *Journal through the North of England and parts of Scotland. With Remarks on the Present State of the Established Church of Scotland, and the different Secessions therefrom.... Also Some Remarks on the Propriety of what is called Lay and Itinerant Preaching.* By Rowland Hill, A.M....(1799), p. 67.

[4] Carus, pp. 120, 122, 125.

[5] 'In country parishes the Communion is generally dispensed twice a year, in town churches four times.'—Art., *The Church of Scotland*, by the Rev. Prebendary Clayton, in *The Churchman*, Oct. 1937, vol. ii, n.s., p. 188.

[6] Rowland Hill, who comments adversely on the Episcopal Church of Scotland ('Their congregations are no where very numerous, but this is made

ao they do in the Kirk of Scotland : and I did so upon this principle; Presbyterianism is as much the established religion in North Britain, as Episcopacy is in the South: there being no difference between them, except in church-government. As an episcopalian, therefore, I preached in episcopal chapels; and as a member of the Established Church, I preached in the presbyterian churches; and I felt myself the more warranted to do this, because, if the king, who is the head of the establishment in both countries, were in Scotland, he would of necessity attend at a presbyterian church there, as he does at an episcopalian church here: and I look upon it as an incontrovertible position, that where the king *must* attend a clergyman *may* preach. I was informed indeed that Archbishop Usher had preached in the Kirk of Scotland;[1] and I know that some very high churchmen had done so; but without laying any stress on precedents, I repeat, that where the king and his court must attend a clergyman may preach. And I believe many will bless God to all eternity that ever I did preach there. But I cannot help recording here, to the honour of the Church of England, that, on all the three times that I have visited Scotland, and have attended almost entirely the presbyterian churches, I have on my return to the use of our Liturgy been perfectly astonished at the vast superiority of our mode of worship, and felt it an inestimable privilege that we possess a form of sound words, so adapted in every respect to the wants and desires of all who would worship God in spirit and in truth.[2]

Indeed, Simeon's powers of endurance were sorely taxed by the long and tedious services of the Church of Scotland. Again

up to them in being mostly *very polite*. They have, however, with them I fear a true sample of what in general prevails with us. The general pre-requisite is, that the Minister should be *a good reader*, that he should not *squall* out the English liturgy similarly to the *twang* of a Scots Precentor, with their doggrel version of the Psalms of David, and so far so good. Next, that he should be a polite and easy gentleman; or, to sum it up in the language of that popular book, the New Whole Duty of Man, that he should produce nothing either in his conduct, or from the pulpit, but what *is made easy to the practice of the present age*'), deplores the *moderation* of Episcopalian preachers, and continues: 'As a proof of this, that good and truly spiritual and respectable man, Mr Simeon, of Cambridge, being asked to preach but once in their chapels, after one sample given was asked no more, though he strictly adhered to a most regular conduct, so far as preaching only in the Established Churches deserves that name' (*Journal*, pp. 103–4 *n*.).—This is an exaggeration: cf. Carus, p. 124 (July 3 and 6, 1796): Brown, p. 29: Preston, p. 45. But it is clear that Simeon was not quite at ease with the Episcopalians, nor they with him.

[1] Cf. Moule, p. 156.—Furthermore, 'The ministrations of the excellent and exemplary Cadogan [of Reading] had also been fully appreciated during his visits to Edinburgh' (Brown, p. 22).

[2] Carus, pp. 112–14. Preston, p. 41.—Cf. *Letters and Verses of Dean Stanley*, ed. R.E. Prothero (letter dated 'Dunkeld, Aug, 4, 1846'), pp. 105, 107.

and again he confided his private feelings to his *Journal*. 'The length of the service wearied me exceedingly.' 'The whole service continued about four hours and a quarter....I would not subject myself willingly to such another season of fatigue.' 'They who could stay there from beginning to end, with any profit to their souls, must be made of different materials from me.'[1]

Moreover, the expediency, if not the propriety, of his conduct was, as he confesses, 'doubted by some on this side of the Tweed'.[2] But he rejoiced to think that it was justified in the light of George IV's visit to Edinburgh in 1822. 'He spent two Sundays there: the first Sunday he went no where; the second Sunday he was constrained to attend at St Giles's Church, (the High Church). Aug. 25, 1822.'[3] However, it was by no means settled that this precedent was binding. When Dr Hook, the new Vicar of Leeds, preached before Queen Victoria at the Chapel Royal in June, 1838, the famous sermon, 'Hear the Church' (Matt. xviii. 17), which so upset the Whigs,[4] he notified Her Majesty very pointedly that

If the mere fact that a religious society is established by the civil government, be sufficient to claim for it our adhesion, see what the consequences must be; we should be obliged, on such principles, to become Presbyterians in Scotland and Holland, Papists in France and Italy; nay, in some parts of the world, worshippers of the Mosque,

---

[1] Carus, pp. 119, 120.   [2] *Ibid.* p. 123 *n.*
[3] *Ibid.* p. 113 *n.*
[4] Hook wrote to his wife: 'It is quite astonishing what a noise my poor sermon at the Chapel Royal has made....The Bishop of London, who was present, was very kind; he told me at the levée (from which I have just returned) that some persons about the Queen wished to make out it was political, and he had just been sent for to give his opinion. He asserted that there was not the slightest allusion to politics, unless it were political to speak of the Church of England as a true Church....' The sermon, which was in fact one that Hook had preached several times before, and had merely adapted to the occasion, excited great commotion in the political and fashionable world, and ran through twenty-eight editions, in which about one hundred thousand copies were sold. (It has been reprinted in *Famous Sermons*, ed. Douglas Macleane, 1911, pp. 223–38.) The Queen was understood to be much displeased, and Hook was obliged to write to the *Times* to deny that he had been forbidden to preach in the Chapel Royal again: actually, as the Bishop of Exeter reported upon unimpeachable authority, she had expressed herself as interested in the subject, and 'seemed to feel it to be *new as well as momentous*'. —W. R. W. Stephens, *Life and Letters of Dean Hook* (7th ed. 1885), pp. 251–4.

and votaries of Brahma! whereas the consistent Protestant could not, of course, conform to the established Church in France or Italy, until those Churches have undergone a thorough reformation; the consistent English Churchman cannot conform to the Presbyterian establishment in Scotland, but in that part of the island, attends the services of the Scottish Episcopal Church, which, though at one time established, was, at the Revolution in 1688, from political considerations, deprived of its endowments, which were then given to the community of Presbyterians, which has there become the extablished religion.[1]

But not all Anglicans are 'consistent English Churchmen': and, to this day, not only those who, like Charles Simeon, with certain reservations which are inapplicable to the Scottish Kirk, regard the fact of territorial Establishment as in itself decisive, but also those who, unlike Charles Simeon, value Low Churchmanship more highly than they value Churchmanship, and do not 'regard Episcopacy as necessary', and, thirdly, those in whose mental processes Erastian and Protestant prejudices are, as far as possible, driven in double harness, notoriously dissent, not less in principle than in practice, from the simple and straightforward attitude of Dr Hook. Thus, for example, the Reader at the Temple Church boasts of having since 1922 'officiated each year in various churches now belonging to the Church of Scotland, though some of them were until 1929 connected with the United Free Church.... If the loyalty of such a course is questioned, we reply that the rules of the Church of England do not forbid its members to worship, communicate, or (if ministers) preach in the Church of Scotland, and that until such action has been declared illegal by the Judicial Committee of the Privy Council we have a right to exercise that freedom.... The fact that the Scottish Episcopalian Church[2] forbids any such inter-communion is irrelevant to those who have never subjected ourselves to the discipline of that church. On the other hand, an English clergyman exercising what is undoubtedly his right incurs the wrath of the Scottish Episcopalian Church and of High churchmen within his own communion, and for the sake

[1] *Hear the Church. A Sermon preached at the Chapel Royal, in St James's Palace, on the First Sunday after Trinity, June xvii, MDCCCXXXVIII*, by Walter Farquhar Hook, D.D., Chaplain in Ordinary to Her Majesty (1838), p. 6.
[2] ['which corresponds to the High-church section of the Church of England.']

of peace he may hold that in his case that which is lawful is not expedient.'[1]

It is, however, worthy of remembrance that when Queen Victoria and the Prince Consort made a triumphal progress through Scotland in 1842, they spent two Sundays across the border, but on neither did they attend the services of the Established Church. On Sunday, Sept. 4, when they were staying with the Buccleuchs at Dalkeith Palace, the Rev. Edward Ramsay, of St John's Episcopal Chapel, Edinburgh, came over to read prayers, and preached (from a temporary pulpit in the dining-room) on Isaiah xl. 9—'Say unto the cities of Judah, Behold your God.' At the same time, possibly as a sop to local feeling, Sir Robert Peel and the Earls of Aberdeen and Liverpool attended divine worship at Dalkeith parish church. On Sunday, Sept. 11, the Royal Party were staying at Drummond Çastle as the guests of Lord and Lady Willoughby D'Eresby, and divine service was conducted in the drawing-room by Lord Willoughby's private chaplain, the Rev. John Douglas Giles, vicar of Swinstead, Lincs.[2] But later, at Balmoral, where they stayed for the first time in 1848, the Royal Family became more careless of ecclesiastical propriety. 'The Prince Consort liked the Scottish service, which he used to say reminded him of the simple Lutheran forms to which in his early youth he was accustomed in Germany,'[3] and the Queen was completely amenable to his influence. Others might be less sympathetic. Writing on April 20, 1850, Disraeli recounted to Lady Londonderry a story, 'which came to me from the highest quarter and in the utmost confidence', of how 'Albert, who has imbibed the ultra Lutheran (alias, infidel) doctrines, and holds that all Churches (reformed) are alike, &c., &c., &c. and that ecclesiastical formularies of all kinds ought to be discouraged', had signified to Mr Birch, the Prince of Wales' tutor, that '*he did not approve of the Prince of Wales being taught the Church catechism*, his R.H. not approving of creeds, and all that.

[1] Art., *The Church of Scotland*, by the Rev. Prebendary Clayton, in *The Churchman*, Oct. 1937, vol. ii, n.s., pp. 189, 192.
[2] *Queen Victoria in Scotland*, 1842, pp. 28, 70: Sir Thomas Dick Lauder, *Memorial of the Royal Progress in Scotland* (1843), pp. 177, 385: John Parker Lawson, *History of the Scottish Episcopal Church* (1843), pp. 422–5.
[3] Patricia Lindsay, *Recollections of a Royal Parish* (1902), p. 99.

Conceive the astonishm^t and horror of Birch, a very orthodox, if not very high, Churchman at this virtual abnegation of all priestly authority! He at once informed H.R.H. that he must resign his post. This c^d not on the instant be agreed to, as the Queen was devoted to Birch, and Albert, himself, had hitherto greatly approved of him. After this, there were scenes for a week—some very violent—it ended by Birch, who was unflinching, consenting to remain, the Prince of Wales being taught the Church catechism, and the utmost efforts being made to suppress the whole esclandre—which, if it were known, would, coupled with the conception and patronage of the National Exposition of 1851, complete, it is supposed, the Prince's popularity. He is already more than suspected by the Church, from making the Queen attend when in Scotland, the Kirk and not the episcopal Church, to which he sends a Lord of waiting, or a maid of honor, every Sunday, instead of the sacred presence.'[1] Even this concession may subsequently have been withdrawn, for when Gladstone stayed at Balmoral in 1863, he was obliged to hire a drag and drive over to Ballater for church: 'I believe this is about the first expedition ever made from Balmoral to an episcopal service', he noted in his diary (Oct. 4, 1863).[2] Mrs Lindsay remembered seeing the Queen and the Prince Consort with their equerries and ladies in waiting in the Balmoral pew in Crathie parish church in 1849, and being disappointed at the absence of the royal children: but 'while they were young they never attended the Presbyterian Church, and I think the rule was that they should not do so until after their confirmation'![3]

The Prince Consort died in 1861, but the Queen, as soon as she emerged from her seclusion,[4] remained a regular attendant

---

[1] *Letters of Benjamin Disraeli to Frances Anne, Marchioness of Londonderry, 1837–1861*, ed. Lady Londonderry (1938), pp. 84–6.
[2] Morley, *Life of Gladstone* (popular ed. 1908), vol. i, p. 549.
[3] Lindsay, *Recollections of a Royal Parish*, p. 34.
[4] When Gladstone visited Balmoral in 1863, 'we had something between family prayer and a service in the dining-room at ten; it lasted about forty minutes. Dr Caird gave a short discourse, good in material, though over florid in style for my taste.... The Prince and Princess of Hesse I think went to the parish church' (Sept. 27). On the following Sunday (Oct. 4) 'there was *no* chaplain here to-day, and so no dining-room service, which for many I fear means no service at all.' (Morley, vol. i, pp. 547, 549.)

at Crathie church. In 1866 she was highly incensed with the Archbishop of Canterbury (Longley) for having so far countenanced and encouraged the reviving Episcopal Church of Scotland as himself to lay the first stone of the Episcopal Cathedral at Inverness. Her valued friend, Dr Macleod, 'than whom there is no better, more liberal-minded, or more thoroughly Christian a man', and under whom she had often sat with so much gratitude and pleasure,[1] had come whimpering to Windsor Castle about the Archbishop's conduct (which had admittedly been indiscreet), and his 'permitting the Bishops to speak of "*the* Church"—implying, as they do, that the *Scotch* establishment is *no* Church, and her Sacraments not to be considered as such, which they openly do', and about the way in which the Episcopal Church was winning back the aristocracy, 'and therefrom establishing a religion for the rich, and another for the poor, and thus alienating the people from their superiors, and producing a want of sympathy between them': a state of affairs which he considered 'as *most serious*, and indeed *alarming* to the safety of the Church of Scotland'. The Queen was easily induced to share his apprehensions, and wrote at once to Dean Wellesley, explaining the position, and asking his advice as to whether she should write to the Archbishop, or summon him to come and see her, 'that she may speak to him as strongly as she can'. For it ought to be remembered that

the Queen takes a solemn engagement, on her accession, to maintain the Established Church of Scotland, and any attempt to subvert it is *contrary* to Law, and indeed subversive of the respect for *existing Institutions* which, above all, the Archbishops and Bishops *ought* to do *everything* to maintain; and she *will* maintain it.

But, quite apart from this, the Queen considers this [Episcopalian] movement as *most* mischievous. The Presbyterian Church is essentially *Protestant*, and, as such, *most* valuable.* The Reformation in this country[2] was *never* fully completed, and had we applied the pruning knife more severely, we should *never* have been exposed to the dangers to which the Church of England is *now* exposed, and for which the Queen thinks it will be *absolutely* necessary to take some measures.

[1] Cf. *More Leaves from the Journal of a Life in the Highlands, from 1862 to 1882* (1884), pp. 209-37 ('Dr Norman Macleod').
[2] [England.]

The Queen feels, more strongly than words can express, the duty which is imposed upon her and her family, to maintain the *true* and *real principles* and *spirit* of the *Protestant* religion; for her family was brought over and placed on the throne of these realms *solely* to maintain it; and the Queen will *not* stand the attempts made to destroy the simple and truly Protestant faith of the Church of Scotland, and to bring the Church of England as near the Church of Rome as they possibly can.[1]

It was evident that Her Majesty, in her indignation, had forgotten how she herself had countenanced, if not encouraged, the Episcopal Church of Scotland twenty-four years earlier: but that was before her 'dear angel', with his odd Lutheran prejudices, had established a complete ascendancy over her mind. In any case, the Archbishop was shown her letter to Dean Wellesley, and had an interview with Her Majesty, in which (as she wrote to her dear Dr Macleod) 'he expressed the greatest concern at having done anything which could cause annoyance to the Queen, or which could have had the effect of injuring the Established Church of Scotland', and professed himself '*quite* innocent and unconscious' of the effect produced by his rash act.

Finally the Queen urged him to take an opportunity of stating publicly that he *never had* intended to do anything hostile to the Established Church of Scotland, which he promised to do.

The Queen hears further that all the English Bishops disapproved what the Archbishop (who is a mild and amiable man) had done.

Is there any chance of Dr Macleod's coming south during the next two months, so that we could see him *here*?[2]

But there was more to follow. On Sunday, Nov. 13, 1871, the Queen was present for the first time at a Communion Service at Crathie. (The service had recently been shortened, and there were now two Sacrament Sundays in the year—spring and autumn—instead of the traditional one.[3]) 'It would indeed be impossible to say how deeply we were impressed by the grand simplicity of the service. It was all so truly earnest, and no description can do justice to the perfect devotion of the whole assemblage. It was

[1] *Letters of Queen Victoria* (Second Series: 1862–78), vol. i, pp. 376–8.
[2] *Ibid.* vol. i, p.381 (Queen Victoria to Dr Macleod, Osborne, Dec. 19, 1866).
[3] Lindsay, p. 105.

most touching, and I longed much to join in it.'[1] *Gefühl ist alles:* and two years later, in November 1873, the Queen indulged that longing, and 'sat down among her Highland tenants and servants to partake with them of the Lord's Supper....Many were found to cavil at the Queen's action in this matter,' writes Mrs Lindsay, 'but it ever seemed to me only one among many instances of her wide sympathy and breadth of view, which could look beyond minor differences of ritual and ecclesiastical government, to the essentials of the Christian faith common to the English and Scottish Churches alike.'[2] 'From that time until the end of her life', adds Dr Stirton, 'the Queen regularly partook of communion at Crathie Church every autumn.'[3] He omits to mention that this practice was firmly discontinued by King Edward VII.

Such is the genesis of the peculiar convention by which Their Majesties, when in Scotland, are virtually forbidden to worship with those with whom they are in communion, and are virtually obliged to worship with those with whom they are not in communion.[4]

The average Englishman of the present day takes all this for granted, so far as he thinks of it at all. He knows little of the religious customs, let alone the history, either of the Church of Scotland or of the Scottish Church, and would probably be embarrassed if asked to tell you which is which. In 1745, when an Episcopalian minister used the Scottish Liturgy in All Saints', Derby, much harm was done to the rebel cause by the resultant rumours that a French priest had said Mass in Latin:[5] and this peculiarly English inability to distinguish between the Scottish Liturgy and the Roman Mass was still observable in the House of Commons during the Prayer Book Debates of 1927 and 1928.

---

[1] *More Leaves from the Journal of a Life in the Highlands*, p. 155 ('Communion Sunday at Crathie, 1871').   [2] Lindsay, p. 106.
[3] John Stirton, *Crathie and Braemar: A History of the United Parish* (1925), p. 279.
[4] The position is peculiarly anomalous when the Queen is herself a member of the Episcopal Church of Scotland. [Her Majesty, however, attended a Confirmation at St Peter's Episcopal Church, Musselburgh, on Sunday, February 25, 1940.]
[5] The best discussion of this incident is in L. Eardley-Simpson, *Derby and the Forty-Five* (1933), pp. 175–80.

To the average Englishman of the present day, therefore, these violations of Church Order on the part of Simeon and Rowland Hill may seem a trivial matter. But the authorities of the Church of Scotland saw them in quite a different light. The Church of Scotland as we know it has lost much of its ancient arrogance: it seems even to exhibit a nervous sense of inferiority, being eager upon any opportunity to entice innocent and well-meaning Anglican dignitaries into its pulpits (and thereby to score off the Episcopalians), and even furtively copying the despised and disestablished Scottish Church in such important matters as the religious observance of Christmas and Good Friday, although this is a very recent innovation and by no means universal. But in 1798 the Kirk exhibited quite another temper: the activities of these itinerant English preachers were regarded by the authorities with a marked distaste: and, under pressure from the so-called Moderate party, the General Assembly passed a resolution 'to prevent any from officiating in their churches who are not in a capacity to receive a presentation in their church'.[1] (Thus, when the Rev. Legh Richmond visited Scotland in 1818 and was indeed received with the utmost kindness, he was none the less made to remember that he had no *locus standi* there.[2]) Rowland Hill thought this 'a very coarse compliment' to Simeon 'for his regularity'.[3] It is, however, clear that the General Assembly was perfectly within its rights in excluding the clergy of the Church of England from the pulpits of the Church of Scotland. But the point is that Simeon had preached in Presbyterian pulpits, not because he was indifferent to Church Order, but because he was peculiarly careful of it according to his lights.

It was not his intention to confront the Church of Scotland with

---

[1] Carus, pp. 158, 163–4. Cf. Rowland Hill, *Journal*, p. 104 *n.*; Brown, pp. 20–1; Moule, p. 153.—It is not clear when this prohibition was relaxed: but Dean Stanley, who had visited Scotland frequently since 1843, preached for the first time in a Presbyterian place of worship (Church of Scotland) in 1872, and repeatedly thereafter, although he never received a similar invitation from either the Free Church or the United Presbyterians (*Life and Letters of Dean Stanley*, by Prothero and Bradley, vol. ii, pp. 392–3: [A. K. H. Boyd], *Twenty-five Years of St Andrews* (1892), vol. i, pp. 59, 205, 258, 281).
[2] Cf. T. S. Grimshawe, *A Memoir of the Rev. Legh Richmond, A.M.* (5th ed. 1829), pp. 372 ff. [3] *Journal*, p. 104 *n.*

a problem, for it was his character rather to solve problems than to set them. That, at least, is the thesis which I have been arguing in this course of lectures. I have concentrated primarily upon two such problems: the problem of Continuity, and the problem of Church Order. There are others which I have mentioned incidentally, and others which I have not had time to mention at all. But these were, in my judgment, the two most crucial problems that confronted the Evangelical Revival: and in each case it seems to me that Simeon's solution was decisive. Not, indeed, exclusively, yet very largely, through his influence, the Evangelical Party established itself within the Church of England, and ceased to stray outside it. 'In this enumeration of faults', wrote a fair-minded critic in 1808, 'I do not acknowledge one which has been laid to their account, and with which many of this class were formerly chargeable; I mean a disregard of that canonical obedience, which every person, receiving holy orders in the Church of England, is considered as pledging himself to observe. This is unquestionably violated, by officiating in places licensed under the act of toleration. But this proceeding being now almost universally condemned by them, may be dismissed without any further notice.'[1]

It is not claimed that Simeon's solution of these problems was original or that it was peculiar to himself,[2] although the commanding influence which he exerted upon young men preparing for the sacred ministry and also upon other undergraduates who were not ordinands—an influence which owed much, indeed, to a combination of external circumstances, but infinitely more to his own qualities of character—lent to his decisions a weight that was probably unique. For these decisions were far-reaching both in their immediate influence and in their ultimate consequences. I would even claim that had these two problems been solved

[1] [James Bean,] *Zeal without Innovation*, p. 155.
[2] Cf., e.g. the Rules and Regulations of the Elland Clerical Society (1787): 'Rules to be observed by the Young Men who are Pensioners on this Charity. —...N.B.—All the young men receiving our pecuniary assistance shall, before the receipt thereof, sign a declaration, purporting that, from and after that time, they will frequent no other places of worship than those of the Church of England.' (*Rules, Regulations, and Forms of Prayer for the use of the Elland Society*, privately printed 1933, Appendix, p. 68.)

otherwise, or had they not been solved at all, the Evangelicals would sooner or later have left the Church of England even as the Methodists had done. And that would have been a great disaster both for the Evangelical Party and for the Church of England. It was Simeon who, more than any other single individual, taught the younger Evangelicals to love the Church of England and enabled them to feel that they belonged within her body.

That is not too high praise, although he himself would have been the first to deprecate it, for a 'chastened humility'[1] was the outstanding characteristic of his piety in his later years. 'I remember dining with him at the house of a mutual friend', said Samuel Thodey, a local Nonconformist minister, 'when the conversation turned upon the increase of Evangelical religion in the Church, and the number of young men who were preparing to enter it. One of the company happened to say in an under tone, "We owe a great deal of this to Mr Simeon". His quick ear caught the words, when he instantly turned to me and said, with great solemnity and tenderness, "No, my dear Sir, you do not owe this to Mr Simeon. It is one of the peculiar circumstances of the present day, that religion is prevailing so generally, that no one can tell whose work it is. Some years ago you could place your finger on the instrument, and say, 'This is Mr Romaine's doing; this Mr Foster's at St Antholin's; this Mr Cecil's at St John's: but now it is so general and diffusive, that you cannot fix upon the man—you must ascribe it wholly to God. Indeed you *do not* owe it to Mr Simeon ": unaffectedly disclaiming a tribute which all felt to be due to him.'[2]

It was in precisely the same spirit that, a few months before he died, he declined to accept the dedication of a certain book. In his reply, he 'spoke highly of the work itself, but added—"As to the dedication, my brother does not know me. If I were a dignitary, I could bear it as official; but as personal, I cannot.

[1] Samuel Thodey, *The Honour attached to Eminent Piety and Usefulness. A Sermon, preached at Downing Street Meeting-House, Cambridge, Sunday, November 20th, 1836, on occasion of the death of the Rev. Charles Simeon, M.A., Senior Fellow of King's College* (1836), p. 47.
[2] Thodey, pp. 47–8.

I had much rather wait for my *Euge* till I stand before my Judge. He does know me, and yet I trust will have mercy on me."'[1] And at another time he said: 'I look, as the chief of sinners, for the mercy of God in Christ Jesus, to life eternal; (then very deliberately) and I lie adoring the *sovereignty* of God in choosing such an one—and the *mercy* of God in pardoning such an one—and the *patience* of God in bearing with such an one—and the *faithfulness* of God in perfecting his work, and performing all his promises to such an one.'[2]

Not less characteristic were his remarks in conversation with a friend, some years before his death. 'He had been expressing his disapprobation of some injudicious and ostentatious narratives of triumphant *death-bed scenes*, as they were termed.[3] "I think," said he, "if you should see me die, you will not see me die in that manner." "No," added he, "*triumph* will not suit me, till I get to heaven. If I am admitted—as I hope to be, there—then, if there be one that will sing louder than the rest, I think I shall be that one. But while I am here, I am a sinner—a redeemed sinner;—that is my style; and as such I would lie here to the last, at the foot of the cross, looking unto Jesus; and go as such into the presence of my God."'[4]

[1] Thodey, p. 48.
[2] *Narrative of his last illness and death*, Carus, p. 811.
[3] Cf. *ibid.* pp. 809–10: also *The Pulpit*, vol. xxix, 1837, p. 213.
[4] Preston, pp. 82–3.

INDEX

313

INDEX

17277607R00204

Printed in Great Britain
by Amazon